RESEARCH METHODS IN CRIMINAL JUSTICE AND CRIMINOLOGY

RESEARCH METHODS IN CRIMINAL JUSTICE AND CRIMINOLOGY

Dr. Anne Wade

SOCIETY Publishing

www.societypublishing.com

Research Methods in Criminal Justice and Criminology

Dr. Anne Wade

Society Publishing
4164 Lakeshore Road
Burlington, ON L7L 1A4
Canada
www.societypublishing.com
Email: orders@arclereducation.com

ISBN: 978-1-77956-393-4 (Hardcover)

ABOUT THE AUTHOR

Dr. Anne Wad has been a researcher and a professor in the Criminal Justice field for over 30 years. She currently holds a position as a Provost/CAO in a University, and Director of Research at another university. She holds an Ed.D. in Educational Leadership and a Ph.D. in Public Safety Leadership/Criminal Justice. Her research interests are in Criminology, Victimology, and the Human Services. She is married to Wesley Wade. She is an artist, writer, researcher, professor, and university administrator.

TABLE OF CONTENTS

LIST OF FIGURES

LIST OF TABLES

PREFACE

Criminology is a field closely related and encompassed in criminal justice that deals with the study of criminal behavior from both individual and societal perspectives. While criminal justice courses and practioners focus on the systems and institutions society employs to respond to crime, criminology explores the philosophical underpinnings of crime. It seeks to understand the causes of criminal behavior, the most effective methods for crime prevention and offender rehabilitation, and how societal reactions to crime evolve. Criminologists influence the criminal justice system by proposing innovative methods and theories to address crime more effectively.

The modern understanding of criminology emerged in the 18th century, shaped by social philosophers. Their work led to the development of three major schools of criminological theory: the Classical, Positivist, and Chicago schools. The Classical school, dominant in the mid-18th century, emphasized deterrence and proportional, swift punishment, grounded in the belief that individuals possess free will and agency over their actions. In contrast, the Positivist school argued that both internal and external factors beyond an individual's control significantly influence behavior.

Criminal justice research employs various methodologies to tackle pressing societal issues, continually evolving to keep pace with changes in crime patterns and technological advancements. This research provides policymakers and criminal justice leaders with the insights needed to address contemporary challenges. For instance, research findings can inform new policies and case laws that guide the daily activities of law enforcement officers. Policy analysis within this research context aims to develop practical solutions to problems in crime and criminology.

"Research Methods in Criminal Justice and Criminology" introduces the theoretical and methodological aspects of criminal justice research, outlining the research process's steps and examining how to select and specify a research problem. It also covers ethics in criminal justice research, experimental models and their variations, alternative data collection strategies, and the Uniform Crime Reports.

The text is structured into 10 comprehensive chapters, each delving into crucial aspects of criminal justice and criminology research. Chapter 1 introduces the fundamental concepts of crime and criminology, setting the stage for an in-depth exploration of criminal behavior and its implications. It provides a foundation for understanding the complex interplay between individuals and societal factors in the manifestation of crime. Chapter 2 discusses research methods specific to the criminal justice system, highlighting various techniques and methodologies that researchers use to examine and address issues within this system. This chapter underscores the importance of employing rigorous research methods to develop effective policies and practices. Chapter 3 extends the discussion to research methods in criminology, focusing on the philosophical and theoretical frameworks that guide criminological research. It emphasizes the necessity of a multidisciplinary approach to understand crime comprehensively. Chapter 4 shifts to socio-legal research, examining how legal principles and social factors intersect in the study of crime and justice. This chapter highlights the importance of contextualizing legal research within broader social dynamics to yield meaningful insights. Chapter 5 guides readers through the process of reading and interpreting cases and statutes, an essential skill for researchers and practitioners in the criminal justice field. It provides practical strategies for analyzing legal texts and understanding their implications for research and practice. Chapter 6 explores crime prevention and control strategies, presenting evidence-based approaches to reducing crime and enhancing public safety. It emphasizes the role of research in developing and evaluating these strategies to ensure their effectiveness. Chapter 7 focuses on juvenile delinquency, discussing the unique factors contributing to youth crime and the specific interventions designed to address it. This chapter highlights the importance of tailored approaches to prevent and mitigate juvenile delinquency. Chapter 8 covers the theories of crime causation, offering a detailed examination of various theoretical perspectives on why crime occurs. It provides a critical analysis of different causative factors and their implications for research and policy. Chapter 9 examines the social context of crime and punishment, exploring how societal norms, values, and structures influence crime and the criminal justice system's response. This chapter emphasizes the need for a nuanced understanding of the social environment in shaping crime and justice outcomes. Finally, Chapter 10 covers advanced topics in criminal justice research, providing insights into cutting-edge methodologies and emerging trends in the field. This chapter equips readers with the knowledge and skills to conduct innovative research that addresses contemporary challenges in criminal justice and criminology.

The book is written for students, educators, and professionals in the fields of criminal justice and criminology. It serves as a comprehensive guide for those seeking to understand and apply research methodologies within these disciplines. Additionally, policymakers and researchers may find it valuable for developing informed, evidence-based strategies and policies.

–Author

Chapter **1**

Crime and Criminology

Contents

INTRODUCTION

The study of criminal behavior's nature, causes, and effects is the focus of both criminology and crime. Crime is the term used to describe behaviors that are illegal under state law and are subject to punishment. These behaviors can range widely, from infractions to major crimes like robbery and murder. The goal of criminology, the scientific study of crime and criminal behavior, is to identify the fundamental causes of these behaviors and create practical strategies for control and prevention. The study of criminology looks at different theories to figure out why people commit crimes. Classical theories, which have their roots in the writings of philosophers such as Jeremy Bentham and Cesare Beccaria, contend that people have free will and make logical decisions based on advantages and disadvantages they perceive.

They contend that by making the costs of crime greater than the benefits, a just and equitable legal system with appropriate penalties can discourage criminal activity. Sociological theories that emphasize the influence of social structures and interactions on criminal behavior, on the other hand, include the strain theory and the social learning theory. Robert K. developed the theory of strain. According to Merton, people may turn to crime as a result of societal pressure to meet certain objectives without offering equal opportunities. According to Albert Bandura's social learning theory, people pick up criminal behavior through watching and copying others, especially when that behavior is rewarded or goes unpunished. Psychological viewpoints, which highlight individual variations in personality, mental health, and cognitive processes, also add to our understanding of crime. Impulsivity, aggression, and early trauma exposure are examples of factors that can make someone more likely to commit crimes.

Furthermore, the environment—which includes peer relationships, family dynamics, and community conditions—plays a critical role in either encouraging or discouraging criminal behavior. In the field of crime and criminology, technological advancements have brought about both new opportunities and challenges. For example, cybercrime uses the digital environment to perpetrate crimes like identity theft, hacking, and online fraud, necessitating creative methods of detection and prevention. Similar to this, globalization has made transnational crimes like terrorism, drug smuggling, and human trafficking easier to commit. As a result, solving these complicated issues will require international cooperation and comprehensive strategies. In order to reduce crime and improve public safety, a multimodal strategy that incorporates social interventions, judicial procedures, and law enforcement is used. Advanced surveillance technologies, predictive analytics, and community engagement have all become part of modern policing strategies. Ensuring that laws are applied consistently and fairly, as well as administering justice, are vital functions of the judicial system. Programs for rehabilitation and reintegration seek to address the underlying cause.

1.1. DEFINITION OF CRIME

A criminal act t that one that is not sanctioned by the government or another authority. In contemporary criminal law, there is no clear-cut definition of what constie the fact thateven though statutes have defined it for specific purpn understandingcollective understanding is that crime is a category that the law has created; in other words, something is a crime if the applicable and relevant law declares it to be one. A proposed definition of a crime or offense (or criminal offence) is an act that harms a community, society, or the state in addition to an individual (a public wrong). Such behavior is illegal and subject to penalties Elizabeth A. 03). All acrossAcross the world, there is a belief that certain actions, like rape, murder, and theft, should be illegal. The criminal laws of all relevant jurisdictions define what exactly constitutes a criminal offence. While many have a comprehensive statute known as the criminal code that lists all crimes, some common law countries do not have one. If someone commits a crime, the state (government) has the authority to impose severe restrictions on their freedom. There are protocols that investigations and trials must follow in today's societies. If found guilty, the punishment for an offender may include community service, life in prison, or, in certain cases, the death penalty, depending on the seriousness of the offense.

1.1.1. Nature of Crime

The definitions, traits, causes, and social effects of crimture of criminalityin criminality. At its core, crime is any act that contravenes the rules set forth by the government and is subject to legal repercussions. Different legal systems and cultures have different definitions of what constitutes a crime, which reflect societal norms and values. Crimes can range in severity from serious felonies like murder, rape, and armed robbery to minor infractions like vandalism or petty theft. The nature of crime is defined by several factors. It is frequently examined from the perspectives of its social, moral, and legal aspects. A crime is defined by law as involving both an act (actus reus) and a guilty mind (mens rea). Mens rea relates to the perpetrator's intention or state of mind at the time of the crime, whereas actus reus refers to the actual physical act of committing the crime. The significance of both action and intention in characterizing criminal behavior is highlighted by this dual requirement. There are many different ways to look at the causes of crime from different theoretical vantage points. Sociological theories frequently highlight how social structures and inequality contribute to criminal activity. According to the strain theory, for example, people may turn to criminality as a substitute forrtunities in order toto fulfill social pressures to succeed. The social disorganization theory emphasizes how higher crime rates in some neighborhoods can be caused by a lack of social control and community cohesion. Psychological theories concentrate on how individual variances and thought processes influence criminal behavior. Personality traits, mental health conditions, and cognitive development are a few examples of factors that can affect a person's likelihood of committing crimes. For instance, there is often a correlation between an increase in criminal activity and antisocial personality disorder and other types of psychopathology. The experiences a person has during their early years, such as being exposed to trauma and vialso have a big impactan enormous impact on how likely they are to commit crimes. Economic conditions, peer pressure, and family dynamics are examples of environmental factors that have a major impact on crime rates. Children's criminal develop as a result ofbecause of abusive, neglectful, or unmonitored dysfunctional family environments. Adolescence is a time when peer influence is especially potent because being around criminal peers can encourage the adoption of criminal behaviors. Poverty and unemployment are two economic conditions that can push people to commit crimes out of need or annoyance. The ramifications and effects that crime has on society are also inherent to its nature. Victims of crime may suffer from physical injury, psychological distress, and financian lower general qualityoverall quality of life, undermine community trust, and increase fear. The judicial system, correctional facilities, and law enforcement are all part of society's response to crime.

1.2. PROPERTY CRIMES

Damage or destruction to another person's property is considered a property crime. It also includes any kind of taking, using, or interfering with the owner's use of the property. Generally speaking, property is classified as either personal or real. Titles or deeds are frequently used to legally represent real property, which is fixed property such as land or real estate. Anything that is movable that an individual owns (such as a laptop, cell phone, car, pencil, or pets) or intellectual property (such as ideas or other intangible items created by an individual) is considered personal property. Property crimes require ownership as a necessary component. Examining proof of ownership is necessary to establish who has the right of ownership, or who we victim in the event thatif something was taken or damaged. Ownership can be established quite clearly by location or usage evidence, but it can also occasionally be established a little less clearly by receipts, deeds, or titles proving proof of purchase (or some other legal documents, too). For instance, someone might be able to prove ownership by displaying a picture of an item in their house. Property value is significant in addition to ownership. Law enforcement and the courts can dete the severity of the crimecrime, and the extent of the owner's victimization b's value. Essentially, youYou are deemed less victimized if someone steals your bicycle than if they steal your car. The severity of property crime increases with the value of the item that was stolen or damaged.

1. **Mens Rea in Property Cri**rea is required in order toto prosecute someone for a property crime. It needs to be demonstrated in some way that the perpetrator knew they were tampering with someone else's property. This knowledge is what proves their purpose and deliberate choice to assert control over something they are aware they do not own. Recall that criminal intent is classified into four "states of mind" by the model penal code, which serves as a guide for defining laws: purposely, knowingly, recklessly, and negligently. When it comes to property crimes like theft, the law requires proof of specific intent, or a mens rea—the conscious or deliberate performance of the criminal act. Higher-order mental states such as knowing and purpose demonstrate volition, ian individual made a decisiondecided. The severity of property crime is determined by how well it can demonstrate that the theft was not merely a loan; rather, it was intended to be permanent, and that the damage was irreparable. Stated differently, the perpetrator must have a clear intention to steal and to never give back the stolen goods. Any defense that they were only "borrowing" the property and planned to return it after they were done using it would be eliminated if this aspect of the crime is proven. In the end, borrowing is not illegal. It might just be thoughtless, and that's okay.
2. **Actus Reus in Property Crimes:** Property crimes encompass a wide range of "interference" with property, hence there is also diversity in the criminal acts that qualify as property crimes. Generally speaking, property crimes that are classified as "theft" are the most identifiable ke offenses necessitate the thefttheft or taking of property. But other acts that may be considered theft include withholding property from someone else, moving someone else's property without authorization, accepting stolenerty, selling property you don'tdo not have the right to sell, and receiving property you don't have the right to have. These would all be the actus reus of theft in this instance. A few more instances of the actus reus of property crimes include breaking into an establishment without authorization, staying there

without authorization, causing damage to property, or destroying property.

1.2.1. Types of Property Crimes

It is unlawful to trespass upon or cause harm to another person's property through theft, break-ins, arson, or criminal damage.

1.2.1.1. Theft

Stealing is a common misconception about theft. Though they refer to different types of crimes, "robbery" and "burglary" are also occasionally used interchangeably with "larceny" and "theft." A variety of actions that result in the destruction of another person's property and prevent them from using it for themselves are collectively referred to as theft. Any deprivation of property from its owner, including theft, is considered theft. This can include receiving stolen property, moving, or withholding something. The goal of theft laws is to deprive a property owner of their possessions. Stealing goods or services is the official definition of theft under the law. For instance, using someone else's Netflix login credentials is just as criminal as stealing a car. Theft of an item by force is regarded as general theft. There are two main steps involved in actually taking an item. The theft must first be initiated by the person taking control of the object. They must then relocate the item. It's known as asportation. Theft typically only pertains to personal property and services since it involves actually taking something. However, this isn't always the case. Cases involving rea rare because it is very difficultexceedingly difficult to steal and relocate real property, such as a house.

Theft is a broad crime that can have many other variations in the law that address specific types:

- Shoplifting (stealing from a retail store);
- Embezzlement;
- Motor vehicle theft (stealing a vehicle);
- Burglary (theft from a residence, or even overstaying at a hotel or rental property);
- Theft of services (stealing utilities or using streaming subscriptions without paying for them);
- Robbery.

The value of the item or service that is stolen determines the level of theft legislation. It should go without saying that thefts with higher values are more serious than those with lower values. The severity of the offense dictates the penalty. Theft of property with significant value is classified as grand theft, the largest and most serious offense. Theft of extremely low-value property is classified as petty theft, which is the lowest and smallest category.

1.2.1.2. Burglary

Due to the common belief that burglary entails theft, it is frequently linked to theft. Only a portion of this is true. The use of real property is impeded by burglary. It is important to keep in mind that interference can take various forms, such as stealing, but it can also involve entering, leaving, or using property without authorization. The distinctions are subtle but significant. Though it varies, the idea of illegal or uninvited entry is usually included in the actus reus needed for burglary. In general, it is against the law to enter any building or vehicle, day or night, if you are not supposed to be there. "Remaining" is one of the entry factors in some jurisdictions. Thus, "breaking and entering" is one thing; "breaking, entering, and remaining for a while" is an even worse offense. When we discuss criminal breaking-in, we typically mean the use of any kind of physical force, including pushing open a closed door, to gain entry into the burglarized area. A partial or total intrusion of the offender, a body part of the offender, or a tool or instrument is referred to as entry. It may be legal in some jurisdictions, but in others, the entry must be unlawful. In some jusridictions, breaking and entering is defined as the breaking of the threshold of the domicile. Literally, walkig in a door can constitute a breaking and entering if the person has no legal right to be there and is without invitation. Usually, knowing entry with the express purpose to commit a crime constitutes the mens rea element needed for a burglary.

1.2.1.3. Criminmage

It is illegal to tamper with,with damage, or destroy property, which is known as criminal damage. It also covers the use of deceit or threats that result in property loss. In certain jurisdictions, criminal damage is also referred to as "vandalism" or "criminal mischief." Physically harming, destroying, tampering with, or interfering with property is the actus reus necriminal damage. Usually, in order toto cause criminal damage, one must act without authorization against another person's property or government-owned property. Depending on the jurisdiction and the severity of the harm, different conditions must be met for there to be criminal damage. There are four types of criminal intent: deliberate, careless, reckless, and negligent. It is typically a less serious offense because the criminal intent is less vicious and directed toward an inanimate object rather than a person, or because the defendant causes property damage in a "safe" or nonviolent manner. Using a golf club to smash someone's car windshield out of rage, frightening someone by hurling a brick through their living room window, piercing a tire with a screwdriver, hitting a mailbox with a baseball bat, or hurling someone's cell phone are a few instances of criminal damage. Each of these instances involves an intentional perpetrator of harm. These are not mishaps. Property damage that occurs by accident is not illegal.

A subset of property crimes known as criminal damage deals with a particular kind of interference with property. Graffiti is a distinct form of criminal property damage that involves the application of graffiti to an object. Criminal damage is applied to any type of marking done with markers, spray paint, or other tools. Both the amount of property damage and the offender's mental state determine the various levels or degrees of criminal damage. Due to the wide range of crimes included in this category, criminal damage may be classified as a felony, misdemeanor, petty misdemeanor, or violation, depending on the severity of the damage or the criminal intent.

1.2.1.4. Arson

Arson is another kind of criminal property damage. The deliberate or malevolent (with the intent to cause harm) burning of property by explosion or fire is known as arson. Most jurisdictions have laws that make burning almost anything illegal, often including the offender's own property. But in order for burning down one's own property to qualify as actual arson, the perpetrator had to have done so specifically with the intention of defrauding the victim (e.g., setting fire to your own house and pretending it was an accident to claim insurance money). Usually, lighting a fire or causing personal or real property to burn is the actus reus necessary for arson. This could apply to vehicles, land, buildings, and other structures. In many jurisdictions, deliberately destroying or setting fire to property is the mens rea required for arson. Arson of residential property may be the primary focus of first-degree arson, whereas arson of other property is the primary focus of second-degree arson. When determining the level or degree of arson, additional factors are taken into account, such as the value of the burned property, the extent of property damage, and the fact that anyone was hurt or killed. Arson charges can result from smoke damage alone, even if there is no burning or charring.

1.3. PUBLIC ORDER CRIMES

Crimes against the law are complex. These are all relatelaws designed to punish people who don'tdo not live or act in the ways that the people who made the laws want them to. Crimes classified as "public order" are those that specifically target transgressions of established norms for "acceptable social conduct" and "community behavior." Public order offenses are frequently contentious and hotly contested because they make illegal behaviors that not everyone agrees are appropriate in society. Public order crimes are intended to deter people from interfering with peaceful and orderly social interactions. Legislators have decided that certain actions should be prohibited because they are damaging and counterproductive to the welfare of society.

The idea of a victimless crime is specific to crimes against public order. The only person involved in this crime is the perpetrator, who is ostensibly only causing themselves harm. There is no victim to defend and no harm to stop when one chooses to commit a victimless crime, which involves no external parties. On the other hand, some contend blic order laws are essential in order toto symbolize society's duty to preserve moral principles. The fine line between individual and constitutional rights and the government's desire to ensure that no one becomes dangerously overzealous in the exercise of those rights is where public order crimes reside. The cautious enforcement of crimes against public order strikes a balance between citizens' rights to engage in legally and constitutionally permitted behaviors ansafety and security of society as a wholesociety. Public order laws are susceptible to constitutional rights challenges under the First Amendment because they frequently make offensive gestures, threats, and language illegal. Free speech is safeguarded by the amendment, which states that "Congress shall make no law abridging the freedom of speech." But some public order offenses do just that, so how is that permissible? Well, the problem is that not all speech is First Amendment protected. Regulating (making laws) obscenity, real threats, and fighting words is both constitutional and entirely legal. You can probably imagine how different people would feel about what constitutes appropriate or obscene behavior that should be subject to legal restrictions. Because of this, any legislation or act that makes speech or expression illegal must pass a rigorous scrutiny process, be drafted with extreme care, and be backed by an undeniable public interest. There must be a compelling government interest in these situations.

The contentious "Don't Say Gay" bill, which was signed into law by Florida Governor Ron DeSantis in 2022, is one example of this exact issue. According to the new law, "sexual orientation or gender identity may not be taught in kindergarten through grade 3 by school personnel or by third parties in a way that is not age-appropriate or developmentally appropriate for students in accordance with state standards."

1. **Mens Rea in Public Order Crimes:** The reasonable person standard is a concept that is used to determine mens rea in crimes pertaining to public order. The reasonable person standard is predicated on an educated guess as to what the typical person would do or believe in

relation to a specific public behavior. A behavior could be deemed offensive and constitute a public order crime if a reasonable person would find it offensive or refrain from acting in a particular way knowing the effect it would have on others around them. This allows for the evaluation of an offender's mens rea to take into account both what a reasonable person would have been thinking and any concrete evidence of the offender's true thoughts (such as words spoken aloud or posts on social media). Public order offenses usually require that the victim had the deliberate intent to cause a disturbance, that they knew their actions could cause a disturbance, or that they knew their actions would cause a disturbance.

2. **Actus Reus in Public Order Crimes:** A "reasonable person" would classify certain behaviors as offensive conduct, which is used to determine the actus reus of public order crimes. Only conduct that is of compelling government interest is regulated by public order laws, or at least that is the intended outcome. These laws are specific in defining actions that constitute violations.

1.3.1. Types of Public Order Crimes

Public order crimes cover acts of disorderly conduct, unlawful assembly or riot, homelessness-related activities, all forms of prostitution, and drug and alcohol-related offenses because the aim is to uphold a peaceful society.

1.3.1.1. Disorderly Conduct

Disturbing the peace, another name for disorderly conduct, is a very general, very ambiguous term that encompas that may be deemed offensive in an effort toto address the majority of disruptive risks and annoyances that a person may encounter. Laws against disorderly conduct specify specific behaviors, but they frequently give no indication as to what a "reasonable person" would or would not do. Disruptions such as making excessive noise, acting in an alarming or threatening manner, blocking traffic, posing a risk to others, or starting fights are among the acts that fall under the purview of disorderly conduct laws. The mens rea of laws pertaining to disorderly conduct is primarily dependent on the specific circumstances of a given case. When someone commits a crime, such as making a loud, unreasonable noise, the noise's qualis assessed in the context of the incident. It'sIt is normal to hear music outside a bar in the downtown area late at night. On the other hand, if the rest of the neighborhood is normally a very quiet place, music coming from someone's backyard during a small party might be deemed excessive noise. Determining the offender's intent is necessary to establish mens rea when taking the context into account. In many jurisdictions, the mens rea element for disorderly conduct is the deliberate infliction of public discomfort, annoyance, or alarm, or the reckless intention to cause a risk thereof. If someone is having a small party in their backyard in a peaceful neighborhood and they are playing music too loudly, it is illegal because they are trying to annoy, disturb, or worry their neighbors. If not, that is just being *1.3.1.2. Unlawful Assembly and Riot*

In order toTo be considered a public order crime, unlawful assembly must include certain elements, such as the gathering or meeting of a group with the express intent to commit a riot, another unlawful act, or a breach of peace. This differs from a protest or demonstration that is protected by the constitution because the actions taken are potentially harmful rather than peaceful. Failure to disperse is the crime committed when a crowd defies law enforcement's request to leave a location because their actions are likely to cause substantial harm or serious annoyance. Interfering with a peace officer is another term for this kind of refusal to comply with law enforcement. A riot is declared when there is dangerously high group behavior. A riot is defined by the increased energy and danger that comes with a group of people acting violently, aggressively, or uncontrollably together. A riot may start as a spontaneous, unplanned event or it may be the product of an unlawful or legal assembly that gets out of control. Group activities that involve the use of force or violence—which are not constitutionally protected forms of assembly or expression—must be classified as riots. The attack on the US Capitol building on January 6, 2021, is a prime illustration of rioting. More than two thousand people stormed the building, looted, and vandalized offices, and threatened government workers in protest of the election results. They attacked multiple Capitol Police officers as well as news reporters in a violent manner. The riot resulted in five deaths, 138 injuries to police officers, four responding officer suicides within seven months of the attack, and over $27 million worth of property damage. As of late 2022, over 900 rioters were being charged with crimes as a result of the ongoing investigations and charges surrounding this riot.

1.3.1.3. Vagrancy and Loitering

Homeless people are frequently the victims of crimes against public order. Some contend that laws prohibiting loitering and vagrancy are motivated by the public's perception of the possibility of heightened criminal activity as well as a decline in the area's health and safety, which aims to keep homeless groups out of particular neighborhoods. Homelessness is referred to as begging, and it is exhibited by someone who doesn't seem to be permanent—they move around a lot and don't seem to have a stable source of income. Historically, laws against vagrancy were drafted broadly to give law enforcement broad latitude in apprehending jobless people, gamblers, drug addicts, alcoholics, and people who frequently visited prostitution houses or othe "ill repute." The argument is that, in order toto protect the safety and security of any given area, vagrancy laws could render people incapable of committing crimes before they even started. In theory, loitering is just aimlessly standing around. However, loitering is defined by law as the act of wandering around or staying in one place specifically with the intention of gambling, begging, or engaging in prostitution (actus reus). If loitering occurs close to a school or a transit hub, it is especially considered unacceptable. Additionally, begging and panhandling are illegal in many places. Since laws prohibiting panhandling say that someone cannot ask someone for money, they run the risk of criminalizing speech. Legislators must therefore exercise caution to ensure that no one's First Amendment rights to free speech are violated. Generally speaking, aggressive behavior and behavior that obstructs public access or the normal flow of traffic are specifically forbidden by law. Sit-lie laws are one relatively new strategy to stop homeless people from congregating in cities, which negatively impacts locals' quality of life, businesses' prosperity, and visitors' experiences. Sit-lie laws make it illegal to sit or lie on sidewalks or public streets, which forces people to move. This makes it illegal for anyone to obstruct roads, businesses, or transit hubs. Essentially, the old laws against loitering and vagrancy, which forbade hanging around without a purpose, can now be used to stop people from lying down or sitting down instead of doing these things. Because these laws specifically target the impoverished, addicted, and jobless, they are already being contested in court. Seattle, Washington, was the first city in the United States to enact a sit-lie ordinance in 1993 that prohibited sitting or lying on a public sidewalk between the hours of 7 a.m. and 9 p.m. in Seattle's downtown area. The ordinance was attacked, but ultimately upheld in 1996.

In 2021, Los Angeles, California enacted a more comprehensive ordinance that banned sitting, lying, or sleeping on public streets and sidewalks at all times and in all places within Los Angeles city limits. Section 41.18 of the Los Angeles Municipal Code (LAMC) prohibits sitting, lying, or sleeping:

- Anywhere that impedes any passage protected by the Americans with Disabilities Act such as ramps on and off sidewalks;
- Within 10 feet of a driveway or loading dock;
- Within five feet of a building entrance or exit;
- Anywhere that impedes the right of way for any activity for which the City has issued a permit;
- Within 500 feet of a property designated for a sensitive use (such as public park or library);

- Within 500 feet of a designated overpass, underpass, freeway ramp, tunnel, bridge, pedestrian bridge, subway, wash, spreading ground, or active railway;
- Within 1,000 feet of a homeless shelter or support center;
- Within 500 feet of a school or day care center; and
- Anywhere else the City has posted a sign prohibiting sitting, sleeping, or lying down.

1.3.1.4. Crimes Involving Prostitution

Sexual activity performed for payment is known as prostitution. Prostitution is illegal in all states but Nevada. In Nevada, legal prostitution is restricted to houses with a license and is subject to strict regulations. Pandering, or street prostitution, is prohibited even in Nevada. Depending on the jurisdiction, different actus reus requirements apply to prostitution. Offering, consenting to, or participating in sexual activity for cash, property, or anything of value is considered prostitution in many states. In most jurisdictions, prostitution is punishable by law, and both agreeing to and participating in prostitution entails the risk of legal action and conviction for both the prostitute and her client. Being the customer or purchasing sexual services from a prostitute is known as patronizing them. This portion of the deal hasn't always resulted in punishment. Most clients, or "johns," were usually permitted to depart even though it was against the law, but the prostitute was the only one who was detained and punished. When authorities realized that focusing on just one aspect of the problem was ineffective and concerns about human trafficking were raised, this began to change in the 1990s. Pimping, or the planning and execution of prostitution, is likewise illegal under the law. A pimp's (or madam's, if she's a female) cut of the money that the prostitutes under their supervision make is typically retained as well. The increased awareness of sex trafficking has led to heightened monitoring and prosecution of all forms of prostitution, including those conducted online. Mens rea for prostitution must include either specific intent to engage in prostitution or strict liability (the act itself s without determining any mental state). It doesn'tdoes not matter what someone was thinking or believing they were doing; the fact that a criminal act was committed is sufficient evidence that a crime was committed.

1.3.1.5. Drug and Alcohol Crimes

The production, distribution, and use of specific drugs are all illegal in every state and by the federal government. Since rehabilitation has been shown to be more successful in reducing reoffending and freeing up space in jails and prisons for offenders who pose a greater security risk to society, many modern statutes place more emphasis on this approach than on incarceration for nonviolent drug offenders. Furthermore, marijuana remains illegal at the federal level despite being legalized for recreational and medical use in many states. A commission tasked with promoting consistency between state and federal laws drafted the Comprehensive Drug Abuse Prevention and Control Act of 1970, also known as the Controlled Substances Act, which includes federal criminal statutes that target illegal drugs. The federal government, along with the states, classifies illegal drugs into drug "schedules" for the purpose of prosecuting drug crimes. The schedules typically highlight a drug's addictive or harmful properties, with Schedule I drugs being the most addictive or harmful. Drugs that are legal with a prescription are included in the remaining schedules, along with less addictive or harmful substances. Scheduled drugs are any substances that appear on these official lists. The constitution does not prohibit the government from punishing drug addicts, but it does not prohibit them from being punished for criminal acts involving controlled substances. The creation and possession of schedule drugs are prohibited in the majority of jurisdictions. Possession is normally classified as either a misdemeanor for simple possession or a serious felony for possession with intent to sell, depending on the quantity possessed, the drug's schedule classification, and whether or not the possession is for the purpose of distribution. Public order crimes include the following: distribution (giving drugs to others to sell), trafficking (moving drugs across state lines), and sale (exchanging drugs for money). These crimes are usually classified as felonies, and the punishments get harsher if drugs are sold in higher schedules, bigger quantities, to minors, or in close proximity to schools. Also known as "being under the influence of a controlled substance," scheduled drug use is usually punished as a misdemeanor, with more severe consequences for repeat offenders.

1.4. VIOLENT CRIME

Violent crime, which includes a broad range of offenses involving the use of force or threat of force against individuals, is a significant social issue. These crimes affect victims, families, and communities by having the potential to cause bodily harm, psychological distress, or even death.

1.4.1. Types of Violent Crime

Understanding the different types of violent crime is crucial for effective law enforcement, prevention strategies, and victim support.

1.4.1.1. Homicide

The term "homicide" describes the unprovoked death of one person by another. With terrible consequences for victims and their loved ones, it is among the most severe and serious types of violent crime. Homicide can be classified into several categories:

1. **Murder:** This involves the intentional killing of another person with malice aforethought. This means that the perpetrator acted with the deliberate intent to cause death or serious harm. Murder charges can vary in severity depending on factors such as premeditation, the degree of violence, and the motive behind the killing.
2. **Manslaughter:** It is the unlawful killing of another person without malice aforethought. Unlike murder, manslaughter typically lacks the element of premeditation or intent to cause harm. It can be further divided into voluntary manslaughter, which occurs in the heat of passion or under provocation, and involuntary manslaughter, which results from reckless or negligent behavior.

1.4.1.2. Assault

Assault involves the intentional act of causing fear of imminent bodily harm or offensive contact in another person. It can manifest in various forms and degrees of severity:

1. **Simple Assault:** It refers to non-aggravated physical attacks that result in minor or no bodily injury. It may involve actions such as punching, slapping, or pushing, with the intent to intimidate or frighten the victim.
2. **Aggravated Assault:** It involves more serious acts of violence that result in significant bodily injury or involve the use of a deadly weapon. This can include stabbing, shooting, or beating someone with the intent to cause serious harm or death.

1.4.1.3. Robbery

The act of robbing someone of their property by using force, threat of force, or intimidation is known as robbery. Robbery differs from theft in that it frequently carries a higher sense of threat and violence and involves direct interaction with the victim. Robberies can happen in a number of places, including homes, businesses, and public spaces.

1.4.1.4. Sexual Assault

Any non-consensual sexual act or behavior committed against another person is considered sexual assault. It is an extremely traumatic type of violence that can affect a victim's physical and mental health for a long time. Sexual assault can take many forms:

1. **Rape:** Sexual contact that is not consenting or that is obtained by coercion, manipulation, or force is referred to as rape. It is an infringement on someone's bodily integrity and autonomy, frequently leaving survivors with severe psychological wounds.
2. **Sexual Battery:** The term "sexual battery" describes the non-consensual groping or touching of a person's private areas. It can happen in a variety of settings, such as relationships, private settings, and public areas.
3. **Child Sexual Abuse:** When adults or older juveniles sexually exploit or molestation minors, it is considered child sexual abuse. It can cover a broad spectrum of actions, from inappropriate physical contact to more serious types of sexual assault.

1.4.1.5. Domestic Violence

A pattern of abusive behavior used by one partner to obtain dominance and control over another in the setting of a close relationship is known as domestic violence. It can include financial manipulation, emotional and physical abuse, coercion into sexual relations, and sexual violence. Domestic violence frequently results in physical harm, psychological distress, and even death for victims and their children.

1.4.1.6. Child Abuse

Child abuse refers to the mistreatment, neglect, or exploitation of children or minors. It can take various forms, including:

1. **Physical Abuse:** It involves intentionally causing physical harm or injury to a child. This can include hitting, beating, shaking, or burning a child, resulting in bruises, broken bones, or other injuries.
2. **Emotional Abuse:** It entails the infliction of emotional or psychological harm on a child through verbal attacks, threats, humiliation, or rejection. It can profoundly affect a child's self-esteem, mental health, and overall well-being.
3. **Sexual Abuse:** This of children involves any sexual activity or exploitation perpetrated against minors. It includes acts such as

molestation, incest, pornography, and sexual assault, causing profound trauma and long-term psychological damage.

1.4.1.7. Armed Robbery

Armed robbery is a particularly dangerous type of theft where victims are intimidated and property thefasier by the use of weapons or the threat of violence. In order toTo elicit fear and compliance from their victims, perpetrators may use knives, firearms, or other weapons, which raises the possibility of serious harm or death.

1.4.1.8. Kidnapping

The illegal taking or detention of another person against their will is known as kidnapping. It can happen for a number of reasons, such as personal grudges, political aspirations, extortion, or ransom. During their captivity, victims of kidnapping may endure physical or psychological abuse, as well as sexual assault, which can cause serious trauma and emotional distress.

1.4.1.9. Terrorism

The deliberate use of force, intimidation, or coercion to further political, religious, or ideological goals is known as terrorism. It can take many different forms, aiming at infrastructure, government institutions, or civilians. Examples include hijackings, gunshots, bombings, and cyberattacks. Since terrorism spreads fear and destabilizes societies, it poses a serious threat to national security and public safety.

1.4.1.10. Stalking

A pattern of intimidating or harassing actions toward a particular percites anxiety, distress, or fear is known as stalking. In order toTo keep an eye on or exert control over their victims, stalkers may use invasive tactics, unwanted communication, or surveillance. Victims of stalking may experience serious psychological consequences that compromise their sense of safety and wellbeing.

1.5. CRIMINOLOGY

Criminology is the scientific study of the non-legal aspects of crime and delinquency, including its causes, remedies, and avoidance, as seen from the perspectives of various academic fields, iuding economics, sociology, biology, psychology, anthropology, and psychology, and psychiatry. Legally speaking, a crime is any individual criminal act (e.g., for example, a burglary) and the way society reacts to those acts (e.g., an imprisonment term of three years). In contrast, criminology integrates and studies a wider range of information regarding crime and offenders. For instance, criminologists have tried to figure out why certain individuals are more or less inclined to act in a criminal or delinquent manner. Additionally, criminologists have looked into and made an effort to explain variations in crime rates, criminal codes, and changes in rates and laws over time among various societies. Many criminologists see themselves as impartial experts in public policy, obtaining information for different government representatives who are in charge of formulating policy decisions. Some criminologists, like their colleagues in disciplines like the atomic and nuclear sciences, contend that scientists are accountable for the ethical and political ramifications of their work. As a result, some criminologists have actively opposed the death penalty and supported a number of legislative changes.

Criminologists who disagree with this activist role argue that political, social, religious, and moral arguments should be considered in addition to the results of criminological research, a task that is best left to political bodies. While acknowledging that criminologists have the same rights as other citizens to voice their opinions, this viewpoint contends that popular will is a less dangerous form of government than expert judgment. During the final decades of the 1900s, criology expanded to include several subfields of study. Among these waswere criminalistics, also known as scientific crime detection, which uses techniques like toxicology, photography, fingerprint analysis, and DNA evidence (also see DNA fingerprinting). It had previously been disregarded in criminology due to its emphasis on specific criminal acts as opposed to a more comprehensive understanding of crime and offenders. By placing a great deal of emphasis on victimology—the study of crime victims, the interactions between victims and offenders, and the role of victims in the criminal events themselves—criminology was able to reach a wider audience. A distinct but closely related academic field known as criminal justice has also grown up, concentrating less on theories of crime and more on the organization and operation of criminal justice institutions such as courts, police, prisons, and juvenile agencies. The academic placement of criminology in universities is significantly diverse due to its relationships with other disciplines. European universities have a tendency to treat criminology as a subfield of legal studies.

1.5.1. Scope of Criminology

As a multidisciplinary field of study, criminology covers a wide range of subjects and methods with the goal of comprehending criminal activity, crime, and the criminal justice system. Fundamentally, the goal of criminology is to identify the reasons behind criminal activity, its trends, and repercussions, and to create practical preventative and intervention plans. To provide a thorough grasp of criminal phenomena, this field incorporates ideas from sociology, psychology, law, anthropology, biology, economics, and other academic fields. The study of criminal behavior is a fundamental component of criminology. Criminologists look for biological, psychological, social, and environmental influences as well as other factors that lead people to commit crimes. Researchers can create theories to explain why some pere likely than others to commit crimes by looking into these factors. In order toTo comprehend the causes, trends, and effects of criminal behavior on society, criminologists also look into a variety of criminal behaviors, such as organized crime, terrorism, and street and white-collar crime. In addition, criminology studies the criminal justice system and its establishments, such as the courts, prisons, and law enforcement. This area of study looks at how these institutions function, how succthey are at preventing crime and advancing justice, and what obstacles they have tomust overcome to get there. In addition, criminologists research issues pertaining to reintegration, rehabilitation, and crime prevention, investigating tactics to lower recidivism rates and advance public safety. Beyond its scholarly endeavors, criminology contributes to the practice and policy of the criminal justice system and other fields. Scholars in this domain work in conjunction with legislators, law enforcement agencies, and community organizations to formulate evidence-based interventions and policies that target the core causes of crime. Criminologists contribute to the identification of best practices and opportunities for advancement in the criminal justice system by carrying out evaluations and assessments of current policies and programs. Furthermore, criminology looks at larger social issues like inequality, discrimination, and social disarray that can fuel crime and victimization, expanding its focus beyond the boundaries of the criminal justice system. Criminologists underlying causes of crime and advance social justice and equity by taking into accountconsidering the structural and social factors that influence people's opportunities and chances in life.

The scope of criminology is expansive and includes various subfields and areas of focus:

1. **Crime Causation:** One of the fundamental aspects of criminology is the study of factors contributing to criminal behavior. This includes examining the influence of socioeconomic conditions, socialization, mental health and even genetic and neurological factors.
2. **Criminal Typologies:** Criminologists analyzes different types of criminals, their characteristics and the patterns of crimes they

commit. This knowledge aids in tailoring prevention and intervention strategies to specific offender profiles.

3. **Victimology:** Understanding the impact of crime on victims and their experiences is a crucial component. This knowledge is used to design support systems and services that cater to the needs of victims.
4. **Criminal Justice System:** Criminology evaluates the functioning of the criminal justice system, which encompasses the police, courts, and correctional institutions. It assesses the effectiveness and fairness of the system in dealing with crime and criminals.
5. **Crime Prevention and Control:** Criminologists are actively involved in developing, implementing, and assessing crime prevention strategies. This includes rehabilitation programs, community policing and measures to reduce recidivism.
6. **Comparative Criminology:** This subfield involves comparing crime rates, criminal justice policies and cultural differences across different countries and societies. The aim is to identify effective approaches to crime control and to learn from international practices.
7. **Specialized Areas:** Criminology also encompasses specialized areas like white-collar crime, which focuses on non-violent crimes committed by individuals in positions of trust or authority and cybercrime, which investigates crimes committed in the digital realm, including hacking, identity theft and online scams.

1.5.2. Nature of Criminology

For legal professionals and policymakers, it is essential to comprehend the nature and application of criminology because it offers insights into the interdisciplinary, empirical, and theoretical approaches used to analyze criminal behavior. It covers a wide range of topics, such as victimology, criminal typologies, crime causation, and the operation of the criminal justice system. With this knowledge, we can create strategies that effectively prevent and control crime and promote justice and efficiency in the legal system.

Criminology is a dynamic and multifaceted field of study that delves deep into the understanding of crime, criminals and the criminal justice system. Its nature can be characterized by several key attributes:

1. **Interdisciplinary:** Since criminology draws from a broad spectrum of social, behavioral, and natural sciences, it is by its very nature interdisciplinary. Knowledge from economics, law, sociology, psychology, anthropology, biology, and other fields is integrated. By

using an interdisciplinary approach, criminologists can comprehend crime auses from a comprehensive angle.

2. **Empirical:** This research is the foundatioology. It lays Empirical research places a lot of emphasis on gathering and evaluating data in order toto research criminal behavior, crime trends, and the efficiency of different crime prevention and control tactics. Criminologists can create evidence-based interventions and policies by utilizing empirical data.
3. **Theoretical:** Many criminological theories aim to explain the reasons and motivations behind criminal behavior, and criminology is largely a theoretical field. These theories cover a wide spectrum, from traditional ones like deterrence to more modern ones like routine activities theory, social learning theory, and strain theory. These theoretical models aid criminologists in comprehending and forecasting criminal activity.
4. **Applied:** The study of criminology is applied and generates solutions to real problems. It employs theoretical and research-generated insights to solve practical issues. Criminologists collaborate with legislators, law enforcement organizations, and other interested parties to create workable plans for enhancing the criminal justice system and preventing crime.
5. **Employs a Scientific Method:** Criminology relies on the scientific method, involving the formulation of hypotheses, data collection, analysis, and the testing of theories. This empirical approach ensures that research in criminology is conducted rigorously and systematically.
6. **Policy-Oriented:** The study of criminology frequently focuses on policy. Criminal justice policy development and reform are directly impacted by research in this area. It assists legislators, judges, law enforcement, and prisons in making decisions based on the best available evidence.

1.5.3. Psychopathological Aspects

The scientific study of crime, criminals, and the reasons behind their actions is known as criminology. The study of personality traits that cause behavior that deviates from accepted social norms in a given social group and are partially unconscious is known as psychopathology. It investigates anomalous personality or emotional phenomena that support symptoms or actions. Psychopathology offers criminology techniques to examine aspects of a criminal act within the framework of personality and seeks to understand the reasons behind the crime. The focus is on the individual, or criminal, as someone who stands out from the crowd due to social or personal flaws that have motivated them to commit a crime. The study and intervention center on the act and the actor. This kind of difference-based criminologyreats crime as a fact and the offender as a specific subject of inquiry. From a broader angle, the context of the criminal behavior should ideally be included in any criminological study. This interpretation includes the victim, the identified victim, the determining fa of the social context in which the crime was committed, and the law's final say. The criminal is sometimes even seen as the victim. According to this criminology of process, a conflict leads to a crime, and the perpetrator is the subject or actor who is entangled in a web of social contexts and legal definitions that make the act qualify as criminal. Without the social and legal identification that situates the actor in a conflict with the group and ultimately qualifies the act as an infraction deserving of sanctions, no act could be classified as a crime.

1.5.4. Criminology Methods

A multitude of fields are included in criminology, which incorporates approaches and strategies from the social and natural sciences. Similar to other academic fields, criminology makes a distinction between applied and pure research, as well as between statistical and intuitive methods of reasoning. However, criminological research, more than most other disciplines, is dependent on the cooperation of public authorities and governmental bodies to provide necessary data. The study of criminology encompasses a broad range of methodologies and constitutes a diverse body of knowledge. It is true that a large portion of research is becoming more quantitative, especially ioking at the causes of crime, even though few current trends can be applied to the entire field of study. Some of this This work uses the statistical approach to explain the crime rates connected to specific societies and social groups; other work uses the Lombroso-initiated approach to explain the likelihood of a person committing a crime based on his social, psychological, or biological traits. Furthermore, the goal of these methods is moving away from deterministic or absolute predictions and toward probabilistic ones. In conclusion, contemporary criminologists have shifted their focus towards pinpointing societal variables linked to marginally elevated crime rates as well as personal characteristics linked to marginally elevated odds of criminal activity. The conclusion that no single factor truly determines whether a person commits a crime or whether a society has high or low crime rates is supported by the fact that all of this illustrates the subject's inherent complexity.

1.5.4.1. Descriptive Statistics

There are significant differences in the methods and scope of data collection between nations, even those with federal systems. A few examples of variables are the frequency of data collection and publication, the items prioritized, the option to choose between comprehensive listings and sample surveys, and the proportion of public versus private research. It has been challenging to develop a useful system of international criminal statistics and to compare national statistics that are collected separately because of these differences, as well as variations in law and legal administration, popular beliefs, and habits. Official statistics, which are gathered as part of the work of criminal justice agencies, are the most frequently used type of data in criminological research. For instance, the police gather information about crimes they are aware of and the individuals they apprehend for committing them; courts gather information about cases that are brought before them and the results of those cases, such as convictions; and prisons, jails, probation and parole offices gather information about the individuals under their control. The value of official criminal statistics is always dependent on human factors, such as the willingness of the police to formally respond to criminal incidents, the willingness of private citizens to report criminal events to the police, and the willingness of court officials to prosecute the case. These rulings are not very reliable as a measure of the amount of crime in a society or of changes in the amount of crime over time because they depend on a number of factors, such as whether the criminal laws at issue are popular or unpopular, whether the criminal event occurs in a high-crime or low crime area, and whether the victim or offender is a member of a minority group.

Researchers in many nations have used victimization surveys—in which random samples of the population are typically asked whether they have been victims of crime within a specified period of time—to get around issues with official statistics. While there are methodological issues with these surveys (e.g., they only use the victims' memories), they have historicpatterns in crime over time with greater accuracy than official statistics. These polls have frequently been carried outconducted by government organizations like the U. S. Census Bureau, which started conducting its yearly poll in 1972. Subsequently, victim sy, Sweden, Canada, Israel, and New Zealand. An international crime victim survey is also sponsored by the United NationsThe United Nations also sponsor an international crime victim survey. Criminologists add self-report questionnaires to the official statistics, asking respondents if they have ever committed any specific types of offenses. These studies are typically carried out by private criminologists rather than by government organizations, and they usually ask respondents about relatively minor criminal incidents rather than very serious ones. They also typically survey juveniles rather than adults. However, the aggregate data from victimization surveys, self-report surveys, and government statistics will typically yield a more realistic picture of crime.

1.5.4.2. Case Studies

A case study, also known as an individual case history, is a method used mainly (though not exclusively) by psychologists, psychiatrists, and psychoanalysts to focus on the life or career of one or more individuals. These histories can shed light on the motivations and personalities of criminals, despite certain limitations in the method. Although there has been a steady increase in the quantity of criminological case studies, there are sometimes concerns about their validity due to their relatively rare publication, professional ethics that prohibit the disclosure of information provided in confidence, and the fact that the studies that are published may not always be representative of the broader topic they aim to investigate. Similarly, books written by criminals, including autobiographies, can shed light on the motivattions of criminals. Yet, these kinds of works usually have serious drawbacks, such as a lack of objectivity, in spite ofdespite their great human and scientific interest.

1.5.4.3. Typologies

Typologies entail categorizing crimes or perpetrators based on a set of relatedness or similarity criteria. A continuum of criminals, for instance, ranging from the "insane" at one extreme through various career criminals, petty offenders, and white-collar criminals to "organized" or "professional" criminals at the other, has been developed by criminologists through numerous attempts to classify offenders into categories such as "normal" or "abnormal" and "habitual" or "professional." Although the typological approach is more comprehensive than the case study, it is not as comprehensive as the statistical approach because it is less individual or specific and more impersonal and heterogeneous. The approach, which was first developed in Germany and Austria, has drawn criticism for its tendency to overlook significant individual differences in favor of simplifying complicated phenomena. It is not widely used because, despite its strong intuitive appeal, its drawbacks appear to outweigh its advantages.

1.5.4.4. Experimental Methods

In a controlled experiment, two closely related circumstances or groups are chosen, one is given a particular stimulus, and the results are compared for both. Historically, the so-called experiments conducted by judicial, penal, and reformatory institutions were not really controlled, nor were they experimental in the scientific sense. This was because public agencies believed that they were obligated by the concept of justice to treat all parties equally, rather than to treat some groups differently than others. However, public criminae organizations started to be more open to conducting experimental research by the 1980s. Minneapolis, Minnesota police.,police, for instance, took part in a controlled, randomized study on the application of arrest in cases of domestior the following six months, police records showed that when they came across domestic abuse, they used random assignmentassignments to decide whether or not to arrest the perpetrator. The findings showed that the likelihood of repeat domestic abuse against the same victim in the following six months was cut in half if the offender was apprehended and held for one night in jail. The study had a big influence on domestic abuse policies for police across the country, and as a result of the important findings, experimental research in criminology and criminal justice increased in popularity. Despite this, the public and justice officials oppose such experimentation, primarily because they still think that equal treatment should be given to equals. However, because it appears to be the most efficient way to ascertain whether police pove the desired effects, its use has been expanding.

1.5.4.5. Prediction Studies

Criminological prediction makes an efforttries to predict how people will behave in the future under specific circumstances. Based on data, ca of the two, the forecasts show how likely it is that a particular person or group will be impacted by particular illnessestherapies. As a result, certain criminals—such as those who commit drug and sexual offenses—are thought to be fairly likelylikely to reoffend, whereas those who commit serious crimes like murder—are thought to be fairly unlikely to do so. Statistical prediction is a useful tool to augment judges' and administrators' naturally limited personal experience, even though it can never be definitive and can only indicate specific probabilities. During the final decades of the 1900s, prediction research gained significant popularity as a criminological technique.

1.5.4.6. Action Research

Action research, which is frequently distinguished from experimental research, involves using the observations of field workers and other individuals who have direct contact with offenders, potential offenders, or prisoners. For instance, social workers have studied the delinquent behavior of children and adolescents in slums, connected it to their surroundings, and assessed the efficacy of youth clubs and other services provided, aling to assist these individuals in resolving their problems. Action research collaborates with field workers in an effort toto produce useful outcomes. It frequently does away with formal hypotheses in favor of identifying and putting into practice strategies and activities that will aid in the prevention of delinquenhis approach attempts to create a bridge between abstract theories and practical work. The most well-known and possibly mostmost effective example was Clifford Shaw's Chicago Area Project, which was implemented in the 1920s and 1930s and applied the ecological theories of sociologists Ernest Burgess and Robert Park of the University of Chicago to encourage locals to addreissues in their neighborhoods.

1.5.4.7. Cross-Disciplinary and Cross-Cultural Approaches

As the 20th century came to an endended, criminology began to emphasize cross-cultural methods more and more. Studies spanning cultures have highlighted similarities between descriptive statistics (e.g., two studies on delinquency among Philadelphia birth cohorts (individuals born in the same year) were repeated using comparable cohorts in China and Puerto Rico. Some research endeavors have endeavored to identify the specific attributes linked to a higher probability of engaging in criminal activity. For example, a study comparing youths born in Dunedin, N.Z., with youths born in Pittsburgh found that crime-prone youths in both countries tended to combine impulsivity with "negative emotionality" (e.g., anger, anxiety, and irritability). Still other studies explored the characteristics of societies that led to higher or lower crime rates; one such study found that the rates of lethal violence in the United States in the 1980s were five times greater than in other industrialized countries but that rates of other types of crimes were similar or even lower. Researchers have attempted to explain why this pattern existed and have also recommended policies designed to reduce lethal violence.

1.5.5. How Is Criminology Supported by Other Academic Disciplines?

As a multidisciplinary field, criminology interacts and draws from other academic specialties. It aims to comprehend, evaluate, and clarify the reasons behind criminal behavior, its repercussions, and how the criminal justice system operates. Here are some of the key academic disciplines that criminology is related to:

1. **Sociology:** It has a strong influence on criminology because both fields study the social structures, processes, and variables that lead to criminal activity and the emergence of deviant subcultures. Criminological research frequently makes use of sociological theories, including labeling theory, social learning theory, and strain

theory.

2. **Psychology:** It is important to criminology, especially when it comes to comprehending the psychological elements that could influence criminal behavior. This covers fields such as forensic psychology, which examines how criminals think as well as how those involved in the criminal justice system are assessed and treated.

3. **Law:** Criminology is closely tied to the legal field, as it deals with the study of laws, legal systems, and the criminal justice system itself. Legal scholars and practitioners often collaborate with criminologists to develop and evaluate policies and practices related to crime and criminal justice.

4. **Anthropology:** It can provide valuable insights into the cultural and societal factors that influence criminal behavior and the functioning of criminal justice systems. Cultural anthropology, for example, may be used to examine how cultural norms and values affect criminal conduct.

5. **Economics:** Economic theories and methods are applied in criminology to analyze the cost-benefit calculations of criminals and the economic consequences of crime. This perspective is often used to study issues like the deterrence effect of punishment and the allocation of resources for crime prevention.

6. **Political Science:** The political aspects of criminology involve the study of how political structures and policies impact criminal justice, law enforcement, and criminal behavior. This includes research on the politics of crime control, criminal justice policies, and the role of government institutions.

7. **Public Health:** Criminology can overlap with public health in the study of crime as a public health issue. This perspective considers the health consequences of criminal activity, such as violence and substance abuse, and explores strategies for prevention and intervention.

8. **Social Work:** These frequently assist those involved in the criminal justice system, such as victims and offenders, by working within the system. They aid in the rehabilitation and reintegration of criminals into the community.

9. **Statistics and Data Analysis:** Criminology makes exse of statistical techniques and data analysis to investigate trends in crime, assess the efficacy of criminal justice initiatives, and carry outconduct empirical research on crime-related subjects.

10. **History:** Historical criminology examines the historical development of criminal behavior, legal systems, and law enforcement. This perspective can provide insights into the evolution of crime and justice over time.

11. **Geography:** It aids criminology by providing insights into the environmental elements influencing criminal behavior, enabling the spatial analysis of crime using tools like Geographic Information Systems (GIS), and enabling crime mapping and predictive models. It is crucial to environmental criminology because it looks at how the social and physical environments impact crime, locates crime hotspots, and provides information for focused interventions and policing tactics. Geographic data also contributes to a more data-driven, evidence-based approach to comprehending and addressing criminal behavior by helping to evaluate the impact of social programs, the efficacy of policing tactics, and the facilitation of predictive policing.

12. **Cyber Sciences and Cyber Criminology:** The field of cyber sciences is vital to the field of criminology because it addresses the changing nature of cybercrime and its investigation. They offer the methods and resources needed to recognize, monitor, and stop crimes that take place online, including identity theft, online fraud, and cyberattacks. Cyber sciences support criminologists in the analysis of digital evidence, the investigation of cybercriminals' methods, and the creation of law enforcement and prevention strategies. These sciences also contribute to the advancement of digital forensics methods, which are critical to gathering and safeguarding evidence for criminal investigations. They also aid in revealing the covert elements of cybercrime networks, which eventually advances our knowledge of modern criminal activity and the creation of practical countermeasures for the digital era.

13. **Forensic Sciences:** A fundamental component of criminology, forensic sciences aid in the gathering, examination, and interpretation of tangible evidence during criminal investigations. These sciences are multidisciplinary fields that include digital forensics, chemistry, and forensic biology. They are essential for determining the identity of criminals, reconstructing crime scenes, and verifying or disputing witness testimony. Forensic experts help law enforcement and criminologists solve crimes and bring offenders to justice by analyzing fingerprints, DNA, ballistics, trace evidence, and other materials. Furthermore, forensic sciences aid in the creation of

contemporary criminological techniques and instruments, improving our comprehension of criminal behavior and the effectiveness of the criminal justice system while upholding the values of justice and fairness in the course of criminal case investigation and decision-making.

These are only a few of the fields that criminology interacts with; interdisciplinary work is frequently done in criminological practice and research. It's crucial to remember that criminology benefits from interdisciplinary research in order to offer a thorough understanding of crime and its varied aspects.

1.5.6. Importance of Criminology

The study of criminology is developing. The definition and effects of wrongdoing have evolved along with advancements and changes in society at large. To be applicable to the justice delivery system, criminology is a field that must adapt to changing times by changing its trendstheses, and approaches. If executed precisely, it would enhance the strategies' fey and create new opportunities for criminologists. Criminology won't will not be able to keep up with the times and will give in to advancements if it doesn't does not change. In this piece, the writer delves into a thorough discussion of various aspects of criminology and explores potential avenues for its advancement to sustain itself going forward.

There are several reasons that explain why criminology is important:

- **Reduction in Crime:** Criminology helps society understand, control, and reduce crime. Studying crime helps discover and analyze its causes, which can be used towards crime reduction policies and initiatives.
- **It Helps Understand the Mindset of Criminals:** Criminology helps understand the mindset of criminals, why they commit crimes, and the factors that affect them. This helps in the proper allocation of resources to control crime.
- **Reform of Criminals:** As well as controlling and reducing crime, criminology can also suggesmeasures for the rehabilitation of criminals.

1.6. HISTORICAL DEVELOPMENT OF CRIMINOLOGY

The field of criminology came into being in the late 1700s as a result ofbecause of a number of humanitarian movements that questioned the injustice, arbitrary nature, and ineffectiveness of the criminal justice and penitentiary systems.

Reformers like Jeremy Bentham, John Howard, and Cesare Beccaria in England, as well as Sir Samuel Romilly in Italy—all members of the so-called classical school of criminology—sought legal and penological reform during this time rather than criminological knowledge. Their main goals were to lessen the severity of the law, force judges to follow the legala poena sine lege (Latin for "due process of law"), lessen the use of the death penalty, and humanize prisons. They had some degree of success, but in an attempt toto create a more "just" criminal justice system, they created fictitious and abstract relationships between crimes and punishments, neglecting the unique needs and traits of each criminal defendant. Furthermore, reformation lagged far behind the primary goal of punishment, which was retribution, and the secondary goal of deterrence.

France released its first annual national crime statistics at the beginning of the 1800s. One of the first people to examine these statistics was the Belgian mathematician, statistician, and sociologist Adolphe Quetelet (1796–1874), who discovered a great deal of regularity in them (e.g., in the number of criminal cases filed each year, the number of convictions, the gender disparity, and the age distribution of offenders). He deduced from these patterns that "those things which are reproduced with astonishing constancy, and always in the same way, must have an order." "Later, Quetelet argued that criminal behavior was the result of society's structure, maintaining that society "prepares the crime, and the guilty are only the instruments by which it is executed. Cesare Lombroso, an Italian physician who lived from 1836 to 1909, investigated the motivations behind the crimes committed by specific offenders, in cho concentrated on the traits of societies and tried to explain the high crime rates that resulted from them. After conducting some research, he came to the conclusionconcluded that some cranial, skeletal, and neurological deformities were biological remnants of a previous evolutionary stage, making the affected individuals "born criminals." Social scientists eventually rejected his theory, which was very contentious when he first proposed it. Lombroso further argued that there were a variety of reasons why crimes occur and that the majority of criminals were not born bad but were instead molded by their surroundings. The research of both Quetelet and Lombroso emphasized the search for the causes of crime—a focus that criminology has retained.

1.6.1. Founding Fathers of Criminology

The study of criminology has changed over time, and its founders are not a single group of people. Rather, it has been influenced by the works of many academics and intellectuals from various fields and eras. Some of the key figures who have significantly influenced the development of criminology include:

1. **Cesare Beccaria (1738–1794):** Beccaria, who is regarded as one

of the pioneers of classical criminology, argued for reasonable and compassionate criminal justice procedures in his work On Crimes and Punishments (1764), highlighting the importance of just punishment and deterrent tactics. He is credited with establishing classical criminology.

2. **Jeremy Bentham (1748–1832):** The English philosopher Jeremy Bentham is well-known for his utilitarian views on criminal justice. His theories have impacted criminological theory, such as the panopticon concept for prison architecture and the maximization of happiness while minimizing pain principle.

3. **Cesare Lombroso (1835–1909):** Cesare Lombroso is another notable figure often regarded as the founding father of modern criminology. Lombroso, an Italian physician and criminologist, is known for his work on "criminal anthropology." He introduced the concept of the "born criminal" and argued that some individuals were biologically predisposed to criminal behavior due to physical anomalies or atavistic characteristics. Lombroso's ideas were influential in the development of positivist criminology, as he emphasized the role of biological and physiological factors in criminality. While his theories have been subject to criticism and revision, his contributions to criminology's early development cannot be overlooked.

4. **Émile Durkheim (1858–1917):** A prominent sociologist, Durkheim explored the social factors influencing criminal behavior. He introduced the concept of "anomie" and emphasized the importance of social cohesion and integration in reducing crime.

5. **Adolphe Quetelet (1796–1874):** Quetelet, a Belgian statistician and sociologist, is often regarded as a pioneer in the application of statistical methods to the study of crime. He examined the patterns and trends of crime in relation to various social factors.

6. **Auguste Comte (1798–1857):** Comte, a French philosopher, contributed to the development of positivist criminology by emphasizing the scientific study of society and the application of the scientific method to understand criminal behavior.

7. **Enrico Ferri (1856–1929):** Ferri was an Italian criminologist who supported the positivist approach to the field. He advocated for treating criminals with greater compassion while focusing on the biological and psychological aspects of criminal behavior.

8. **Raffaele Garofalo (1851–1934):** Another Italian criminologist, Garofalo, focused on the idea of natural crime and had a significant

impact on the field of criminal anthropology, which studied the psychological and physical traits of criminals.

9. **Edwin Sutherland (1883–1950):** The differential association theory developed by Sutherland is well-known, and it highlights the part that social learning plays in criminal behavior. He advanced knowledge about deviance and white-collar crime.

The foundation for the broad field of criminology was established by these academics among others. It is still developing and absorbing ideas from other fields, such as sociology, psychology, law, and more. Although criminology owes much to these individuals, it is crucial to recognize that the discipline has evolved and become more diverse over time, with modern researchers continuing to add to our knowledge of it.

1.6.2. Criminology as a Separate Branch of Study

The field of criminology in this country suffers from preventable disdain and apathy despite its immense promise and potential. Degree-granting and post-degree criminology programs are not easily accessible because there aren't many institutions offering criminology instruction, research, or practices. The situation has resulted in a number of negative outcomes. For instance, India was unable to develop a large system of academicians in criminology or academic openings in the field. There was no way for Indian criminology to develop a clear audience. There are murky and unexamined connections between criminology training and calling. The experts who made commendable commitments to criminology remained uninterested in the advancement of criminology in India because they were mostly associated with their parent-teachers. The crucial investigations in Indian criminology that have led to the development of theories elucidating the grave questions of accountability in this country have been essentially nonexistent. Furthermore, most criminologists have not had the opportunity to support methods and initiatives that place research findings. India's criminology also required attention and recognition on a global scale. When combined, criminology is lars a roadblock with limited vertical mobility for success in the workplace in India.

1.6.3. Evolution in the Field of Criminology

The study of criminology began in the late 1700s as a result ofbecause of various philanthropic developments that called into question the justice system's and the criminal justice system's brutality, discretion, and wastefulness. Reformers like Jeremy Bentham, John Howard, and Cesare Beccaria in England, as well as Sir Samuel Romilly in Italy, addressed the so-called traditional school of criminology during this time and sought out penological and legal reform rather than criminological knowledge. Their main goals were to reduce the use of the death penalty, relieve judges of legitimate sentences, make judges observe the principle of nulla poena sine lege, and modify corrective organizations. Even though they were somewhat successful, their attempts to gradually "justify" criminal justice system were based on fabricating a fake and easily assimilated relationship between offenses and penalties, rather than taking into account the unique characteristics and needs of the offender. Furthermore, renewal lagged far behind as the goal of discipline was retaliation and optional discouragement.

The first national wrongdoing measurements were distributed in France in the middle of the 19th century. Among the first to dissect these insights, Adolphe Quetelet (1796–1874), a Belgian mathematician, analyst, and humanist, found notable consistency in them (e.g., in the quantity of people found guilty of infractions each year, the number of sentences imposed, the ratio of men to women, and the age distribution of those found guilty). "There must be a request to those things which are duplicated with amazing consistency, and consistently similarly," he concluded after looking at these examples. Subsequently, Quetelet maintained that society "readies the wrongdoing, and the blameworthy are just the instruments by which it is executed," and argued that criminal behavior was the result of society's structure. While Quetelet focused on the characteristics of social orders and explain the ensuing crime rates, Cesare Lombroso (1836–1909), an Italian clinical specialist, investigated individual criminals to determine the reasons behind their wrongdoings. Based on some of his examinations, he concluded that people with specific skeletal, neurological, and cranial abnormalities (Phrenology) were "brought into the world lawbreakers." Social scientists eventually disproved his hypothesis, which was extremely dubious when he first proposed it. Both Quetelet and Lombroso's research focused on identifying the causes of crime, an emphasis that criminology has continued to hold.

1.6.4. Criminologist and Their Work in the Field of Criminology

The people who study and work in t criminology are known as criminologists. They view wrongdoings from an interdisciplinary perspective and look at various angles, such as personal conduct norms, brain science, and so on, in order toto understand the motivations behind particular wrongdoings or criminal behavior.

A criminologist's work includes investigating crimes based on the type of offense committed, the offenders, the historical context of the crime, the overall impact of the crime on society, and potential legislative measures to deter future crimes. Because of this, criminology can be isolated into 3 channels of works which are:

- Investigation of a crime;
- Finding the reason behind wrongdoing, in this manner comprehend the crooks; and
- To devise measures to forestall wrongdoing and top off provisos which are existing in the criminal law.

1.7. THEORETICAL PERSPECTIVES IN CRIMINOLOGY

The broad field of criminology is an interdisciplinary one that includes the study of criminal behavior and the criminal justice system. The field of criminology studies the causes, effects, and victimization of crime as well as the functioning of the criminal justice system, with a particular focus on the judicial, correctional, and police sectecause criminology covers such a broad range of subjects, researchers have needed to employ a number of distinct approaches to tackle different issues. It is crucial to note right away that there is no oneno ideal way to research crime and the criminal justice system in all of its facets. Instead, the kind of method that is employed should be the most appropriate to address the research question, as this discussion explains. Penology, prophylactic criminology, criminal psychiatry, criminal psychology, criminal anthropology, criminal sociology, and criminal politics are all included:

- **Criminal Anthropology:** According to Darwinism, humans descended from animals via an evolutionary process. When this idea is applied to criminology, we can draw the conclusion that criminals are less evolved than other people and are unable to suppress their urge to commit crimes. Atavism is the theory that claims criminals are descended from a group of humans who underwent a regression in their evolutionary history. The founder of anthropological criminology, Cesare Lombroso, proposed that certain regressive physical characteristics are shared by criminals. Criminal anthropology seeks to provide answers to queries like what unusual physical traits the offender possesses. What connection exists, if any, between criminality and race?
- **Criminal Sociology:** It is the study of crime as a social phenomenon in science. Its main goal is to determine the degree to which societal factors contribute to criminal behavior (social etiology). It is, broadly speaking, the study of the physical environment, including meteorological, climatological, and geographic aspects. According

to Dr. Sutherland's "Differential Association Theory," criminal activity can be linked to an offender's associations with other offenders and the company they keep. As many a parent has told a teenager "You are who you hang with."

- **Criminal Psychology:** It is the study of the thoughts and behavior of criminals. It answers the question: why do criminals do what they do? It also studies the psychology of other persons connected to the crime as witnesses, judge, counsel, etc., and psychology of confession. Criminal psychologists can act as profilers, helping agencies create a psychological profile to help apprehend suspects. Criminal psychology is based on the works of Alfred Binet, Prof. Jerman.
- **Criminal Psycho-Neuro-Pathology:** Pathology of crime, then, can be called the study of crime; the psychological and general aspects of it, by careful examination of the various constituents and factors of crime, such as disruption of existing social norms and values, mental illness, stress, disorganization in society, anti-social psychopathological mindsets, physical disorders, etc., when a crime is considered to be a disease, an abnormality among humans. An emerging field within criminology and bio-criminology called "neurocriminology" uses concepts from neuroscience and brain imaging methods to analyze, forecast, and prevent crime. The research of Gluek and Sigmund Freud has an impact on this area of criminology studies.
- **Penology:** It is the study of the causes, progression, importance, applications, and laws pertaining to punishment. The study of punishment in connection to crime is known as penology. It is a science that studies the nature, scope, and severity of punishment.

1.7.1. Applied Criminology or Pragmatic Criminology

It encompasses the application of scientific techniques from other fields, including experimentation, statistical analysis, synthesis, comparison, analysis, and psychology.

- **Applied Criminology:** It is a science that focuses on using the field of criminology to address "real world" issues with crime and criminal justice. It aims to problematize proposed approaches and find solutions to specific crime and justice issues. It is both critical and compelling.
- **Criminalistics (Police Science):** This applied science aims to

identify the methods used in crime and its detection, i.e., gathering and examining tangible evidence in legal matters. This science combines knowledge of goods and materials, chemistry, physics, graphology, and the psychology of crime and the criminal.

1.7.2. The Internationalization of Crime and Criminology

Despite having its roots in Italy and other European countries, criminology evolved and flourished in the US. In the United States, criminology was growing as a social and behavioral science; however, it continued, if it existed at all, as a component of the study of law in other parts of the world. Two changes have happened recently. One of the changes is expounded upon in this encyclopedia's article on "International/Comparative Criminology." Around the world, criminology has become a social science with an emphasis on empirical research (though criminology has a longer history in England and some Scandinavian countries; even in those countries, criminology research has increased over the past 50 years). The scope of crime has expanded globally. As a result of these two advancements, the value of an international perspective in criminology is becoming increasingly acknowledged. Even in nations without a well-established criminology field, there is a strong desire to learn more about the subject and its potential applications. For instance, China and Vietnam have developed master's degrees in criminology in partnership with the University of Maryland in order to promote the growth of the criminological study of crime and justice in their respective nations. An international focus is unavoidable in the investigation and management of cybercrime, drug markets, human traffickinaundering, organized crime, and terrorism. In other words, criminology can no longer be limited to the study of crime in the US.

1.7.3. Benefits of Criminology to the Legal System

The discipline of criminology has improved almost thethe entire equity conveyance framework. It has altered how people react to crime, which has had a significant impact on both victims and offenders. It advances our knowledge of crime's origins, consequences, and impact on society at large. It has led to the establishment of more specialized areas, such as ecological criminology, which has made progress, police tactics, networks set up for law enforcement, and so forth. It tries to explain why some events awrongdoing in some social orders and not in others, and then it sets up laws to make the laws better. This further strengthens the differences between societies and social orders, as well as between what is legal and illegal. In order toTo help us understand why violations are reported, psychology investigates a few novel theories, such as positivist, old-style, and so forth. It suggests that people commit violations when they perceive an advantage or due to internal and external variables, such as social or organic factors, through a variety of conjectures. All of this aids in the understanding of wrongdoing by the legislative branch and the executive branch after more robust and powerful laws are passed. Depending on the severity of the infraction, it proposes a reasonable plan for controlling and preventing it while also striking a balance with bad behavior. Disciplines that are progressively more severe make criminals aware of the possible repercussions of their illegal behavior. Consequently, this lowers the percentage of crime. An additional path in criminology, i.e., explains the rationale, causes, and motivation behind a criminal's act as well as the state of mind that led to it. Overall, criminology makes us understand crime and criminals on a deeper level. It conveys the idea that people are free to make their own decisions and that, as a result, breaking the law puts one at risk of rejection. It emphasizes how strict the criminal justice system is, which can deter wrongdoing. Additionally, it equips the legal executive to understand and enact laws that prohibit infractions with reasoned measures. By encouraging us to understand the primary causes of wrongdoing and providing the best means of addressing and preventing it, contemporary criminology supports the equity delivery system in all of these ways.

1.7.4. Future of Criminology

The most recent developments have been welcomed by the criminal equity framework as a step ahead of the thugs. Law and innovation work hand in hand to stay abreast of the changing times. Modern developments in the legal sciences, for instance, are extremely energizing to the field of criminology, which discourages wrongdoing in general. Through scientific research, criminology has progressed and integrated ballistic fingerprinting, linking the marks and scratches on projectile housings to the weapons that fired them. This could be useful in explaining crimes for which there is little evidence and no clear criminal. In criminology, there exist multiple systems that advance their methods towards the future. The criminal value system will function more realistically thanks to these techniques. One such structure might be the DNA Indexing System, which is widely utilized in India and has the best chance of growing in the future due to advancements in general. Devices that gather unique information in this manner by jeopardizing an individual's security are referred to as spyware. With the advancement of artificial intelligence and scientific advancements, criminology can make strides in these domains. Cybercrimes were a severely underregulated crime at first, and India never had any special laws dealing with them. However, changes to the legal system have made it recognized as a dangerous crime that is increasingly prevalent in today's society. India still needs a lot of motivation to enact stricter laws governing it and protect people from serious online threats. Since the field of electronic development is evolving quickly, law implementation organizations must also adapt to the current landscape. This needs to be completed by implementing significant changes to the criminology-managed wrongdoing control approach. Improved GPS reference points and biometric identification systems may be the fundamental steps toward achieving notable advancements in this area. The best tool could be an Iris Scan and Facial Recognition Device combined into a simple device for identifying people. In this sense, one could argue that criminology could eventually be greatly advanced through the use of mechanical advancementsh would offer completely different guidance to the nation's equity conveyance arrangement.

1.7.5. Future Trends to Be Followed

Criminology examines a distinct set of facts that incorporates a broad range of methodologies. Even though there aren'tare not many current trends that apply to the entire field of study, there are still instances where the examination is becoming increasingly quantitative, particularly nsidering and analyzing the causes of crime. Some works use the methodology proposed by Lombroso to explain the likelihood of an individual committing a crime in relation to his natural, mental, or social attributes. A portion of this work appliesapplies to the quantitative process initiated by Quetelet to explain the crime rates associated with explicit social gatherings. Furthermore, these approaches are increasingly centered around probabilistic predictions rather than absolute or deterministic ones. Finally, criminologists are now concentrating on identifying social order factors that are associated with relatively little increases in the percentage of crimes committed, as well as individual factors that are associated with relatively little increases in the likelihood that a person will commit crimes again. All of this reflects the inherently complex nature of the issue and concentrates on the conclusion that no one for determines whether a person commits misconduct or whether the general population has a high or low rate of crime. The study of criminology integrates a diverse range of methodologies to examine a distinct set of facts. Even though there are n'tnot many examples from today that can be used to the entire field of study, a large portion of assessment is dynamically quantitative, especially when looking into the causes of bad behavior. Some of this work uses the Lombroso-initiated strategy to explain the likelihood of an individual engaging in bad behavior to the extent that it is consistent with his regular, mental, or social qualities; other work applies the quantifiable approach started by Quetelet to explain the wrongdoing rates related to explicit social requests and get-togethers. Furthermore, instead of being based on deterministic or incomparable gauges, these procedures are dynamically centered around probabilistic ones. Ultimately, criminologists eventually focus on identifying social demand factors associated with relatively small increases in rates of criminal activity as well as individual factor associated with relatively small increases in the likelihood that an individual will continue to engage in criminal activity. All of this illustrates the subject's innate complexity and culminates in the conclusion that no one factor can definitively determine whether a person engages in bad behavior or whether the rate of wrongdoing in a population is high or low.

1.8. CYBER CRIMINOLOGY

The frequency of online victimization is rising as cybercriminals have improved their methods for staying anonymous. Furthermore, even infrequent users are vulnerable because networked computers are storing more personal data than ever before. Researchers in the multidisciplinary field of cybercriminology come from a variety of backgrounds, including computer science, victimology, sociology, criminology, and internet science. The body of knowledge pertaining to cybercrimes ought to be separated from investigation and combined with cyberforensics; additionally, a separate field should be established to examine and investigate cybercrimes from a social science standpoint. Since the International Journal of Cyber Criminology was established, both online and offline academic circles have adopted the term "cyber criminology" as their own. Information and communications technology advancements have given rise to a number of new crime issues that did not exist 20 years ago. Because of the ease with which different types of criminal activity can now be conducted online, cybercriminology has become a recognized field within the criminology framework. Since computers and the Internet are becoming more and more integrated into everyday life, it is critical to comprehend the dynamics of cybercrime and the people who fall prey to it. Cybercrime and Criminological Theory: Foundational Readings on Hacking, Piracy, Theft, and Harassment is an anthology that examines the factors that lead to involvement in different types of cybercrime and deviance, ranging from common issues like media piracy to more specialized crimes like computer hacking. It's unclear how criminological theories might relate to virtual offending because the majority of them were created to explain street crimes. This work offers important perspective on the applicability of various theories to explain cybercrimes. Using data sets from populations across the country, Cybercrime and Criminological Theory provides direct insight into the rates and prevalence of cybercrime offenses. It describes potential predictors of both offending and victimization and provides readers with a basic understanding of and appreciation for various forms of cybercrime. The readings that have been chosen highlight research issues that need to be resolved in order to enhance the legal, technological, and policy reactions to cybercrimes.

Cybercrime and criminological theory begins with an introduction to cybercrime and virtual criminality.

- Routine activities theory;
- Deterrence theory;
- Social learning and self-control;
- General strain theory;
- Space-transition theory.

1.8.1. Routine Activity Theory

The scope of cybercrime and the threat it poses is expanding in tandem with the comparable expansion of information technology. Because cybercrime transcends national borders via the Internet, some countries account for a greater variation in cybercrime activity than others, which also affects less criminally involved nations. Cybercrime at the individual level has been explained by routine activity theory (RAT), but not at the national level. Numerous studies have concentrated on nations with high rates of cybercrime; however, these studies are typically carried out by cyber security companies and are purely descriptive, drawing no conclusions. The goal of this study was to identify the traits that indicate a country's propensity for phishing or spamming. Cybercrime activity was found to be higher in wealthier countries with a higher per capita Internet user base (a sample of 132 countries). It was also discovered that Internet users and unemployment interacted, with the result that countries with higher unemployment rates had stronger effects from the percentage of Internet users on spam.

1.8.2. Deterrent Theory

Global cyber threat landscape is rapidly growing, making it difficult for corporate executives and national security officials in the US and other countries to keep up with increasingly complex and varied attack techniques while also keeping up with the quickly accelerating pace of technological advancement. Significant cyberattacks targeting American interests, both public and private, have increased recently. There is still more work to be done in creating cyber policies that are audacious and sophisticated enough to consistently disarm and deter hostile actors, even though this has prompted the current Administration to take action to strengthen our cyber security posture. America does not have the luxury of time when it comes to addressing this problem. Rather, dedication and haste are crucial elements in the competition to advance US cyber capabilities beyond those of its enemies and to take the lead and excel in this new field of defense strategy. Even though the government's strong ties with the private sector already help American cyber security, strengthening these crucial alliances must continue to be a top priority. Of course, investing in the training of a skilled cyber workforce is also essential if the United States is to become the most capable cyber power in the world. Finally, it is critical that American leaders make the most of these new opportunities to establish a framework that will protect this country and its interests from cyberattacks and allow for the implementation of a strong cyber deterrence policy.

1.8.3. Social Learning and Self-Control Theory

Control theory provides an explanation for why people obey rules, in contrast to most criminology theories that claim to explain why people commit crimes. The explanation for how behavior conforms to societal norms can be found in control theory. Certain control theories highlight how internal constraints emerge during childhood development. However, the main focus of social control theories is on outside variables and the mechanisms through which they become effective. Inadequate restrictions lead to deviance and criminality. The idea of free will is central to the social control theory's understanding of human nature, which endows criminals with agency and accountability for their actions. Therefore, rather than being more in line with positivist or determinist viewpoints, social control theory is more in line with the traditional school of criminology. Social control theory primarily assumes that people share a common value or respect for social norms. The general consensus that laws and social norms should be obeyed is probably shared even by those who disobey them. Deviance and crime are seen as normal behaviors that society has not suppressed. For criminologists, cyberspace offers an exciting new frontier. The traditional discourse of criminology is challenged by virtual reality and computer-mediated communications, which introduce new forms of crime, deviance, and social control. Scholars have noted that cyberspace has become a new hub for criminal activity since the 1990s, but criminology has generally under researched the phenomenon of cybercrime and has been slow to acknowledge the significance of cyberspace in altering the character and extent of victimization and offense. Thus, there areications for cybercrime.

1.8.4. General Strain Theory

According to recent research, people can more easily express their frustration and rage onling to make physical contact with others, which lowers the risk of harm. In actuality, cyberbullyingCyberbullying has been the main focus of the few experiments conducted on the general strain theory in the virtual world. Agnew (2011) notes that the majority ofmost of the restricted experiments on the general strain theory in the virtual world have concentrated on cyberbullying. According to four criteria, bullying has been previously identified as a specific relevant strain that raises the risk of delinquent behavior:

- Bullying is perceived as unjust by the victim.
- The importance of peer relationships between victim and offender will place a high level of significance on the bullying.
- Bullying typically occurs away from traditional forms of social control, such as parents.
- Bullying provides a model for the victim to express his or her own aggressive behavior.

These claims are supported by research on bullying both online and offline. Young people who are under a lot of stress—for example, by performing poorly in school, feeling mistreated by those in positions of authority, or going through difficult personal experiences—are more likely to bully others both online and offline. Furthermore, a number of academics have investigated the impact of stress resulting from cyberbullying. Wright (2013) discovered that even after adjusting for prior cyber-aggressive behavior, cyberbullying victimization and peer rejection led to an increase in online aggression. The effect of cyberbullying on future offending was greater than that of physical bullying. While general strain theory has been shown to be useful in addressing cyberbullying and victimization, it has not been extensively studied in relation to other forms of cyber-offending. It makes sense to attribute online predatory crimes, like some types of computer hacking, to stress and bad feelings. General strain theorists would contend that going through life experiences, like splitting up with a long-term partner or girlfriend, losing a job, performing poorly in school, or struggling with authority, can cause people to feel bad. In response, someone might try to break into someone else's computer or guess their social media account password in an effort to harm people they believe have wronged them. Therefore, researchers must address how general strain theory can be applied to different types of cybercrime both theoretically and empirically.

1.8.5. Space-Transition Theory

Another unique theory proposed to account for cybercrimes is K. Jaishakar's (2008) space-transition theory, which integrates various theoretical paradigm into single model. This theory operates on the basic argument that people behave differently while online than they otherwise would in physical space, leading to different behavior patterns in online environments which are not identified by traditional theories of crime. Jaishankar presents seven basic propositions about behavior on and off-line:

- Individuals who repress their desire to engage in crime in the real world due to either status or position have a propensity to engage in crimes online.
- Offenders may be more likely to engage in cybercrime because of the ability to utilize various identities, hide their location, and the lack of deterrence in online spaces.
- Crime in online spaces is likely to move into physical space, and vice versa.
- Cyber criminals may have the opportunity to desist because of the temporary nature of the internet and its spatio-temporal disconnect from theorld.
- The nature of technology allows strangers to come together in cyberspace in order to plan and commit offences in real world, and those who know one another in real world may partner in order to engage in cybercrimes.
- Closed societies may produce greatera greater level of cybercrime than open societies due to repressive nature of government regime.
- The disconnect between norms and values of a society in real world and those of the internet may lead some individuals to engage in cybercrime.

Although several of the propositions are sensible and are supported by basic characteristics of the internet, other propositions are somewhat difficult to test and may be contrary to either the current research on cybercrime, or be specific to a certain form of cybercrime.

1.8.6. Prevention of Cyber Crimes

As always, the best defense against cybercriminals is prevention. The most def are typically the ones targeted first in criminal activity. Though there are some gencautions you can take that will significantly lower your risk of attack, it is ideal to work with an IT security expert to evaluate your unique needs and vulnerabilitiesvulnerability. Cybercrime prevention is not always difficult; with a little technical know-howknowledge and common sense, many attacks can be averted. Cybercriminals aim to profit as fast and conveniently as they can, in general. The harder you make it for them, the more likely it is that they will give up and find an easier target.

1. **Ke Current with the Latest Patches and Updates:** Whenever patches and other software fixes are released, applying them to your computer is one of the best ways to keep hackers away from it. You can prevent hackers from exploiting software defects, or vulnerabilities,vulnerabilities that they might otherwise use to access your system, by updating your computer on a regular basis. Even though keeping your computer updated won't shield you from every attack, it will make it far more difficult for hackers to access your system, completely prevent many simple and automated attacks, and possibly deter a less determined attacker from looking for a more vulnerable computer elsewhere.
2. **Make Sure Your Computer is Configured Securely:** Remember that the level of security on a recently acquired computer might not be sufficient for you. Make sure your new system operates securely when installing it on your home computer in addition to making it function.
3. **Choose Strong Passwords and Keep Them Safe:** Today, passwords are a necessary part of using the Internet; we use them for everything from online banking and flower orders to checking the miles we have accrued on our favorite airline website.

The following tips can help make your online experiences secure:

- Selecting a password that cannot be easily guessed is the first step toward keeping passwords secure and away from the wrong hands. Strong passwords have eight characters or more and use a combination of letters, numbers and symbols Avoid using any of the following as your password: your login name, anything based on your personal information such as your last name, and words that can be found in the dictionary. Try to select especially strong, unique passwords for protecting activities like online banking.
- Keep your passwords in a safe place and try not to use the same password for every service you use online.
- Change passwords on a regular basis, at least every 90 days. This can limit the damage caused by someone who has already gained access to your account. If you notice something suspicious with one of your online accounts, one of the first steps you can take is to change your password.

4. **Protect Your Computer with Security Software:** Basic online security requires a variety of security software types. Firewall and antivirus software are essential components of security software.

Generally speaking, a firewall is your computer's first line of defense since it restricts what and who can communicate with it over the internet. A firewall functions as a kind of police officer, monitoring all data that tries to enter and exit your computer over the Internet. It lets through communications that it deems secure while preventing malicious traffic, likerom ever getting to your system.

5. **Protect Your Personal Information:** Be careful when disclosing personal information online, including your name, home address, phone number, and email address. You will unavoidably need to provide personal information in order toto use many online services, as they handle the billing and shipping of gyou have purchased. As it is rarely possible to disclose no personal information at all, the following list offers some guidelines for sharing personal information securely online:

- Never reply to emails requesting personal information. Reputable businesses won'twill not request personal information from you via email. If in doubt, give the business a call or enter its website address into your browser. The links in these messages lead to malicious and fraudulent webclicking on them.
- Pay attention to privacy policies on Web sites and in software. It is important to understand how an organization might collect and use your personal information before you share it with them.
- Take care of your email address. In an attempt toTo identify a possible victim, spammers and phishers occasionally send millions of messages to email addresses that may or mnot exist. You will be added to their lists for future communications if you reply to these messages or even download images. Additionally, exercise caution when sharing your email address on blogs, newsgroups, or online communities.

6. **Online Offers That Look tooToo Good to be True Usually are:** The proverb that states there is no such thing as a free lunch is still applicable today. The enticing hooks used by companies to get your attention include purportedly free software like screen savers or smileys, investment secrets that will make you untold fortunes, and contests that you've surprisinglyring. Even though the program or service you requested may not have required a cash payment up front, it's possible that it came attached with adverti software (adware) that monitors your usage and shows you unsolicited adverts. To claim your purported contentcontent winnings, you might need to give up

personal information or make another purchase. Ask for a second opinion, check the fine print, or, better yet,yet just ignore an offer that seems too good to be true.

REFERENCES

1. Applin, S. (2014). Her American Dream: Bringing gender into institutional-anomie theory. *10*, 36–59. https://doi.org/10.1177/1557085114525654.
2. Braithwaite, J. (2000). The new regulatory state and the transformation of criminology. *British Journal of Criminology, 40*(2), 222–238. https://doi.org/10.1093/bjc/40.2.222.
3. Bunei, E. K., & Barasa, B. (2017). Farm crime victimization in Kenya: A routine activity approach. *International Journal of Rural Criminology, 3*(2), 224–249.
4. Deflem, M. (Ed.). (2006). *Sociological Theory and Criminological Research: Views from Europe and the United States*. Elsevier.
5. Gilman, S. (2008). Freud and the making of psychoanalysis. *The Lancet, 372*(9652), 1799–1800. https://doi.org/10.1016/S0140-6736(08)61746-8.
6. Hayward, K. J. (2004). *City Limits: Crime, Consumerism and the Urban Experience*. Routledge.
7. Hayward, K. J., & Young, J. (2004). Cultural criminology. *Theoretical Criminology, 8*(3), 259–273. https://doi.org/10.1177/1362480604044608.
8. Hillyard, P., Pantazis, C., Tombs, S., & Gordon, D. (2004). *Beyond Criminology: Taking Harm Seriously*. Pluto Press.
9. Hughes, L. (2015). Economic dominance, the "American Dream," and homicide: A cross-national test of institutional anomie theory. *85*, 100–128.
10. Jaishankar, K. (2016). *Interpersonal Criminology: Revisiting Interpersonal Crimes and Victimization* (1st ed.). CRC Press.
11. Jaishankar, K., & Ronel, N. (2013). *Global Criminology: Crime and Victimization in a Globalized Era* (1st ed.). CRC Press.
12. Lochner, L. (2004). The effect of education on crime: Evidence from prison inmates, arrests, and self-reports. *American Economic Review, 94*(1), 155–189. https://doi.org/10.1257/000282804322970751.
13. Martin, E. A. (2003). *Oxford Dictionary of Law* (7th ed.). Oxford University Press.
14. Naegler, A., & Salman, M. (2016). Feminist criminology. *SAGE Journals: Your Gateway to World-Class Journal Research, 11*(4), 354–374. https://doi.org/10.1177/1557085116660609.
15. Rhodes, R. (2000). *Why They Kill: The Discoveries of a Maverick Criminologist*. Vintage Books.

16. Siegel, L. J. (2015). *Criminology: Theories, Patterns, and Typologies*. Cengage Learning.
17. Stallwitz, A. (2014). Community-mindedness: Protection against crime in the context of illicit drug cultures? *International Journal of Rural Criminology, 2*(2), 166–208.
18. Uggen, C., & Inderbitzin, M. (2010). Public criminology's. *Criminology & Public Policy, 9*(4), 725–749. https://doi.org/10.1111/j.1745-9133.2010.00666.x.

Chapter **2**

Research Methods in Criminal Justice System

Contents

INTRODUCTION

Researchers can address some of the most important problems affecting our society by using research methods in criminal justice. There is constant change in the criminal justice system. It adapts to the constantly evolving patterns of crime and technology. Policymakers and leaders in the field of criminal justice can address many of their challenges with current, pertinent insights from criminal justice research. Research on criminal justice, for instance, can result in new regulations and even case laws that serve as daily guidelines for law enforcement personnel. Criminology and crime issues are resolved via the application of policy analysis. The socioeconomic background of society has shaped the evolution of crime. It has always been reliant on the momentum and shift of national public opinion as well as social sanctions. The degree of crime seems to differ between societies and communities, andincludeincludes the behavior itself as well as the response to it over time for a particular society or community. National and local governments utilize the criminal justice system, which consists of organizations and policies, to uphold social order, deter and manage crime, and punish lawbreakers. The main organizations in charge of these responsibilities are law enforcement (police and prosecutors), courts, defense lawyers, and local jails and prisons. They also supervise the processes for the arrest, charging, decision-making, and sentencing of those found guilty. The process of addressing crime is referred to as criminal justice administration. When a criminal act happens, the criminal justice system has a duty to ascertain whether the action has infringed upon people's rights and liberties and, if so, to take the appropriate action to remedy the imbalance that the criminal act has caused. Because of this, the criminal justice system is designed to deal with just one facet of the crime problem, which is justice. The criminal justice system is compelled to adopt a purely post-orieny in order toto fulfill this role, concentrating on previous criminal acts. The state's decision to enforce the high standards of behavior necessary to safeguard individuals and communities gave rise to the necessity for criminal justice administration. By decreasing the likelihood of crime and catching, questioning, finding guilty of, and sentencing of those who violate society's laws and regulations, it seeks to accomplish its protection goal through enforcement.

2.1. OVERVIEW OF CRIMINAL JUSTICE SYSTEM

The criminal justice system is a complex framework that includes the organizations, guidelines, and procedures put in place to protect the rule of law, preserve soc, and carry outconduct justice in society. Fundamentally, the role of this system is to deter and address criminal activity by identifying, looking into, prosecuting, deciding, and punishing offenders. The judicial system, corrections, and law enforcement make up its three primary parts. Enforcing the law, looking into crimes, and detaining suspects are the responsibilities of law enforcement organizations, such as police departments. The judiciary, which consists of courts and judges, upholds defendants' rights to due process, interprets and applies the law, and decides criminal cases through trials or plea agreements. The oversight, rehabilitation, and provision of services aimed at easing the reintegration of convicted criminals into society falls within the purview of corrections agencies, which include prisons and probation departments. The criminal justice system functions within a legal framework that is defined by statutes, constitutional clauses, and court rulings that specify the rights and obligations of those who are engaged in the criminal justice system. Important tenets that protect the rights of defendants, victims, and society at large include the presumption of innocence, the right to a fair trial, and the ban on cruel and unusual punishment. These tenets also serve as the foundation for the system's operation. Furthermore, the policies, practices, and results of the criminal justice system are influenced by a wider range of social, political, and cultural facthe system as a wholesystem. Problems with the effectiveness of rehabilitation programs, the use of force by law enforcement, and racial disparities in arrest and sentencing are just a few examples of the difficulties and complexities that come with working in the criminal justice system. To achieve its overarching goals of public safety, accountability, and justice, the criminal justice system's various components must effectively collaborate and coordinate with one another. Improving the system's efficacy, efficiency, and fairness requires sustained evaluation and reform initiatives, evidence-based practices, and interdisciplinary approaches. Moreover, encouraging legitimacy and accountability requires developing openness and trust between criminal justice organizations and the communities they serve. In the end, preserving the rule of law, defending individual rights, and promoting a safer and more equitable society for all depend on a functional criminal justice system.

2.1.1. Purpose of the Criminal Justice System

It may be appropriate to note that only a small percentage of crimes are reported to the police, and even then, not all of those crimes are taken to court for prosecution. Finally, only a very small percentage of cases tried in a court of law end in a logical conclusion. Unreasonably long delays in case resolution put undue strain on the criminal justice system and cause people to lose faith in it. The fundamental goals of the criminal justice system are to protect people's person and property to the fullest extent possible and to prosecute those who break the law. Stated differently, the fundamental idea behind the Criminal

Justice System is to deliver justice to both the offender and the victim. Every society strives for justice, peace, and order, but there are always certain people or groups that cause issues with law and order. A civil society's quality is largely determined by how well the criminal justice system performs. As a result, even with a high arrest and concretion rate, a CJS may not be ideal if the public perceives it as having a low credibility rate.

2.1.2. Evolution of the Criminal Justice System

Humanity has always developed a variety of strategies and tools to uphold social order, curb criminal activity within its population, and prevent natural tendencies toward crime. The systems in place to curb criminal activity differ from one society to the next and occasionally even within a single society. But the mechanism mostly consists of the arrest, prosecution, and sentencing procedures. With the advancement of civilization and the socio-economic and political circumstances that have prevailed throughout history, the mechanisms of arrest, trial, and punishment have undergone significant changes that have an impact on the system's development. According to Pillai (200), the development of penal law has occurred in three main stages. The first stage is characterized by strict liability, while the second stage is centered on moral wickedness or guilt consciousness. The test of foresight of the consequences was added to the idea of moral wickedness. The Criminal Justice System has a rich historical background. The English Crown gradually came to control the administration of justice in the 12th century, and the Crown was to be compensated rather than the victim. Nevertheless, no formal methods were developed. The informal methods and uncodified law that typified the criminal justice system before the 18th century. It is a historical fact that the criminal justice system's operational framework can be traced back to certain codified legal codes and state-administered processes from antiquity. TCode of Hammurabi developed bythe King Hammurabi of Babylon in 18th century B.C. was the earliest known system of laws. This code was designated to regulate a wide variety of human affairs.

According to Dwivedi (2004), the law of dharma, as outlined in the Vedas, governed the criminal justice system in ancient India because it was regarded as the highest law. The king had the authority to punish the transgressor. The distinction between criminal and civil wrong was not made explicitly in ancient Hindu law, but as society advanced and developed, the King began enacting laws and regulations that took into account regional usages and customs. The system underwent very gradual but slow changes. Muslim law was introduced to India following the Muslims' conquest of the nation, and Muslim criminal law was used by Indian courts to administer justice. According to Misra (2004), the holy Quran and Hadis served as the primary sources for Muslim criminal law. The laws needed to be clarified and explained by the Qazis. Crimes against God, such as adultery and intoxication, and crimes against man, such as murder and robbery, were separated under the Muslim Criminal Law. The community or society punished the crimes against God because they were considered public wrongs. The victim or the victim's next of kin played a crucial role in determining the type and severity of the punishment for crimes against humanity, which were considered private and subject to legal consequences. By paying compensation—what was referred to as "blood money" in the majority of the cases—the matter could be resolved. There were four main categories of punishment: Hadd (defined punishment), Qisas (retaliation), Diyut (blood money), and Tazer and Siyasa (exemplary and discretionary punishment). Up until the East India Company assumed control of the administration of justice, there were numerous operational challenges.

In 1765, the Nizamat of the three provinces of Bengal, Bihar, and Orissa was purchased by the East India Company. The Companys as they were at first in order toto administer justice, but changes were made gradually and on a regular basis. Numerous modifications were made to the trial process and the types of penalties meted out. Warren Hastings made the first attempt to change the nature of punishments, and Lord Cornwalis then brought about a number of changes to the substantive criminal law. Many laws were introduced piecemeal, but each presidency had its own set of laws and regulations that were very different from one another. The differences in the Rules and Regulations became apparent when all the Presidencies were placed under a single administrative unit. It was then recognized that piecemeal reforms might not produce the desired outcomes, so in order to resolve the conflicting rules, the All India Legislature, the Office of the Law Member in the Council of the Governor General, and the Law Commission were established by the Charter of 1833. In 1834, Lord Macauley was appointed as the chairman of the First Law Commission. The Legislative Council received the draft report from the Commission. It was recommended by the Legislative Council to the Governor General for approval. The amended draft penal code was approved by the governor general and went into effect on January 1st, 1862. The Criminal Procedure establishes the process for trial of the offenses, the Law of Evidence deals with the evidence, the Penal Code defines crimes and criminal behavior, and the Constitution, among other important matters, deals with the rights and obligations of both the State and the subjects. There are numerous other laws that specify offenses, assign responsibilities and rights, and establish the protocols for handling particular offenses. In addition, courts have had a part to play in interpreting the law. Indeed, judicial activism has played a significant role in the expansion of the criminal justice system.

2.1.3. Components of the Criminal Justice System

The administration of justice is facilitated by a number of interconnected components that criminal justice system. In order toTo maintain the rule of law, protect public safety, and treat those involved in the criminal justice system fairly, these elements cooperate. The main components of the criminal just system include:

- **Law Enforcement:** It oOrganizations are in charge of upholding the rule of law, investigating criminal activity, and maintaining public order. Examples of these organizations include police departments, sheriff's offices, and federal agencies like the FBI. When a person contacts the criminal justice system, police officers are usually the first to respond to an emergency, initiate investigations, make arrests, and gather evidence.
- **Courts:** The federal, state, and local courts make up the judicial branch of the criminal justice system. Courts have the authority to interpret and apply the law, decide criminal cases, and guarantee defendants' rights to due process. Judges preside over court cases, make legal decisions, and sentence criminals who have been found guilty. Courts can help prosecutors and defendants reach plea agreements by supervising pretrial procedures like bail hearings and arraignments.
- **Prosecution:** In criminal cases, prosecutors—also referred to as district attorneys or state attorneys—represent the government and are in charge of filing charges against those who are suspected of committing crimes. Assessing the evidence, prosecutors decide whether to press charges, bring cases before the court, and attempt to secure convictions through trial or plea agreements. By standing up for victims, holding offenders accountable, and advancing public safety, they are essential to the criminal justice system.
- **Defense:** These lawyers stand up for the rights of people who are accused of crimes and defend them throughout the criminal justice system. Defense lawyers give defendants legal advice, look into the case's facts, refute the prosecution's evidence, and make sure the law is applied fairly to the defendants. They are essential in defending the constitutional rights of defendants, such as the right to a fair trial and the right to competent legal representation.
- **Corrections:** Those who have been found guilty of crimes and given prison, probation, or other types of supervision must be managed by the criminal justice system's corrections division. Correctional

agencies are in charge of the custody, treatment, and rehabilitation of criminals. These agencies include prisons, jails, probation offices, and parole boards. Their main objectives are to safeguard public safety, assist in the rehabilitation of offenders, and encourage a smooth transition back into society.

Together, these elements of the criminal justice system guarantee the administration of justice, the holding of criminals accountable for their deeds, and the protection of the rights of all parties involved in the criminal justice system. The integrity and efficacy of the criminal justice system depend on the cooperation and coordination of law enforcement, courts, prosecution, defense, and corrections.

2.2. TYGY OF RESEARCH METHOD

1. **Fundamental Research:** It'sIt is also referred to as basic or pure research. In this type of study, information is gathered purely for intellectual purposes. Creating and evaluating theories and hypotheses is required for this. The results could be useful theoretically.
2. **Applied Research:** In applied or analytical research the main aim is to solve implementation problems of different laws.
3. **Action Research**: It is similar to applied research but mainly related to the actual operations connected with an institution or problem.
4. **Evaluation Research**: It is a systematic collection of information about activities and outcomes of actual programs. The aim is to evaluate the impact of the program.
5. **Doctrinal Research**: Legal doctrine is analyzed, legal reasoning and logical deduction are applied to the study of legal institutions, and legal propositions are arranged, ordered, and systematized. The doctrinal study is primarily proposition-based and focuses on the specific legal doctrine, not the reasons behind its creation. Legal theories and law reports/case laws are the data sources used by doctrinal researchers. The doctrinal research looks at the following issues:
   - The aim of preferred values;
   - The problems posed by the gap between the policy goal and present state of achievement;
   - Availability of alternative choice for the implementation of goals;
   - The predictions and consequences that were made.

6. **Non-Doctrinal or Empirical Research**: The legal decision-making process is the primary focus of empirical or non-doctrinal research, i.e., the factors that affect decisions and how those decisions affect society are the focus of researchers. Thus, one definition of this research could be "research into the relationship between law and other behavioral sciences." Fieldwork is necessary because people, social values, and social institutions are given more weight in this context. It looks for ways that extralegal events affect the legal system and how decisions about it affect individuals and society at large.

2.2.1. Historical Survey of Development of Criminal Justice Research

2.2.1.1. Classicism

The earliest school of criminology that is still regarded seriously to offer current discussions is probably classicismclassicism. Classicist writers discussed the guiding principles that ought to direct to criminal activity. They were essentially politicalpolitical theorists. Hence, classicism serves as a crucial reminder that the term "crime" is more than just a term used to describe a particular type of behavior among people. Instead, by designating a particular behavior as a "crime," a society ascribes to that behavior a significant component of societal censure; the acts that are subject to this kind of censure can and do differ between societies as well as over time within a single society. As crime is ultimately a normative category, meaningful discussions about what behaviors should be classified as "criminal" (i.e., the content of the criminal law) as well as the procedures for investigating, proving, and, in the event that a crime is proven, punishing the perpetrator (penology) can anated in any given society. Although the classicalistsclassicalists were very good at this type of normative theorization, they also occasionally made empirical claims that were later proven to be untrue, though not always. These empirical claims were derived from common sense observations and introspective thoughts rather than any kind of systematic research.

2.2.1.2. Natural Science- Based Positivism

The triumphs of natural science and engineering were everywhere in the second half of the 19th century, from Darwin to the railway network, daring bridge-building, and medical science advancements. It should come as no surprise that fearless pioneers in sociology, psychology, and psychiatry aimed to apply the natural scientific method to the study of behavior in people. By then, "the natural scientific approach" was defined as positivism, which is the belief that causal laws of behavior can be found, a strong emphasis on observations, and a neutral, dispassionate approach from the scientist. "The classical school bade men study justice, but the positivists bade justice study men," was the famous aphorism that contrasted the positivists with their classicist forebears. Stated differently, the positivists argued that the armchair theorization of the classicists would become obsolete. It is imperative for criminologists to conduct empirical research on criminals, criminal justice systems, and related areas. Subsequently, policymakers should carefully consider the insights these criminologists provide.

These can be characterized as follows:

- It was assumed t natural science could and should be unproblematic allyunproblematically applied to the social world (while making allowance, of course, for the fact that the context was empirically different). Since such methods were taken to include assumptions of determinist causation, it was assumed that human behavior should be studied within a determinist framework.
- It was assumed that the foundation of all science, natural and social, was 'sense-data,' i.e., information that our senses were able to observe. It was believed the scientific observer would have direct access to thesethis sensory data and could report on them objectively, Empiricism. Thus, carefully gathered, theory-neutral facts by scientists formed the foundation of science. These "real facts" that serve as s for knowledge were regarded as being far more reliabledependable than the classicists' "metaphysical speculations."
- It was believed that "facts" and "values" were distinct from one another. The former could be observed and verified by science, while the latter could not and were instead based on "taste" or individual preferences. It was, in fact, a widely accepted belief in scientific positivist philosophical circles in the 1950s and early 1960s that rational discourse regarding substantive moral principles was impossible. All of this, along with the focus on empirical observation, signified a total break with the presumptions of the classicists, whose work was occasionally disparagingly referred to as "pre-scientific."
- It was acknowledged that positivism struggled with the idea of "crime," since the definition of "criminal" in any given society was set by the powerful, and societies varied, sometimes dramatically, in what behaviors they considered to be "crimes." All of this appeared to be extremely distant from the consistent and "natural"

explanandum (to be explained phenomenon) that is ostensibly necessary for a completely "natural-scientific" criminology. Primarily, positivists avoided this significant challenge by arguing that certain types of crimes (such as theft, murder, etc., made up the main topics of criminology, and that these, as opposed to other types of "administrative" crimes, were the "natural crimes."

- Because of its desire to follow as closely as possible the methods of the natural sciences, positivist criminology that focused on the explanation of criminal behavior was and is primarily concerned ' with how accurate facts can be obtained and how theory can thereby be more rigorously tested' (Glaser & Strauss, 1967) That is to say, the ideal research method was seen as an initial collection of facts, the formulation by logical processes of a theory in the shape of a formal hypothesis, and then the rigorous testing of that hypothesis, to verify or falsify it. If a modified hypothesis then seemed necessary in the light of the results of the first testing, then that h hypothesis (Hypothesis B) was formulated and formally tested and so on.
- Of course, not all criminological research focuses on explaining criminal behavior; for instance, a significant portion of it assesses the efficacy of different criminal justice interventions, like community policing or intentionally designed rehabilitative prison programs. In keeping with their fundamental principles, positivist criminologists once more looked to natural science for a model for their investigative work. This was particularly evident in the "clinical trial" experimental design that is commonly employed in scientific medicine. Therefore, positivists supported randomizing the assignment of participants to one of two "treatments" (e.g., ProlongedProlonged, and regular probation), with the aim of removing erroneous results stemming from pre-treatment variations between the experimental and control groups. (For the promotion of the random assignment technique in criminological assessment.
- A strong preference for quantitative data over qualitative data resulted from positivists' preference for techniques similar to those used in the natural sciences, the experimental method in evaluative research, and the hypothetical deductive approach to explanatory research. In post-1970 criminology, each of the aforementioned presumptions has been called into question, frequently seve Space does not allow for a thorough discussion, but let'slet us say a few things quickly. Nowadays, there is a general consensus that social science differs from natural science primarily because its subjects

are human, with the ability to give meaning to the circumstances in which they find themselves and the potential to respond to and even change those circumstances.

2.2.1.3. Subject Socially-Oriented Criminologist

Two dimensions have beeStuart Henry & Dragen Milovanovic (1996) as a very helpfulan extremely helpful way to categorize mainstream criminological theories. The first dimension categorizes theories based on how much they consider humans to be active subjects (i.e., do they have the ability to create and shape their own world, or are their behavior limited and determined by their unique biology, upbringing, and/or the social environment around them?). The second dimension categorizes theories based on whether they consider human behavior to be primarily social or individual. Although it may be more beneficial to view each of these dimensions as a continuous distribution, both can be treated as dichotomies for heuristic purposes. When this is done, active-subject individually oriented theories (i), active-subject socially oriented theories (ii), passive-subject individually oriented theories (iv), and passive-subject socially oriented theories (v) are considered to be the four main categories of mainstream criminological theories. Of course, the primary exemplar of the third and fourth (passive subject) types—though not the only one—is the positivist tradition in allof its forms. An extensive and illustrious history exists of criminologically-oriented ethnographic research; among the prominent supporters of this tradition during the interwar years were the Chicago School of Socio whose members, particularly Clifford Shaw, conducted some criminological research. When positivist criminology's hegemony began to wane after the mid-1960s, ethnographic work in criminology saw a resurgence, drawing on this earlier tradition.

It must be acknowledged that authors in the ethnographic tradition are typically wary of theoretical generalizations when it comes to the relationship between theory and research. They tend to find it difficult to draw generalizations from the specifics because they place so much importance on the unique contexts of each social situation. When it comes to building theories, they are more inclined toward the inductive than the deductive methods. This means that instead of formally testing hypotheses, they would rather develop theories "upwards" from an understanding of particular social situations.

2.2.1.4. Active Subject Individually Oriented Criminologist

Several iterations of active subject individually oriented criminology have gained prominence in the 1980s and 1990s. The emphasis that these criminologists place on the fact that people make actual decisions rather than viewing them as the result of a variety of biological, familial, and social factors at play—as is the case with positivist perspectives—is reminiscent of the ethnographic approach. On them. However, this type of criminology is very different from ethnography in that it places more of an emphasis on human reasoning and rationality than it does on cultural contexts and normative ties. Within this type of criminology, it is useful to distinguish between the main strands. First, there is the economic theory of crime and punishment, which was first presented in a groundbreaking 1968 paper by eminent economist Gary Becket. The second line of inquiry is rational choice theory, which emerged partly from the now substantial corpus of research on "situational crime prevention." Routine activities theory, the third strand, shares many characteristics with rational choice theory but also differs from it in some significant ways. These three threads have all significantly of criminology. They have proven, beyond a shadow of a doubtany doubt, that decisions made by participants occasionally have aspects of prudential rationality. Prudent rationality can frequently be deduced from aggregate data, which makes this most evident. One such study found that bus passenger vandalism was significantly more common on the (unsupervised) upper deck. The application of situational crime prevention and routine activities approaches has also made criminologists more aware of the role that opportunity plays in the genesis of crime; on the other hand, limiting opportunities will frequently result in a decrease in criminal activity. But these developments have come at the expense of a decontextualized understanding of the human subject, as the ethnographic research of Wright & Decker (1994) on active burglars amply illustrates. Similar to this, the routine activities approach has placed a strong emphasis on decisions made at the scene (or probable scene) of a criminal act, but it has largely disregarded the social perceptions and biographical histories of the potential offenders who may actually have to make these decisions.

2.2.1.5. Political-Activist Criminologist

Anyone familiar with the evolution of criminology in Britain since 1970 will know that a great deal of the analysis put forth has taken an overtly political stance in addressing its subject. This is especially true for criminologists who are Marxist-oriented, feminist criminologists, and members of the theoretical movement known as "left-realism." Henry and Milovanovic's four-fold typology of mainstream criminologists and this category of criminology overlap because political-activist criminologists can be, as these authors clarify, (i) active – subject socially – oriented (like in left realism), (ii) active – subject individually – oriented (like in liberal feminism), or even (iii) passive – subject socially – oriented (like in some forms of Marxism). But from the perspective of this chapter, there are some unique points to be made by focusing on political-activist criminologists, since the explicit combination of poism and these theories naturally brings up some rather uniqueunique questions regarding the connection between theory anarch in criminology. But at this point, that viewpoint has tomust be considered untenable. Because the idea of crime itself and the type of criminal justice system that a particular society adopts are inherently the result of moral and political decisions. Furthermore, political ramifications can arise from criminological research, even the most meticulous, objective, and rigorous studies. Therefore, the main advantage of political activist criminology is that it serves as a reminder that, whether criminologists like it or not, conducting research and developing theories in the field of criminology is inextricably linked to the political environment. Thus, political-activist criminology brings criminology full circle to its classical beginnings, where the normative aspects of the field were highlighted.

Any criminologist worth their salt will have witnessed instances of political advocacy in which unfavorable empirical evidence is "forgotten" for a while, or even in which strong empirical claims are made in an effort to further the political cause, despite the argument's clearly inadequate empirical foundation. This kind of strategy has even been used by professional criminologists. However, it is risky to proceed in this way because, at worst, it may put political objectives ahead of scholarly pursuits. And doing so would be a decisive and disastrous turn away from the pursuit of truth. Many people are familiar with John Rawls's claim that justice is the primary virtue of social institutions, just as truth is of philosophical systems, which appears on the first page of his famous book on justice. No matter how beautiful and well-organized a theory may be, if it is false, it must be rejected or revised; similarly, if laws and institutions are unfair, they must be changed or eliminated. Although Rawls emphasizes the primacy of truth as a criterion when trying to explain the natural and social worlds, this passage is most frequently cited for its emphasis on the primacy of justice within normative debates.

2.2.2. Relationship Between Theory and Research in Crime and Justice

In crime and justice, theory and research have a fundamentally symbiotic and cyclical relationship in which each component continuously informs and improves the other. Theories offer crucial conceptual frameworks for comprehending the intricate phenomena of victimization, criminal behavior, and the operation of legal systems. They provide answers on why crimes happen, who is most likely to commit them, and how communities can effectively deal with them. These theoretical frameworks ensure that research efforts are targeted and pertinent by providing guidance for the creation of hypotheses, research questions, and empirical study designs. For example, the strain theory, which holds that social pressures can influence people to commit crimes, encourages researchers to look into things like social inequality anhardship. On the other hand, research is essential to the testingtesting, confirming, and improvement of these theories. Researchers obtain information through thorough empirical research that either confirms or refutes theoretical hypotheses. Research results that support theoretical predictions strengthen the theory's validity; those that do not force theoretical constructs to be reexamined and revised. This process of iteration is essential to the advancement of knowledge within the field. Additionally, empirical research can reveal novel patterns and anomalies that current theories fail to explain, which can result in the creation of fresh theoretical viewpoints. For instance, new theorieess criminal behavior in the digital age are required in light ofconsidering the rise in cybercrime. Theory and research are ensured to evolve in response to new evidence and shifting social contexts through their dynamic interplay. In the end, the integration of theory and research in the field of crime and justice has practical implications that influence policy-making, intervention strategies, and the creation of more just and equitable justice systems, in addition to advancing academic understanding. Together, theory and research advance the field and promote a more comprehensive and nuanced understanding of crime and justice through their ongoing influence on one another.

2.2.3. Common Obstacles in Criminal Justice Research

Starting wie practical observations could be beneficial. As much emphasis asemphasis is placed on the relationship between theory and research, the reality is that younger researchers face significant obstacles in their attempts to gain a deeper understanding of the relationships between theory and data and to acquire the abilities required to manage these connections.

1. **Disciplinary Specialization:** The first challenge comes from younger researchers' natural desire to break out in the world. Furthermore, it appears that successful academic careers are frequently built on a narrow specialization; in any case, to land one's first academic permanent position, one must position themselves as an authority in a particular field (for instance, a theorist or a quantitative researcher accustomed to working with big data sets). These demands may undoubtedly work against the growth of a comprehensive comprehension of the relationships between theory and research.
2. **Discouragement of Theory by 'Practical People':** The Second obstacle is perhaps, a particular problem in the phere of criminology. There is undoubtedly, in many instances, and impatience with theory

from those wanting simply to 'get on with the job' of reducing crime, or of running a just and efficient criminal justice system.

3. **Pigeonholing:** It is the third barrier to complex criminological research that incorporates both theory and empirical data. This comes in two flavors: "methodological pigeonholing" and "theoretical pigeonholing." The tendency to assume that specific research methods "go with" specific theoretical approaches, to the exclusion of other types of data, is known as "methodological pigeonholing." Thus, for instance, participant and non-participant observation, in-depth interviews, and other qualitative research techniques are frequently used in ethnographic research projects. From this research angle, it is not difficult to come to the conclusion that quantitative data are, at most, meaningless. Or, in the worst case, deceptive due to their inability to accurately capture the actual, ground-level contexts of the meanings of social life in a particular milieu. Nevertheless, this categorizing Indeed, there is no reason at all why quantitative data shouldn't beshould not be used to supplement an ethnographic study in its main mental obstacles that some qualitative researchers have erected to prevent the application of quantitative data. Moreover, some of the most detrimental aspects of the British criminological landscape over the past 25 years have been the corresponding barriers that certain quantitative researchers have erected against qualitative research data. Though there is no valid reason for them, there are indications that these obstacles are beginning to be removed; let us hope this is the case for the topic's long-term health.

4. **Eclecticism and Synthesis:** The misunderstanding of eclecticism and synthesis is another barrier to a fruitful and productive collaboration between theory and empirical research. Even though the confusion is typically implicit rather than explicit, it still plays a significant role in impeding advancement. Criminology theories frequently cover only a portion of the field; for instance, we cannot reasonably expect "labeling theory" or "strain theory" to explain all criminality, even though they can be very helpful in some particular situations. If there were a widespread "culture of openness" in criminology—that is, a culture of being receptive to the insights provided by many theories and willing to examine their potential contribution to social scientific explanation within a specific set of circumstances—then this narrow coverage of individual theories would mean absolutely nothing.

5. **The Problem of Conceptual Hegemony:** If methodological and

theoretical silos are avoided, and if a researcher is generally content to work toward synthesis, there is still an additional barrier that could prevent theory and research from developing to their full potential. We could use a study on whether and under what conditions harsher sentences discourage crime to demonstrate this issue. We may try a comprehensive conceptual analysis of general deterrence policies as part of our research, i.e., any deliberate deterrent measure designed to make the general public less likely to commit crimes in the future by instilling fear of the potential consequences. In that analysis, we stressed that deterrence is a subjective concept because it is based on fear as the reason to refrain from taking a particular action. We then outlined five that we contend are simulative (i.e., logically required) in order toto successfully attain marginal general deterrence in a particular instance. As an example, the first of these five requirements stated that "a potential offender must realize that the probability of conviction or the severity of punishment has changed" in cases where a newly introduced general deterrent policy is in place.

2.3. FUNCTIONING OF CRIMINAL PROCEDURE LAW

Current procedural laws subtly represent the concepts of natural justice. Regarding the criminal side, it addresses ideas like representation, fair play, adversarial systems, avoidance of double jeopardy, wrongful detention, and so forth. The civil side has incorporated the following principles: finality, avoidance of diversity, protection of the poor and incompetent parties, protection of women in money decrees, and provisions protecting judgment debtors without compromising the rights of the decree holder. There has been a focus on using alternative dispute resolution techniques to settle conflicts. The Criminal Procedure Code of 19contains provisions for the administration of justice to all as few of important points are:

2.3.1. Protection to the Accused atTime of Arrest

The process guarantees that an individual detained won'twill not be subjected to more restrictions than what's required to keep them from escaping. According to Section 50, the person who has been arrested has to be told of their right to bail as well as the reason for their arrest. When someone is arrested without a warrant by a police officer or another official, they have an obligation to tly inform the arrested person of the reason(s) for their arrest. Let'sLet us say a police officer makes an unauthorized arrest for any reason other than a crime for which there is no possibility of bond. Then, he has to inform the person who was arrested that they are eligible for bail and that he can make arrangements for sureties on their behalf. If someone has been arrested, whether on a charge or not, and they claim at any point while they are being held in custody that a physical examination will reveal information that refutes their involvement in any crime, the Code guarantees that they have the right to have a medical professional examine them at their request.

2.3.2. Fair Trail and Principles of Natural Justice

No one should be sentenced without a hearing, according to natural law. As a result, the fundamental requirement of the principle is that the person being prosecuted be informed about the circumstances in w in violation of the law. To accomplish this, the court must as per Theproduce to the accused who is entitled to a copy of the police report and all documents under Section 207. It stipulates that in any case where the investigation is based on a police report, the Magistrate shall without delay furnish to the accused, free of cost, a copy of each of the document as- "the police report; the first information report recorded under section 154; the statements recorded under sub-section (3) of section 161 of all persons whom the prosecution proposes to examine as its witnesses, excluding there from any part in regard to which a request for such exclusion has been made by the police officer under subsection (6) of section 173; the confessions and statements, if any, recorded under section 164; any other document or relevant extract thereof forwarded to the Magistrate with the police report under sub-section (5) of section 173; is voluminous, he shall, instead of furnishing the accused with a copy thereof, direct that he will only be allowed to inspect it either personally or through pleader in Court."

Defendants in other cases tried by the Court of Session are required to receive copies of statements and documents pursuant to Section 208. "The Magistrate shall promptly provide the accused, free of charge, with a copy of each of the documents namely: the statements recorded under section 200 or section 202, or all persons examined by the Magistrate; the statements and confessions, if any, recorded under section 161 or section 164; any documents produced before the Magistrate on which the prosecution proposes to rely." This is because the Magistrate is required by section 204 to issue process in cases where it appears to the Magistrate that the offense is only triable by the Court of Session. "

2.3.3. Notice to the Accused Regarding the Trial

Natural justice principles are still upheld at the beginning of the proceedings. The charge or notice of accusation that includes the allegation is sent to the defendant. In warrant cases or cases that can only be tried by the Court of

Session, the charge is framed. On the other hand, a clear notice of indictment is given in summons cases. The victim is informed of the nature of the offense and has the opportunity to defend it in summary trials.

Section 211 is concerned with Chargeable content:

1. "Every charge under this Code shall state the offence with which the accused is charged."
2. "If the law which creates the offence gives it any specific name, the offence may be described in the charge by that name only."
3. "If the law which creates the offence does not give it any specific name so much of the definition of the offence must be stated as to give the accused notice of the matter with which he is charged."
4. "The law and section of the law against which the offence is said to have been committed shall be mentioned in the charge."
5. "The fact that the charge is made is equivalent to a statement that every legal condition required by law to constitute the offence charged was fulfilled in the particular case."
6. The charge must be written in the official language of the court. If the accused has a prior conviction for any offense and is therefore subject to an increased punishment or a different kind of punishment for a subsequent offense, the charge must include the factual information about the prior conviction in order to influence the punishment the court may determine is appropriate for the subsequent offense. If this information has not been included, the court may add it at any point before sentencing."

2.3.4. Proceedings of the Cases

To guarantee that the fair trial regulations are adhered to in letter and spirit, specific guidelines have been incorporated into the code. Section 273 mandates that proof be taken in the accused's presence. Unless otherwise ordered, the accused or, if his presence is not necessary, his pleader, must be present during all testimony taken during a trial or other proceeding. The court that is trying the accused is always open, with the exception of certain situations, like rape, where the judge may order the trial to be held in secret.

2.3.5. Right of the Accused against Double Jeopardy

The protection against being prosecuted and being punished for the same offense more than once is guaranteed by the Constitution. Section 300 of the Code of Criminal Procedure (1973) enshrines this principle in a broader manner, encompassing situations where the accused is found guilty or even exonerated. Section 300 stated that a person cannot be tried for the same offense again after being found guilty or found not guilty. It is a protection against double jeopardy.

1. "A person who has previously been tried for an offense by a court of competent jurisdiction and found guilty or not guilty of that offense shall not be subject to another trial for that same offense, nor on the same facts for any other offense for which a different charge than the one made against him might have been made under subsection (1) of section 221, or for which he might have been found guilty under sub-section (2) thereof, as long as that conviction or acquittal remains in effect. "Under sub-section (1) of section 220, an individual who has been found not guilty or acquitted of any crime may, with the approval of the State Government, be tried again for any other crime for which he may have been charged separately during the first trial."
2. "If the consequences had not occurred or the court was unaware that they had not occurred at the time of the conviction, an individual convicted of any offense comprised of an act that resulted in consequences that, when combined with the act, constituted an offense distinct from the one for which they were found guilty, may subsequently be tried for the aforementioned offense."
3. "If the court that tried him initially lacked the authority to try the offence he is now charged with, then a person acquitted or found guilty of any offense constituted by any acts may, notwithstanding such acquittal or conviction, be charged with and tried for any other offense constituted by the same acts which he may have committed."
4. "A person discharged under section 258 shall not be tried again for the same offence except with the consent of the Court by which he was discharged or of any other Court to which the first-mentioned Court is subordinate."
5. "Nothing in this section shall affect the provisions of section 26 of the General Clauses Act (1897) or on 188 of this Code."

2.3.6. Accused Right to be Defendeeader Attorney of His Choice

Section 303 provides the right to a defensedefense for the person against whom proceedings are broughs the subject of liion under this Code or who has been found guiltybeen charged with ae in a Criminal Court is entitled to legal representation from a pleaderan attorney of their choosing.

2.3.7. Legal Aid to Accused at State Expense in Certain Cases

1. "Where, inbefore the Court of Session, the accused is not represented by a pleaderan attorney, and where it appears to the Court that the accused has not sufficient means to engage a pleader, the Court shall assign a pleader for his defense at the expense of the State."
2. "The High Court may, with the previous approvaState Government make rule providing for the mode of selecting pleaders attorneys for defense under sub-section (2); the facilitiellowed to such pleaders by the Courts; the fee payable to such pleaders attorneys by the Government, and generally, for carrying out the purposes of sub-section (1)."
3. The State Government may order, by notification, that the provisions of sub-sections (1) and (2) apply to any class of trials before other courts in the State as they apply to trials before the Courts of Session as of the date specified in the notification. The right to free legal assistance does not require the accused to request it, and the Court is required to remind the accused of his right to free legal assistance.

2.3.8. Provision Deal with When the Accused Person Is Unsound Mind

Section 328 provides procedure in case of accused being lunatic.

1. "When a magistrate conducting an inquiry has cause to suspect that the subject of the inquiry is mentally ill and thus unable to present a defense, the magistrate will investigate the possibility of this ill-being and will arrange for the subject to be examined by the district's civil surgeon or another medical officer at the direction of the State Government. The magistrate will then call the surgeon or other officer in question as a witness and will put the examination in writing."
2. "The Magistrate may deal with such person in accordance with section 330 provisions pending such examination and inquiry."
3. "The Magistrate shall record a finding to that effect and shall postpone further proceedings in the case if he believes that the person mentioned in subsection (1) is not of sound mind and is therefore unable to present his defense."

   "In that case, the Magistrate or Court can dismiss the case., the Magistrate or Court shall, in the first instance, try the fact of such unsoundness and incapacity, and if the Magistrate or Court, after considering such medical and other evidence as may be produced before him or it, is satisfied of the fact, he or it shall record a finding to that effect and shall postpone further proceedings in the case."

4. "The trial of the fact of the unsoundness of mind and incapacity of the accused shall be deemed to be part of his trial before the Magistrate or Court."

2.3.9. Provision as to Bail and Bonds

Following are the provisions in what cases bail to be taken like:

1. A person shall be released on bail if, aside from those found guilty of non-bailable offenses, they are arrested or detained without a warrant by a police officer, or they appear in court and are willing to post bail at any time while in the officer's custody or during the court's trial.
2. "In spite of what is stated in sub-section (1), the Court may decline to grant someone bail if they have not complied with the bond's requirements regarding the time and location of attendance. This refusal will not affect the Court's ability to demand payment of the bond's penalty under section 446 from anyone who is bound by the bond when they appear in court again or are placed under custody. It is true that the Supreme Court does not overturn a bail order, but if jurisdiction under Article 136 is denied, judicial discretion will be compromised at the expense of judicial discipline."

2.3.9.1. Section 437 Provides When Bail May Be Taken in Case of Non-Bailable Offence

1. If an individual has been found guilty of a non-bailable crime and is being held without a warrant by a police station officer, or if they are appearing in court outside of the High Court or Court of Session, they may be released on bond. However, this will not happen if there are reasonable grounds to believe that they have committed an offense for which they could be executed or imprisoned for life; it also won't happen if the offense is one that is cognizable and the individual has been previously convicted of an offense punishable by death, lifelong imprisonment, or imprisonment for seven years or more, or if he has been previously convicted on two or more occasions of a non-bailable and cognizable offense.
2. In the event that an officer or court determines, at any point during the investigation, examination, or trial, that there are no reasonable

grounds to believe the accused has committed an offence for which there is no bail, the accused may be released; however, if an officer or court determines that there are sufficient grounds to conduct a further investigation into the accused's guilt, the accused may be released on bail, subject to the provisions of section 446A while the investigation is ongoing, or at the officer or court's discretion upon the accused's execution of a bond without sureties for his appearance as specified below.

3. When a person is convicted or suspected of committing an offence punishable by seven years or more in prison, or an offence of the Indian Penal Code (1860) or abetment of, or conspiracy or attempt to commit, any such offence, is released on bail under sub-section (1) the Court may impose any condition which the Court considers necessary in order to ensure that such person shall attend in accordance with the conditions of the bond executed or in order to ensure that such person shall not commit an offence similar to the offence of which he is accused or of the commission of which he is suspected or otherwise in the interests of justice.
4. When releasing someone on bail under subsection (1) or subsection (2), an officer or a court must document their special or unique justifications in writing.
5. If a court determines that it is appropriate, it may order an arrest and commit the person to custody after releasing them on bail under subsection (1) or (2).
6. A person convicted of any non-bailable offense who is in custody for the entirety of the trial period and whose trial is triable by a magistrate will be released on bail upon the magistrate's satisfaction if the trial is not completed within 60 days of the first date scheduled for the collection of evidence in the case, unless the magistrate orders otherwise in writing.
7. Upon the accused's execution of a bond without sureties and his appearance to hear the judgment, the court will release the accused, if he is in custody, if it determines at any point after the conclusion of the accused's trial and before judgment is delivered that there are reasonable grounds to believe the accused is not guilty of any such offence.

2.3.10. Saving of Inherent Power of High Court Under Section 482

Nothing in this Code may be interpreted to limit or impair the High Court's inherent authority to issue orders as necessary to implement any directive made pursuant to this Code, prevent abuse of any court process, or further advance the interests of justice.

- "The charges under section 302 read with section 120B, IPC against the accused were quashed by the High Court in the exercise of its powers under section 482 after the investigation was turned over to the CID due to the police's inadequate investigation. This decision was made despite the fact that the Court was not required to carefully consider all relevant material and evidence at the time the charges were framed."
- "The High Court would not investigate whether or not the allegations in the complaint are likely to be supported by evidence when exercising its jurisdiction under section 482."
- "The High Court may, in the exercise of its inherent powers under section 482, quash the proceedings to prevent abuse of the Court's process; however, interference would only be warranted in cases where the complaint revealed no offense or was frivolous, vexatious, or oppressive."
- "There is no justification by the High Court to interfere with the prosecution at the preliminary stage where there was some discrepancy, primarily with regard to the implications of respondent by name in the FIR and the statement of the witnesses recorded during the investigation. The Supreme Court has repeatedly found fault with the practice of the High Court prejudging the question without giving the prosecution a reasonable opportunity to substantiate the allegations."
- "The criminal proceedings established on the basis of such a First Information Report should be quashed if the allegations made in the report are taken at face value and accepted in their entirety as not constituting an offense."
- "It amounts to abuse of the process of the Court if without prima facie case having been made out a person is summoned to face trial in a criminal proceeding."
- It is well established that the inherent powers under section 482 may only be used in situations where the litigant has exhausted all other options, not in situations where the statute specifies a particular remedy. Furthermbecause the power is extraordinary, it must be used carefully. There won'twill not be any contradiction between this Code's sections 397(2) and 482 if these factors are taken into account.

- "There is no need to produce any sanction if the prosecution was started within six months of the Bengal Excise Act (1909), under Section 92 allegations, as the Magistrate would then be free to take cognizance under the Act." The learned single judge's reasoning that the proceedings should not have been quashed and that the steps to obtain sanction should have been taken before the first six months had passed is not supported by section 92.
- "Necessary ingredients of offence of cheating or criminal branch of trust have not been made out but the attendant circumstances indicate that the FIR was lodged to prompt the filing of criminal complaint against the informant under section 138 N.I. Act Quashing of FIR was proper to avoid the abuse of process."
- "FIR lodges to preempt the filing of criminal complaint against the informant under section 138 N.I. Act Quashing of FIR proper."
- Regarding the quashing of grievances and inquiries based on the complainant's FIR, the High Court was not justified in intervening with the process and quashing the proceedings by an elaborate judgment on the merits. It was premature to conclude that section 195 of the Cr. P. C. will be a limit. Order quashing the two comaint set aside.
- The extra-ordinary power under section 482 of Code hasve to be exercised sparingly and should not be resorted to like remedy of appeal or revision.
- The complaint may be dismissed if there is no claim in it that the petrector on the day the company issued the check or that he was in charge ofoversaw and accountable to the company.
- When the provisions under section 37 of N.D.P.S. are applicable and operative with non-obstinate clause, the powers of High Court remains restricted by limitation under section 37 (1)(b) of Act in considering bail application of accused charged for offence under N.D.P.S. Act, then the accused not entitled to grant of interim bail.
- In absence of any valid ground, the F.I.R. lodged against immigration consultant for violating sections 10, 16 of Emigration Act by issuing advertisement, High Court cannot interfere at the stage of F.I.R.

2.3.11. Order for Maintenance of Wives, Childrents

Criminal law has enacted the civil rights of maintenance in order toto expeditiously address maintenance needs, with the social objective of averting poverty and homelessness among vulnerable women and children. To give the clause teeth, penal effects are added to the respondent's default. The maintenance orders for spouses, kids, and parents are outlined in Section 125. A Magistrate of the first class may, upon proof of such neglect or refusal, order such person to make a monthly allowance for the maintenance of his wife or such child, father or mother, at such monthly rate as such magistrate thinks fit, and to pay the same to such person as the Magistrate may from time to time direct. If any person with sufficient means neglects or refuses to maintain his wife, who is unable to maintain herself, or his legitimate or illegitimate minor child, whether married or not, unable to maintain itself, or his legitimate or illegitimate child (not being a married daughter) who has reached majority. To grant such an allowance, up until the time she reaches adulthood, if the magistrate is convinced that the minor female child's married spouse does not have adequate resources.

2.4. STRUCTURE OF CRIMINAL JUSTICE SYSTEM

The term "criminal justice system" describes a group of national, state, and local government organizations that address the issue of crime. These organizations handle suspects, defendants, and convicted criminals. They are reliant on one another insofar as decisions made by one organization have an impact on those made by others. The governmental branches of the legislative, judicial, and executive provide the fundamental framework for the system.

1. **The Legislature:** Legislatures, both state and federal, define crimes, fix sentences, and provide funding for criminal justice agencies.
2. **The Judiciary:** Trial courts determine whether or not a person accused of a crime is guilty, and appellate courts apply constitutional principles to their interpretation of the law. Legislative decisions are reviewed by state and federal appellate courts, which then determine whether or not they are in accordance with federal law, state law, or ultimately the US Constitution. Courts have the authority to assess legislative actions for constitutional compliance through judicial review. An appeal court has the authority to overturn a law if it is unconstitutional.
3. **The Executive Branch:** The president, governors, and mayors are granted executive authority. They have the authority to name judges and agency heads, including police chiefs and directors of correctional departments, when it comes to criminal justice issues. Furthermore, by presenting legislative agendas and influencing public opinion, elected officials can spearhead initiatives to enhance criminal justice.

The major components of the justice system:

- The justice system's major components—police, courts, and corrections—prevent or deter crime by apprehending, trying, and punishing offenders.
- Police departments are public agencies whose purposes are to maintain order, enforce the criminal law, and provide services. Police officers operate in the community to prevent and control crime. They cooperate with prosecutors in criminal investigations, gathering evidence necessary to obtain convictions in the courts.
- Judges or juries decide a person's criminal responsibility in a courtroom when they are accused of breaking the law. Finding the truth and pursuing justice are the goals of the legal system. The main players in the legal system are the judges, defense lawyers, and prosecutors.
- Probation, parole, jail, prison, and various new community-based sanctions like house arrest and electronic monitoring are all included in the category of corrections. Correctional agencies have three main goals: to punish, to rehabilitate, and to protect the public.

2.4.1. The Differences Between Federal and State Justice Systems

While the roles of the federal and state justice systems are similar (enforcing the law, trying cases, and punishing offenders), their respective legal frameworks and administrative structures are different. The majority of criminal laws are made by state legislatures and are upheld by local and state law enforcement. In state courts, those accused of breaking state laws are put on trial by city and county prosecutors. Judges assign criminals found guilty of breaking state laws to serve their sentences in state-run prisons or locally run jails. At the federal level, Congress enacts criminal laws, and federal law enforcement agencies, such as the Federal Bureau of Investigation, enforce these laws. U.S. attorneys prosecute persons accused of committing federal crimes, and U.S. courts try the cases. To punish and rehabilitate those convicted of federal crimes, the Federal Bureau of Prisons provides programs and institutions.

2.4.2. The First Line of Defense against Crime

In the United States, state and local governments are primarily in charge of administering justice. Two-thirds of all criminal justice workers are employed by state and local governments, which also bear a far higher portion of the criminal justice system's expenses than does the federal government. Additionally, the majority of the defense against robbers, rapists, and killers is supplied by state, county, and local criminal justice systems.

2.4.3. Criminal Justice as a Non-System

Criminal justice, according to critics, is not a system at all. They draw attention to the fact that criminal justice organizations are, in some ways, autonomous entit their funding and powers from various sources. Towns and cities provide the majority ofmost of the funding for police departments; county governments fund trial courts, public defenders, prosecutors, and jails; and the state provides the majority of funding for prisons and appellate courts. Criminal justice organizations establish their own policies in addition to having distinct funding and authority sources. Lastly, age frequently overlook the cffects of their decisions on other agencies because they don'tdo not coordinate their efforts.

2.5. THE POLITICS OF CRIMINAL JUSTICE

The distribution or allocation of resources takes place through the process of politics. Politics, according to a well-known political scientist, is "who gets what, when, and how." Political factors are an essential but occasionally problematic aspect of criminal justice. Politics involved in decision-making Criminal justice decision-makers are chosen through appointments or elections. Judges are appointed by governors in some states, and elected by voters in others. The selection process is political in both scenarios. Attorneys who have taken on political roles for their party frequently run for judicial positions. The Senate confirms federal judges after the president appoints them. The political system has a significant impact on the ourt. The Court's opinions on matters pertaining to criminal justice change as a result ofbecause of retircments from the bench and new appointments.

2.5.1. Politics of Lawmaking

The lawmaking process is arguably the most significant way that the democratic political system affects criminal justice: Politics has an impact on the laws that legislatures pass. State lawmakers and the U.S. during the 1980s and 1990s. Legislators hurricd to draft politically conservative, harsh sentencing legislation. These laws require fewer chances for parole and lengthier sentences. A lawyer who played a key role in the rewriting of federal drug laws in 1986 and 1988 claims that politicians' pranks and whims led to the harsh sentencing laws that made headlines right before elections. 'There was level of hysteria that resulted in a complete breakdown of the legislative process,' stateds lead U.S. attorney Eric Sterling. The laws imposing lengthy mandatory sentences for various drug-related convictions were drafted by the House Committee on the Judiciary. After 20 years of strict sentencing guidelines, the number of people incarcerated has skyrocketed. Correctional costs have increased dramatically. Revenue allocations within state governments have shifted to prioritize funding for prisons over education and other vital human services.

2.5.2. Politics and Policing

While politics does not directly influence the day-to-day decisions made by police officers while on patrol, the political climate of a community does influence the type of departmental policy and the manner in which law enforcement is conducted. The degree to which politics influence policing varies depending on the type of government (commissioner, mayor/council, city manager). In municipalities where a mayor and council form of government is in place, politics is ingrained in the police force. A competent city manager, on the other hand, reduces the likelihood of political interference with law enforcement.

2.5.3. Politics of Prosecution

Prosecutors are directly influenced by political factors. In most states, prosecutors are elected officials who play a significant role in local politics. In the U.S. at the federal level. Since they are political appointees, attorneys frequently align their professional goals with the demands of their political party. State and federal prosecutors frequently use their positions as stepping stones to more senior political positions. Sometimes a dishonest prosecutor will abuse their position of authority in the most egregious way possible: acting out of political animosity, the prosecutor will bring criminal charges against political opponents. One could argue, for instance, that independent counsel Kenneth Starr's investigations into President Clinton's extramarital affairs in the late 1990s were driven by his conservative political views.

2.5.4. Politicsecision-Making

There is a lot of political pressure on judges. As judges consider whether or notwhether to apply the death penalty, dubious political factors are taken into consideration. The fact that elected judges apply the death penalty more frequently than appointed judges is not an accident. This disparity results from elected judges' concern over coming across as tolerant of crime. A judge who refuses to execute someone is open to criticism from political rivals who hope to utilize the judge's decision against them in the upcoming judicial retention

Politics of Corrections

Politics is a factor that corrections officials also take into accountconsider. Parole board decisions about release can be influenced by politics. e parole board are vulnerable to the sway of the governors who select them. Members almost alwaysalways choose releases with caution. The governor may be blamed by the media, the governor's political rivals, or both if parolees commit crimes.

2.5.6. Politicization of Criminal Justice

The politicization of criminal justice, a process by which political leaders take advantage of opportunities to use criminal justice issues to enhance their own popularity, electability, or power, can lead to serious problems for citizens and the criminal justice system. Politicization is most noticeable during campaigns where there is a lot of talk about law and order. Politicians are prone to demagoguery when criminal justice issues become overly politicized, appealing to people's passions, emotions, and prejudices rather than their intellect. The enemy of reasoned solutions to the crime problem is political demagoguery.

2.5.7. Politics of Stymie

The justice system can be severely harmed by needless political squabbling over criminal justice issues, which can occur when public officials start prioritizing winning political battles over reducing crime and enforcngthe law. One unwanted outcome is that the legal system comes to a complete standstill. In America,. fFor the final three months of 1998, the Sentencing Commission remained empty as Republicans and Democrats were unable to reach a consensus on the seven available commission seats. Congress established this commission in 1984 with the primary goal of establishing guidelines for the sentencing of individuals found guilty of federal offenses. It was initiated to help create an efficient and successful criminal justice system and to lessen disparities in federal sentencing.

2.6. LAW ENFORCEMENT AGENCY

Any government organization that employs and deploys law enforcement officers and their resources to enforce the law within a particular jurisdiction is known as a law enforcement agency (LEA). The police are the most prevalent kind of law enforcement agency, but there are other kinds as well, such as agencies that concentrate on particular legal infractions or are arranged and managed by particular authorities. They usually have a range of legal privileges and powers that enable them to carry out their responsibilities, including the ability to make an arrest and use force.

2.6.1. Importance of Law Enforcement

The primary goal of all law enforcement personnel, including security guards, parole officers, police officers, and drug enforcement agents, is to serve and protect the public. These experts protect our states, nations, cities, and neighborhoods from criminal activity and other undesirable occurrences. They are also an essential part of the larger, three-part criminal justice system, which includes courts (which administer justice in a court of law), corrections (which works with offenders), and law enforcement (which apprehends criminals). In an effort to keep society safe, the criminal justice system works to provide "justice for all" by defending victims, finding guilty parties, and overseeing the due process of law for those who are accused of crimes. Law enforcement officers, first responders, and others who work to investigate crimes, collect, and preserve evidence, and respond to reports of various crimes are among those who support the criminal justice system. A world without law enforcement and our criminal justice system could be one in which violence, theft, mayhem, and danger are commonplace. Law enforcement personnel should be proud of and satisfied with the work they do to protect society and hold criminals accountable for their deeds.

2.6.2. What Do Law Enforcement Professionals Do?

A career as a law enforcement officer might be a great fit for people who are passionate about helping and defending the public. In addition to upholding law and order, law enforcement officials foster mutual respect and trust among the people they serve, institutions, and communities.

While day-to-day activities vary, especially when responding to emergencies, this line of work can involve:

- Informing the public about policies, services, or procedures;
- Investigating illegal or suspicious activities;
- Apprehending criminal suspects;
- Escorting prisoners;
- Preparing incident or investigation reports;
- Serving court-ordered documents;
- Testifying during legal proceedings.

Furthermore, there are a variety of job opportunities in the criminal justice system, and law enforcement is no different.

Possible positions and job descriptions include:

1. **Police Officers**: While some police officers have specific geographic jurisdiction, such as working for public school districts

or transportation systems, most police officers conduct their business primarily at the local level in cities and towns. According to U.S. government data, they can anticipate a median yearly salary of $69,160 while protecting people and property Labor Statistics Bureau (BLS).

2. **State Troopers**: As state police officers, state troopers patrol state highways, enforce driving laws, and arrest criminals at the state level.
3. **Drug Enforcement Agents (DEA)**: This, who work for the federal government, are in charge of stopping and intercepting drug trafficking in the country while also being on the front lines of drug investigations.
4. **Fish and Game Wardens**: These people labor outside in national parks, public waterways, and forest preserves. Game and fish wardens ensure the safety and protection of the natural habitats, wildlife, and tourists.
5. **Security**as well as small and large businesses and facilities can hire security guards. They safeguard particular individualsindividuals and property, just like many other law enforcement jobs.

2.7. COURTS AND THE LEGAL PROCESS

Courts are essential to the legal system because they provide unbiased settings for settling conflicts, interpreting the law, and enforcing the law. There are various steps in the legal process, from the filing of a lawsuit or the filing of criminal charges to the settlement or adjudication of the case at the end.

2.7.1. The Relationship Between State and Federal Court Systems

Due to the dual nature of the American legal system, which consists of both federal and state jurisdictions, the relationship between the state and federal court systems is intricate and multifaceted. Although every system functions autonomously, they are linked together by a number of connections, exchanges, and legal precepts. Here's an overview of the relationship between state and federal court systems:

- **Jurisdiction:** The U.S. has established separate jurisdictional boundaries for state and federal courts. State laws, the Constitution, and federal statutes. State statutes give state courts the authority to hear cases involving state law, including family law, probate, contracts, and criminal offenses. Federal courts have jurisdiction over cases arising under U.S. law, cases involving federal law, and disputes between parties from different states (diversity jurisdiction) the federal statutes, the Constitution, or treaties.

- **Hierarchy:** Both state and federal court systems are organized hierarchically, with multiple levels of courts, including trial courts, appellate courts, and supreme courts. Each state has its own system of trial courts, intermediate appellate courts, and a state supreme court, while the federal court system includes district courts, circuit courts of appeals, and the US. Supreme Court.
- **Concurrent Jurisdiction:** Parties may choose where to file their case when state and federal courts share concurrent jurisdiction over a specific issue. This frequently happens in cases involving diversity jurisdiction, where the parties are from different states and the amount in controversy exceeds a threshold, or in cases involving federal question jurisdiction, where the dispute arises under both state and federal law.
- **Removal and Remand:** If there is diversity of citizenship among the parties or if the case involves federal law, the parties may attempt to transfer the case from state court to federal court. On the other hand, federal court cases that don't fit the requirements for federal jurisdiction may be remanded to state court. The procedures of removal and remand aid in guaranteeing that cases are heard in the proper forum according to pertinent legal principles and jurisdictional requirements.
- **Precedent and Supremacy:** Federal law, including decisions of the U.S. Supreme Court, serves as the supreme law of the land and takes precedence over conflicting state laws or court decisions. State courts are bound to follow applicable federal law, including the U.S. Constitution and federal statutes, as well as binding precedent established by the U.S. Supreme Court. However, state courts are not bound by decisions of lower federal courts and may interpret federal law independently.
- **Cooperative Federalism:** Principles of cooperative federalism, in which both systems cooperate to administer justice, settle disputes, and preserve the rule of law, define the relationship between state and federal courts. State courts may look to federal courts for guidance on matters pertaining to federal law, and federal courts may defer to state courts on matters pertaining to state law. State and federal courts may also practice judicial comity, accepting one another's

judgments and, when necessary, yielding to jurisdictional expertise.

All things considered, the dynamic and complex relationship that exists between the state and federal court systems reflects the shared responsibilities, jurisdictional boundaries, and legal principles that direct the administration of justice in the United States. Even though each system functions independently, they cooperate to guarantee that legal disputes are settled equitably, consistently, and in line with the rule of law and federalism.

2.7.2. The Problem of Jurisdiction

Understanding jurisdiction is crucial to comprehending courts and the legal system. Combining the Latin terms juris (law) and diction (to speak), we get jurisdiction. The fundamental jurisdictional question is which court has the authority "to speak the law." Before a judge will hear a case, two questions regarding jurisdiction must be resolved: the question of subject matter jurisdiction and the question of personal jurisdiction. We will address subject matter jurisdiction first because judges have the authority to do so; they will dismiss a case if they conclude, based solely on the case's pleadings, that they lack the authority to hear and decide that type of case.

2.7.2.1. The Federal-State Balance: Federalism

The United States Constitution's concept of federalism creates a distinct form of government that allocates authority between the federal and state governments. The goal of this structure, referred to as the federal-state balance, is to guarantee an authority and responsibility distribution that upholds state autonomy and national unity. Fundamentally, federalism is a commitment to shared governance, in which state governments maintain control over local issues like public safety, education, and transportation while the federal government handles matters of national importance like defense, foreign policy, and interstate commerce. Instead of being absolute, this power structure is defined by the federal and state governments' dynamic interaction and cooperation.

States are free to implement federal policies in a way that best suits the particular needs and preferences of their citizens, even though the federal government establishes the general guidelines and standards. States can act as democratic experimentation grounds by experimenting with various forms of government and policy-making thanks to this flexibility. Federalism also prevents any one branch or level of government from growing overly dominant by acting as a check on centralized power. The federal-state balance is not without difficulties, though, as there are disagreements regarding policy priorities, resource distribution, and jurisdiction. Federalism, however, continues to be a pillar of American democracy, offering a framework for cooperation, creativity, and the defense of individual liberties and rights within a broad and dispersed form of governance.

2.7.2.2. Exclusive Jurisdiction in Federal Courts

A plaintiff (or the plaintiff's attorney, if applicable) must choose between filing a case in the federal or state courts when there are two separate legal systems. Certain types of cases are exclusively under the jurisdiction of federal courts. The reason for this comes directly from the Constitution. Article III of the US Constitution provides the following:

All cases pertaining to ambassadors, other public ministers and consuls; all cases involving admiralty and maritime jurisdiction; all disputes in which the United States shall be a pParty; all disputes between two or more states; all disputes between a state and its citizens; all disputes between citizens of different states; all disputes between citizens of the same state claiming land under grants of different states; and all disputes between a state, or its citizens, and foreign states, citizens, or subjects are all covered udicial power.

By excluding diversity cases, we can assemble a list of the kinds of cases that can only be heard in federal Federal courts. The list looks like this:

1. **Suits Between States:** Cases in which two or more states are a party.
2. **Cases Involving Ambassadors and Other High-Ranking Public Figures:** Cases arising between foreign ambassadors and other high-ranking public officials.
3. **Federal Crimes:** Crimes defined by or mentioned in the US Constitution or those defined or punished by federal statute. Such crimes include treason against the United States, piracy, counterfeiting, crimes against the law of nations, and crimes relating to the federal government's authority to regulate interstate commerce. However, most crimes are state matters.
4. **Bankruptcy:** The statutory procedure, usually triggered by insolvency, by which a person is relieved of most debts and undergoes a judicially supervised reorganization or liquidation for the benefit of the person's creditors.
5. **Patent:** The federal government's exclusive right to manufacture, use, and sell an invention for a predetermined amount of time (often 17 years), provided the invention is new, practical, and not readily apparent.
6. **Copyright:** The body of legal precedent pertaining to a property

right in an original work of authorship, defined as any tangible medium of expression (film, photography, music, painting, or other creative works), that grants its holder the sole authority to copy, modify, distribute, perform, and exhibit the work.

7. **Trademark:** A manufacturer or seller may use a word, phrase, logo, or other graphic symbol to set their product or products apart from competitors.
8. **Admiralty:** The legal framework that resulted from admiralty courts' operations, which are courts with authority over all maritime contracts, torts, injuries, and crimes.
9. **Antitrust:** Federal laws intended to prevent price discrimination, price fixing, and monopolies from impeding trade and commerce.
10. **Securities and Banking Regulation:** The legal framework that safeguards the public by controlling the listing, exchange, and purchase of securities as well as banking operations.
11. **Other Cases Specified by Federal Statute:** Any other cases specified by a federal statute where Congress declares that federal courts will have exclusive jurisdiction.

2.7.2.3. Concurrent Jurisdiction

When two or more courts are able to hear the same case, it is referred to as concurrent jurisdiction. Concurrent jurisdiction in law refers to the ability of several courts, such as state and federal courts, to decide a particular kind of case based on the parties or subject matter at hand. For instance, in the US, some cases may fall under the concurrent jurisdiction of state and federal courts. These cases may include federal law (federal question jurisdiction) or disagreements between parties from different states (diversity jurisdiction). Therefore, depending on a number of variables, including the type of claim, the amount in dispute, and tactical considerations, plaintiffs may choose to bring their case in state or federal court. Concurrent jurisdiction facilitates the enforcement of legal rights and obligations across legal systems, guarantees that parties have access to multiple forums for resolving their disputes, and increases judicial efficiency. But it can also result in forum shopping and the possibility of contradictory rulings if various courts come to different conclusions about the same matter. As a result, mechanisms for transferring cases between state and federal courts as well as comity principles to encourage collaboration and uniformity across various judicial systems are in place to manage concurrent jurisdiction.

2.8. CORRECTIONS AND REHABILITATION

The process of addressing and changing the behavior of people who have been found guilty of crimes while they are under the supervision of the criminal justice system is known as "correctional rehabilitation." Reducing the probability of reoffending, fostering positive change in offenders, and assisting their successful reintegration into society are the three main objectives of correctional rehabilitation. A broad range of services and interventions are included in correctional rehabilitation programs, such as educational initiatives, life skills instruction, mental health counselling, drug and alcohol treatment, vocational training, mental health counselling, and cognitive-behavioral therapy. The underlying causes of criminal behavior, such as substance abuse, a lack of education or work experience, dysfunctional family dynamics, and antisocial attitudes or beliefs, are the focus of these programs. The correctional system, which consists of jails, prisons, probation, parole, and community-based supervision programs, is the larger framework within which correctional rehabilitation functions. Rehabilitation programs, such as pretrial diversion programs, sentencing alternatives, and post-conviction interventions, can be offered at different phases of the criminal justice system. Programs for correctional rehabilitation are usually designed to meet the specific needs and risk factors of each offender, with the aim of encouraging responsibility, development, and constructive behavior modification. Studies have demonstrated the efficacy of evidence-based rehabilitation programs in decreasing recidivism rates and enhancing the outcomes of offenders, thereby promoting safer communities and lowering societal costs. However, a number of factors affect the effectiveness of correctional rehabilitation, such as the degree of offender motivation and engagement, the availability of resources and support services, the quality of program implementation, and the coordination of efforts among criminal justice agencies, community organizations, and other stakeholders. Successful rehabilitation may also face difficulties and impediments, such as restricted access to programs for treatment, the stigma attached to criminal convictions, structural injustices, and the difficulty of meeting the various needs and risk factors of offenders. Correctional rehabilitation is still a vital part of the criminal justice system in spite of these obstacles because it demonstrates a dedication to encouraging rehabilitation, lowering recidivism, and creating favorable outcomes for both offenders and communities.

2.8.1. Policy Issue: Does Rehabilitation Work

The debate over whether rehabilitation in the criminal justice system is a successful policy involves many different viewpoints, research conclusions, and pragmatic considerations. The ability of intervention programs and services to encourage positive behavior change, lower recidivism rates, and enhance outcomes for people involved in the criminal justice system is at the heart of the effectiveness of rehabilitation debate. Proponents of rehabilitation contend that antisocial attitudes, drug addiction, mental health problems, a lack of education or work eand other underlying causes of criminal behavior can all be effectively addressed by evidence-based programs and interventions. In order toTo assist offenders in reintegrating into society as law-abiding citizens, these proponents of a rehabilitative approach to criminal justice emphasize the significance of giving them opportunities for education, treatment, counselling, and skill development. They cite studies and meta-analyzes that demonstrate the positive effects that well-thought-out rehabilitation programs can have on people, families, and communities, as well as the significant decline in recidivism rates. Conversely, those who doubt the efficacy of rehabilitation contend that the results of intervention programs are frequently insignificant or transient. They bring up issues with the standard of rehabilitation services, the availability of standardized assessment instruments, and the difficulties in determining long-term results. Critics also draw attention to the difficulties in addressing the various needs and risk factors of criminals, as well as the shortcomings of intervention programs in resolving systemic problems like social marginalization, poverty, and inequality. Furthermore, some detractors contend that harsher penalties, like imprisonment and deterrence, might be more successful in lowering crime and preserving public safety.

Practical issues, such as financial limitations, conflicting priorities within the criminal justice system, and political beliefs, further muddle the discussion over the efficacy of rehabilitation. The costs and benefits of funding rehabilitation programs must be weighed by policymakers against alternative strategies for crime prevention and control, taking into account elements like program fidelity, scalability, sustainability, and cost-effectiveness. Furthermore, individual factors like the gravity of the offense, the offender's motivation and engagement, and the accessibility of community support services can all affect how effective rehabilitation is. Given these intricacies, tackling the policy question of whether rehabilitation is effective calls for an all-encompassing and sophisticated strategy that incorporates practical considerations, stakeholder viewpoints, and research findings. The strengths and weaknesses of rehabilitation programs must be carefully considered by policymakers, who should also pinpoint areas for improvement and create evidence-based practices and policies that support offenders' successful reintegration into society while maintaining public safety and accountability. In the end, a number of variables, such as program quality, individual needs, community support, and the larger social, economic, and political framework in which interventions are carried out, determine how successful rehabilitation is within the criminal justice system.

2.8.2. The Rehabilitative Ideal

It is modeled after the medical paradigm that treats physical illnesses in many ways. Thus, in the same way that illness is not viewed as a choice because it results from the exercise of free will at the moment of offense, neither is crime. Rather, causal factors—which are now commonly referred to as "risk factors"—influence, if not completely determine, the decisions that are made. These elements may be internal to the person (biological or psychological) or external to the person (social). Nevertheless, criminals will not be cured and their deviant behavior will persist if they are not appropriately identified and treated. On the other hand, rehabilitation is feasible if the underlying reasons for a person's criminal behavior are found and the necessary treatment is then recommended.

The traditional legal approach of matching punishment to the nature of the crime—a practice that supposedly achieves equal justice and, some would argue, deterrence—is viewed by the rehabilitative ideal as unscientific, if not uncivilized. The obvious challenge is that two individuals who commit the same crime—shoplifting, for instance—might do so for very different motives (e.g., a low level of self-control, peer pressure, and a desperate need for money). It makes no more sense to apply a sanction that is one size fits all than it does to treat every patient with a disease in the same way. It also makes no sense to punish offenders, whether it be with a fine or a jail sentence. In particular, this is one reason why academics who support rehabilitation predict that punitive interventions will have minimal effects: they do not target for change the engines of criminal behavior—risk factors. How can inflicting pain—a "cost"—on offenders cure the underlying causes of their behavior?

But the possibility of rehabilitating criminals rests on two difficult presumptions. First, the rehabilitative ideal presupposes that individuals engaged in rehabilitation possess the knowledge necessary to identify criminogenic risk factors and then successfully implement a suitable treatment intervention. Treatment knowledge and experience have actually frequently been woefully inadequate, with offenders receiving interventions that could be best described as "correctional quackery." Secondly, the rehabilitative ideal presupposes that correctional personnel will utilize their discretion in accordance with therapeutic principles and the best interests of rehabilitated offenders. The trust must be allocated because providing tailored interventions that can address the reasons behind each person's criminal activity requires discretion. The unavoidable fact is that rehabilitation takes place inside a correctional system, where staff choices are subject to the influence of political and custodial factors in addition to legitimate treatment priorities. As Rothman has warned, under such conditions, the need to satiate "convenience" frequently corrupts "conscience."

At the National Congress on Penitentiary and Reformatory Discipline in 1870, the rehabilitative ideal was first articulated clearly. Following the Civil War, the country's jails were overflowing with inmates who belonged to the so-called "dangerous classes of impoverished immigrants." Elites in the prison system may have labeled these criminals as the "other" and unredeemable. The leading advocates and administrators of corrections instead reaffirmed at a conference in Cincinnati that "the supreme aim of prison discipline is the reformation of criminals, not the infliction of vindictive suffering." They favored the classification of inmates, the use of rewards rather than punishments, inmate education and industrial training, the special training of guards, and efforts to reintegrate prisoners back into society by providing work and encouragement," according to their Declaration of Principles, a list of policies that could be written today. The indeterminate sentence, which would keep criminals behind bars until they were reformed rather than for a predetermined amount of time depending on the seriousness of their offense, was their main recommendation, though. They pointed out that "the prisoner's destiny be placed measurably in his own hands" only in this manner.

These concepts came to direct the creation of the contemporary penal system during the first two decades of the 20th century, also known as the Progressive era. With the development of the social sciences came increased assurance that crime causes could be pinpointed with greater accuracy, and social engineering was encouraged by the political atmosphere of this "age of reform." Notably, the redesign of the system was conceptually supported by the rehabilitative ideal. As parole boards were established to determine when prisoners had recovered and could be safely released, sentencing became increasingly arbitrary. The n and parole supervision made sense because of the need for community-based offenders to be assisted in preventing crime and, in the event thatif they were unable to do so, to be sent to prison. Pre-sentence reports, which were created by probation officers and included information about the livesrs, were crucial in helping judges decide which offenders should be imprisoned and which should be kept in the community. Finally, in order toto save misbehaving children, a distinct juvenile justice system focused solely on treatment was necessary. There was a lot to be said for the rehabilitation ideal. The logic of matching treatments to individual differences instead of crimes and punishments fell apart as soon as it was acknowledged that criminal behavior was caused. Thus, accepting rehabilitation—the individual treatment model—seemed civilized and reasonable rather than irrational and vindictive. The emphasis on science in secular humanism and the universal potential for salvation in sacred belief combined to create a positive correctional paradigm where the aim was to improve offenders. Children would receive special consideration and, once more, a justice system tailored to their unique needs. And all of this would happen without compromising social defense. Recalcitrant inmates would be kept behind bars—for life, if necessary—until they were cured, and ever-vigilant probation and parole officers would keep an eye out for offenders unable to remain crime-free in the community.

2.8.3. The Abuse of Discretionary Powers

The individual treatment model is the foundation of the rehabilitative ideal. However, granting judges, parole boards, and correctional staff broad discretionary authority is necessary to individualize interventions. Just as doctors need to have the freedom to recommend specific drugs or services to each patient, rehabilitation specialists also need to have the freedom to work with each offender individually. Allotting essentially unrestricted discretionary powers is predicated on the belief that state representatives are rational, well-informed decision-makers who prioritize the rehabilitation of offenders—that is, that they are not quacks or blatantly self-serving. Advocates for rehabilitation have long recognized that this standard is frequently more of an ideal than a practicality. However, imperfections were seen as justification for pursuing the rehabilitative ideal more vigorously rather than giving up on it.

Trust in the state was rapidly declining by the late 1960s, according to polling data that revealed a "virtual explosion in antigovernment feeling." There was now a crisis of legitimacy or a gap in trust. By the mid-1970s, less than 40% of the public still held the belief that public officials would "do what is right just about always or most of the time," down from 73% in 1958. A number of significant social events, including political assassinations, the violent suppression of civil rights demonstrations, violent insurgencies in inner cities, persistent protests against the Vietnam War, and revelations of political corruption, best illustrated by the Watergate affair, are well documented as the causes of this profound shift in public opinion. Critiques of the rehabilitative ideal found a more accepting audience in this setting. As a result, rehabilitation's standing changed from that of a progressive ideal that ought to direct reform initiatives to that of a "noble lie" or mask of benevolence that was being used to cover up and allow the repression of people who were subject to the state's iron grip. It was being said that the rehabilitative ideal was to blame for the abuse of discretionary power by state officials, who were supposed to be doing good. A portion of this abuse was the result of incompetence on the part of government officials working in the correctional system, who lacked the scientific knowledge necessary to diagnose patients accurately or determine when they were cured. However, the more serious criticism was that these officials were malicious. Judges were charged, for instance, with discriminating against the poor and racial minorities instead of individualizing treatment. Prisons were a particular focus of attention because they were portrayed as being fundamentally cruel. In this depressing setting, correctional officers would use the threat of permanent incarceration as a stick rather than a carrot to compel compliance with their orders. This kind of thinking encouraged progressive academics and reformers to support initiatives aimed at reducing discretion. Determinate sentencing, which included set prison terms codified in legislation, equal rather than individualized punishments, and the elimination of parole release, was the cornerstone of their preferred "justice model." Conservatives were eager to get on board with this. Conservatives perceived the rehabilitative ideal as allowing the victimization of innocent citizens, while liberals condemned it for allowing the victimization of offenders. They had long viewed the discretion as giving judges the power to impose light sentences and as giving parole boards the ability to be duped into releasing predators before their time. A massive movement to remove discretion from the sentencing system had begun by the middle of the 1970s, with conservatives advocating for longer prison terms and liberals hoping for shorter ones. Every state would limit judges' and/or parole boards' discretion over the ensuing several decades by implementing measures like determinate sentencing guidelines and policies.

REFERENCES

1. Bennett, W. J., & Hess, K. M. (2018). *Criminal Investigation* (12th ed.). Cengage Learning.
2. Clear, T. R., & Frost, N. A. (2018). *The Punishment Imperative: The Rise and Failure of Mass Incarceration in America*. NYU Press.
3. Clear, T. R., & Latessa, E. J. (1993). Probation officers' views on intensive supervision: Is it effective? *Journal of Criminal Justice, 21*(3), 235–248.
4. Cole, G. F., & Smith, C. E. (2018). *The American System of Criminal Justice* (16th ed.). Cengage Learning.
5. Cullen, F. T., & Jonson, C. L. (2017). Rehabilitation and treatment programs. In J. Q. Wilson & J. Petersilia (Eds.), *Crime and Public Policy* (pp. 213–250). Oxford University Press.
6. Feeley, M. M., & Simon, J. (1992). The new penology: Notes on the emerging strategy of corrections and its implications. *Criminology, 30*(4), 449–474.
7. Festinger, L., & Katz, D. (Eds.). (1976). *Research Methods in the Behavioral Sciences*. New Delhi.
8. Garland, D. (2001). *The Culture of Control: Crime and Social Order in Contemporary Society*. University of Chicago Press.
9. Garland, D. (2013). *Punishment and Modern Society: A Study in Social Theory*. University of Chicago Press.
10. Goldstein, H. (2018). *Policing a Free Society*. Ballinger Publishing Company.
11. Greene, J. R., & Pranis, K. (2007). The new criminal justice thinking. In J. Petersilia & K. Reitz (Eds.), *The Oxford Handbook of Sentencing and Corrections* (pp. 811–834). Oxford University Press.
12. Johnson, E. (1951). *The Research Report: A Guide for the Beginner*. Ronald Press.
13. Lynch, M. J., & Stretesky, P. B. (2003). The harmful effects of ineffective assistance of counsel. *Crime & Delinquency, 49*(1), 35–52.
14. Maguire, E. R., & Radosh, P. H. (2019). *The American Prison: Imagining a Different Future*. Sage Publications.
15. Miethe, T. D., & Lu, H. (2005). *Punishment: A Comparative Historical Perspective*. Cambridge University Press.
16. Peak, K. J. (2018). *Justice Administration: Police, Courts, and Corrections Management* (9th ed.). Pearson Education.

17. Reiman, J., & Leighton, P. (2017). *The Rich Get Richer and the Poor get Prison: Ideology, Class, and Criminal Justice* (11th ed.). Routledge.
18. Schmalleger, F. (2019). *Criminal Justice Today: An Introductory Text for the 21st Century* (15th ed.). Pearson Education.
19. Siegel, L. J., & Worrall, J. L. (2018). *Introduction to Criminal Justice* (16th ed.). Cengage Learning.
20. Tandon, B. C. (1979). *Research Methodology–Social Sciences*. Allahabad.
21. Travers, R. M. W. (1978). *An Introduction to Educational Research* (4th ed.). Macmillan Publishing Co. Inc.
22. Verma, R., & Wani, M. (2001). *Legal Research Methodology* (2nd ed.). Indian Law Institute.
23. Walker, S., & Katz, C. M. (2017). *The Police in America: An Introduction* (9th ed.). McGraw-Hill Education.
24. Wilkinson, T. S., & Bhandarkar, P. L. (1979). *Methodology Techniques of Social Research*. Himalaya Publishing House.

Chapter 3

Research Methods in Criminology

Contents

INTRODUCTION

In criminology, research methods are fundamental to comprehending the intricate relationships between criminal activity, crime, and the criminal justice system. This multidisciplinary area uses a wide range of approaches to investigate and assess the reasons, relationships, and effects of criminal activity in addition to assessing programs meant to lessen crime and advance social justice. In order to understand the patterns, trends, and underlying mechanisms that influence criminal behavior and the responses of the criminal justice system, criminology researchers conduct thorough investigations and systematic inquiry. Both quantitative and qualitative methods are used in criminology research, which enables a thorough analysis of crime-related phenomena from several angles. In order to test theories and find statistical relationships, quantitative methods entail gathering and analyzing numerical data, whereas qualitative methods concentrate on comprehending the social settings and personal experiences of those who commit crimes.

Criminologists can contribute to the advancement of knowledge in the field, clarify the complexities of crime and justice, and inform evidence-based policies and practices by utilizing a range of research methods. With the ultimate goal of improving our understanding of crime and assisting in the development of more successful crime prevention and criminal justice strategies, this introductory overview lays the groundwork for an exploration of the various methodologies and ethical issues inherent in criminological research. Researchers with an interest in criminology and criminal justice have access to a variety of research techniques. The particular research question being studied will determine which specific research methods are used. There are four main types of research questions: (1) exploratory, (2) explanatory, (3) evaluative, and (1) descriptive. The goal of descriptive research is to characterize and define the social phenomenon that is being studied. Exploratory research looks for the deeper meanings underlying behaviors and actions. Determining the cause(s) and effect(s) of social phenomena is the goal of explanatory research. The goal of evaluation research is to ascertain how an intervention affects a person's behavior. These four research domains are intended to be utilized in conjunction with one another to enhance comprehension of the topic being studied, rather than to be mutually exclusive. Given this context, the goal of this entry is to acquaint the reader with the two main research paradigms and concerns—qualitative and quantitative research strategies—that structure the field of criminology and criminal justice.

3.1. QUANTITATIVE RESEARCH METHODS

Measuring the reality of criminology or criminal justice is usually the focus of quantitative research methods. A few terms must be definedoto comprehend this process. Concepts are numerically assigned, abstract tags that are applied to reality, making them variables. Next, patterns of relation, covariation, and cause and effect are examined through the study of variables. At the most fundamental level, there is one independent variable and one or more dependent variables. The outcome variable is another name for the dependent variable. This is the outcome that the researcher hopes to forecast. The variable that causes, determines, or comes before the dependent variable in time is known as the independent variable, also known as the predictor variable. Think about the following instances. The link between criminal behavior (dependent variable) and impulsivity (independent variable) may be of interest to criminological theorists. Scholars investigate this relationship by developing a summated scale of items intended to measure impulsivity in an indirect manner. Then, criminal behavior involvement is predicted using this impulsivity scale. Scholars studying criminal justice may find it interesting to examine how future patterns of domestic violence are affected by mandatory arrest policies (independent variable). When investigating this kind of question, academics usually compare the impact of an arrest to another form of punishment in terms of the arrestee's potential for future criminal behavior. Therefore, a pattern of examining the relationship(s) between sets of variabletoto ascertain cause and effect is involved in quantitative research methods.

To prove causation, three requirements must be satisfied. Association comes first. In other words, there needs to be a relationship between the independent and dependent variables. The second is temporal order, which requires the independent variable to occur before the dependent variable. And lastly, the question of no spuriousness. This happens when there is no variation in an unobserved third variable explaining the relationship between the independent and dependent variables. Researchers can choose from a variety of quantitative research methods, most of which are categorized under the general heading of research design, which is loosely defined as the study plan that covers the who, what, where, when, why, and how of an investigation. Survey research, experimental and quasi-experimental research, cross-sectional research, longitudinal research, time series research, and meta-analysis are some of these research techniques.

3.1.1. Survey Research

Survey research is the most commonly employed mode of observation in the social sciences, including criminology. It entails gathering data from a sample of people by asking them questions. Typically, survey research is conducted in person, over the phone, via mail, or on a computer.

Surveys typically include both closed- and open-ended questions. Respondents are asked to answer specific questions in open-ended questions. For instance, the question might be, "What do you think is the most important problem facing residents in your neighborhood today?" The respondent would then give his or her response in their own words. Conversely, answers to closed-ended questions must be chosen from a predetermined list of options. For example, the question above would still be asked, but respondents would now have a list of options to choose from: (a) crime, (b) drugs, (c) education, (d) employment, (e) family structure, (f) poverty, (g) health care, (h) child care, (i) extracurricular activities, and (j) other. What do you think is the most important problem facing residents in your neighborhood today? Surveys are a popular research method because they provide many appealing features. They are adaptable, cost-effective, efficient, and broadly applicable. However, issues with sampling, measurement, and survey design as a whole may restrict the use of certain survey methods. Researchers should take care to ensure that the survey's items are concise and easy to understand when designing one.

3.1.2. Experimental and Quasi-Experimental Research

According to some academics, experimental research is the most effective kind of study for determining cause and effect. At least three elements are required for an experiment to be considered valid: (1) there must be two comparison groups (an experimental group and a control group); (2) the independent variable must vary before the dependent variable's change is evaluated; and (3) the two (or more) comparison groups must be assigned at random. Both a pre- and post-test are common in experiments. While the latter test measures the outcome variable after the experimental group has received treatment, the former measures the dependent variable before the experimental intervention. In a true experiment, the comparison group is a powerful tool for determining the treatment's effects because of randomization. Systematic bias is prevented from influencing the assignment of subjects to groups by randomly allocating groups to the experimental and comparison groups. This is crucial if researchers hope to apply their findings to the larger picture of the relationships between important variables both within and between groups. A traditional experimental design consists of a pre-test for each group, an intervention for one of the groups (i.e., the experimental group), and following that, both groups took a post-test. Take a look at the following criminal justice scenario. A study looking at neighborhood fear of crime selects two police precincts that are identical to each other in every way. To gather data on crime rates and public opinion of crime, pre-tests would be conducted in both precincts. Something would be done to the experimental precinct (i.e., a rise in police presence), but no intervention would be given to the comparison precinct. Both precincts would then undergo a post-test a year later to assess any changes in crime rates and public opinion.

In criminology and criminal justice, there have been a number of experimental designs. One such design is the Domestic Violence Experiment, in which criminals were randomized to one of three interventions: separation, mediation, or arrest. An experimental design was also used in the Jersey City Police Department's Program to Control Violent Places. In a randomized block field experiment, one participant from each pair of 24 high-activity, violent crime locations was assigned to one of two treatment conditions for the purposes of this study. Conversely, quasi-experimental research can be roughly modeled by closely and carefully matching subjects across the two groups on several important variables, but it does not involve random assignment to experimental and control groups. Quasi-experimental designs fall into two main categories: (1) nonequivalent control group designs, in which the comparison and experimental groups are predetermined and not formed by random assignment; and (2) before-and-after designs, in which there is a comparison group but no pre- or post-test. An examination of the impact of police actions on seat-belt law violations is one instance of a nonequivalent control group design. Watson, for instance, chose two similarly sized towns with lax police enforcement of the law. Watson launched a media campaign in the experimental community to encourage people to wear seat belts, and he then stepped up police enforcement of the law. According to Watson, the percentage of drivers in the experimental community who used seat belts rose, while in the comparison community it either stayed the same or slightly decreased.

The Pierce and Bowers analysis of the effects of the Massachusetts Bartley-Fox gun law is an illustration of the before-and-after design. This law imposed a minimum one-year prison term for carrying a firearm without a permit. Their preliminary analysis indicated a decline in assaults, robberies, and killings involving firearms, but this was countered by an increase in assaults without firearms and robberies involving other weapons.

3.1.3. Cross-Sectional Research

Studies using cross-sectional designs focus on a single group at a single point in time. As a result, they provide a brief overview or snapshot of the phenomenon under study. They typically make reference to a representative sample of the population, enabling researchers to extrapolate their results. Research in criminology and criminal justice is heavily reliant on cross-sectional research designs. In his well-known investigation into the origins of delinquency, Hirschi used a cross-sectional design and questioned male participants about their engagement in delinquent behavior and emotional connections to social networks.

3.1.4. Longitudinal Research

Panel and cohort studies are the two types of longitudinal research designs most frequently utilized. Both look at the same group over time and are primarily interested in evaluating changes within and between groups. Panel studies track an individual or sample over time, whereas cohort studies focus on more specialized populations (e.g., cohorts) as they evolve with time. In panel studies, the same individuals are usually interviewed twice or more. The National Crime Victimization Survey (NCVS), for instance, chooses a set number of households at random from throughout the United States and conducts seven interviews with a member of each household every six months. Cohort studies track the movements of particular cohorts or individuals over time. Marvin Wolfgang and associates in Philadelphia carried out a cohort study that is a prime example of one. All boys born in Philadelphia in 1945 up to the age of 18 had their criminal histories tracked down by the writers. Tracy, Wolfgang, and Figlio also investigated the criminal records of men and women born in Philadelphia in 1958.

3.1.5. Time-Series Designs

Many observations of the same group are usually varied in time-series designs (i.e., Person, Town, Region, and so forth, over an extended period of time or at different times. In most cases, they examine a single variable (like the crime rate) over time, and they are particularly helpful in research on the effects of recently implemented legislation or social programs. An instance of a time-series design would be analyzing the murder rate in the US over the previous 20 years or contrasting the rates in the US and Canada during the same time frame. Measurements taken prior to some type of interruption (i.e., one variable at a time) are analyzed in an interrupted time-series design, observation made following the intervention) as well as additional observations. See Spelman & Eck (1987) for an illustration of an interrupted time-series design. These writers investigated how many car-related larceny cases there were in Newport News, Virginia. A program of problem-oriented policing, which included crime incident investigation and special tracking, was the intervention used in this study. Based on the findings, there was a significant decrease in the number of larceny cases right away following the intervention, and the number of cases continued to decline for more than a year. D'Alessio and Stooked intoinvestigated the effect of Minnesota sentencing guidelines on jail incarceration in another interrupted time series study. Their discovery went beyond the influence of previous patterns to show that the introduction of the sentencing guidelines led to a rise in the use of jail sentences by judges.

Researchers should be aware of one important aspect of time-series fact thateven though they are particularly helpful in examining trends over time and how interventions affect those trends: the inability to account for all possible spurious effects. Think about the example that follows. Let's say a researcher is looking at how a law requiring convenience stores to have at least two clerks on duty during business hours affects robberies. The researcher found that there were significantly fewer robberies following the enactment of the law after comparing the number of robberies that occurred before and after it took effect. As a result, the researcher asserted that the law contributed to a drop in the number of robberies that were commconclusionconcluded that other locations should adopt the law. The researcher might not have realized, though, that two criminals who were responsible for 75% of convenience store robberies were recently apprehended around the time the law went into force. In conclusion, scientists must exercise caution when interpreting interrupted tis analyzesanalysis to ensure that they account for as much empirical and nonempirical data as feasible.

3.1.6. Meta-Analysis

Meta-analysis is a newer addition to research methodology. This method of research involves quantitatively analyzing the results of several studies. Fundamentally, meta-analysis is the process by which scientists synthesize findings from multiple studies and provide concise, factual claims regarding a cause-and-effect relationship. Wells and Rankin conducted a seminal example of meta-analysis in criminology, focusing on the connection between delinquency and broken homes. Wells and Rankin found 50 studies that examined the broken-homes-causes-delinquency hypothesis after observing a number of results indicating that this theory was inconclusive. The average effect of broken homes across the studies was to increase the probability of delinquency by roughly 10 to 15%, the authors found after classifying the important features of the studies, such as the population sampled, age range, and measures (both independent and dependent) used. More significantly, they discovered that a large portion of the variation in estimating the impact of broken homes could be explained by the various methodologies applied in the various studies. For instance, research employing official records as opposed to self-report surveys tended to find a stronger correlation between broken homes and delinquency. One thing ie fact thateven though opinions on the value of meta-analysis are divided among researchers: meta-analysis raises awareness among researchers that drawing conclusions from a single study's results is inappropriate. Meta-analysis has gained popularity in criminological and criminal justice research due to this crucial lesson.

3.1.7. Threats to Validity

Validity pertains to the precision of the measurement or the extent to which the instrument is truly measuring the intended object. Though they are widely used in criminological and criminal justice research, quantitative research methods are not without issues. The most serious threats to validity are probably those that need to be recognized. Some of these threats are internal, asking whether the findings were the result of the observational process itself; external threats, on the other hand, ask whether the findings were distinct and limited to the group or target under study.

3.1.7.1. Internal Threats

As per Campbell and Stanley, there are several internal threats that must be taken into account. These threats include history, maturation, testing, instrumentation, statistical regression, selection bias, experimental mortality, and selection maturation interaction. There are also other threats that need to be taken into account. Cook and Campbell suggest that estimating the internal validity of a relationship is a deductive process in which the investigator has to systematically consider how each of the internal validity threats can be ruled out in order to determine whether a particular design rules out threats to internal validity.

3.1.7.2. External Threats

In addition, Campbell and Stanley list a number of factors that could compromise external validity, such as selection bias, testing effects, reactivity or awareness of being a subject, and interference from multiple treatments. These risks are higher fors carried outconducted in more meticulously regulated environments. Replication, or repeating experiments or studies using the same methodology, is perhaps one of the best ways to evaluate threats to external validity. Researchers can be more confident that results from a study aren'tare not the result of threats to external validity if important findings are replicated. A notable instance of replication took place in the latter part of the 1980s when six Ames carried outconducted replications of the Minneapolis Domestic Violence Experiment. Crucially, the results of thesee in agreementagreed with the original experiment's findings as well as in contradiction with it.

3.2. QUALITATIVE RESEARCH METHODS

Qualitative research methods, in contrast to quantitative research methods, aim to record life as it is experienced by participants, instead of categorizing it into predefined categories. Inductive reasoning, an awareness of social context and human subjectivity, exploratory research questions, and the interpretations that participants make of events and their own lives are all common components of these methodologies. Within this paradigm there are several unique research designs: (1) case studies and life histories; (2) focus groups; (3) participant observation; and (4) intensive interviewing. We shall talk about each of these one by one.

3.2.1. Participant Observation

Participant observation, at its most basic, is a range of data collection techniques wherein a researcher watches a group by engaging in varying degrees of group activities. In this context, Gold examines four possible roles that field researchers might take on: (1) complete participant; (2) participant-as-observer; (3) observer-as-participant; and (4) complete observer. When the researcher actively participates and starts directing group activities, it is considered complete participation. The researcher typically introduces himself and attempts to watch the group's activities objectively when using the participant-as-observer strategy. When interviewees are also short-term participant observers, the observer-as-participant approach resembles a one-visit interview quite a bit. Generally, these interviews are carried out with people who are known to take part in a certain activity. To better understand how the crack trade functions on the streets, for instance, Jacobs spoke with well-known drug dealers who are currently active in the community. Lastly, without the researcher's involvement, the full observer strategy depends only on observation.

While conducting this kind of research, a number of issues need to be addressed, but two are particularly crucial: (1) objectivity and (2) going native. The first one concerns the researcher's capacity to refrain from becoming overly identified with the study group as well as hostile toward it. The latter deals with a scenario in which the researcher gives up on his or her position as an impartial researcher and identifies with the study group. Despite these warnings, numerous significant participant observation studies in criminology and criminal justice have been conducted, such as Marquart's study of prison life and Polsky's study of pool hustlers and con artists.

3.2.2. Intensive Interviewing

During an intensive interview, the interviewer asks open-ended, mostly unstructured questions to elicit detailed information about the interviewee's thoughts, feelings, and experiences. Intensive interviewing does not necessitate the systematic observation of respondents in their natural environment, in contrast to the participant observation strategy. Interviewing sample members and finding and speaking with additional sample members usually go on until the point known as the saturation point, at which conducting new interviews appears to provide little new data. A number of studies conducted with current residential burglary and robbers in St. Louis provide a notable illustration of the intensive interviewing technique. Louis. Thave carried outconducted comprehensive interviews with convicted felons in their actual settings. Important theoretical insights that might not have been obtained through conventional survey methods have been obtained from some of these interviews. Additional noteworthy instances can be discovered in the research conducted by Fagan and Wilkinson on gun-related violence in New York and Jacobs on crack addicts in St. Louis.

3.2.3. Focus Groups

Focus groups are made up of unrelated people who are gathered by a researcher and guided through group discussions on a given subject. The information that is produced is often hat unstructuredunstructured; however, the researcher usually poses targeted questions and facilitates the conversation to make sure that group members address these issues. Research indicates that focus group data, when paired with survey data, can be fairly consistent, even though exact generalizations from focus groups to target populations are impossible. Schneider and her colleagues provide one such example in criminal justice. The implementation process and the function of risk/need assessment tools in determining the appropriate degree of supervision for parolees and probationers were investigated by these writers. They were able to gain a deeper understanding of the survey results from the probation officers they spoke with by using focus groups.

3.2.4. Case Studies and Life Histories

A case study or life history is typically a comprehensive qualitative analysis of one or a small number of representative examples. This approach has been used in a number of criminological cases; several in particular have yielded some of the most significant baseline data currently available in the field. The classic example is Sutherland's *The Professional Thief* (1937). In this case study, Sutherland's informant, Chic Conwell, described the world of the professional thief. Other examples include Shaw's *The Jack-Roller* (1930), which tells the autobiographical story of a delinquent's own experiences, influences, attitudes, and values. Last but not least, Horatio Alger's account of street life in New York tells the tale of Young Dick, a street kid who leads a troubled life but is also trustworthent. In order toTo get a thorough understanding of either a singular or representative person, life-history methods typically entail the analysis of diaries, letters, biographies, and autobiographies.

3.2.5. Future of Research Methods in Criminology and Criminal Justice

The discussion that came before it may have depicted the two primary research paradigms—qualitative and quantitative research methods—as opposite poles of a continuum, but it did not mean to suggest that they are incompatible. Conversely, the amalgamation of quantitative and qualitative research methodologies is the way forward for research methodologies in the fields of criminology and criminal justice. Two successful integrations are shown below.

In the first, conducted in 1985, Eric Hirsch employed a range of techniques, such as participant observation, in-depth interviews, and a standardized survey, to examine the student movement advocating for Columbia University to divest its holdings in businesses that dealt with South Africa. Hirsch thought that the combination of research approaches offered a more complete view of the reasons behind students' actions.

Robert Sampson and John Laub provide the second example. The Unraveling Juvenile Delinquency (UJD) study, which was started by Sheldon and Eleanor Glucck in 1940, is one of the classic data sets in criminology, and these two academics have been working on its reanalysis for a while now. The data include detailed archival life records that contained information from the home investigation, which included family interviews and provided the investigators with an opportunity to observe the homes and lives of sample members, in addition to the original case records of all one thousand sample members. In addition, key informants including social workers, settlement house workers, clergy, teachers, neighbors, employers, and representatives of the criminal justice and social welfare systems were interviewed as part of the UJD study. One can start to appreciate the richness with which Laub and Sampson have been able to document these one thousand lives and contribute much needed information regarding crime over the life course when one combines this detailed information with the statistical data on criminal behavior and other life events.

Research on criminology and crimll probably returnreturn full circle in the future. Quantitaas almost entirelyentirely superseded by qualitative observations in the early studies of crime and criminality. Researchers who wanted to advance our knowledge of crime and criminality kept an eye out for and highlighted new research topics. After these subjects gained attention from experts in the field, quantitative research was the preferred technique of analysis. Research in criminology has to concentrate on combining the two in the future. According to John Clausen, understanding the influences on the lives of people who have experienced a specific period of American history requires both case history and statistical data.

3.3. ETHICAL CONSIDERATIONS IN CRIMINOLOGICAL RESEARCH

Almost every study that criminologists conduct has l problems. We're We are not talking about matter here. Animal experiments raise serious moral and ethical issues. When people are involved, these become more significant. Growing awareness and enlightenment about ethical issues have led to costly legal battles. To avoid the severe consequences that follow each of these ethical principles when they are broken, criminologists must be fully aware of these issues and adhere to due process.

3.3.1. Ethics

The goal of research ethics is to safeguard the integrity, safety, and rights of human subjects. Throughout history, numerous instances of heinous violations of human rights have been documented byom the majority ofmost Euro-American nations. Due to the medical experiments conducted on Jews, African Americans, and other ethnic nationalities in concentration camps, Germany bears the greatest responsibility. Unquestionably, some researchers used placebos, misled participants about the nature of the research problem, or gave participants substances that would be classified as first-class poison as trial vaccines. The question that is pertinent in this context is: at what cost of human dignity are medical breakthroughs achieved?

The international agencies that have been at the forefront of the battle against human abuse in research include:

- **The Hellenistic Declaration (1964):** In this declaration, the world medical Association outline, ethical principles guiding human experimentation – The pacts to informed decisions. Furthermore, provisions were made for the welfare and interests of subjects to take precedence over the neeence.
- **The Bemouth elmont Report (19768):** This was instituted by the United States of America. It provided specific guidelines for

safeguarding humans participating in research. The document introduced the concept or informed consent and some cardinal principles such as respect for people, justice and beneficence.

- **Office of Human Research Protection:** This office was responsible for articulating the general principles contained in the Hellenistic declaration and the Beaumont Report into law to protect the people involved in research. The key fact to note at this stage is that the protection offered is to the researcher and subjects in research. Some ethical considerations attract heavy penalties when violated by researchers.

Ø **Example:**

- As a criminologist involved in research on strategies for rehabilitating drug addicts with particular reference to the use of cocaine.
- The research problem involves identifying lower addictive substances that could gradually replace cocaine particularly when participants begin to exhibits withdrawal syndrome.
- The research is conducted in a government social welfare institution.
- The researchers, evaluators and administrative officers are afforded effective protection by military policy officers.
- The drug addicts include males and females within the 18–40 years' age range.
- The researchers and evaluators are male within the already stated age range. Females are excused because of the dangers involved in interacting with drug addicts.
- The research involves the use of placebo as replacement for cocaine.
- The addicts are informed that the experiment is guided by the problem of controlling violence in communities.
- Addicts are deceived and tricked into the welfare institution by relatives.

3.3.2. Principles of Ethics in Research

There are many principles of ethics in research:

- Respect;
- Beneficence;
- Justice.

3.3.2.1. Respect

Respect is the first ethical rule in research. The idea of respect implies that people should be allowed to make educated decisions as long as they have access to the fundamental knowledge needed to do so. If you conducted research on drug-related gang warfare and insecurity in a specific state as a criminologist. In the event that you choose to pay drug users 30,000 Naira per month to compel them to take part in the study, how much of an informed choice can the participants make if they are informed that the main goal of the research is to lessen drug addiction in the community? On the other hand, given the behavior of drug users, particularly when addiction sets in, how can we make any case that the participants volunteered to participate? Should the N30,000 payment ensure the ability to purchase drugs, would drug users consider opting out of the researcher to be their only option? Any researcher could undoubtedly contend that coercion was used in the recruitment process.

The safeguarding of the weak is the subject of the following section of the principle of respect. During research, the vulnerable are identified with the help of the research problem. This social category is forced to comply wuirements in order toto deal with other social forces or poverty. Those who are mentally or physically challenged are also considered vulnerablwith autism shouldn'tshould not be able to weigh the advantages of taking part in a study. Applying the concept of respect becomes extremely challenging in Nigeria, where social disillusionment, unemployment, and extreme poverty are commonplace. When conducting research, a researcher who may be tempted to take advantage of the social conditions in Nigeria should keep in mind that the principle also applies to the respect that should be shown to participants.

3.3.2.2. Beneficence

The necessity of safeguarding against bodily, psychological, and socioeconomic harm is highly valued by the beneficence principle found in research. Flashbacks to past events can cause psychological harm to participants, assuming that you need information about these events from your sample for research purposes and that these events have the potential to scare them. Researchers sometimes forget to explain to participants why they are participating in a study. This is done to stop zealous units in the sample from displaying the expected results. As alt, participants won'twill not be expecting any negative effects. The victims might not identify the connection between the experiment and the side effects when they materialize. Whether through ignorance or deliberate action, the research may also fall short of fixing the problem. Additionally, the materials and methods used in the research could cause bodily harm. Substance use can cause allergies, which can have dangerous physical repercussions. Stigmatization may be linked to the procedure. As a unit in the sample, a participant in a drug trial for the treatment of psychological disorders may experience stigma. The process has made the candidate more vulnerable to stigma related to mental illness. Participants may suffer socioeconomic harm if research procedures reveal information about individual members of the sample, such as mental health or HIV status which could result in job loss or exclusion from particular professions.

3.3.2.3. Justice

During the Second World War, Jews were the subjects of some German experiments. The focus of these experiments on Jews will be questioned by the justice principle. The principle of justice in research ethics suggests that the burden of research should be borne by the appropriate groups and social categories in society. If the answer is no, why were they subjected to bearing the burden of the experiments alone? Experiments should not be conducted on any particular community, ethnic group, or nationality. Consider the suggestion to test COVID-19 vaccines initially in Africa.

The United States of America code of ethics are:

1. Researchers must endeavor to maintain objectivity and integrity in their research by disclosing their research findings in full and including all possible interpretations of the data (even those interpretations that do not support their viewpoints.*)*.
2. Researchers must safeguard the participant right to privacy and dignity while protecting them from harm.
3. Researchers must protect confidential information provided by participants even when this information considered not to be — privy ledged —(legally protected as is the case between doctor and patient, and between attorney and cheat).
4. Researchers must acknowledge research collaboration and assistance they receive from others and disclose all source of financial supports.

3.3.3. Ethics and Criminological Research

Research ethics has seen groundbreaking work from three criminologists. Professor Mark Israel of Australia's Flinders University is well-published on ethical matters.

Moreover, the Canadian professors Ted Palys and John Lowman of Simon Fraser University have written deeply and in-depth about the topic. Their writings and the author's personal research experiences with victims and offenders in

Ireland and the UK inform the discussion that follows. The University College Dublin (UCD) ethical code, a notable illustration of an institutional ethical framework, is also taken into consideration in this paper.

3.3.3.1. Confidentiality

It is crucial to guarantee the confidentiality of participant information when conducting research. The law may conflict with this responsibility in criminological research. Irish researchers are not currently required by law to disclose offenses that they become aware of while conducting a study investigation. Section 8 of the Criminal Law Act of 1997 eliminated the offense of misprision of felony, which classified failure to report certain serious offenses as a crime. However, a lot of professions support an obligation to report specific crimes. Additionally, criminological researchers may be held to stricter ethical standards if they belong to professional societies. Additionally, in certain jurisdictions, criminologists have been asked by law enforcement to divulge private information; those who refuse have been threatened with legal action. The Sunday Tribune's northern editor, Suzanne Breen, was sued in Northern Ireland for failing to give the police access to information she had obtained from Real IRA interviewees. The judge found in her favor, citing legal protections for journalistic confidentiality and the possibility of death if those protections were violated. To the best of my knowledge, Irish researchers have not yet faced legal requests for disclosure; however, given other nations' experiences, this could present a problem in the future, especially if Ireland's research capacity keeps expanding. The advice given to researchers on how to handle these problems varies depending on whether the legal or ethical requirements are given priority. The UCD Ethical Guidelines support limited confidentiality as a common solution. As per the guidelines, the researcher has an obligation to safeguard the confidentiality level that was agreed upon during the informed consent process, to the extent that it is legally feasible. The degree of confidentiality that can be upheld and the steps taken to guarantee it must be disclosed to research participants.

In general, limited confidentiality means that information is kept private unless it contains information about actual or planned harm to oneself or others. "Harm" is characterized as an obvious threat (i.e., aimed at a specific person), grave (i.e., would cause grave physical injury) and soon. Serious harm is defined as "an event, which is life-threatening and/or traumatic, from which recovery, whether physical or psychological, can be expected to be difficult or impossible" in the UK by the Multi-Agency Public Protection Arrangements Guidance. The British Society of Criminology Code of Ethics (s4.iv) and the ASA Code (s11.02.a) also make it clear that offers of confidentiality can be overridden by legal obligations. Both codes recommend that researchers educate themselves about the legal circumstances under which disclosure to legal or other authorities is required. They stress that participants should be fully and clearly informed about the limitations that apply to confidentiality before they take part in the research.

The Irish Prison Service Research Ethics Committee permits researchers to breach confidentiality if the welfare of the participant or another person is at risk, if the disclosure will prevent a serious crime or if the researcher is legally obliged to disclose the information, for example because of a court order. They advise that, where possible, this information should be shared with the agreement of the participant. The Protection for Persons Reporting Child Abuse Act 1998 (s3) protects people who disclose child abuse from civil liability.

In contrast, the ACJS states that research participants are entitled to their 'right' of personal confidentiality. Section 19 of the code (*see* also s11.01b of the ASA Code) explicitly prioritizes ethical above legal obligations:

Ø Confidential information provided by research participants should be treated as such by members of the Academy, even when this information enjoys no legal protection or privilege and legal force is applied. The obligation to respect confidentiality also applies to members of research organizations (interviewers, coders, clerical staff, etc.) who have access to the information.

For several reasons, Palys & Lowman (2001) oppose the use of limited confidentiality. They note that information about a person's criminal activity may be used against them if it is revealed to law enforcement. Therefore, limited confidentiality is against the duty to do no harm, or the ethical principle of non-maleficence. In addition, individuals might not provide an honest response if they think their answers might be revealed to a third party, especially if the information is private or if the revelation might have unfavorable effects. If the research relies heavily on data with restricted confidentiality, this raises significant methodological problems. Lastly, there might be safety issues because participants might hold researchers accountable if they are later arrn come to the conclusionconcluded that if researchers cannot ensure complete confidentiality for theiubjects, they should n't not be doing the study.

There are numerous additional ways to resolve this conundrum. One strategy is to gather the data in an anonymous manner to prevent it from being connected to a specific person. As an alternative, names and other identifying information about participants can be promptly removed from their records. In studies that require linking separate files, such as ethnographic research, this may not always be possible. Restricting the type of information that is asked of participants is a third option. For instance, it is best to steer clear of questions that ask for specific details about criminal activity that has escaped police notice or about any crimes that participants hope to commit. Additionally, very serious offenses like rape and murder are typically left off of self-report questionnaires.

A few nations, most notably the United States and Canada, have created legislative remedies for the issue. Researchers looking into sensitive subjects can apply for certificates of confidentiality from the US National Institute of Justice. The certificate offers statutory defense against mandates from the law requiring information disclosure. Under the Statistics Act (1985; s17), researchers at Statistics Canada, the country's national statistics agency, are also permitted to ensure research participants' confidentiality; however, other Canadian researchers are not covered by this provision. Common law has also been successfully used by Canadian researchers to claim privilege. According to the Wigmore test, personal data can be shielded if four requirements are met: (a) the data was shared in confidence; (b) maintaining confidentiality is crucial to the professional relationship; (c) the study is in the public interest; and (d) the harm that would arise from sharing the information outweighs the benefit. Limited confidentiality, as noted by Palys & Lowman (2001), goes against the first principle since it forces researchers to reveal their findings upon request. Participants run an increased risk as a re*3.2. Privacy*

In order toTo safeguard personal information, data protection laws have been enacted in many nations, which has made it more challenging for researchers to access data sources. The Data Protection Acts of 1988 and 2003 govern access to personal information in Ireland. Guidelines regarding the implications of this legislation for researchers were released by the Data Protection Commissioner in 2007. In the following three situations, they clarify, written consent is not necessary. To begin with, since anonymized datasets don't include personal data, they are exempt from the data protection laws. Second, the Commissioner acknowledges that connecting various datasets can occasionally be essential for research objectives. It is permissible to use pseudonymized data in these situations; that is, to remove any personally identifiable information and link the data together using codes or reference numbers. The law also permits a data controller to perform research on protected data, provided that the data is not disclosed to a third party. In all other situations, the researcher needs to get the individuals' "unambiguous" written consent before being able to access their information. Consent must be voluntary and informed, and consent forms must expressly state the purposes for which the data will be used. Consent may need to be renegotiated if the data are to be used for purposes other than those listed on the form, according to the Data Protection Commissioner.

Legitimate research has been accommodated by more accommodating data protection legislation in other countries. In Australia, if the research is in the public interest, access to personal records may be permitted under Privacy Act (1988; s95). This clause only relates to health and medical research. According to the National Health and Medical Research Council guidelines, personal so be released in order toto link datasets, provided that the data is later deleted. As an alternative, researchers can request that agencies prepare a dataset that has been anonymized or pseudonymized. This isn't always possible because anonymizing data takes a lot of time and resources, which can be too much for smaller agencies to handle. In these situations, it might indicate that the research cannot be started or will take a long to complete. Lastly, it'sit is critical to emphasize that public records, including court transcripts, are typically exempt from data protection laws under ethical codes, provided that researchers treat the people whose files they are dealing with the appropriate decency and respect. For instance, information obtained from public records is not protected by guarantees of confidentiality or privacy, according to section 15 of the ACJS Code.

3.3.3.3. Informed Consent

A basic ethical principle that guides research involving human subjects is informed consent. As a result, information regarding the study's objectives, methods, participant rights, possible risks, and rewards, degrees of confidentiality, potential applications for the research, and the researcher's contact details must be given to participants. Its goal is to make sure everyone knows exactly what is involved in taking part. Every research subject must give written informed consent in accordance with UCD guidelines. Presenting the participant with an information sheet and a copy of the consent form is required. These documents are required for applications to be accepted by the UCD Human Research Ethics Committee (HREC).

Roberts & Indermaur (2003) examined the issues surrounding obtaining informed consent in the field of criminology. The process of getting informed consent may be hampered by the fact that offender populations frequently have literacy or comprehension issues. Due to the high literacy and educational requirements of standard university consent forms, participants who struggle with comprehension or literacy frequently sign without understanding what they are signing and feel as though they have given up their legal rights in the process. According to the UCD guidelines, participants should be involved in the writing of documents and their cold be discussed in order toto address this problem.

This guarantees that participants comprehend the information given, but it doesn't fix other problems. People who are involved in crime are less likely to participate in criminological research when they are asked to divulge personal information, according to Roberts and Indermaur's findings. They also have a higher propensity to hide important information. This has an impact on the research's value and, consequently, its quality. Moreover, consent forms that have been signed actually raise the risks of participation because they establish a connection between the individual and their data, which may cause problems in the event that disclosure is required by law. There are more ways to get informed consent that should be taken into account. A protocol was created by Roberts and Indermaur to acquire verbal informed consent. Participants were first given a script detailing the necessary information to read. After that, the researchers had a conversation with them to make sure they understood. The participant and the researcher did not share any personal information.

This is in line with the guidance provided by the majority of codes, which accept that verbal consent is sufficient in some circumstances. According to the American Anthropological Association (s4): 'It is the quality of the consent, not the format, that is relevant.' The ACJS guidelines (s17) state that 'special actions' may be required for certain populations and that, in some circumstances, 'culturally appropriate' methods must be used. Similarly, the NHMRC guidelines (s3.1.16) recommend that procedures for obtaining consent should be influenced by the cultural context, the sensitivity of the information required, the potential risks involved and the vulnerability of the participants. The ASA (s12.02) permits informed consent to be obtained in writing or orally, as long as the researcher keeps a record.

In addition, many guidelines recognize that it is not always necessary or appropriate to obtain informed consent. Under the ASA guidelines (s12.01c), informed consent does not apply to publicly available information such as public records or archives and is not required for research conducted in public places. Obtaining consent in naturalistic observation may change the participants' behavior and thereby invalidate the research findings. According to the NHRMC guidelines (s2.3), researchers may request a waiver of the requirement for informed consent for research that represents minimal risk to participants, is beneficial and does not breach participants' rights to anonymity and confidentiality. The ASA guidelines (s12.01b) also allow for waivers if there is minimal risk to participants or if the research could not be done with informed consent. These waivers have to be approved by the institutional ethics committee.

3.3.3.4. Participant Distress

It is the duty of researchers to make sure that participation in their study does not negatively impact participants' psychological, social, or physical wellbeing. A list of pertinent support services should be given to participants who experience distress, as per the British Society of Criminology's guidelines (s4i) (also refer to the ASA's guidelines, s11.02b). In further detail, the BSC recommends that the particular circumstances of each case should be taken into consideration when deciding whether to disclose potential self-harm to third parties.

It is customary to have a brief debriefing session after the interview when doing research on delicate subjects. This gives participants a chance to "wind down" following the interview and ask inquiries regarding the study. Furthermore, a participant distress protocol can be created to address any potential discomfort. McGee et al., conducted a nationwide survey on sexual violence in Ireland (2002) created an advanced protocol. In these circumstances, their protocol was to listen, calm the individual, and, if required, find a source of support. It is beneficial to first find out if the participant would be open to discussing the issue with someone in their life (e.g., family member, physician) prior to providing details regarding assistance programs. Individuals are frequently more inclined to talk to a familiar and trusted person than to seek help from a qualified source. McGee and associates (2005) then conducted follow-up interviews with a portion of the initial SAVI participants to investigate the impact of involvement on wellbeing. The vast majority of participants reported only positive or neutral outcomes, with a minority reporting some short-term distress following participation. Nearly all (94%) stated that if they had been aware of what was involved beforehand, they would still have taken part.

3.3.3.5. Voluntary Participation

It is crucial to make sure that participants' consent is freely provided when doing research. In actuality, this means that the researcher has to let them know that they can leave the study at any time and that there won't be any consequences for declining to take part. Making sure that participation is voluntary is more challenging when working with probationers and prisoners. Due to their uneven interactions with criminal justice authorities, these populations are viewed as potentially vulnerable. It's reasonable to worry that they might feel pressured to participate in research. Moser along with others (2004) investigated the vulnerability to coercion in inmates receiving psychiatric care, a potentially highly susceptible group. Their results imply that these populations do not feel coerced if protocols are followed to ensure voluntary participation. A majority of the inmates contacted for the research said they would not participate, indicating that coercion was not a problem. The motivations of those who opted to take part were largely benign. The most popular ones were to: stay out of boredom, make new friends, seem helpful, and contribute to society. "Prisoners are a vulnerable population that needs to be protected from abuse, but it is also concerning that they are routinely left out of many studies involving human subjects."

3.4. EXPERIMENTS AND EVIDENCE-BASED RESEARCH IN CRIMINOLOGY

The experiment serves as the cornerstone or standard by which all other research techniques are measured. By the study's very design, it is the most efficient way to account for error or competing factors before the fact. The classic experimental design serves as the starting point or prototype for the countless variations of the experiment. The classic experimental design contains three key elements:

- Equivalence;
- Pretests and posttests; and
- Experimental and control groups.

Equivalency is essentially the process of allocating participants to experimental and control groups in a way that makes the assumption that they are similar in all significant ways. Either random assignment, in which each subject has an equal chance of appearing in either group, or matching, a process where subjects with similar age, sex, and other characteristics displayed by the experimental group are recruited for the control group, can be used to accomplish this. In order to compare the experimental group's experience with the control groups, the experimental group will receive treatment (X), while the control group will not receive any treatment at all. Pretests, or pre observations to document conditions that exist before treatment, are given to both groups. These are denoted as 01, or observation time 1, and posttests, or observations made after the experimental treatment (X) has occurred. Since both groups were equal during the pretest, the experiment's logic presupposes that any discrepancies in the posttest observation must result from one group receiving a specific treatment while the other did not. These kinds of experiments are increasingly being used to help make decisions about public policy.

3.4.1. Some Examples of Experiments in Criminology

3.4.1.1. Housing for Prisoners

The Maryland Opportunities through Vouchers Experiment (MOVE) was recently assessed in a randomized controlled trial. For the duration of this project, free housing outside of their hometown was provided to formerly incarcerated individuals (the treatment group); the control group received free housing in their hometown. After that, the experiment was carried out once more, but this time the control group was not given free housing. After a year of the program, the treatment and control groups' rates of reoffending were analyzed. The program's outcomes demonstrated that the treatment group that relocated to new locations fared better than the group that stayed put in terms of rearrest. Additionally, compared to individuals who did not receive the free housing, it was discovered that those who did receive free housing in their hometown experienceess rearrest or recidivism.

3.4.1.2. Scared Straight

In the United States, a novel program that involved having frank, heartfelt conversations with specially chosen inmates in prison to prevent misbehaving youth from progressing to more serious criminal activity generated a lot of excitement in the late 1970s. The original Rahway, New Jersey, prison project, as shown in the movie Scared Straight, was designed to combat the romanticized perception of a life spent behind bars. Even though a lot of jurisdictions hurried to adopt what seemed to be the newest miracle in the field of corrections, more investigation revealed that this enthusiasm was unwarranted. Youth were randomized to experimental and control groups in an assessment of the Jackson State Prison's JOLT (Juvenile Offenders Learn Truth) program in Michigan. When delinquency rates were assessed three and six months later, there were no discernible differences between the experimental group (those who had attended JOLT sessions) and the control group.

3.4.2. Evidence-Based Research

The questions "So what?" and "Of what practical use are all of these research projects?" are frequently raised by those who are impatient with or doubt the necessity of criminology or criminal justice research. Perhaps in response to s, in 1996 the U. S. In order toTo help communities and state and local law enforcement prevent crime, the Department of Justice awards over $3 billion in grants each year, and Congress mandated that the attorney general provide a "comprehensive evaluation of the effectiveness" of these grants.

The goal of evidence-based research is to provide well-researched support for knowledge and practice. The Department of Justice's "what works" in criminology and criminal justice approach is predicated on the idea that funding ineffective programs makes little sense. This evidence-based research employs a problem solving approach using local, national, and international evidence on what works; the most ambitious effort in this regard is the Campbell Collaboration (C2). Why not identify which programs do work or are promising and allocate our limited funding into those programs? The organization was founded to honor the late Donald Campbell, a trailblazer in the field of research design, and its goal is to make systematic program reviews easier to prepare, maintain, and make accessible. The group maintains a register of systematic studies in order to support this. The extremely effective Cochrane Collaboration in healthcare, which aimed to address the dearth of evidence directing medical and health care practices, served as the foundation for C2. Over the course of a year, C2, chaired by David Farrington at Cambridge University, requested program reviews in 25 areas, such as hot spots policing, boot camps, street lighting, restorative justice, and child skills training. The goal of the Campbell Collaboration is to generate the best available data to assist researchers, policymakers, and the general public in making informed decisions. "Best evidence" refers to rigorous systematic reviews that are updated in response to new research and criticisms, are pertinent and easily understandable by end users, encompass research published globally, and are receptive to feedback.

3.5. OFFICIAL POLICE STATISTICS: THE UNIFORM CRIME REPORT (UCR)

Official police statistics constituted the primary source of information about crime statistics on a global scale until quite recently. These data had a tendency to be uneven in quality and were not collected or recorded in any systematic way; they were collected for government administrative purposes, with social science research being gieration. Basically, criminologistsBasically, criminologists had no reliable statistics to turn to when trying to determine the answers to even simple questions like whether crime was rising or falling. The U.S. Department of Justice has compiled national crime statistics, the Uniform Crime Report (UCR), with the Federal Bureau of Investigation (FBI) assuming responsibility as the clearinghouse and publisher. The FBI receives reports from police departments after they compile the data. Local police departments are completely free to participate in the UCR program, but over time, the quantity of departments reporting and the quality of the data have increased. Historically, police departments from big cities have been the most consistent participants.

3.5.1. Sources of Crime Statistics

Examining the UCR and its connection to sources of information on crime and offenders can help us answer our original question about the amount of crime. The relationship between crimes committed and the UCR and other sources of crime statistics is depicted in Figure 3.1. For a number of reasons, it is difficult to determine with precision how much crime has been committed. For starters crime that is committed gets caughtresults in an arrest. Furthermore, in certain cases, the victim is not aware of loss because the perpetrators are the only ones who know about the crime. In the event of a gambling infraction, there might not be a victim that can be identified. A statistical source is less helpful in gauging the scope of crime the further it falls under the "crimes committed" category. Not every crime is reported to the police, just as not every crime that is discovered is reported to them.

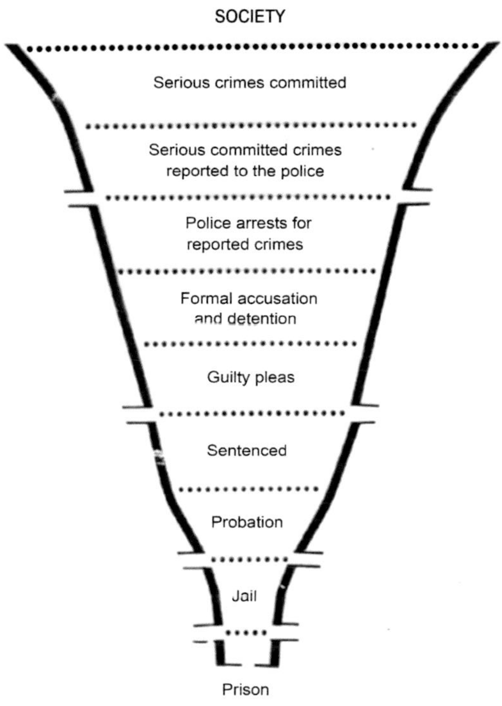

Figure 3.1. *Sources of crime statistics: The flow of offenders through the criminal justice system.*

Furthermore, some law enforcement organizations might knowingly fail to disclose crimes that have been reported, and some offenses might be deemed by investigating authorities to not be crimes at all or to be unfounded. For example, when an attempted burglary is reported by a complainant, investigating officers might determine that there is insufficient evidence to prove that a crime was committed. The UCR, as discussed later in this chapter, represented the best available statistics on crime commission until recently, despite this problematic relationship between crimes committed and crimes recorded. As demonstrated in Figure 3.1, we are once more moving away from an accurate assessment of crime as we go beyond crimes reported as a gauge of crime commission. As a result, information about arrests, convictions, indictments, jails, and other sentences like parole and probation is less helpful. These figures are not useful for gauging the severity of the crime problem; rather, they are more closely related to the effectiveness of the police, funding for the criminal justice system, and broader societal attitudes toward crime control.

The UCR's annual summary serves as the foundation for the majority of media reports on shifts in the crime rate. The UCR offers numerous qualifiers about the significance of these figures, but generally speaking, the media presents these facts carelessly and frequently in an alarmist fashion. It goes without saying that the researcher who decides to use UCR data needs to familiarize themselves as much as possible with any flaws or potential sources of bias in these data. Local police departments provide information to the FBI regarding the UCR. State penal codes differ significantly in what constitutes a crime and how it is defined, but participating departments are trained in uniform crime recording so that their reports are consistent and can be used to aggregate data across the country. UCR systems mandate that all local departments submit their statistics to the state in most states. The FBI is then given access to these data. According to Census Bureau estimates, the report covers approximately 97% of the entire population of the United States.

3.5.2. The Crime Indexes: Violent and Property Crime

The UCR has historically been classified into two categories. The index crimes, which are major felonies that are deemed to be serious, frequent, and more likely to be reported to the police, make up type I crimes. Type I crimes are included if the police are made aware of them. The index offenses are as follows:

- Murder and nonnegligent manslaughter;
- Forcible rape;
- Robbery;
- Aggravated assault;
- Burglary;
- Larceny-theft;
- Motor vehicle theft;
- Arson.

The original index and the one used for historical comparison consist of the first seven offenses. Arson was added as a result of a law passed by the U.S. Congress in October 1978. As we will see shortly, the crime rate is calculated with the index offenses. In 2004, the FBI decided to stop reporting the crime index and to report a violent crime index and property crime index instead. An advisory board felt that the crime index had been distorted by including the category of larceny-theft.

The violent crime index consists of the following:

- Murder and nonnegligent manslaughter;
- Forcible rape;

- Robbery;
- Aggravated assault.

The property crime index consists of the following:

- Burglary;
- Larceny-theft;
- Motor vehicle theft;
- Arson.

Type I and Type II offenses are separated into two categories in Uniform Crime Reports. Law enforcement reports every month on the quantity of Type I offenses that they are aware of, the number of people who have been arrested, and the number of cases that have been cleared through arrest or other extraordinary measures. Type II crimes are excluded from the calculation of the crime rate because they are non-index offenses. Reports are limited to arrests related to Type II offenses.

Type I offenses are the following:

3.5.2.1. Criminal Homicide

1. **Murder and Nonnegligent Manslaughter:** the deliberate (nonnegligent) murder of a person by another. Deaths brought on by carelessness, murderous attempts, murderous assaults, suicides, and accidents are not included. The program classifies justifiable homicides separately and limits the definition to:

i. The killing of a felon by a law enforcement officer in the line of duty; or

ii. The killing of a felon, during the commission of a felony, by a private citizen.

2. **Manslaughter by Negligence:** the heinous negligence that results in another person's death. Manslaughter by negligence does not include deaths caused by personal negligence, accidents that do not result in extreme carelessness, or fatalities from traffic accidents.

i. **Rape:** The penetration, no matter how slight, of the vagina or anus with any body part or object, or oral penetration by a sex organ of another person, without the consent of the victim.

ii. **Robbery:** The taking or attempting to take anything of value from the care, custody, or control of a person or persons by force or threat of force or violence and/or by putting the victim in fear.

iii. **Aggravated Assault:** An unlawful attack by one person upon another for the purpose of inflicting severe or aggravated bodily injury. This type of assault usually is accompanied by the use of a weapon or by means likely to produce death or great bodily harm. Simple assaults are excluded.

iv. **Burglary (Breaking or Entering):** The unlawful entry of a structure to commit a felony or a theft. Attempted forcible entry is included.

v. **Larceny-Theft (Except Motor Vehicle Theft):** The illegal taking, transporting, leading, or riding of property out of another's legal or constructive ownership. Examples include pocket-picking, shoplifting, stealing bicycles or auto parts and accessories, and stealing any other item that isn't taken by coercion or fraud. This includes attempted larceny. The following are not included: check fraud, forgery, embezzlement, and confidence tricks.

vi. **Motor Vehicle Theft:** The taking of, or attempting to take, a car. A motor vehicle travels on the ground without the assistance of rails and is self-propelled. This category expressly excludes motorboats, aircraft, farm equipment, and construction equipment.

vii. **Arson:** Any willful or malicious burning or attempt to burn, with or without intent to defraud, a dwelling house, public building, motor vehicle or aircraft, personal property of another, and so on.

Type II offenses are the following:

a. **Human Trafficking, Commercial Sex Acts:** Inducing a person by force, fraud, or coercion to participate in commercial sex acts, or in which the person induced to perform such act(s) has not attained 18 years of age.

b. **Human Trafficking, Involuntary Servitude:** The obtaining of a person(s) through recruitment, harboring, transportation, or provision and subjecting such persons by force, fraud, or coercion into involuntary servitude, peonage, debt bondage, or slavery (not to include commercial sex acts).

The Type II offenses, for which only arrest data are collected, are the following:

a. **Other Assaults (Simple):** Assaults and attempted assaults where no weapon was used or no serious or aggravated injury resulted to the victim. Stalking, intimidation, coercion, and hazing are included.

b. **Forgery and Counterfeiting:** The act of changing, duplicating, or mimicking something without authorization or permission, with the intention of misleading or defrauding others by passing off the copied or mimicked item as authentic or original; or the sale, purchase, or acquisition of something that has been changed, copied, or mimicked with the intention of misleading or defrauding others.

Attempts are included:

1. **Fraud:** The deliberate distortion of facts in order to coerce someone else or some other entity that depends on them to give up something of value or a legal right fraudulent conversion and obtaining goods or money through deceitful means. Included are confidence games and fake checks, excluding forgeries and counterfeiting.
2. **Embezzlement:** The unlawful misappropriation or misapplication by an offender to his or her own use or purpose of money, property, or some other thing of value entrusted to his or her care, custody, or control.
3. **Stolen Property—Buying, Receiving, Possessing*:*** Buying, receiving, possessing, selling, concealing, or transporting any property with the knowledge that it has been unlawfully taken, as by burglary, embezzlement, fraud, larceny, robbery, and so on. Attempts are included.
4. **Vandalism*:*** To willfully or maliciously destroy, injure, disfigure, or deface any public or private property, real or personal, without the consent of the owner or person having custody or control by cutting, tearing, breaking, marking, painting, drawing, covering with filth, or any other such means as may be specified by local law. Attempts are included.
5. **Weapons – Carrying, Possessing, and So On*:*** The violation of laws or ordinances prohibiting the manufacture, sale, purchase, transportation, possession, concealment, or use of firearms, cutting instruments, explosives, incendiary devices, or other deadly weapons. Attempts are included.
6. **Prostitution and Commercialized Vice*:*** The unlawful promotion of or participation in sexual activities for profit.
7. **Sex Offenses (Except Rape, Prostitution, and Commercialized Vice):** Offenses against chastity, common decency, morals, and the like.
8. **Drug Abuse Violations:** The breaking of laws that forbid using, producing, or distributing specific controlled substances. The illegal production, distribution, sale, acquisition, use, possession, transit, or importation of any kind of controlled substance. Arrests for breaking municipal and state laws, particularly those pertaining to the production, manufacturing, growing, and possession of illegal

narcotic drugs. The following drug categories are listed: marijuana; synthetic narcotics (manufactured drugs that can lead to true addiction, such as methadone and Demerol); opium or cocaine and their derivatives (morphine, heroin, and codeine); and dangerous nonnarcotic drugs (barbiturates, Benzedrine).

9. **Gambling:** In order to obtain a gambling advantage, one must: manufacture, sell, buy, possess, or transport gambling equipment, devices, or goods; assist, promote, or operate a game of chance for money or another stake; possess or transmit wagering information; or tamper with the results of a contest or sporting event.

10. **Offenses Against the Family and Children:** Unlawful nonviolent acts by a family member (or legal guardian) that threaten the physical, mental, or economic well-being or morals of another family member and that are not classifiable as other offenses, such as assault or sex offenses. Attempts are included.

11. **Driving Under the Influence:** Driving or operating a motor vehicle or common carrier while mentally or physically impaired as the result of consuming an alcoholic beverage or using a drug or narcotic.

12. **Liquor Laws:** The violation of state or local laws or ordinances prohibiting the manufacture, sale, purchase, transportation, possession, or use of alcoholic beverages, not including driving under the influence and drunkenness. Federal violations are excluded.

13. **Drunkenness:** To drink alcoholic beverages to the extent that one's mental faculties and physical coordination are substantially impaired. Driving under the influence is excluded.

14. **Disorderly Conduct:** Any behavior that tends to disturb the public peace or decorum, scandalize the community, or shock the public sense of morality.

15. **Vagrancy:** The breaking of a court order, rule, ordinance, or law that mandates that people leave the streets or other designated areas; forbidding people from loitering aimlessly in one place or another; or forbidding people from moving from place to place without a clearly visible means of support.

16. **Suspicion:** Released from custody without formal charges after being detained for an unspecified offense.

17. **Curfew and Loitering Laws (Persons Under Age 18):** Violations by juveniles of local curfew or loitering ordinances.

18. **All Other Offenses:** All violations of state or local laws not

specifically identified as Part I or Part II offenses, except traffic violations.

3.6. SURVEYS

The majority of readers are aware of the applications of surveys in marketing research, voting prediction studies, and public opinion polls. In criminology, surveys are also utilized, especially for the purposes of examining victimization, self-reported crime, public assessments of the seriousness of crimes, crime fear measurements, and opinions regarding law enforcement and the criminal justice system. Questionnaires are used in surveys to collect data in an organized manner. Survey researchers try to control for error and competing causal factors after the fact through the use of statistical procedures, just as experiments control for these factors by design. There are several ways to administer surveys: you can design a paper survey, an email or web survey, or a phone survey. A survey can be self-completed by the individual or it can be asked by an interviewer. Occasionally, an interviewer will ask a research participant a few survey questions, then allow them to read and respond to the remaining questions on a computer on their own.

3.6.1. Victim Surveys

The failure to include unreported or undiscovered crimes in official police statistics, such as the UCR, is one of their main flaws. Early European criminologists referred to these crimes as the "dark figure of crime," meaning they escaped official notice. The premise was that there were an unknown number of unreported crimes—the dark figure—for every crime that was brought to the attention of the authorities. The purpose of victim surveys is to gather data on the approximate number of reported victimizations from a representative sample of the general public. One significant discovery, starting with the US. surveys conducted in the late 1960s revealed that, on average, interviewers reported roughly twice as much crime as what was documented in official police records.

3.6.2. National Crime Victimization Survey (NCVS)

Commencing in 1972, the National Crime Surveys were initiated. These surveys, now known as the National Crime Victimization Survey (NCVS), encompassed the Central City Surveys and the National Crime Panel Surveys. The Central City Surveys primarily targeted households and commercial establishments in selected urban areas. Initially, around 10,000 households and 1,000 to 5,000 commercial establishments were surveyed in 26 major cities using probability samples. However, the high cost of such surveys in each city led to their discontinuation. In its place, the National Crime Panels implemented a complex probability sample, covering housing units and businesses across the United States. Unlike the Central City Surveys, which were cross-sectional or one-time studies, the panels were longitudinal, tracking a specific group over time. This approach enabled the establishment of a reference point for victim reports or the utilization of pretests during the survey period. The initial interview served as a benchmark, allowing for comparisons of future reported victimizations. The national panels conducted interviews with approximately 50,000 households every six months and 15,000 (later increased to 50,000) businesses, repeating the process twice a year to achieve the aforementioned benchmark. Each housing unit remained in the sample for three years, with a 10,000-household subsample rotating out every six months and replaced by a new group. By 2014, 90,380 households with 158,090 individuals aged 12 and above participated in the NCVS (Truman & Langton, 2015). Participants in the NCVS were queried about various victimization experiences that occurred within the preceding six months. The initial findings were celebrated as the first reliable crime statistics, but subsequent analysis suggests that this assessment may have been overly optimistic. As with the UCR, any measure of crime, including victim surveys, may have limitations.

3.6.3. Issues and Cautions in Studying Victim Data

The cost of gathering large samples, inaccurate or erroneous reports, memory loss or deterioration, telescoping of events, sampling bias, over- or underreporting, interviewer effects, coding and mechanical errors are just a few potential issues with victim surveys.

1. Although large-scale public opinion polls such as those by Gallup or Roper can be conducted with sample sizes of fewer than 1,000, the rarity of some types of victimization, such as rape, requires large samples to turn up a few victims. Hundreds may need to be surveyed to find one victim.
2. A parallel could be drawn with attempting to survey lottery winners on the basis of a sample of the general population. Many would have to be canvassed before turning up only a few winners. If the chances of winning the lottery were 1 in a million, to discover one winner by chance, the researcher would have to interview 1 million players.
3. False or mistaken reports can result in error. For example, found inaccuracies in respondent reports regarding their voting behavior, finances, academic performance, business practices, and even sexual activity. Should we assume greater precision in victim reports?

4. Memory failure or decay tends to increase with the distance between the actual time of the event and the interview concerning the event.
5. Telescoping of events, a type of memory misfire, involves the moving of events that took place in a different time period (e.g., before the reference period) into the time studied. A victimization of 2 years ago is mistakenly assumed to have occurred this past year. Subjects may even unconsciously telescope events to please interviewers. Such demand characteristics or over-agreeability on the part of respondents can certainly bias victim studies.
6. Sampling bias may produce an under-numeration of the young, males, and minorities. These very groups that tend to be undercounted by the U.S. Census are also more heavily victimized.
7. Over-reporting in victim surveys generally involves subjects reporting incidents to interviewers that they normally would view as too trivial or unimportant to call for police involvement. Much of the dark figure of crime consists of minor property crime, much of which could be considered unfounded by police.

3.6.3.1. Controlling for Error in Victim Surveys

The use of panels and boundary-drawing of target groups, assessments of coding and other sources of human or mechanical error in data processing, reverse record checks of known groups (if someone claims to have been victimized and reported to the police, you can check police records to see if this is accurate), reinter views of the same group, behaviorally specific questions (which provide specific details about the behavior in question instead of using labels that the respondent has to define for themselves), and interviews with significant others are some methods of controlling for error in victim surveys. Panels, which are longitudinal studies conducted on the same group, have been previously discussed as a way to control for forward telescoping, or the tendency to incorporate earlier incidents into the time period under study, by bounding, or establishing the time period during which events were recalled as having occurred. The National Crime Panel's reinter view views of the same group make it possible to monitor reported crime incidents and cross-check respondent responses with close friends and family members. The main advantage of victim surveys is that they give us an additional, independent way to measure crime outside of official statistics. Both official statistics and victim surveys significantly underestimate the extent of crime in this regard because they do not fully capture the scope of corporate, public order, and occupational crime.

3.6.3.2. Redesign of the National Crime Victimization Survey

The NCVS was criticized for its shortcomings, most notably its incapacity to collect reliable data on domestic abuse and sexual assaults. This led to the creation of an enhanced methodology that improved respondents' recall of incidents. The number of reported rapes and simple and aggravated assaults increased as a result of the survey modifications. For the first time, data on non-rape sexual assault and coerced or unwanted sexual contact were also collected using the redesigned tool. The new design took into account advances in survey methodology and technology. Currently, the NCVS is undergoing yet another significant redesign. A review of the data that is currently available shows that our understanding of the percentage of crimes committed by different groups or individuals within a given society is severely limited. If we base our discussions solely on official statistics, then this is undoubtedly the case.

3.6.3.3. The National Crime Statistics Exchange (NCS-X)

The Bureau of Justice Statistics is making a very large effort called the National Crime Statistics Exchange to develop a national crime statistics program that will take the place of the nearly century-old summary-based uniform crime report. A project called NCS-X is being developed to produce incident-based crime data that is nationally representative. In order to improve the country's capacity to provide more precise national measures of crime incidents, new agencies are added to the database, which is reported to law enforcement agencies and combines data from over 6,000 police agencies as compiled by the FBI's National Incident-Based Reporting System (NIBRS). To promote participation, the NCS-X will offer incentives to state reporting programs and agencies. Many organizations are going to take part. The National Consortium for Justice Information and Statistics will be creating the plan. These include RTI International, the International Association of Chiefs of Police, the Police Executive Research Forum, the Integrated Justice Information Systems Institute, and SEARCH. During NCS-X's first phase, 400 more law enforcement agencies will be invited to join and the costs will be evaluatmore, it will consult with current state NIBRS programs. In order toTo improve the operational capabilities of NCS-X agencies, the Bureau of Justice Statistics is looking into a number of options for participating agencies, such as extending reporting capabilities, technical solutions, analytical tools, and other incentives.

3.6.4. Self-Report Measures of Crime

Similar to victim surveys, self-report measures aim to offer a substitute for official statistics when gauging the level of criminal activity within a community. Criminologists question people about their criminal histories and delinquent behavior. This can be accomplished by using anonymous surveys or questionnaires, where the respondent's identity is verified by follow-up interviews or official police documentation. Furthermore, validated information through follow-up interviews or threats of a polygraph (lie detector) test, signed instruments that can be compared to official records, interviews conducted alone, and interviews that are subsequently compared to official records can all be employed. In the US, the majority of self-report surveys have been done on "captive audiences," like students or faculty. Studies on the adult population are scarce. Around 99% of the adult sample in one of the first studies, conducted by Wallerstein and Wyle in 1947, had committed at least one offense. The following were some of the percentages of admission for males and females, respectively: 89% and 83% for larceny; 77% and 74% for indecency; 49% and 5% for assault; 13% and 11% for grand larceny (except auto); and 57% and 40% for tax evasion. These numbers point to a remarkably high level of criminal activity among a population that is generally thought to be law-abiding.

3.6.4.1. Controlling for Error in Self-Report Surveys

The relationship between claimed behavior and actual behavior is seriously questioned when using self-reported data as a gauge of crime commission. "Asking people about their behavior is a poor way of observing it," according to Nettler (1978). If individuals report other aspects of their behavior inaccurately, like voting, receiving medical care, and the like, it might be dangerous to assume that they will admit deviant behavior more accurately. Potentially erroneous reports, the use of subpar or inconsistent instruments, inadequate research design, and a poor subject selection are some issues with self-report studies. The number of minor infractions that are classified as delinquent in the US and are included in such studies is questionable, even though erroneous or inaccurate reports may have an impact on these surveys. They draw attention to the fact that juvenile criminality is synonymous with delinquency in Europe. Problems arise from small and unrepresentative samples as well as the potential for lying, poor memory, and telescoping in self-report surveys.

The National Institute of Justice's ADAM (Arrestee Drug Abuse Monitoring program), formerly known as the Drug Use Forecasting (DUF) program, was one particularly creative program for verifying self-reports. After being questioned about their drug-using habits, groups of people who had been arrested were asked to voluntarily submit urine samples so that they could be checked for drug use. The program offered a clever method of estimating drug use among criminal populations in addition to serving as a gauge for the effects of different policies on drug usage. In order to conduct local research and evaluation and to inform local policy decisions, ADAM provided information to state and local drug policy makers, courts, law enforcement agencies, treatment providers, and prevention specialists. With the establishment of International ADAM in 1998, the NIJ was able to provide a worldwide evaluation of drug use through collaboration between criminal justice agencies across numerous nations. In conclusion, self-report surveys provide an independent measure of crime commission, similar to victim studies, despite certain drawbacks.

3.7. PARTICIPANT OBSERVATION

Through a range of techniques, a researcher can study or observe a group through varying degrees of participation in its activities. This technique is known as participant observation. In Hustlers, Beats, & Others (1967), Ned Polsky makes a powerful case for the application of this tactic and offers helpful guidance on the subject.

3.7.1. Participant Observation of Criminals

Uncaught criminals can be studied in the field of criminology, despite the advice that was once given in most criminology classes. For an extended period, biologists have observed that gorillas in zoos behave differently from those in their natural environment. It is crucial that criminologists abandon the practice of focusing solely on incarcerated offenders in jails and prisons. In support of field studies of criminals, Polsky (1967) asserts that a criminologist can only be a veranda anthropologist until he learns to set aside his personal distaste for the beliefs and ways of life of the wild savages, until he visits cannibals and headhunters in the field and observes them without attempting to r civilize or turn them over to colonial officials. That is, he won'twill not be able to provide anything approaching a truly scientific picture of crime; instead, he will only be a sociologist working in a jail or courthouse. The idea that the researcher needs to pose as a member of the criminal underworld is one of the arguments frequently used to discourage this kind of research. In actuality, employing such a tactic would be extremely risky and unfeasible. Polsky contends that the barriers to accessing criminal and conventional types are greatly exaggerated and that the gap between them is not as great as many would have us beieve.

There are, of course, problems in studying criminals au naturael. The researcher must realize that he or she is more of an intruder than would be the case in a prison setting. Un-incarcerated criminals have more to lose than those already in jail do. And on their own turf, criminals are freer to put the researcher down or to refuse to be observed. Having successfully employed participant observation in studying uncaught pool hustlers, organized criminals, and drug addicts, Polsky offers some sage advice regarding procedures to employ in studying criminals in the field:

- Avoid using gadgets such as tape recorders, questionnaires, and the like. Construct field notes later, after leaving the scene for the day.
- Keep your eyes and ears open, but keep your mouth shut.
- In the argot, the specialized language or jargon of a group, but don'tdo not overuse it.
- You can often gain entry into the setting through common recreational interests, for example, card games, the track, or poolrooms.
- Do not pretend to be one of them. As soon as practicable, make them aware of your purposes.

3.7.2. Evaluation of the Method of Participant Observation

Participant observation is an excellent procedure for studying little-understood groups. Some examples of participant observation studies with criminological ramifications have been Whyte's Street Corner Society (1943/1955); Polsky's Hustlers, Beats, & Others (1967); Yablonsky's Synanon (1965); and The Violent Gang (1962); Ianni's A Family Business (1972); Albini's (1986) study of the Guardian Angels; and Humphreys's Tearoom Trade (1970). In addition, Eleanor Miller (1986) did field research interviewing 64 prostitutes in Milwaukee, Marquart (1986) worked as a prison guard, Hopper (1991) studied outlaw motorcycle gangs, and SanchezJankowski (1991) spent 10 years living with and studying street gangs in Los Angeles, Boston, and New York.

The usefulness of such field studies in exploring settings that would not readily lend themselves to quantitative analysis is illustrated by some studies. Philippe Bourgois, author of In Search of Respect: Selling Crack in El Barrio (1995), spent the 5 years from 1985 to 1990 in East Harlem studying young Puerto Rican men on street corners and in crack houses, bars, and homes. Elijah Anderson's A Place on the Corner (1981) took place in the 1970s and reported on Chicago ghetto life from Jelly's, a bar and liquor store that he studied for more than 3 years. Anderson's Streetwise (1990) describes two other Philadelphia neighborhoods. Mark Hamm's American Skinheads (1993) reports on his field study of neo-Nazi hate groups, which included communications with skinheads via the WAR (White Aryan Resistance) website. Jim Aho in This Thing of Darkness (1994) conducted a participant observation study of Idaho Christian Patriots until he defined such involvement as increasingly too dangerous. J. M. Miller and Tewksbury in Extreme Methods: Innovative Approaches to Social Science Research (2000) and Ferrell, Hamm, and Adler in Ethnography at the Edge: Crime, Deviance, and Field Research (1998) provide very interesting collections of articles on difficult-to-access deviant groups that require more innovative, and sometimes controversial, means of investigation.

The primary benefits of participant observation are associated with the qualitative information it can yield. By employing this technique of sensitization, also known as verstehen (derived from the German word meaning "to understand"), the researcher is less susceptible to bias. The method allows the researcher to watch subjects in their natural habitat and is very adaptable and natural-feeling. These ethnographic techniques give students firsthand information and introduce them to the subjects' points of view. This method has resulted in literature that is both thrilling and captivating, on par with some of the best modern fiction. Chapters that follow provide examples from this genre. Participant observation can have certain drawbacks, such as being a very time-consuming technique that can place a lot of demands on the observer's personal life. Both over-identification with and aversion to the group under study pose risks to the observer, which frequently push the boundaries of the researcher's commitment to objectivity. Participant observation can present significant ethical challenges in addition to the possibility of observer bias and the difficulty of interpreting a large amount of non-quantitative data.

The study of a culture is called ethnography. Critics have pointed out that one issue with this type of research is that it is difficult to tell if the researcher made anything up. Alice Goffman's On the Run: Fugitive Life in an American City (2014) caused quite a stir when it was published. The late, well-known Erving Goffman's daughter is Alice Goffman. Regarding how she conducted her fieldwork, there has been much discussion. When investigating young black men involved in Philadelphia's criminal justice system, questions were raised about whether she had committed a felony (accessory to a planned murdeks of going on drives with a gun-wielding subject of hers in order toto find the person who killed another subject. Sknowledged embellishing and exaggerating her story, according tosome critics.

REFERENCES

1. Academy of Criminal Justice Sciences. (2000). *Code of Ethics*. Greenbelt, MD: ACJS. Retrieved from: www.acjs.org/pubs/167_671_2922.cfm (accessed on 16 August 2024).
2. American Anthropological Association. (1998). *Code of Ethics of the American Anthropological Association*. Arlington, VA: AAA. Retrieved from: www.aaanet.org/committees/ethics/ethicscode.pdf (accessed on 16 August 2024).
3. American Sociological Association. (1999). *Code of Ethics and Policies and Procedures of the ASA Committee on Professional Ethics*. Washington, DC: ASA. Retrieved from: www.asanet.org/cs/root/leftnav/ethics/code_of_ethics_standards#12 (accessed on 16 August 2024).
4. Australian and New Zealand Society of Criminology. (2000). *Code of Ethics*. Canberra: ANZOC. Retrieved from: www.anzsoc.org/cms-the-society/code-ofethics.phps (accessed on 16 August 2024).
5. Babbie, E. R. (2015). *The Practice of Social Research* (14th ed.). Cengage Learning.
6. Bachman, R., & Schutt, R. K. (2019). *The Practice of Research in Criminology and Criminal Justice* (7th ed.). SAGE Publications.
7. Breen, S. (2009). A victory to savor. *Sunday Tribune*.
8. British Society of Criminology. (2006). *Code of Ethics for Researchers in The Field of Criminology*. London: BSC. Retrieved from: www.britsoccrim.org/ethical.htm (accessed on 16 August 2024).
9. Bryman, A. (2016). *Social Research Methods* (5th ed.). Oxford University Press.
10. Data Protection Commissioner. (2007). *Guidelines on Research in the Health Sector*. Retrieved from: www.dataprotection.ie/docs/Guidelines_on_research_in_the_Health_Sector/573.htm (accessed on 16 August 2024).
11. Engel, R. S., & Schutt, R. K. (2016). *Fundamentals of Social Work Research* (2nd ed.). SAGE Publications.
12. Gadd, D., Farrall, S., Gray, P., & Sparks, R. (2019). *Doing Criminological Research* (3rd ed.). SAGE Publications.
13. Hagan, F. E. (2018). *Research Methods in Criminal Justice and Criminology* (12th ed.). Pearson.
14. Maxfield, M. G., & Babbie, E. R. (2017). *Research Methods for Criminal Justice and Criminology* (8th ed.). Cengage Learning.

15. McGee, H. M., Garavan, R., Leigh, C., Ellis, C., & Conroy, R. (2005). *SAVI Revisited: Long-Term Effects of Disclosure of Sexual Abuse in a Confidential Research Interview*. Dublin Rape Crisis Centre.
16. McGee, H., Garavan, R., de Barra, M., Byrne, J., & Conroy, R. (2002). *The SAVI Report: Sexual Abuse and Violence in Ireland. A National Study of Irish Experiences, Beliefs and Attitudes Concerning Sexual Violence.* Liffey Press.
17. Moser, D. J., Arndt, S., Kanz, J. E., Benjamin, M. L., Bayless, J. D., Reese, R. L., & Martin, R. (2004). Coercion and informed consent in research involving prisoners. *Comprehensive Psychiatry, 45*(1), 1–9.
18. National Offender Management Service. (2007). *MAPPA Guidance 2007*. NOMS Public Protection Unit, Ministry of Justice.
19. Palys, T., & Lowman, J. (2001). Social research with eyes wide shut: The limited confidentiality dilemma. *Canadian Journal of Criminology, 43*(2), 255–267.
20. Rennison, C. M., & Hart, T. C. (2019). *Introduction to Criminal Justice: Systems, Diversity, and Change* (3rd ed.). SAGE Publications.
21. Roberts, L., & Indermaur, D. (2003). Signed consent forms in criminological research: Protection for researchers and ethics committees but a threat to research participants? *Psychiatry Psychology and Law, 10*(2), 289–299.
22. Weisburd, D., & Braga, A. A. (2015). *An Introduction to Experimental Criminology*. Cambridge University Press.
23. Worrall, J. L., & Schwartz, D. (2019). *Criminological Theory: Context and Consequences* (7th ed.). SAGE Publications.

Chapter **4**

Socio-Legal Research

Contents

INTRODUCTION

Socio-legal research is an interdisciplinary approach to investigating the relationship between law, society, and human behavior that combines social science methodologies with legal studies. This area of study aims to comprehend how society uses law, how norms and values impact the making and application of laws, and how legal institutions both influence and are influenced by social change. Socio-legal research frequently uses both qualitative and quantitative techniques to collect data on legal practices, institutions, and their effects on different social groups. These techniques include surveys, ethnography, interviews, and statistical analysis. Aiming to offer a more thorough understanding of legal phenomena than traditional legal studies alone, socio-legal researchers integrate theoretical frameworks from sociology, anthropology, political science, and other social sciences. This method makes it possible to investigate how laws work in actual situations, illuminating the subtleties and complexity of legal procedures as well as their effects on justice, equality, and human rights. Socio-legal studies could look into how underprivileged communities interact with the legal system, how judges and attorneys influence the way cases are decided, or how legal changes affect institutions and social behaviors.

Legal systems can be conceptualized in three principal ways. First, a legal system can be said merely as an aggregate of legal norms, as a sum of its parts. In this conception, the typical questions are:

- What makes a system out of a vast and heterogeneous mass of normative materials?
- By what concepts and criteria can we identify the existence of a legal system?
- How is the unity of the systems to be established?

Second, legal systems may be seen as structured relationships between those who create, interpret, violate, uphold, and comply with the rules of law. These systems encompass roles, status, and institutional behavior.

Thirdly, legal systems can be likened to social control systems due to their shared characteristics such as distinct institutional environments, varying normative requirements and sanctions, and distinct bases of social authority and power. The distinction made here is between social control systems that are maintained and/or supported by the state and those that are supported by non-state organizations or groups. Therefore, a study of the criminal justice system would be lacking if it did not consider social behavior, roles and status, and the institutions that are part of the criminal justice administration.

4.1. LEGAL RESEARCH

Research is the process of gathering data in order to conduct an extensive investigation of a specific topic. The word "recherché," which translates from French to mean "thorough inspection," is the source of the English term "research." Research is the methodical, systematic analysis of data with the use of scientific methods to investigate and analyze a specific research problem. Research is done to investigate and comprehend novel issues, identify potential solutions, or learn new information about an already-known subject. Legal research is an organized approach to researching legal issues in a scientific manner. It entails gathering new information, confirming that which already exists, examining subject relationships and sequences, and creating tools and concepts based on the data. Legal research primarily aims to test theories, modify concepts, and promote fair and just laws. There are several ramifications for the significance of legal research. It affects how laws are made, deals with business issues, backs court rulings, raises legal awareness, advances legal knowledge, directs attorneys, and strengthens the nation's legal system (Shipra, 2003).

According to Collis and Hussey, research is essentially an exhaustive, methodical, and rigorous process of inquiry that advances knowledge. The study of legal issues and problems is the main focus of legal research. It covers an organized analysis of legal cases, norms, regulations, and statutes. It is employed to improve the legal system, resolve legal disputes, bolster arguments made in court, and offer direction to judges when making decisions. Legal research encompasses tasks such as data collection, legal knowledge updating, necessary modifications, and introduction into our legal system. Through the introduction of new regulations, Codes, and Acts, it plays a significant role in framing a relationship between law and society. Scientific research is also conducted in this area of law. It helps in the discovery of new facts, the confirmation of old facts, the introduction of new knowledge, the analysis of old and new facts, their proper explanation, and their development.

4.1.1. Types of Legal Research

The majority of legal research has been divided into two categories. There are two types of legal research: the first is doctrinal, which analyzes the theoretical aspects of legal issues, and the second is non-doctrinal, which identifies practical issues and provides solutions.

4.1.1.1. Doctrinal Legal Research

Research on a legal theory known as doctrinal legal research is carried out by applying reasoning to analyze the current statutes and case law. This study is theoretical in nature since it examines legal concepts and principles in detail from a variety of sources, including laws, case law, and other sources, in order to arrive at a sound conclusion. The word "doctrine," which meaning "principle" or "normal governing tenet," is where the term "doctrinal research" originated. Legal doctrines, rules, concepts, and their interrelationships are studied, analyzed, and critically evaluated in a methodical and rigorous manner. Another name for this study is "Pure Theoretical Research." The majority of doctrinal legal research is conducted in libraries (online and print), where one can find statutes, court rulings, periodicals, articles, legal journals, and other materials. It would be simpler to come to a decision by critically analyzing the pertinent data and information after going through them in order to address a specific legal issue. The present study employs conventional legal research methodologies. The information and data are analyzed, interpreted, and synthesized by this research to address legal issues and create new legal theories:

1. **Objectives of Doctrinal Legal Research:** The process of conducting doctrinal legal research involves reading theoretical study materials from libraries in-depth. To find a clear answer to a legal question, one must conduct a book-based analysis of various statutes, legal books, laws, and other legal literature and journals. Since fieldwork and experimentation are not necessary, it primarily relies on secondary sources of information. The inspection starts with a few legal propositions, and its whole goal is to ascertain whether the underlying hypothesis is sound. Its goal is to acquire information from various legal documents and other sources and apply it to the process of using logical and rational reasoning and interpretation to arrive at a sufficient answer to the legal question.
2. **Sources of Doctrinal Research:** Conventional legal sources are the primary sources utilized in doctrinal legal research. The sources include legislative history, judicial rulings, committee reports, and more in addition to statutes and enactments. This group of sources also includes the Acts that the Legislature has passed. Additional resources for doctrinal legal research include the rulings and decisions of the Supreme Court and the various High Courts. When conducting doctrinal legal research, textbooks, commentaries, and periodicals are occasionally used as resources. However, they lack the authenticity of original sources such as Acts, enactments, and cases that are published in books, articles, journals, and authorized websites.
3. **Characteristics of Doctrinal Legal Research:** The essential characteristics of doctrinal legal research are as follows:

- It involves the analysis of legal concepts or propositions.
- It mainly used conventional sources of information.
- It may include legal concepts derived from enactments, regulations, administrative guidelines, or judicial decisions.
- It is used for doing research into legal concepts and principles in all kinds of cases, rules, and statutes. This research mainly focuses on legal information and data that are collected from legislation, law journals, reports, case laws, textbooks, and so on.
- It is more concerned with research in law than research about law. This type of research focuses only on the current state of the law instead of seeking public opinion on how it should be.
- It is closely linked with the doctrine of precedent.
- It is research into the black letters of the law.
- This research is based on secondary data that is available and relevant to the study.

4. **Normative Character of Doctrinal Legal Research:** When legal research and doctrines are developed for publication in textbooks and journals that challenge the definition of law, they take on a normative quality specific to a given legal problem. Legal rules and regulations are normative in nature, as they instruct us on how each individual should behave. This question, "What is law?" is addressed by doctrinal legal research. Just having a conversation about human behavior does not require any effort to explain, forecast, or even comprehend it. To sum up, doctrinal legal research focuses on the purposes of law rather than the content of the law.

5. **Purpose of Doctrinal Research:** The following are the purposes of the doctrinal legal research:
   - It constructs new legal principles, doctrines, and theories. Then it tries to verify its validity and add new knowledge to it.
   - It helps in maintaining continuity, consistency, and certainty of law in society.
   - It tries to resolve disputes with clients in various matters by applying statutory laws and related cases. The outcomes become more predictable as they are derived from established sources.
   - It provides assistance or advice to the courts or clients about applying legal doctrines to a particular case or legal event at the time when required.

- It is also helpful for examining judicial opinions and determining which opinion is to be preferred. If there is a conflict in the decisions of the courts, it provides suggestions for resolving those conflicts.
- It also provides tools for reaching a conclusion for lawyers and judges on multiple legal problems, usually for those who have very limited time at their disposal.
- It is also useful for conducting comparative and historical inquiries that deal with a contrasting legal regime.
- It is useful for developing legal theories that try to provide an explanation of how laws or areas of law fit together.
- It helps in identifying problems or tensions within a body of law or a legal institution.
- It also helps to separate helpful information from useless ones.

6. **Tools Used for Doctrinal Research:** The various tools that are used for doctrinal legal research are as follows:
   - Legal resources include statutes, regulations, and others.
   - Legal commentaries, which include law journals and legal articles.
   - Legal reviews like academic journals.
   - Legal treaties.
   - Case laws by studying the judicial pronouncements.
   - Online resources include various online legal websites and blogs.
   - Government reports.
   - Reports of committees.
7. **Methodology of Doctrinal Legal Research:** The focus of doctrinal legal research is theoretical, or library-based, investigation. The majority of researchers employ it since it is the most widely used methodology in legal research. The analysis, development, and application of legal concepts and principles are the goals of doctrinal legal research. Interpreting legal documents, such as statutes, case laws, treaties, and regulations, is another use for it. It also offers a thorough comprehension of the theories, concepts, and principles of law. The process for doctrinal research methodology consists of various steps, which are as follows:
   - **Identifying the Research Problem:** The first step is to

identify the research problem. It entails choosing a research topic, then elaborating on and specifying its parameters.

- **Collecting Legal Sources:** In order to solve research problems involving statutes, case laws, regulations, and judicial decisions, this step entails gathering legal sources. This is the most crucial step because it calls for a thorough background investigation of a specific issue using a variety of sources, including legal articles, treatises, dictionaries, encyclopedias, textbooks, and journals.
- **Evaluating Those Legal Sources:** After collecting information regarding the research problem, the researcher must evaluate them to check their relevancy, trustworthiness, and credibility.
- **Analyzing the Legal Sources:** Once the evaluation is done, the researcher then must analyze the legal principles, ideas, concepts, and arguments. The researcher should take into consideration all aspects of the legal sources.
- **Synthesizing Legal Principles:** After analyzing the legal sources, the researcher must synthesize the legal concepts and principles so as to frame a rational, logical, and coherent understanding of the legal problem.
- **Applying Those Legal Principles:** The last step in the synthesizing process is to apply the previously analyzed and synthesized legal principles to frame the legal problem or question and ultimately reach a conclusion.

8. **Examples of Doctrinal Legal Research:** Some of the examples of doctrinal legal research are as follows:
   - Studying a series of court judgements to find out how a legal doctrine works and evolves over a period of time, like the 'basic structure doctrine' of the Indian Constitution.
   - Evaluating legal articles, textbooks, journals, commentaries, and other legal documents to understand the ways in which scholars and jurists are interpreting various aspects of the law.
   - Analyzing a specific statute that has been implemented by the Legislature and its effect on different jurisdictions.
9. **Merits of Doctrinal Legal Research:** Some of the advantages of doctrinal legal research are as follows:
   - **Helpful at the Initial Stage:** It is beneficial to those who

are conducting preliminary legal education research. This method is commonly used to obtain information or carry out legal research. Since there will be an abundance of resources available to them, this method will be much easier for most scholars and law students.

- **Provides Clarity to the Researchers:** The researchers benefit from clarity because it can offer succinct, straightforward solutions to legal issues. Its primary foundation consists of authorized legal resources and legal sources. It aids in the methodical and impartial identification and analysis of legal doctrines, concepts, and ideas by the researchers.
- **Cost-Effective/Less Expensive Method:** This research methodology is economical because there are no costs associated with data collection. Legal documents, libraries, and internet websites all provide easy access to the data and information. The information can be easily analyzed by the researcher to arrive at a specific conclusion.
- **Consumes Less Time:** It is also a time-efficient research methodology, as the legal sources are easily available. The researcher can at any time search for information on a particular matter and analyze it quickly and efficiently.
- **Foundation for Further Research:** It also offers a starting point for additional study of a specific legal matter. With a clear understanding of the research problem, the researcher is able to spot any ambiguities, contradictions, or gaps in the specific legal issue at hand. They assist the researchers in finding new information, formulating fresh hypotheses, putting forth fresh legal amendments, and, if necessary, carrying out additional study.
- **Helps in Professional Development:** The legal profession—which comprises judges, attorneys, academics, and law students—benefits from the advancement of knowledge and expertise in related fields. It provides them with a broad and in-depth comprehension of legal theories, concepts, principles, and doctrines that researchers can utilize to practically apply them in the real world.
- **Provides Quick Solutions:** It is useful as it provides quick answers to legal issues that are at hand. The information can be analyzed by collecting it from all the secondary legal sources that are easily available.

- **More Predictable and Easily Manageable:** Finally, because it draws from reliable and approved sources, it is more predictable and in control. Because it concentrates on the sources of jurisprudence, it is easily manageable.

10. **Demerits of Doctrinal Legal Research:** Some of the disadvantages of doctrinal legal research are as follows:

- **Based on the Theoretical Method:** The library's theoretical resources serve as the primary basis for research. Because it ignores the social, political, and economic ramifications of the legal issue in society, it is extremely technical, conservative, and trivial in nature. It is limited to analyzing and interpreting them theoretically. When compared to non-doctrinal legal research, it is less innovative.
- **Subjective in Nature:** It is also subjective in nature because different researchers may have different perspectives on the same legal issue. It implies that two people can ask the same question and come to completely different conclusions.
- **Limited Scope:** Its scope is restricted because it is based solely on the analysis of legal sources, which frequently include non-legal factors that may influence the outcome of the legal process. Given its restricted scope, it might not offer a thorough and in-depth comprehension of a specific legal issue.
- **Lack of Empirical Evidence:** Since it excludes the gathering of empirical data through surveys or interviews, it is not backed by empirical data. Its projection is far from social reality because it ignores the effects that laws and legal procedures have on people and society. As a result, it lacks any basis in social facts and a working knowledge of social issues. This research isn't very helpful because using this approach won't result in social transformation.
- **Biassed in Nature:** The majority of the theoretical legal sources used in this research may occasionally be biased in favor of a specific legal interpretation. This could result in prejudices from a biased examination of a specific legal issue.
- **It Cannot be Updated:** This type of research is primarily reliant on the laws that Parliament enacts and passes. The social changes that are occurring in people's daily lives within society are not taken into account. Therefore, it's possible that

this research won't yield a useful finding that will benefit the community as a whole.

- **Difficulty in Predicting the Practical Outcomes:** The analysis and synthesis of legal sources obtained from earlier court rulings and precedents is the main objective of this study. Therefore, it might not always be adequate to forecast future legal outcomes and offer assistance for future legal decision-making.
- **Limited Applicability:** The applicability of doctrinal research findings to other legal systems or jurisdictions may be restricted to its participants within a specific legal system.

11. **Non-Doctrinal Legal Research:** The foundation of non-doctrinal legal research is real-world data. This research is fact-based. Compared to doctrinal legal research, it has a far broader scope. Fieldwork or first-hand observation by an academic is the primary method used in research. There are no secondary sources used in this study. Primary data collection is necessary in order to address that research problem. This study investigates how law and society intersect from a practical standpoint. Because it combines social science and legal principles to examine the relationship between law and society, this research is also known as "socio-legal research." It entails the empirical technique of data collection followed by an examination of the institutions, policies, and legal practices in relation to society. It investigates how a person's attitude and how that attitude affects society are impacted by the law, these institutions, and policies. In discussing consequences, non-doctrinal research is also sometimes called "purposive" research because it focuses on how laws affect individuals and society or the reason behind a particular law's enactment. The primary approach used in this study is multidisciplinary. It conducts this research using a variety of methodologies. The researchers arrive at a conclusion following the application of all techniques required for gathering primary legal data. Observations, demonstrations, surveys, questionnaires, and interviews are a few techniques that have been employed in non-doctrinal research. The significance of this research increased when it became necessary to bring legal issues into the real world. The belief was that legal research ought to focus on the practical implications of laws for society in the real world, in addition to theoretical studies grounded in written laws. The primary focus of researchers when choosing a topic is on legal factors, such as law,

and non-legal factors, such as social, economic, or political variables. Data, which can be either quantitative or qualitative, are then used to examine and analyze the relationship and interconnection between these factors. This study's main goal is to understand how the law functions in real-world situations.

12. **Objectives of Non-Doctrinal Legal Research:** The primary goals of non-doctrinal legal research are to shed light on the intricate interactions between the law and society and identify legislative changes and initiatives that could advance social justice and equity. Studying how the law functions in a social and cultural context is its goal. Through questioning and observation, it also attempted to learn more about how individuals actually apply, comprehend, and abide by a given law. It demonstrates the practical application of a law in the day-to-day activities of members of society.

13. **Sources of Non-Doctrinal Research:** The framework offered by non-doctrinal legal research is sufficient for assessing how the law affects institutions and society. For analysis in non-doctrinal legal research methods, primary data and information, or first-hand research, is necessary. The following techniques are used to gather primary data: questionnaires, interviews, schedules, and observations.

14. **Characteristics of Non-Doctrinal Legal Research:** The essential characteristics of non-doctrinal legal research are as follows:
    - It is conducted to find out the effect of non-legal events on the process of law-making or legal provisions.
    - It tries to determine and evaluate the extent to which the different variables influence the legal process.
    - It tries to identify the effect of legal decisions on individuals in society.
    - It tries to identify the societal consequences of any legislation or legal principle that can be traced.
    - It determines the correlation between the law and other non-legal facts.

15. **Purpose of Non-Doctrinal Research:** The following are the purposes of the non-doctrinal legal research:
    - It alters the research tools to cope with the present legal problems or finds out various measures to resolve different social issues.

- It organizes society in a systematic manner and maintains peace by tracing social evils and eradicating them.
- It finds out the consequences of the legal decisions and judgements that the courts pass and their effect on society.
- It assesses the impact of non-legal events like technological improvement, economic development, and technical changes on legal decisions.
- It also identifies and assesses the magnitude of variable factors that influence the decision-making process, like the effect of capital punishment awarded by the courts to convicts of dangerous crimes at a certain place at a given time.
- It traces the practical consequences of the legal principles for society.
- It finds out whether a law that has been passed is actually helping the people of society in the real world.

16. **Tools Used for Non-Doctrinal Research:** The various tools that are used for non-doctrinal legal research are as follows:
    - Surveys;
    - Judgements;
    - Schedule;
    - Sampling;
    - Case study;
    - Published sources;
    - Interviews.
17. **Methodology of Non-Doctrinal Legal Research:** The main focus of non-doctrinal legal research is fieldwork. It is founded on first-hand knowledge. This study's data was gathered through experimentation and observation. Surveys, interviews, questionnaires, and other tools are part of the methodology. Data may be displayed using pie charts, bar graphs, and other formats after it has been collected. The process for doctrinal research methodology consists of various steps, which are as follows:
    - **Identifying the Research Question:** It entails defining the scope of the study and choosing or identifying the research problem.
    - **Collecting Data:** This step entails obtaining data on variables of interest and measuring it, which is required for research

problems. The procedure ought to be carried out in a way that makes it simpler to respond to the research question, test theories, and assess the outcome. In order to guarantee that the information is accurate and correct, this approach places a strong emphasis on gathering primary data. Methods of gathering information include local surveys, interviews with judges, attorneys, and other legal professionals, as well as with members of the public who may be impacted by a particular legal issue. It also includes advocacy groups with local organizations, and groups that watch court cases and other legal proceedings as participants.

- **Classifying Data:** Classifying the data is the next step after gathering it. It refers to the process of classifying data into homogeneous groups based on the shared characteristics found in the data. Organizing information so that similarities and differences can be quickly understood is the primary goal of data classification.
- **Analyzing Information**: The researcher then conducts an analysis of the data after correctly classifying them into groups with related features. After distilling the data to a narrative, the researchers conduct an analysis. By dividing the data into more manageable, smaller pieces, the process of data analysis helps to lessen the burden of large amounts of data.
- **Findings:** This step deals with the conclusion that the researchers reached after examining the gathered data. Even if the final result deviates from the hypothesis, its objective is to use this data to answer the research question that was posed at the beginning.
- **Conclusion:** This is the last step of non-doctrinal legal research. It may be concluded that a reformation is needed in the legal system for the welfare of society. It can also be used to portray that certain rights of communities have been violated. Therefore, greater attention should be given to rectifying them, as well as examining how social issues influence legal decisions.

18. **Examples of Non-Doctrinal Legal Research:** Some of the examples of non-doctrinal legal research are as follows:

- Conducting interviews and surveys with incarcerated individuals to study the impact of criminal justice policies on the real world, like the effect of capital punishment on the offenders.

- Investigating human rights abuses in a particular region or locality through field work involves questioning and interviewing those whose rights are being violated.
- Evaluating the effectiveness of the regulations that have been implemented for the protection of the environment and collecting information about pollution levels.

19. **Merits of Non-Doctrinal Legal Research:** Some of the advantages of non-doctrinal legal research are as follows:
    - **Based on Field Research:** This research is field-based, as opposed to doctrinal legal research. It is not restricted to purely theoretical research. Compared to the doctrinal legal research methodology, it covers a far larger ground. It considers how society's legal issues have an impact on the social, political, and economic spheres. Being field-based research, it doesn't rely on information from secondary sources.
    - **Determines the Practical Efficiency of Laws:** It aids in assessing how effective laws are in practice across all non-legal domains. It draws attention to the discrepancies between practicality and legislative objectives. It demonstrates the distinction between a statutory law that is referenced in the statutes and its actual social applicability. It also offers a thorough and in-depth comprehension of a specific legal issue.
    - **More Credible:** Unlike doctrinal legal research, this research is more credible as it is based on first-hand information, which is the primary source of data.
    - **Improves and Simplifies Policy Making:** This research shows what laws society requires, where laws are lacking, what laws are needed to be implemented, and what the reactions of individuals are to a particular law. This detailed and in-depth research helps in providing assistance and improving and simplifying policy making.
    - **Always Updated:** This approach to research addresses not only laws that have been passed but also those that must be put into effect in order to ensure the well-being of society. It makes allowances for the social transformations that are occurring in people's daily lives within society. It actually yields a useful outcome that will benefit both legislators and the general public.

– **Becomes Easier to Predict Practical Outcomes:** It is useful for analyzing the real-world effects of laws that are being put into effect. It is based on current laws and their impact on society's members as well as on earlier court rulings and precedents. As a result, forecasting future legal results and offering assistance for future legal decision-making become simpler.

– **Provides Expert Advice:** It provides legislators, judges, and other policymakers with crucial information and professional counsel regarding a range of social issues, enhancing the creation, application, and interpretation of legal regulations.

20. **Demerits of Non-Doctrinal Legal Research:** Some of the disadvantages of non-doctrinal legal research are as follows:

– **Time-Consuming:** It takes longer than doctrinal legal research work because it is field-based research. Since the research is grounded in actual events, the sources are not readily accessible. To gather information, the researchers must travel to various locations. Following data collection, the researcher thoroughly examines the information and draws a firm conclusion. As a result, this research cannot be completed soon.

– **Expensive Method of Research:** This type of research is more costly than doctrinal legal research. This research methodology is not cost-effective because it necessitates fieldwork in addition to relying on readily available data from libraries, legal documents, and internet websites. To travel to various locations and gather primary evidence, the research requires funding. He has numerous difficulties as he conducts this research.

– **Needs Special Training for Doing This Research:** This research project is unable to use the standard research instruments for gathering data. To create and use instruments for gathering data, one requires a specific kind of training. It calls for specialized knowledge, proficiency, effectiveness, and training at every level, from preparation to implementation. More time and effort must be invested in order to get significant results.

– **Needs Strong Background Research:** Before starting a non-doctrinal research work, a strong background research is necessary to get a detailed understanding of a particular matter.

If a researcher is weak in doctrinal legal research, it would be difficult for him to conduct non-doctrinal legal research in a meaningful and proper way.

– **Does Not Provide Instant Results:** This research takes a long time to comprehend a specific problem and its impact on people, identify a solution, and specify the steps that must be taken to address the problem, in contrast to doctrinal research work, which yields results immediately.

– **Needs Financial Support:** This research methodology requires funding. It is challenging for a researcher or a law student from an impoverished background to carry out non-doctrinal legal research. One of the primary flaws in this research is the lack of funding.

– **Not Easily Manageable:** It is not easily manageable, as it is not based on established and authorized sources only. It deals with actual facts, which requires the collection of primary information by visiting different places, classifying them in different categories, and finding an appropriate solution.

– **Difficulty in Collecting First-Hand Information:** Additionally, gathering primary data on some contentious or sensitive topics can be a challenging and dangerous undertaking. People differ in their comprehension of information, and their judgment may contain bias and prejudice to some extent, which can occasionally be confusing to researchers.

21. **Difference between Doctrinal and Non-Doctrinal Legal Research:** There is a close relationship between non-doctrinal legal research and doctrinal legal research. The legal research lies in the middle of these two groups. Legal theories and principles drive the research process in doctrinal legal research, whereas in non-doctrinal legal research, the legal doctrine is only one factor among many. There isn't much of a difference between them. However, there are a few differences between these two categories of legal research.

The difference between doctrinal and non-doctrinal legal research can be understood by reading the points given in Table 4.1.

Table 4.1. *Difference between Doctrinal and Non-Doctrinal Legal Research*

SL. No.	Doctrinal Legal Research	Non-Doctrinal Legal Research
1.	Doctrinal legal research deals with legal doctrines and principles.	Non-doctrinal legal research emphasizes the practical impact of the law on society.
2.	In doctrinal research, the research is mainly dependent on traditional or conventional sources of data.	In non-doctrinal research, the research is not solely dependent on traditional sources but also includes current problems at hand.
3.	Doctrinal legal research is library-based theoretical research.	Non-doctrinal legal research is field-based socio-legal research.
4.	Doctrinal research work is based on secondary sources of data, which include textbooks, legal articles, commentaries, and others.	Non-doctrinal legal research is based on primary sources of data, which include surveys, interviews, and case studies.
5.	The origin of doctrinal legal research came from the analytical or positivist school of thought.	Non-doctrinal research comes from the realist school of thought.
6.	The scope of doctrinal legal research is narrower as compared to non-doctrinal legal research, which deals with law in isolation.	The scope of non-doctrinal legal research is much wider as compared to doctrinal legal research, as it gives a detailed and comprehensive understanding of law.
7.	Doctrinal legal research is used by the advocates for framing legal arguments and policy recommendations.	Non-doctrinal legal research is used by advocates in forming policy decisions for social and legal reforms.
8.	Special training is not required for doing doctrinal research.	Non-doctrinal research needs special training, a conceptual framework, particular skills, and knowledge of other disciplines.
9.	Doctrinal legal research is mainly concerned with legal propositions.	Non-doctrinal legal research is mostly concerned with social values and individuals.

10.	In doctrinal legal research, it is not required to collect first-hand information.	Non-doctrinal legal research requires the collection of first-hand information for case studies.
11.	A researcher doing doctrinal legal research only answers questions about one or two legal propositions.	A researcher doing non-doctrinal legal research answers more questions as it involves large areas of research work.
12.	Doctrinal legal research is less expensive and consumes less time.	Non-doctrinal legal research is a more time-consuming and expensive method.
13.	The basic sources of the doctrinal research are taken from established sources like legal norms and principles.	Non-doctrinal research incorporates interdisciplinary perspectives and empirical data to provide a significant understanding of the law's impact on society.

Source: https://blog.ipleaders.in/all-about-doctrinal-and-non-doctrinal-research/.

4.2. OVERVIEW OF SOCIO-LEGAL RESEARCH

The social sciences provide the theoretical and methodological foundation for socio-legal research. It aims to comprehend law as a social construct. It is easily distinguished from other legal research traditions, like the black letter tradition. Rather than being doctrinal, its methodology is primarily empirical and social-theoretical. Law is more than just a bunch of letters. Instead, it serves as a tool for social control. It comes from and serves a society as well as society at large. Without sociological inquiry, it is impossible to better understand the need for new legislation, the need to amend current legislation, and the challenges associated with putting it into practice. In any social study, law is a crucial variable. If a researcher is not familiar with the fundamentals of law, the legal system, and legal institutions, they cannot conduct any sociological research. In a similar vein, a legal researcher devoid of knowledge regarding the workings of social research methods cannot adequately represent the legal inquiry. Law is acting as a catalyst in a planned society to aid in the process of social transformation. Legal research needs to adopt a multi- or inter-disciplinary approach in today's dynamic society because legal problems are linked to social, political, economic, and psychological problems (Ambekar & Sanjay, 2020).

The socio-legal research is comprised of the following key elements:

- To undertake theoretical and empirical analyzes of the nature of law and its relationship to society and the State in the context of a rapidly changing world;
- Analyze, both historical and contemporary, of the social, economic and political factors leading to the development of the law and legal process;
- An examination of the operation of the law in formal contexts; for example, the courts, or in informal contexts, for example, the law office;
- Analyze of the process of decision-taking by those responsible for the administration of the law; and
- An analysis of the experience of those affected by the process of law.

4.2.1. Utility of Socio-Legal Research

The socio-legal research has following utility:

- Socio-legal research can be useful in formulating new theories;
- Socio-legal research gives clue to the decision-making;
- Socio-legal research gives a lead and molds public opinion;
- Socio-legal research is useful in framing new laws;
- Socio-legal research is useful in finding root causes of crimes and differential behavior among different tribes and races;
- Socio-legal research provides the knowledge which widens the outlook of legislators, executives and judiciary;
- Socio-legal research paves the way for broad based social reforms.

4.2.2. Areas of Socio Legal Research

Society and the law cannot be divided into airtight compartments. They are connected to one another. Since socio-legal research takes an interdisciplinary approach that crosses into the social science domains, cooperative interdisciplinary research is necessary to address social-legal issues. According to Upendra Baxi, both sociologists and lawyers need to have a solid understanding of law and sociology. Prof. Baxi proposed the socio-legal research in the following vital areas:

1. Mapping of Indian legal system and formal and informal legal systems;
2. Studies on the beneficiaries and victims of administration of justice;

3. Law and poverty;
4. Compensatory, discrimination of a second of people such as Scheduled Castes and Schedule Tribes;
5. Study of legal system in connection with cultural, social and national legal systems.

We can include a few more specific areas of socio-legal research, such as the following: the Indian Constitution's guiding principles and the impact of their implementation; criminal tendency in some Indian tribes and sections; tax imposition and social change; international economic law and the growth of international trade; white-collar crimes and their impact on society; labor laws and the welfare of the working classes; Land Reform Acts and the social and economic change; the provision of contributions to political parties in Company Law and its implications; sexual offenses and their impact on society; the relationship between physical abnormalities and criminality; the influence of social customs on crime rate; alcoholism and crime rate; and the rise in crime rate in urban areas. Programs to reduce crime and delinquency; the impact of bribery on administrative effectiveness; public opinion and preventive detention; the effectiveness of the police department and the rate of crime; the state of criminals awaiting trial and the need for reforms; the consequences of punishment and the necessity for reforms; the delay in trials and its effect on judicial administration; the desirability of abolishing the death penalty; prison reforms for the treatment of inmates; and protection for tenants under the Rent Control Law.

4.2.3. Different Approaches to Socio-Legal Research

It is possible to think of the socio-legal approach as existing in the middle of a methodological spectrum. A rigorous doctrinal approach, on the other hand, is primarily based on an informed examination of laws and rulings from higher courts. On the other extreme are methods that are focused on the issues, theories, and sources of information from outside viewpoints, such as critical legal studies and economic analysis of law. A socio-legal approach requires external informants even though contextual analysis is becoming more common in legal scholarship. As operational and everyday legal situations are observed through the socio-legal lens, a variety of textual sources, disciplinary viewpoints, and cultural considerations are taken into account.

4.2.3.1. Socio-Legal Field

H. L. A. Hart's Concept of Law, offers an accessible analysis of a mature legal order which is attuned to law's social character and its role in ordering a society.

The two main ideas in Hart's explanation of law are official acceptance of the law and social rules, of which legal rules are one type. It looks at the idea of a social rule, what it means to follow the rules, the rule of recognition as the supreme law, the function of officials in the legal system, and Hart's distinction between citizens and officials. At this point, the question of whether there exist other legal systems outside state law and, if so, why state law is given priority comes up. This raises concerns regarding legal pluralism, which is the existence of multiple legal orders coexisting, overlapping, or one superseding the other. A law and society approach begins with an understanding of the legal system and law as a social formation. The second component is the interaction of the legal system with other facets of society. One concern is the relationship between the legal system and other social rule systems, including those of private institutions, civil associations, religious organizations, family networks, and so forth. The idea of social spheres is developed and applied here to explain the inter-relationships between legal rules and other networks of rules, and what happens when legal rules try to modify or conflict with those networks?

The question of why we even need laws is another. One way to answer the question of what additional value law adds to society when society is made up of sets of social rules that all work together to uphold social order, achieve social goods, and advance social values is to say that law serves specific social functions that other rule-based systems are unable to carry out. Another response, which is skeptical of functional approaches, asserts that law—that is, state law—can help achieve social goods because it is supported by state institutions and organizations. Law must be divided into several categories in order to develop this analysis, including criminal, civil, constitutional, and regulatory laws. The final concern is the efficacy of the law. It is assumed that law is effective in influencing behavior if state law is justified and explained on the grounds that it has certain social advantages over social rule systems.

4.2.3.2. Political Science Approaches to Socio-Legal Research

1. **Legal Mobilization:** The interaction between social movements and the law is nuanced. A wide range of legal strategies, such as litigation, administrative advocacy, and lobbying, are employed by social movement actors in their pursuit of social, political, and economic change. Movements rely on rights, on the one hand, to articulate their complaints, to establish and strengthen their collective identity, and to inspire activists. Social reform movements may find it possible to influence laws, regulations, and enforcement procedures by working within the legal system. Conversely, the employment of legal tactics and dependence on attorneys may place

social movements under conservative pressure by directing protest and other radical actions through established political and legal channels. The inherent tensions in legal mobilization activity have given rise to a number of theoretical and empirical questions: What are the circumstances in which individual and collective actors will use the legal system to pursue political or social goals? How can social movement researchers best assess social movement success in the legal system, policy domain, and beyond? How does legal mobilization affect a social movement's collective identity? The literature on social movements' use of the law to mobilize draws from, complements, and differs from court-centric studies of social reform by offering a "bottom-up" viewpoint.

2. **Judicial Review and Human Rights:** An essential component of safeguarding and upholding human rights is judicial review. Judicial review serves as a check on governmental power by enabling courts to judge whether actions taken by public authorities are lawful, preventing the arbitrary or unjustified violation of an individual's rights. Through this procedure, people can legally seek accountability and redress for decisions that infringe upon their fundamental rights. Courts interpret and apply human rights provisions found in legislation and the constitution through judicial review, influencing future case law and the evolution of human rights law. This dynamic process serves to safeguard individual rights while also encouraging public institutions to uphold a human rights culture. Judicial review also plays a vital role in strengthening the human rights framework by ensuring that national laws are consistent with international human rights norms. By keeping national laws in line with international human rights standards, this alignment improves the defense of individual rights. Because courts are able to address issues of discrimination, inequality, and unfair treatment, judicial review also provides a means for vulnerable and marginalized groups to pursue justice. Judicial review upholds the rule of law, encourages openness, and fosters good governance by holding authorities responsible.

   However, the independence and impartiality of the judiciary are necessary for judicial review to effectively protect human rights. To guarantee impartial and equitable decision-making on human rights matters, a judiciary free from political influence is necessary. Equal access to judicial review is also necessary, as is the availability of the resources and information needed for people to use the legal system to defend their rights. To sum up, judicial review is an essential part of protecting human rights because it creates a legal framework in which everyone can access justice, governmental actions are closely examined, and individual rights are respected.

4.2.3.3. The Role of Courts in a Democracy

The court system has a significant influence. When it works well, it has a significant impact on social cohesion, promotes economic growth, and protects the person from arbitrary state power. A judiciary with the authority to uphold the constitution is universally recognized as crucial to the consolidation of democracy in nations making the shift from authoritarian to democratic governance. It is not surprising that sociologists and political scientists have become more and more interested in judicial affairs in recent decades given the significant role that courts are thought to play. A diverse subset of these investigators has identified, documented, and analyzed a post-World War II trend that is particularly prevalent due to its global expansion of domestic and supranational judicial power. Many people now perceive the judiciary as a check on the purported evils of unbridled democracy, thanks to a paradigm that attributes the horrors of World War II to the weaknesses of parliamentary democracy. Courts have been able to "strike down" with finality statutes of Parliament and even plebiscites that they interpret to be unconstitutional in a number of jurisdictions, even the most conservative and authoritarian civil law traditions. Judges are no longer limited to their traditional role of reviewing cases where people's rights are in jeopardy because of the judicial assumption of power to legislate new general norms in all spheres of life in addition to nullifying legislation that has been democratically enacted.

A range of theoretical questions and long-standing controversies can be seen in this, like:

- What ought to be the role of courts in a democratic society?
- Ought judges to intervene in policy processes or should they confine themselves to deciding the guilt or innocence of individual persons?
- Is judicial supremacy incompatible with the democratic ideal of popular sovereignty?
- If activism becomes excessive, how and by whom ought it to be curtailed?
- Do any alternatives to the judicialization of politics exist that are more compatible with democracy yet do not compromise the rule of law?

4.2.3.4. Sociological Approaches to Socio-Legal Research

1. **Placing Law in a Socio-Cultural Context:** Understanding how legal systems, norms, and practices interact with and are influenced by the larger social and cultural environment is essential to placing law in a socio-cultural context. Law is not an isolated system; it both influences and is influenced by the society in which it is practiced. Lawmaking, legal interpretation, and legal enforcement are greatly influenced by cultural values, customs, beliefs, and social norms. For example, cultural attitudes toward justice, morality, authority, and individual rights are reflected in the legal practices and principles of various societies. A complex legal environment is produced in many societies where formal legal systems coexist with customary laws and traditional practices. These customary laws address topics like marriage, inheritance, and conflict resolution in ways that are consistent with regional values and customs, frequently reflecting the social and cultural norms of the community. Comprehending the interplay between socio-cultural contexts and legal reform is imperative, since neglecting them can result in laws that are not aligned with the intended beneficiaries, leading to opposition or non-adherence.

   Law enforcement officers, judges, and attorneys all interpret and apply the law differently depending on the sociocultural context. Their decisions can result in different interpretations of the same legal principles because of the influence of their own cultural backgrounds and societal norms. This emphasizes how crucial it is to have a culturally sensitive judiciary that can handle these nuances and apply the law in a way that honors and represents the diversity of the community. Furthermore, sociocultural elements affect how the general public views and accepts the law. Laws that are consistent with public values and norms have a higher chance of being embraced and obeyed. On the other hand, laws that go against strongly held cultural beliefs may encounter resistance and prove challenging to implement. Setting the law in a sociocultural framework emphasizes how crucial it is for legal procedures to take social and cultural factors into account. It emphasizes that laws must be in line with the social and cultural realities of the communities they govern in order to be just and effective. This strategy promotes a more comprehensive and inclusive legal system that honors and incorporates society's varied cultural heritage.

2. **Can Law Control?:** The law serves as a potential tool of control by

outlining the legal and social contexts that affect its application and enforcement and by tackling the contentious concept of compliance in the context of business regulation. First, laws regulate conduct by establishing expectations for individuals and organizations to abide by certain standards and norms. These norms establish a framework for society's operations and are frequently codified in laws, rules, and court decisions. Laws prohibiting theft or violence, for example, set limits on appropriate behavior and safeguard people's rights and property. The desire to stay out of legal hot water and avoid fines, jail time, or other penalties is usually what drives people to abide by these laws. Second, the mechanisms of enforcement are how law establishes control. Enforcing the application of the law is a critical function of courts, law enforcement organizations, and other legal institutions. Illegal behavior is discouraged when there is a possibility of legal repercussions. For instance, police patrols, fines, and license plate points are used to enforce traffic laws, which promote observance of speed limits and safe driving techniques. Law's ability to control behavior, however, is not absolute and is dependent on a number of factors. Laws can be interpreted and obeyed differently depending on social conventions, cultural values, and economic circumstances. Laws that are perceived as unfair or inconsistent with society values may occasionally be disregarded or actively opposed. This emphasizes how crucial social acceptance and legitimacy are to the efficiency of legal control. Furthermore, the scope of what the law can regulate is limited. Although the law can control outward behavior, it has less power to affect people's inner attitudes and beliefs. Beyond the legal system, social control is embodied in the family, the school system, religion, and other institutions of society that mold values and conduct. For example, although anti-discrimination laws may forbid specific forms of discrimination, a more comprehensive social and cultural shift is necessary to eradicate ingrained prejudices.

4.2.3.5. Anthropological Approaches: Law beyond Government

Anthropological perspectives on law highlight the diversity and complexity of law in various cultural contexts by examining the ways in which legal systems and practices transcend formal government structures. This viewpoint highlights the fact that laws originate from social practices, customs, and local traditions in addition to state institutions. Anthropologists investigate how different groups establish, interpret, and uphold their own laws and procedures for resolving conflicts, frequently independently of or in conjunction with established legal frameworks. Legal pluralism, which acknowledges the coexistence of multiple legal systems within a single society, is a fundamental idea in anthropological approaches. For instance, customary laws pertaining to marriage, property rights, and resolving conflicts may be observed by indigenous communities. These customary laws, which represent the group's values and customs, are frequently ingrained in the community's social and cultural fabric. Legal pluralism recognizes that, in their particular contexts, these non-state legal systems may have the same authority and legal force as state law. Anthropologists also look at how informal customs and social norms contribute to upholding law and order and settling conflicts. Social structures like community councils, kinship networks, and religious organizations are essential for controlling behavior and resolving disputes in many societies. The principles of restorative justice, reciprocity, and consensus-building are frequently the foundations of these mechanisms, which function in contrast to formal legal systems that are more punitive and adversarial. In certain African societies, for example, customary courts or elders' councils settle disputes and uphold rulings based on customary law, giving precedence to communal peace and harmony over punitive measures. Anthropological research also demonstrates how marginalized and disenfranchised groups can establish substitute legal spaces to meet their unique needs and difficulties. To handle matters such as land tenure, resource distribution, and social behavior, for instance, urban informal settlements frequently create their own regulations and systems of enforcement. For community members, these informal legal systems can offer justice that is more accessible and culturally appropriate than formal state institutions, which can be far away, costly, or seen as corrupt. The relationships between state law and other types of regulation are also examined through anthropological perspectives. Customary practices and state law may coexist or be incorporated in various situations where there is a dynamic interaction between formal and informal legal systems. The result of this interaction may be hybrid legal structures that combine local customs and state authority. Certain nations, for example, have recognized traditional leaders and courts as official components of the legal system and have formalized customary laws within their legal frameworks.

4.2.3.6. Economic Approach to Socio-Legal Research

The application of economic theories and methodologies to the study of law and legal institutions, along with an examination of how economic principles can guide legal decision-making, is known as the economic approach to socio-legal research. This method, which is related to the study of law and economics, places emphasis on the relationship that exists between the three: law, economic efficiency, and societal well-being. This method relies heavily on the notion of efficiency, specifically Pareto and Kaldor-Hicks efficiency. When resources are distributed such that improving the lot of one person does not improve the lot of another, this is known as Pareto efficiency. The opposite of this is known as Kaldor-Hicks efficiency, which views a situation as efficient if those who gain from a change could theoretically compensate those who lose out, leading to a net gain for society. The capacity of legislative regulations and policies to produce these kinds of efficiencies is evaluated. For instance, property laws that specify ownership rights precisely can lessen disputes and transaction costs, which promotes more effective use of available resources. The analysis of incentives is another crucial component. In socio-legal research, economic approaches look at how laws encourage or discourage particular behaviors. Tort law, for example, is researched because it encourages people and businesses to adopt safer practices in order to avoid liability. Tort law deals with compensation for harm or injury. Comparably, criminal law is evaluated for its ability to deter illicit activity; the possibility and severity of punishment have an impact on potential offenders' cost-benefit calculations. A crucial instrument in this strategy is cost-benefit analysis. In order to ascertain the overall influence of laws and policies on the welfare of society, it is necessary to weigh their advantages and disadvantages. Regulations, court rulings, and legal processes can all be assessed using this methodology. For instance, the economic costs of business compliance with environmental regulations could be compared to the advantages of environmental preservation and public health. The analysis of legal structures and their effects on economic growth is also covered by the economic approach. Establishing a stable environment for economic activities is largely dependent on institutions like courts, regulatory agencies, and law enforcement units. For example, by upholding property rights, enforcing contracts, and lowering the risks involved in business transactions, fair and efficient legal systems can promote economic growth. On the other hand, by raising transaction costs and fostering uncertainty, ineffective or dishonest legal systems can impede economic growth. Additionally, the economic approach to socio-legal research frequently employs empirical analysis, analyzing the effects of institutions and legal rules on economic outcomes through statistical methods. This empirical research can demonstrate the impact of legal changes.

4.3. PERSPECTIVES OF SOCIO LEGAL RESEARCH

The Indian Constitutions revised by Parliament and construed by theirour Supreme Court, has a long history of legal and political legitimacy. It is imperative to consider sociological theories pertaining to "anomic" alienation, legitimacy, violence, and the normlessness of criminal justice. In the Indian literature on social deviance, there is little to no attempt made in the research to integrate theoretical perspectives and "anomic." Whether we define anomic as "overweening ambition" and the collapse of regulatory norms according to Durkheim, or as the disjunction between "cultural goals" and "socially structured" opportunity or mercy in terms of "differences in the availability of illegitimate means" according to Mertonian theory, a wide range of Indian criminology materials require theoretical perspectives produced by "anomic" theorizing. In connection with this. Is the issue of violence related to the rule of law and politics? It is necessary to consider how the boundaries between acceptable and prohibited violence are changing in Indian society, as well as how legal political orders can respond to both intragroup and intergroup violence. Additionally, we must consider the viability of legal political ideological controls over the use of acceptable violence by law enforcement officials. Throughout his lifelong commitment to sociological jurisprudence, Roscoe Pound consistently articulated and reaffirmed his belief that the law should be used as a tool to maximize de-facto human demands while minimizing friction and waste.

4.3.1. Collection of Data in Socio-Legal Research

The phase of research that is considered most fascinating is data collection. The real thrill of research starts to get to the researcher through the gathering and processing of data. A researcher has two options for gathering data: he can do it himself or he can rely on others to gather data or information that they have on hand. High-quality data are greatly needed in both situations. This calls for a high level of expertise. What is manifest, phonotypical, or observed is called a datum. Similar to other sciences, data in socio-legal studies are derived from our sense-observations. In this context, "observation" refers to any kind of perception that is used to note reactions as they interact with our senses. Reaction, however, is not a datum. A datum is the outcome of the response's recording process, while a response is some sort of manifest action. The respondent (subject) is shown stimuli (questionnaires, examinations, images, or other objects) during the data collection process. It is possible to categorize the stimuli as either unsystematic or systematic. When we refer to systematic stimuli, we mean those that remain unchanged when objects undergo changes. The stimuli that lack standardization, for example, are considered unsystematic queries posed during casual interviews. It is also possible to categorize the responses of the subjects, or respondents, to the stimuli into two groups: systematic and unsystematic. Response categories that are constant (definite and standardized) are referenced in systematic responses. As a result, the subject's reactions to a stimulus are noted. The subject's erratic reactions to a stimulus are noted. There is a reference to constant (definite, standardized) response categories in the unsystematic responses. The responses that are verbatim recorded while taking into account all potential individual variances and character logical nuances are considered unsystematic. Bringing these categories of stimuli and responses, we can decide the settings for the collection of data as:

- Informal;
- Formal unstructured; and
- Formal structured.

The subjects' answers could be referred to as "acts." Verbal and non-verbal acts can be distinguished. One can further categorize the verbal acts into written and oral forms. Acts that use spoken symbols for communication are referred to as verbal acts. Signals such as bowing, clapping, etc., are examples of non-verbal acts. The oral-verbal acts comprise the subject's verbal response to a stimulus. The other type of verbal acts consists of recording the stimulus responses in writing.

The main forms of data collection responses can be presented in break-down Table 4.2.

Table 4.2. *Collection of Data in Socio-Legal Research*

Settings	Responses		
	Non- verbal	Oral-verbal	Written-verbal
Formal	Participant observation	Conversations	Letters, articles, biographies
Formal unstructured	Systematic Observation	Unstructured Interviews	Open–ended Questionnaires
Formal structured	Experiments	Structured interviews	Structured questionnaires

Source: https://egyankosh.ac.in/bitstream/123456789/39096/1/Unit-4.pdf.

4.3.2. Primary and Secondary Sources of Data

Data collection is related to:

- Primary and secondary sources data;
- Census and sampling techniques; and
- Methods of data collection.

Legal data sources can be categorized according to a number of factors, including availability, dependability, and individual efforts. They can be roughly categorized into two groups based on reliability: primary data and secondary data. Some separated the data sources into field sources and documentary sources. They were categorized by Lundberg as field and historical sources.

1. **Primary or Field Source or Internal Source of Data:** It is first-hand, original data that has been gathered. Because the data is obtained directly from the subjects, it is also referred to as an internal source of data. They are gathered through observation or from live individuals who are directly involved in the issue. Once more, there are two categories for these primary sources: (a) Direct Primary and (b) Indirect Primary.

   – **Direct Primary Sources:** The researcher goes and watches things, activities, behavior, events, and so forth. He needs to demonstrate extreme objectivity and skill. Observation can be of three sub-types:

     i. participant observation;

     ii. non-participant observation; and

     iii. quasi – participant observation.

   Direct observation is the best, but difficult. In some cases it may be either legally inadmissible or physically impossible.

   – **Indirect Primary Sources:** The researcher must get in touch with those who have made observations that are pertinent to his work because he is unable to observe events that happened in the past. Schedules, questionnaires, and interviews can be used for this.

2. **Secondary or External Source of Data**: This data comes from sources other than published works or other people who have done prior research on the topic. They spare a researcher from having to laboriously gather data again and avoid needless expenses. They fall into two main categories: published documents (b) and personal documents (a). Memories, letters, diaries, and life histories are examples of personal documents. Getting hold of them or using them properly is extremely challenging. Public documents come from public bodies, Government and private organizations. Apart from books, available in libraries, this category includes records, published statistics, reports of newspapers and journals and special reports, film or T.V. programs, tapes and so on. Unpublished documents are not easily available. Documentary sources are very important because past events can be known only thorough them. They may reveal certain secrets. They can help to save time, money

and energy. But a researcher should verify the contents with the help of other sources. The secondary materials of low possess only on persuasive value but not authoritative value.

3. **Relationship Between Primary and Secondary Sources:** When primary data is gathered, it becomes secondary data for other users. The researcher who is gathering primary data is aware of the constraints and realities of the issue. Theories about the issue are supplied by second-hand data. On the basis of first-hand information, these theories can be investigated or confirmed. If secondary sources are cited as the most trustworthy, they become third-hand sources of information. There is a small library with the secondary sources.

4.4. ORIGINAL MATERIAL SOURCES OF LAW

The source from which law derives its substance rather than its validity is known as the material source of law. The two categories of material sources are legal and historical. The authoritative sources are the legal sources of law. The law itself acknowledges them as such. These are the low's immediate causes. The law which comes through the legal source may be divided into the following classes:

1. **Enacted Law, Having Its Source in Legislation:** The nation's sovereign power makes the ultimate legislation. Parliament in democracies. Is the one in charge. It is regarded as both legally omnipotent and supreme. However, its authority might be limited by certain provisions of the constitution. Any authority other than the nation's highest authority can enact subordinate legislation. It is made using the authority that the highest authority has granted. Such laws are regarded as legal as well. Local laws passed by local bodies and executive orders are examples of subordinate laws.
2. **Case Law, Having Its Source in Precedent:** Precedent refers to a prior instance or case that serves as a model or precedent for future cases, or that provides support or justification for a comparable act or set of circumstances. Within the legal sphere, it refers to the precedent or power of earlier rulings on cases to come. Judicial precedents are only those rulings that establish new guidelines or precepts. Every court is bound completely by the rulings of the courts above it, according to the first general rule of doctrine precedent. The second rule states that higher courts are somewhat constrained by the rulings of other courts.
3. **Customary Law, Having Its Source in Custom:** The most

significant source of law is customs. However, as society develops, they progressively disappear and are replaced by laws and court rulings. Certain socially accepted customs exist in every legal system and at every stage of legal development. The customs that are sanctioned are those that the state upholds. Legal customs function based on the immutable rule of law. They are now a part of the national law after being acknowledged by the courts. They are incorporated into national law and are upheld by the courts. They are upheld by the legal system.

4. **Conventional Law, Having Its Source in Agreement:** The customs that control the parties to an agreement are known as conventional law. The parties accept them. These customs are enforceable because they are the result of an agreement between the parties involved, not because they are supported by any independent legal authority. Every nation has a large body of conventional law.
5. **Statutory Interpretation**: Actuarial law, also known as statute law, is the body of law created by legislation. It is up to the courts to apply these formulas to particular situations. For the purpose of applying the enactment, the court must determine the meaning of its letters and expressions. The process by which the court determines the meaning of the letters and expressions is known as interpretation. The judge has a significant impact on the statute law during this process. Literal and liberal interpretations make up the two main categories of interpretation. The literal interpretation principle states that a judge cannot determine the true intention of a statute by interpreting its words.
6. **Codification**: It is the process by which a State's authorized authority promulgates, compiles, collects, and organizes the body of law into a logical structure. The codes of Manu, Yajnavalkya, Brihaspathi, Narada, Parashara, and others are found in India. Different regions of the nation used different codes. The Indian Law Commission created several codes in the modern era, including the Civil Procedure Code and the Indian Penal Code. Numerous of the Law Commission's extensive and detailed recommendations have been put into practice.

There are other sources of law like: (1) morals and equity and (2) opinions of experts. All these sources are available in documentary form in general and legal libraries.

4.4.1. Case Law as a Source of Law

Since "neither a judge nor a lawyer knows more than a relatively tiny part of the law," the legal professional, judge, and researcher all search for the law to be applied to a particular case. However, they must be aware of where and how to locate the law. Attorneys obtain pertinent legal propositions to be utilized in a given case from two primary sources: rulings rendered by superior courts, etc., the laws, and the precedents. A fact situation covered by one source of law does not always correspond to a single law. Frequently, one cannot infer the legal conclusion to be applied in a given factual scenario from a specific body of law. A lawyer who is well-versed in both substantive and procedural laws can sift through a client's mountain of information to find the pertinent facts for a case. A lawyer employs reasoning to establish a correlation between pertinent facts and the law that must be applied to them.

A precedent is essentially a body of case law that directs the resolution of a case that is similar to it. Case laws have frequently been crucial in determining how to interpret statutes. Case law is the set of guidelines and precepts that judges articulate and apply when rendering judgments. In a case-law-based system, a judge must render a decision in a subsequent case in the same manner as the previous case, unless there is a valid reason why they cannot. This implies that when cases have identical material facts, they must be decided in the same manner. Naturally, this does not mean that every fact must be the same.

Case law is the set of guidelines and precepts that judges have articulated and applied when rendering judgments. The case laws are an essential component of any doctrinal investigation since the decisions made by the High Court and Supreme Court bind the lower courts. A system of case law makes up the majority of Indian law. In other words, the ruling in a specific case sets "precedent." The precedent doctrine states that a judge's decision when rendering a judgment does not necessarily set a precedent. However, the judgment's justification for the ruling is the only thing that makes it precedent. Thus, the rationale given in the decision of an appeal becomes an essential topic for a lawyer to research and consider.

The researchers' secondary source of data is case laws. A legal issue may arise while the researcher is reading case laws. In this situation, he can formulate a hypothesis, carry out an empirical investigation, and conduct research. The arguments in deductive analysis are supported by case laws as the evidentiary source. Case laws are used by judges, attorneys, and researchers to support their logical arguments. As a result, case laws serve as legal studies' official source of data.

4.4.1.1. Documentary Source of Data for Socio-Legal Studies

Data can be made available from different sources. P.V. Young (year) has classified the data into two groups:

- Documentary; and
- Field sources.

Published or unpublished material that has already been gathered is included in documentary sources. Public documents, libraries, and individuals can provide such information. Anything that includes information of socio-legal significance is considered a legal document. The majority of the documents are not specifically designed for the analysis of the current issue. Documents can be divided into two categories:

- Primary; and
- Secondary.

The same body that created the primary documents also collected the primary data for those documents. Secondary documents offer information that has been assembled or transcribed from primary sources.

Ø **Personal Documents (Direct Source):** Personal documents include all such written material as is written by an individual to narrate his views upon personal relationship or social phenomena. Most of these documents are written from personal point of view. There are many kinds of personal documents such as:

- Life histories;
- Diaries;
- Letters; and
- Memories.

All biographical materials, including autobiographies, are included in life histories. All biographical writing, including autobiographies, is attributed to the author of a life history. A life history writer expresses his personal opinions about current events. These publications serve as a valuable resource for scholars. Diaries are yet another valuable information resource. Events are routinely documented in a diary. An author's diary contains reflections of their own experiences. Another useful tool for socio-legal researchers is the letter. They include the phenomena's facts. However, letters have their own constraints. Some people jot down their recollections, listing some of the most significant moments from their social lives.

4.4.1.2. Importance of Personal Documents

The writer's innermost thoughts are conveyed in these personal writings, which occasionally shed light on facets of life that would have been challenging to learn through observation or interview. In general, they are more trustworthy in terms of the subject's description and the writer's emotions. They include just the right kind of socio-legal information required to describe a social group's way of life.

4.4.1.3. Limitations of Personal Documents

- The availability of personal documents may be difficult if they contain some confessions which are likely to damage his reputation.
- Unreliability of the data may be there due to personal bias of the writer.
- Personal documents do not provide a representative sample and the document may not be considered as a valid one.

4.4.2. Public Documents or Official Documents

Official documents, sometimes referred to as public documents, are records kept and produced by governmental bodies that offer a formal account of decisions, actions, and procedures in the public sector. These records are a trustworthy source of information for citizens, scholars, and decision-makers, and they are crucial for accountability, transparency, and governance. Legislative acts, court rulings, administrative regulations, and executive orders are a few examples of public documents that describe a nation's legal and regulatory framework. Public documents also include official statistics, white papers, and government reports that provide information on a range of socioeconomic issues and the effects of policy. This category also includes records of public meetings, proceedings, and official correspondence, guaranteeing that public participation and scrutiny are allowed in government operations. Public documents are essential for maintaining the rule of law, promoting informed public discourse, and building public institution trust because they offer a record of government actions.

4.4.2.1. Documentary Sources of Legal Material

The different kinds of records and documents that serve as the cornerstone of legal systems and the practice of law are referred to as documentary sources of legal material. The text of laws, rules, court rulings, and other legal documents that control society can be found in these sources. Comprehending these sources is essential for legal practice, research, and teaching. Here are the primary documentary sources of legal material:

- **Constitutions:** These are the supreme law of a country, establishing the framework for government and delineating the fundamental rights and responsibilities of citizens. They outline the structure of government, the separation of powers, and the relationship between different branches of government. Examples include the U.S. Constitution and the Constitution of India.
- **Legislation:** The laws passed by legislative bodies like parliaments, congresses, and assemblies are known as legislation, or statutory law. These laws address many different topics, ranging from environmental regulation to criminal law. Acts, statutes, and ordinances are a few examples.
- **Regulations:** Governmental organizations issue regulations in accordance with the authority that they have been given by law. They offer comprehensive instructions for putting laws into effect and upholding them. Executive orders and administrative regulations are two examples.
- **Judicial Decisions:** Court rulings are known as case law or judicial decisions. These rulings establish precedents that direct subsequent cases by interpreting and applying the law to particular situations. Opinions, decisions, and decrees from supreme courts, appellate courts, and other judicial bodies are a few examples.
- **International Treaties and Agreements:** Treaties and international agreements are binding agreements between countries. They cover various areas such as trade, human rights, and environmental protection. Examples include the United Nations Charter and the Paris Agreement on climate change.
- **Legal Commentaries and Treatises:** Commentaries and treatises are scholarly writings that provide analysis and interpretation of laws and legal principles. These documents help lawyers, judges, and scholars understand and apply the law. Examples include legal textbooks, annotations, and law review articles.
- **Legal Codes:** These are methodical sets of rules and laws arranged according to topic. Commercial, criminal, and civil codes are a few examples. They offer a thorough and well-organized explanation of the law in a specific field.
- **Government Publications:** These include official documents issued by government bodies, such as legislative debates, committee reports, and white papers. These documents provide insights into the legislative process and the intent behind laws.

- **Legal Encyclopedias:** These provide a comprehensive summary of legal topics, offering an overview of the law and references to primary and secondary sources. Examples include American Jurisprudence (AmJur) and Corpus Juris Secundum (CJS).
- **Case Reporters:** Publications known as "case reporters" gather court rulings from multiple courts. The complete text of court opinions is accessible through their chronological and jurisdictional organization. The Supreme Court Reporter and the Federal Reporter are two instances.
- **Law Journals and Reviews:** Legal scholars, practitioners, and students write articles, essays, and notes that are published in law journals and reviews. Recent court decisions, legal developments, and current legal issues are frequently covered in these publications.
- **Statutory Instruments:** Legislation created by an individual or organization using authority granted to them by a parliamentary act is known as a statutory instrument. They are employed to draft specific rules and guidelines that fall under the purview of the enabling statute.

Legal knowledge and practice are derived from a vast array of documents found in documentary sources of legal material. These resources are necessary for comprehending, interpreting, and using the law in different situations. To effectively represent their clients, maintain compliance, and negotiate the complexities of the legal system, legal professionals rely on these documents.

4.4.3. Method of Using Libraries and the Use of Computer

4.4.3.1. Use of Libraries

Using library books, pamphlets, periodicals, and documentary materials is a necessary part of conducting legal research. In order to obtain the background information required for the problem under investigation, general source materials must be reviewed. Legal researchers must also be aware of prior findings in cases that are comparable to their own. A library has a wealth of these source materials on hand. Every researcher needs to use the library. Therefore, a researcher ght to be familiar with using library resources. The researcher He should be familiar with the fundamentals of bibliographic and reference materials as well as how libraries arrange their collections. Because all libraries provide similar resources for users and arrange their collections according to general principles, the general procedure for maintaining libraries is the same in all libraries. Every library has a card catalogue, a subject classification system, and specific reference and bibliographic materials.

4.4.3.2. Library Card Catalogue

Researchers have to head straight to the card catalogue as soon as they walk into a library. The card catalogue is arranged alphabetically by the first word on each card on a shelf at the library's entrance. All of the publications in the library collection are listed in the card catalogue, which is an index that frequently includes author, subject, and title lists. It is essential to search under the heading that most closely describes the subject when looking up information by subject. It is helpful to know the author's given name and last name in order to locate their publication in the card catalogue. There might be multiple authors with the same name or one that sounds similar, and occasionally some of the authors write books about the same topic. The call number is the information that appears on the cards' front.

4.5. SOCIOMETRY IN SOCIO-LEGAL RESEARCH

The researcher in socio-legal studies must quantify data that is qualitative in nature otherwise. The development of scientific laws of scaling technique was made easier by the quantification of the data. A scale is a tool used for measurement. The process of measuring involves numbering objects to indicate the relative amounts of a property that each object possesses. In socio-legal research, there are two kinds of scales: (1) personality and social behavior scales, and (2) scales used to gauge other facets of the social and cultural milieu.

- Ø **Definition of Scale**: If it is possible to derive a quantitative variable from the multivariate frequency distribution of a universe of attributes for a given population of objects, such that each attribute is a straightforward function of the quantitative variable, the distribution will be referred to as a scale. The subjects of an investigation are referred to as the "Population of objects" in this definition. The term "Universe of attributes" describes a set of quantitative characteristics that are defined for research and are connected to these objects. These variables could be qualitatively recorded observations of any kind. The quantitative variable that is derived in this manner is called a "Scale score."
- Ø **Properties of Scale Scores:** The scale scores possess the following properties:
  - – The recorded observations on a large number of variables in the defined universe can be summarizes by a single score

which will reproduce the original records with a specified degree of reproducibility.

– Individuals can be arranged in a rank order on the scale score in a manner that will be consistent with their rank order on any of all of the variables in the defined universe of attributes.

– As in a multiple regression equation with the external criterion as the defendant variable, the scale score can be used to predict any outside variable or criterion with an accuracy as high as can be attained by the direct use of all the variables in the defined universe.

4.5.1. Types of Rating or Intensity Scales

The goal of rating or attitude scales is to place people in positions with varying numerical values so that degree distinctions can be made. The rater positions the person or item being rated at a certain point along the continuum, assigning a numerical value to each point, in one of the following main categories of rating scales.

- **Graphic Rating Scale:** With this scale, the rater just needs to put a check at the right spot on a line that connects the two extremes of the attribute to indicate his rating. The purpose of the scale points, which may be indicated along the line with brief descriptions, is to assist the rater in localizing his rating. By taking certain precautions, such as avoiding the use of extreme end statements and making the descriptive statements as close as possible to the numerical scale, this scale can be used with relative ease.
- **Itemized Rating Scale:** The rater chooses from a restricted set of categories (typically five or seven categories) arranged according to their scale position in this scale. With an equal number of categories on either side, this scale offers a central neutral point. The rater chooses the item on this scale that most accurately describes the act from a list of ones that each describe a different act. When categories are defined correctly, one can obtain trustworthy ratings.
- **Comparative Rating Scale:** In this scale, the rater gives relative rating. The positions on the rating scale are expressly defined in terms of a given population or social group.
- **Rank Order Scale:** In this scale, rank of each one of the individuals in relation to one another on the characteristic is being measured.

4.5.2. Rating Techniques

There are forced choice rating technique and self –rating. Technique in the use of scales.

- **Forced Choice Rating Technique:** Using this method, pairs of items with similar popularity but different discriminating powers are selected. A tetrad is formed by joining two of these pairs. It is necessary for the rater to indicate which tetrad item most closely resembles the individual and which one does not. The main challenge with this method is that there's a chance the four tetrad items aren't comparable.
- **Self-Rating Technique:** When a person rates the attribute being measured, they are using this technique. There are situations when a person is unwilling to disclose the existence of an attribute being measured in themself or may not even be aware that it is being measured. This approach has worked well.

4.5.3. Attitude Scales

With this method, the person indicates whether or not he agrees with a number of statements that are pertinent to the topic rather than explicitly describing his position on the dimension in question. He receives a score, or a numerical value, based on his replies. This method has been widely employed in the assessment of attitudes. The statements that make up the attitude scales are different, or objects pertinent to a problem. To these statements, the individual subjects react differently. Specific scores are allocated to these response modes.

4.5.3.1. Types of Attitude Scales

There are three types of techniques of attitude scales. They are:

1. **Technique of Differential Scales (Judgment Method):** A scale's ability to discriminate between people is dependent upon how it is constructed and how points are assigned. Differential scales are those in which a person's response determines his position. These scales consist of statements or items that form a gradation of such a nature that the individual agrees with only one or two of these and disagrees with the remaining statements on either side of those agreed to L.L. Thurstone employed this kind of measure. This scale is made up of several statements, each of whose place on the scale has been decided by a ranking process carried out by judges. Many techniques have been employed to obtain scales-position judgments,

namely the social distance technique, the equal-appearing interval method, the paired comparison method, etc.

2. **Technique of Summated Rating:** R. Likert Formulated this technique. Rather than indicating his agreement for a small number of items, the respondent on this scale indicates his various degrees of agreement or disagreement with each item that makes up the scale. Based on either a three- or five-point response category, each response is assigned a numerical score that represents how much the respondent agrees or disagrees. The total score, which is calculated by adding the individual response scores to each of the individual items, represents the respondent's position on the scale of favorable to unfavorable attitudes toward the object.

3. **Technique of Cumulative Scales (Scaloram Method):** When using a cumulative scale, the times are correlated so that, in theory, a person who answers favorably to item two also answers favorably to item one, and a person who answers favorably to item three also answers favorably to items one and two. The items on the scale are sometimes arranged randomly, and other times they are arranged in the order of favorableness. Usually, there is no attempt to check if the distances between items are equal. Therefore, cumulative scales are ordinal scales in actuality. L. Guttman employed this method. The scalogram method is the name for it. Scalogram analysis is the general process used to ascertain whether or not subjects' responses to items from the scale. Its foundation is an examination of the subjects' response patterns to a series of items, where a response pattern represents the collection of answers to questions provided by a subject. In actuality, scalogram analysis is best defined as a process for assessing sets of statements or pre-existing scales to see if they satisfy the specifications of a specific type of scale.

   Every method has its own benefits, including procedural refinement, analytical nature, scoring, and nature. Each of them has drawbacks of its own, including length of time required, suitability of specific measurements, and complexity brought on by laborious scaling procedures. The type of data and the nature of the research determine which technique is used.

4.5.3.2. Problems in Preparing Scales

1. **Definition of Continuum:** This phenomenon ought to be scalable. A phenomenon's capacity to scale depends on its continuum. Instead of using isolated, conclusive facts, the numerous variables to be

measured should be logically related to one another and should be measured continuously. Only those elements that are distinct, unambiguous, and crucial points on the scale may be chosen as determinant factors.

2. **Reliability:** When two scales are given the same measurement in comparable circumstances, the scale is considered reliable. The split half method, multiple form method, and retest method are used to assess the scale's reliability.

3. **Validity:** When a scale accurately measures what is intended to be measured, it is considered valid. Validity and Scale reliability are two different things. While validity depends on accurate measurement, reliability is attained when there is uniformity in the measurements. A scale would be dependable but unquestionably invalid if it consistently made the same error. A scale is considered reliable when its measurements are consistent and accurate; it is not valid otherwise.

   Goode and Hatt have given the following criteria for validity of a scale:

   - It should stand to our commonsense reason.
   - It should stand on the judgment of a number of persons.
   - It should tally the experience of persons who are known to hold a particular opinion with the known. Fact.
   - All or most of the tests should show the same result.

4. **Problem of Weights:** If all the attributes involved are not of equal importance, they must be provided with proper weights. On the basis of the commonsense test and the validity test, the weights have to be decided.

5. **Difficulties in Scaling:** The following difficulties are experienced in preparing scale:

   - The socio –legal phenomena are very complex and cannot easily be quantitatively defined.
   - There is no universally accepted measure of values.
   - Human behavior is constantly changing.
   - Human beings are most heterogeneous in nature.
   - Most of the social phenomena are intangible in nature.
     - § Socio-legal phenomena cannot be put to laboratory type test. In terms of statistical methodology, scales of

all kinds can be subsumed under the following headings:

- § Arbitrary scales
- § Scales in which the item's scale values and other characteristics are determined by a panel of judges.
- § Scales based on item analysis.
- § Scales constructed in accordance with the "Scale analysis" technique devised by Liuis Guttman.

4.5.3.3. Disadvantages of Rating Scales

There are the following disadvantages in the use of rating scales:

- There is room for systematic error in one's rating through the influence of personal bias of the rater or raters which is commonly referred to as Hole effect.'
- Another type of constant error is the 'generosity error' where the rater develops a tendency to over –estimate the desirable qualities of the rater whom he likes.
- There is another type of error known as 'contrast error' where there is a tendency on the part of the rater to see others as opposite to himself on a trait.

4.5.4. Sociometric Technique

In socio – legal research, the researcher has, often, to study group behavior. The socio-metric technique has been developed by J.L. Moreno to study the closed community. Sociometry is the measurement of what draws and repels members of a particular group. Typically, it entails each group member individually designating a range of other group members with whom he would like to participate in a specific activity as well as a range of individuals with whom he would prefer not to.

Moreno has advocated the following requirements of the sociometric test:

- the limits of the group should be indicated to the subjects;
- the subjects should be permitted an unlimited number of choices or rejections;
- the subjects should be asked to indicate the individuals they choose or reject in terms of specific criteria;
- results of the sociometric questions should be used to restructure the group;
- the subject should be permitted to make their choices and rejections

privately without other members of the group being able to identify the responses; and

- the questions used should be ranged to the level of understanding of the members of the group.

4.5.5. Characteristics of a Good Socio-Metric Scale

1. **Reliability:** The sociometric scale needs to be consistent across judges. Over time, the socio-metric scale ought to remain constant. Equivalent forms of measurement must be consistent. It's crucial to maintain internal consistency.
2. **Validity:** The validity of a test is determined by how well it can accomplish its stated objectives. The intelligent concept of face validity is equally relevant in this case if the sociometric investigator restricts his focus to a measure of interpersonal choice. Second, in cases where a criterion variable is observable, criterion-related validity is significant. Finally, the network of relationships between test performance and a variety of pertinent measures must be considered when designating a test to measure a hypothetical quality construct.
3. **Simplicity:** The scale should be simple and intelligible even to the common man. A simplest scale creates confidence in the minds of the people and the scale thus derived is more acceptable to the people.
4. **Universality:** The scale should be widely applicable as possible. The various attributes of socio-legal phenomena differ from place to place according to difference in culture, religion and social values. Too much universality may impair the precision and validity of a socio-metric scale.
5. **Practicability:** It implies that factors which are included for the construction of the scale must be capable of being measured and gathered.
6. **Based on Norms:** We must use norms or standards with which the measurement is to be compared for all comparison purposes.
7. **Properly Weighted:** Not every item on the scale is significant in some way. Their total measurement wouldn't be representative if appropriate weights weren't assigned to the different attributes.

There are, in addition to the above, certain characteristics of socio-metric tool that make it a desirable and useful instrument.

- The subjects should express themselves spontaneously in their choice of companions.
- Directions should be clear about tools and situations and the methods of recording choices.
- The Confidential nature of choices made should be emphasized.
- Each student would have a companion out of the choices given by him.
- The word test cannot be used anywhere because it is associated with right and wrong answers and would probably distort the meaning of the choices of the students.

4.5.6. Techniques of Sociometry

The following are some of the techniques which deserve consideration:

1. **Sociometric Self-Rating or Related Analysis:** The application of sociometric self-rating on the prediction of an individual's sociometric choice is an extension of the sociometric test. One more step involved giving the subjects the task of guessing every sociometric choice made by every member of the group. Important additional variables in the sociometric situation appear to be the accuracy with which the individual perceives the choices and rejections of his associates, as well as the circumstances under which systematic distortions of these perceptions occur. Moreno brought up this technique.
2. **Scaling Method:** Gardner and Thompson developed a trustworthy set of measures intended to elicit ratings from the individual regarding a group member's ability to meet needs related to recognition, occurrence and achievement, and affiliation. The scales produced ratings on each variable from each subject, for each other group member, through a series of forced choice comparisons of group members.
3. **Group Preference Record:** This is a variation of the sociometric techniques which requires the members of the group to respond in terms of like, dislike or reference to every member of the group.
4. **Multi Relational Sociometric Survey:** By this method it is possible to establish a large number of meaningful indices for the classification of rational patterns in an organization. In this adaptation two classes of criteria are utilized, that is organizational 'goal-directed' and 'non –goal directed.'

5. **Estimate of Time:** This procedure requires the investigator to ask the members of the group to estimate the proportion of time given a finite limit; that they would like to spend interacting with the other members of the group in a given activity.
6. **"Guess Who" Technique:** This method entails giving the subjects a variety of behavior descriptions and asking them to "guess who" in the group best fits the description. This method has an advantage because it is a little more deceptive and the subjects are less aware of the researcher's intentions.

4.5.7. Procedure of Constructing Sociometric Scales

The following steps are taken for the construction of socio-metric scales:

- **Selection of Institution:** This initial phase involves choosing the organization, community, or behavior that needs to be measured. For generalizations about an institution to be valid, it must be stable and adhere to strict standards.
- **Selection of Aspect to be Measured:** The specific elements to be measured must be chosen. We will never be able to measure every aspect on a single scale. The indices may combine different measurements.
- **Selection of Component Attributes:** The majority of socio-legal institutions are intricate in design. Unless they have been dissected into meaningful component parts, they can be measured. Internal consistency or factor analysis may be used as the basis for the process.
- **Weighing of Attributes:** Even when the component attributes have been selected, they have to be properly weighed in order to provide a more precise and accurate measurement.
- **Standardization of Scale:** Since no sample can be considered completely representative of the universe, applying scales based on one sample to another sample may present some challenges with regard to validity and precision. The scale is adjusted as needed in light of fresh knowledge. The scales need to be changed and adjusted in order to eliminate the disparity. The scale becomes completely valid and reliable after multiple trials, at which point it is adopted as a standard.

4.5.8. Analysis of Sociometric Data

To analyze social-choice data, there are the following methods:

- **Graphic Method:** Moreno presented a method, the sociometric, for summarizing the choices and rejections among members of a group. It employs geometric figures to represent members of the group and various kinds of lines, joining the figures to represent choices and rejections. Its purpose is to discover group structure and the relation of a group member to the group as a whole.
- **Simple Quantitative Method:** Sociometric data are summarized completely in the sociograms but an equally complete method of the summarization is the N X N table or matrix, in which N refers to the number of subjects.
- **Scores and Derived Indices:** Moreno's book "Who Shall Survive?" includes the explicit formulation of a number of indices and implicitly assumes a large number. The number of mutual choices in a group serves as the basis of several indices. The sum of acceptance plus the sum of rejections divided by one less than the group size is an index for social intensity.
- **Statistical Methods:** Statistical techniques are widely used in analysis of sociometric data both to test the significance of observed findings and to provide derived scores of indices.
- **Limitations:** The limitations a researcher employing sociometric technique ought to be familiar with: (a) the manner of employing these techniques, and (b) shortcomings inherent in the very nature of socio-metric techniques.

4.5.8.1. Advantages

- Sociometry is a simple, economical and materialistic method of observation and data collection through questionnaires and schedules. It is easy to administer.
- It has the virtue of considerable flexibility. It can be adapted to a wide variety of research.
- It improves social – relations. The sociometry is highly useful in identifying leadership, attitudes, beliefs and values.
- It provides relatively acceptable indices for a large number of empirical concepts.
- It has implications for action research.
- It has interdisciplinary popularity.

REFERENCES

1. Aggrawal, S. (2003). *Legal Research Methodology*. Sri Sai Law Publications.
2. Ambekar, S. J. (2020). *A Socio-Legal Research & Citation Methods*. Educational Publisher and Distributor.
3. Anwarul Yaqin. (2008). *Legal Research and Writing Methods*. Lexis Nexis.
4. Apuke, O. D. (2017). Quantitative research methods: A synopsis approach. *Kuwait Chapter of Arabian Journal of Business and Management Review, 6*(11), 40–47. https://doi.org/10.12816/0040336.
5. Arundell Esdaile. (1954). *Student's Manual of Bibliography*. Barnes and Noble Publication.
6. Banakar, R., & Travers, M. (2005). *Introduction to Theory and Method in Socio-Legal Research*.
7. Finch, E., & Fafinski, S. (2011). *Legal Skills*. Oxford University Press.
8. Kothari, C. R. (2008). *Research Methodology: Methods and Techniques*. New Age International Publishers.
9. Myneni, S. R. (1997). *Legal Research Methodology*. Allahabad Law Agency.
10. Singh, R. (2013). *Legal Research Methodology*. Lexis Nexis.
11. Tiwari, H. N. (1999). *Legal Research Methodology*. Allahabad Law Agency.
12. Verma, S. K. (2000). *Legal Research and Methodology*. Indian Law Institute.

Chapter 7

Reading Cases and Statutes

Contents

INTRODUCTION

An essential component of legal studies and practice is reading statutes and cases. Analyzing these legal texts needs to be done methodically. Finding the important facts should be your first step when reading a case because they serve as the basis for the court's ruling. To comprehend how the case moved through the court system, pay attention to the procedural history. The matter at hand is significant because it formulates the legal query that the court is trying to answer. The resolution to this matter is the court's holding, or decision. Just as crucial is the reasoning, in which the court provides an explanation of how it arrived at its ruling, frequently referencing legal precedents and statutory interpretations. If they are present, dissenting and concurring opinions provide different points of view and can be useful in figuring out the case's larger ramifications. Any legal research, including that conducted in the field of criminal justice, must be founded on a specific legislation or collection of related laws. Additionally, a researcher must frequently consult Indian Constitutional provisions and cases pertaining to the rights of victims or accused parties. Furthermore, implementation or evaluation processes are frequently the focus of criminal justice research. Analogously, a study on criminal justice administration might be limited to using data from Superior Court reports alone. Additionally, it is standard procedure for research to concentrate on laws pertaining to any specific area of criminology or criminal justice. Therefore, in order to conduct criminal justice research, we must be able to read and apply statutes and cases.

5.1. RESEARCHING BY READING

The processes of gathering and analyzing various forms of information from a variety of sources, such as personal experience, rumors, political discourse, scientific data, and the media, are how we as researchers and regular members of the public learn about crime. One of the most fundamental ways to collect and evaluate data in a variety of fields is through reading research. In order to gain knowledge and insights on a particular topic, it entails a methodical approach to reading written materials, including books, academic journals, articles, reports, and other documents. The first step in the process is to identify and define the research question or interest topic. The choice of pertinent materials and sources is guided by this focus. Separating primary from secondary sources is necessary for conducting effective research. Original research articles, court documents, and historical records are examples of primary sources that provide firsthand information or proof. Critical essays, textbooks, and review articles are examples of primary sources that are analyzed, interpreted, or commented upon by secondary sources. We will be examining the various approaches we take to gaining knowledge about crime, and we will accomplish this by concentrating on the ways in which researchers collect and evaluate data through "reading," "seeing," and "talking/listening" about crime. Much of our authoritative knowledge about crime comes from reading, which makes sense for this section of the book to start with when we start working as researchers. We're going to talk about research methodologies that use previously published research findings that have been documented and made accessible. Although some materials (e.g., studies, reports, statistics, books written by academics or government agencies) may be created specifically with the intention of increasing our understanding of crime, we also want to think about other uses for these materials news, entertainment, which could still advance our knowledge of crime.

5.1.1. Reading and Reviewing the Literature Critically

The literature review is arguably the most crucial component of any research project. We should emphasize right away that before beginning any research project, a researcher has an obligation to gain a thorough understanding of the body of literature in the field in which they are interested. The literature review is a crucial first step in the majority of research projects, but it's important to understand that it's more than just a brainstorming session for research design. At several stages of the research process, including before a topic is chosen, when formulating a research question, during the stage of methodology design, and during data analysis, it may very well be required to refer to and expand the literature review. As researchers, we also need to be aware of the chance that new information could be released during a project that conflicts with, overlaps, or changes the course of the ongoing work. To put it simply, the majority of the work used by researchers is published in the form of books, reports, and articles in academic journals. Perhaps it would be worthwhile to take a moment to clarify what we mean exactly by "literature" in the context of research? But there's also another category of sources that O'Leary (2004) refers to as "grey literature," which comprises sources like unpublished conference papers, newspaper articles, and student theses. The multidisciplinary and policy-driven nature of criminology means that there is an especially large body of literature available to criminological researchers. It is often necessary to read literature from other disciplines, such as sociology, psychology, law, and geography. We also need to familiarize ourselves with pertinent research conducted by a variety of entities, including academic researchers, government departments, public and private sector agencies, and interest groups.

Therefore, there is a very broad potential range of sources, and finding and reviewing the literature can be a difficult and time-consuming process. The research design needs to take into account the substantial time and effort that a researcher will need to devote to reading and evaluating the work of other researchers in the field. Since a lot of time is spent working alone at computers and/or libraries, it is important to incorporate some variety into the workday and make an effort to engage with colleagues about research problems or recent discoveries. It is worth noting that this can be an isolating task. It also necessitates a high degree of organization because multiple lines of inquiry must be pursued concurrently to develop a comprehensive picture of the work in a given area. A literature review can be approached in a variety of ways, so it's critical to start with a well-defined plan. Getting started is often the hardest part, but once you've located a few initial sources, more will appear and start to accumulate (kind of like a snowball effect). To get things going, it might be necessary to use a few different search tactics. For instance, using a bibliographical database—many of which are now accessible online—is a good way to locate journal articles; however, for books, it might be more effective to look up local bookshop databases and library catalogues. Furthermore, searching the websites of these organizations or, if needed, using an internet search engine might be the best way to locate reports and studies that are published by interest groups and agencies in the public and private sectors. Creating a strong set of search terms that can be derived from the topic, subtopics, main ideas, theories, and named authors is essential to success in all of these search strategies. Thus, for instance, your search terms might be "fraud" and "credit card" if you were looking for literature about techniques used by credit card fraudsters. Subsequently, as you become familiar with the relevant literature, you'll find that the terms "plastic card" and "payment card" are frequently used; you'll use these new terms in subsequent searches. More search terms will surface as you go on; using identity fraud, card-not-present fraud, skimming, and counterfeiting as examples, you'll see that these are all techniques used in credit card fraud. It's also possible to identify theories or use the names of the authors as search terms.

After locating and identifying each piece of literature, the researcher needs to organize and assess the data. As previously mentioned, it is typical for a researcher to amass a sizable collection of literature for a project. There are two problems to be solved: first, how to organize the sources into a catalog, and second, how to document the data that is contained in them. Building a catalogue or bibliographic database required the use of card indexes and manual filing systems in the past, but computers have made this task much simpler today. Although many people prefer to use their own personal system of cataloguing, there are several excellent bibliographic computer programmes that are especially helpful because they are automatically formatted and particularly simple to search. Whatever method you choose, the most crucial thing to keep in mind is to make sure you record a complete reference for every item when you acquire it. Nothing is worse than realizing later that you have forgotten where or how you found an item because you haven't recorded a reference. You will need to select which category of information you will use to organize the materials and decide which details—such as author names, year of publication, article/book title, journal title, page numbers, ISBN/ISSN, http address, date source was recorded, where it was found/how it was acquired, and whether a copy is held on file—are important to record.

After you have located and accurately recorded an item in the catalogue, the next step is to actually sit down and read it! Because reading involves critical analysis, this is probably the most difficult part of the literature review process. Obviously, one cannot memorize everything that they have read, so they must maintain some sort of record of the information found in each source. However, recording a brief synopsis of the source's content is neither productive nor efficient; these summaries are typically long and have little meaning when consulted later. Rather, it is preferable to evaluate a source and distill its "contribution to the field" through critical analysis. By doing this, the investigator can formulate research questions by identifying gaps or inconsistencies and creating a meaningful picture of the state of knowledge regarding a specific subject. Critical analysis is not an easy process, though; it takes confidence and experience. While we won't go into great detail here, O'Leary (2004) offers some very helpful advice, particularly for those who are unfamiliar with research methodology. In addition, we believe that one last note regarding context is necessary, which is especially significant for those of us who conduct research on crime and crime policy. Periodically taking a step back to examine the environments in which the literature has developed is crucial. In our work as crime researchers, we typically address current social issues that have their roots in particular political, economic, and legal environments. The arguments surrounding ASBOs are one example. It is best to understand the emerging literature in this field in light of the public discussions surrounding knife possession, binge drinking, and the "respect agenda." Similarly, it's best to consider the contentious identity card proposals in the light of the post-9/11 terrorism concerns and the status of illegal immigration. If the larger context is not known, we can imagine that in 10 years, researchers reviewing today's literature on identity cards or anti-social behavior may not fully comprehend the significance of its conclusions and recognize its contribution to criminology and policy.

5.1.2. Analyzing Other People's Data

We covered how published research—articles, books, reports, etc.—is obtained in the section before this one.) should be examined in order to develop a knowledgeable and critical understanding of the suggested field of study. You will frequently be reading and reviewing data that has been summarized and analyzed by researchers (as there is a limit to the number of points that can be covered in a single publication!). You'll have moments when you wish the information was in your possession. Maybe you can think of alternative lines of inquiry beyond those that are offered, or maybe you just want to learn more about the connections between sets of variables that you find interesting. Should the latter scenario hold true, you might be able to envision a whole research project that could be completed with data that has already been gathered by someone else! In certain circumstances, such as when the data is provided by a government agency, a significant survey series, or a project supported by a Research Council, it might be feasible to obtain access to other people's datasets and carry out original analysis on the raw data. In criminological research, this strategy—known as secondary analysis—is frequently employed. To put it simply, secondary analysis is the process of having a "independent" researcher (i.e., who was not involved in the data collection process or who was not initially intended to be the main "user" of the data) analyzing the data and making inferences from it. Secondary analysis typically entails a fresh interpretation of the data, making it an innovative and fascinating method of conducting research. It is appealing as a research methodology for several useful reasons as well. First, there is a strong incentive to use data that has already been gathered by someone else because the process of gathering and evaluating empirical data is frequently costly and time-consuming. Data analysis can take up more time, which is a luxury that empirical work does not always afford. Access to high-quality datasets is also getting easier. In the UK, this is undoubtedly the case, but it's also getting simpler to access data from abroad. The UK is lucky to have the UK Data Archive, which serves as the "curator" of the country's largest digital data collection in the humanities and social sciences.

5.1.3. Secondary Analysis of Qualitative Data

The utilization of secondary analysis for qualitative data is growing in popularity, particularly with the expansion of data availability via the Economic and Social Data Service (ESDS) offered by Essex University's UK Data Archive (UKDA). The service contains digital data sets from modern mixed-methods and entirely qualitative research, including all pertinent ESRC-funded studies. For the purpose of managing research projects, providing data creators and depositors with specialized advice on matters of consent and confidentiality, as well as data documentation for archiving, general guidelines are offered. Analyzing qualitative data that has been gathered by another person can be challenging. Unlike quantitative analysis, qualitative analysis is not subject to the same set of regulations and guidelines. As a result, it is crucial that the researcher create a unique analytical approach, guaranteeing high standards of validity and reliability all along the way. This necessitates a thorough comprehension of the project's methodology as well as the circumstances surrounding the data collection. Indeed, some contend that secondary analysis of qualitative data is impractical due to the impossibility of a third party understanding the data completely, such as an observer or interviewee. But the fact that there is so much space for investigation and conceptual development, along with the potential for a fresh analyst to offer an insightful, unbiased viewpoint to the data, seems to outweigh the possible drawbacks.

5.1.4. Secondary Analysis of Quantitative Data

The secondary analyst can access a wider variety of quantitative datasets, including official statistics gathered and generated by government agencies as well as significant survey series carried out by research organizations. Some of these quantitative datasets are managed by specialized research institutions, but the majority are held by the UKDA and accessible for secondary analysis. Because the data are gathered by large, reputable research organizations using carefully thought-out sampling techniques, they are typically of exceptionally high quality. The datasets are frequently repeated (either annually or less frequently), which makes them appropriate for longitudinal or trend analysis. However, there are also a lot of drawbacks. You have to take a lot of time to fully comprehend the data before you can start analyzing it because you were not involved in the operationalization of the measures, the data collection, or the dataset preparation. This is especially troublesome when it comes to big datasets like the British Crime Survey. Additionally, there will be several limitations on what you can do with the information. For instance, you might have data that only functions at the individual level (as opposed to the household, local, or national levels). It's also possible that some important variables are absent, either because they weren't there in the first place or because they were eliminated to anonymize the data (for instance, postcode variables are occasionally eliminated from datasets, which can be annoying if you want to try area-level analysis). Arber (2001) concludes with a great point: creating theoretically grounded research questions and exercising sociological imagination are both necessary for secondary analysis. You will find value in two different forms of quantitative data as a criminological researcher. Firstly, we will take a quick look at the main survey series that are currently accessible. These are not specifically "crime surveys," but they frequently include data on social traits and markers of social change that criminologists find interesting (such as political views, unemployment, poverty, and health). Subsequently, we examine the set of data gathered by the government, which we commonly refer to as official statistics.

5.1.4.1. Major Survey Series

Numerous extensive surveys and long-term studies that have been conducted over many years offer a more comprehensive and in-depth picture on a range of subjects. While some of these are funded and conducted by independent organizations, others are government surveys. They include:

1. **The OPCS Longitudinal Study:** Based on records of significant events pertaining to 1% of the people in England and Wales who were born on four different dates every year beginning in 1971 (roughly 500,000 individuals). Rather than being a sample taken at a specific moment in time, it represents a continuous sample of the population.
2. **The National Child Development Study (NCDS):** A long-term study involving 17,000 people who were born in Great Britain between March 3 and March 9, 1958 intended initially to look into infant health and perinatal mortality. The sample has undergone seven primary follow-ups to date to track its development; the most recent one was conducted in 2004 at the age of 46 by the Social Statistics Research Unit, which is now known as the Centre for Longitudinal Studies (CLS).
3. **The 1970 British Cohort Study:** Similar to the NCDS, based on a cohort of 17,000 people born in the UK between 5th and 11th April 1970. Also being carried out by SSRU and was last followed up in 1999/2000.
4. **The Millennium Cohort Study:** All live births in the UK during a 12-month period, beginning on September 1, 2000, in England and Wales and December 1, 2000, in Scotland and Northern Ireland, comprised the sample population for the study. The goal is to investigate the crucial first year of life and possibly find answers to many of the questions regarding its long-term effects. These include matters of fundamental interest to policy, such as the underpinnings of cohesiveness and social capital. To date, the survey has been swept three times; the most recent one took place in 2006, the year the kids began primary school.
5. **Labor Force Survey:** An 80,000-person quarterly survey with a primary focus on employment and training activities. Its definition of unemployment is founded on an internationally accepted

definition, in contrast to the monthly claimant count, and its findings are frequently contrasted with the claimant count.

6. **General Household Survey:** A yearly survey that was started in 1971 and surveyed roughly 10,000 households was used to track the impact of different government policy areas over time.
7. **British Social Attitudes Survey:** An annual survey that tracks how British social, political, economic, and moral values have changed and remained consistent with other societal shifts. Newspaper readership, political parties and trust, public spending, welfare benefits, health care, child care, poverty, the workplace and labor market, education, charitable giving, rural areas, transportation and the environment, Europe, economic prospects, immigration, sentencing, prisons, and race and religion are just a few of the topics covered.

5.1.4.2. Official Statistics

A broad range of statistics produced by government departments and agencies are referred to as "official statistics." When you stop to consider it, the majority of a person's life's significant occurrences and activities are documented by government organizations. As a result, the government gathers an enormous quantity of data about its citizens. An individual's contacts with state organizations, including the NHS, Benefits Agency, Passport Office, HM Revenue and Customs, Land Registry, and criminal justice system, are documented as soon as their birth is registered. Naturally, in the contemporary era of potent electronic data exchange and storage systems, this is becoming more and more true. While each government department is in charge of gathering and producing statistics on subjects falling under its purview, the Office for National Statistics (ONS) has served as the central government organization in charge of organizing government statistics since 1996. Naturally, the criminological researcher is most interested in the Crime Statistics, which are a subset of the Official Statistics. As demonstrated previously in this chapter, it is imperative to construct an overview of existing knowledge regarding a particular topic or research idea prior to delving deeper into it. A summary of the pertinent official statistics is frequently included in literature reviews, and this is helpful for creating the theoretical framework and context. Policy-makers, the public, the media, and researchers are interested in finding answers to questions like: How much crime is there? Is crime rising or falling? Are the police doing their jobs? How do criminals get punished for their crimes? The data has been used as a kind of barometer of the moral health of the country for more than a century (Maguire, 2007). Researchers may also be able to access the datasets and use them for secondary data analysis. The Scottish Executive and the Police Service of Northern Ireland, respectively, independently collect and publish crime statistics for Scotland and Wales; the Home Office is currently in charge of these statistics. Historically, the data have been disseminated through three primary statistical reports or series, each with well-established advantages and disadvantages.

1. **The Criminal Statistics:** The government has been producing criminal statistics for over 150 years. They are a national compilation of local police and court records that are produced at the national level. They concentrate on the number of police-recorded notifiable offenses, the number of cautions issued, and the number of offenders found guilty of particular offenses. The Criminal Statistics were the primary metrics used for many years to track changes in crime throughout the nation. However, a shift in criminological theory in the 1970s led to requests for new types of data. After police and court records came under fire for serving as more of an indicator of institutional needs than a neutral source of information about crime, new research on victims and situational crime prevention was initiated. Formerly, the Criminal Statistics served as the exclusive official source of information about crime; today, however, they are only one piece in a larger "kaleidoscope" (Maguire, 2007).
2. **The Recorded Crime Statistics:** A nationwide compilation of crimes reported to the police and maintained since 1876 is known as the Recorded Crime Statistics (RCS). The Home Office compiles and disseminates the information supplied by various forces and establishes regulations that dictate the manner and timing of crime reporting. By comparing different crime types and trends, the statistics can be used to identify changes in crime issues. For instance, they can show whether property crime is more common than violent crime or whether auto crime is on the rise. The statistics are helpful in providing overall totals of all recorded crimes). You must interpret the data with extreme caution, though, as the RCS have drawn a lot of criticism for their validity and reliability. Maguire notes that there are three main factors which need to be taken into consideration:
    - i. **Conceptual Consistency:** The definitions of offenses are subject to change over time as new laws and policies are introduced. Therefore, you need to be cautious that the crime you are looking at now meant the same thing to people who were employed, say, in the 1950s. The most recent significant modifications were made in 1998 to introduce a whole new

range of recordable offenses and alter the guidelines for recording multiple offenses in an effort to promote uniformity amongst police forces. The result was a sharp increase in the number of crimes reported, which has made historical comparisons extremely challenging.

ii. **Consistency in Recording Practice:** Despite the Home Office's regulations controlling recording procedures, police discretion remains an option, potentially leading to disparities in the methods employed by different units. Numerous people contend that the attitudes and actions of the police have a big impact on the statistics. It is still concerning that the police have the capacity and, in an increasingly managerial and performance-driven culture, the motivation to conceal certain offenses and/or over record others, despite the fact that adjustments have been made to help assure consistency. Therefore, you still need to be aware of potential differences both within and between forces.

iii. **Reporting of Crime by the Public:** It is common knowledge that individuals report crimes to the police or not for a variety of reasons, such as ignorance, trust, apathy, or accessibility. When interpreting the statistics, you should always keep in mind that the RCS are subject to any changes in reporting behavior.

3. **The British Crime Survey:** The British Crime Survey (BCS) was launched in 1982, during a period of growing criminologists' interest in the victim perspective and harsh criticism of official statistics based on police and court work. The BCS is a nationwide household survey that aims to find out if any household members have ever been victims of crime and, in the event that they have, to learn more about that experience. It is therefore claimed to give a more accurate picture of crime as it captures all crimes that are either not reported to the police or wind up in court. Along with self-completion questionnaires for drug use and domestic violence, it also includes questions measuring attitudes toward the police and the criminal justice system. It used to be done on a four-year cycle, but it is currently done on a continuous annual cycle with 40,000 respondents as the sample size each year. The questionnaire's content has not changed significantly from its original format, and maintaining it is highly valued in order to enable precise trend analysis. This has, however, drawn a great deal of criticism because

it has made it difficult to make adjustments to certain measures that have been acknowledged as being conceptually weak or badly designed.

Additionally, the BCS only covers a narrow subset of crimes, which complicates comparisons with RCS data. Researchers and the media have most frequently used the RCS and BCS statistics as measures of crime over the last 20 years. They were previously released separately as different but complementary data sources, but the Home Office decided to combine the two in an annual report titled "Crime in England and Wales" recently. This choice has drawn a lot of criticism because it seems to have produced "analysis with political spin" rather than an objective presentation of the available facts. The most severe criticism may have come from the Statistics Commission's 2006 review of crime statistics (Statistics Commission, 2006), which suggested that the distinction between BCS data and Recorded Crime Statistics be restored as soon as feasible. The Criminal Statistics, the British Crime Survey, and the Recorded Crime Statistics are still undoubtedly three of the most significant sources of data for criminological researchers, despite the clear shortcomings in all three methods. Nonetheless, there are regular reviews of the crime statistics, and it is crucial for criminological researchers to remain up to date with the modifications that are made. There are variations in the amount and variety of data gathered, as well as in the methods used for conducting and sharing analysis. In fact, Maguire (2007) speaks of a "data explosion" that has recently taken place in the field of crime statistics. This explosion has been fueled by a new managerialism and performance management culture in government departments and agencies, as well as notable technological advancements that have revolutionized the ways in which we can store and analyze electronic data. He notes that more data—both quantitative and qualitative—is currently being gathered in a variety of new areas, such as crimes that go unreported or are not recorded, the circumstances surrounding the crime, the geographic distribution of crimes, the improvement of concepts like "street crime," the amount of information on hidden crimes and hidden offenders, victims, and public perceptions. Additionally, it appears that there is a willingness to consider crime statistics in a more creative way and that the idea that crime is a social construct rather than one based on "legal definitions" of crime is becoming more prevalent.

The Simmons Report proposed a 'national index' of crime which would focus on the most serious and high volume crimes, for example. However, it would appear that we are some way from developing a meaningful 'index' of crime. Therefore, it is evident that utilizing the official crime statistics can lead to confusion. In fact, there has been increasing criticism that the public is given confusing statistics, and it has been suggested that the general misinformation about crime rates and distributions is undermining public confidence. How these issues are resolved remains to be seen but it is perhaps worth concluding by reflecting on the six key recommendations made by the Statistics Commission aimed at improving the availability, usability and accuracy of official crime statistics:

- The structure of the Home Office should be changed to separate the policy-making and information provision/publication functions.
- Improved communication with users.
- Better data at the small area level.
- Furthering of research opportunities.
- Improvements to the comparability of data (especially with Scotland and Northern Ireland).
- Further work on index measures of 'total crime.'

5.1.4.3. Criminological Research, Policy, and Politics

We believe it is necessary to discuss the connection between criminological research and politics before moving on from the subject of official crime statistics. A wide range of individuals functioning in various capacities actually use crime statistics. Statistics are used, for instance, by the government and local delivery organizations to manage performance, create policies regarding criminal justice and crime reduction, and inform the public about crime. Crime statistics are used by the general public to assess risk in their daily lives, to understand the justification for government policy, to hold local delivery organizations accountable, and to learn about the experiences and perceptions of others regarding crime and disorder. As a result, public concern about crime, where crime is on the political agenda, and government investment in data collection are closely related (Maguire, 2007), and research must always take this relationship into account.

It is difficult to recall a period in which criminological research did not have some bearing on politics. For instance, The New Criminology (Taylor et al., 1970). embodied a radical critique of criminology, which was previously thought of as a branch of the criminal justice system. However, there was a period of time before the 1980s when issues related to party politics did not include crime and the treatment of offenders. But in recent decades, criminological research has inevitably become more politicized due to changes in criminal justice policy. Parallel to this (though we do not necessarily propose a direct causal relationship), discussions concerning the methodology of criminological research and its applicability to policy have emerged. These have addressed the two primary criminological fields of assessment and criminal statistics. The so-called "paradigm wars" were a discussion about the nature of evaluation that took place in the 1990s. That being said, this was primarily a disagreement about various assessment models rather than something obviously political. Nonetheless, the Labor Government's announcement in the late 1990s that it was dedicated to "evidence-based" research increased the importance of evaluation. Later, this commitment was called into question when it appeared that some of the evidence did not support the government's claims. As a result, Tim Newburn, President of the British Society of Criminology, spoke of "the rise and fall of evidence-based research."

Tim Hope, a former Home Office researcher, has been one of the Home Office's most scathing critics. Hope addresses the role of "scientific" evidence in politics within the framework of a contentious project he worked on (Hope, 2004). He points out that the conventional Enlightenment paradigm views science as distinct from policy. On the other hand, more contemporary scholars—such as Beck in his 1992 analysis of the Risk Society—have contended that when scientific data serves as the foundation for policy choices, "science itself becomes a site for politics." The methodology of science is no longer the only thing that gives it value; it now also has the promise of application and utility. The emergence of a purportedly new "crime science" that aims to apply methods in ways that could improve the work of criminal justice agencies and views research as primarily something that is intended for policy utilization has added to this promise in recent years. The previously held belief that criminology is primarily concerned with comprehending and explaining crime and criminality, with policy relevance being incidental, is in contrast to the "reflexive" role of science. The Treasury's role is another aspect of the relationship between research and politics. Government departments must provide evidence of the cost-effectiveness of their programs to HM Treasury, in accordance with guidelines provided by the Treasury in the form of The Green Book, which lays out a framework for project appraisal. The government social research context is enhanced by the addition of the Magenta Book, which provides guidelines for policy analysis and evaluation. While it makes sense that a government would want to show that its expenditures are worthwhile, doing so can limit the scope and speed of research. Raynor and Robinson have argued that: The policy of recruiting as many offenders as possible to programmes to meet Treasury targets has probably tended to undermine the fit between offenders' needs and programmes and contributed to increasing attrition and non-completion, which in turn reduces the overall impact of the programmes if non-completers reconvict more.

Furthermore, a frequent grievance expressed by researchers is that meticulously planned and developed programs are expedited to yield outcomes before they have had adequate time to settle in. In conclusion, the Home Office does contribute significantly to funding criminological research and sets the research agenda, even though it is not the only authority on the field. The point we are trying to make here is that these issues should alert criminological researchers to the fact that their field of study does involve politics, disagreements, and values, all of which must be taken into account before beginning any new project.

5.1.5. Analyzing Documents

The last research strategy through reading that we would like to discuss in this chapter is the content analysis method of document analysis. A multi-method strategy frequently includes content analysis as an auxiliary method. Both quantitative and qualitative data—such as the quantity of pertinent words or paragraphs or the style of the pictures—may be gathered and analyzed in this process. The majority of criminological studies that have employed a content analysis approach have concentrated on official policy documents and printed news media. However, as a reading-based research method, we should talk briefly about content analysis here. Finding a specific research question and, when appropriate, developing hypotheses are the first steps in the process. Formulating a strategy for sampling is the next step. The selection of the sample frame will be contingent upon the specific research question. For instance, if the objective is to investigate the correlation between news reports of criminal activity and public perceptions of crime rates, then the sampling frame would be comprised of pertinent national and local newspapers, as well as news programs broadcast on radio and/or television. Once more, the nature of the research question will dictate how the sample is drawn. Some possible criteria include time, publication, author, and reference to specific events. Content analysis has advantages and disadvantages, just like any other research methodology. The documents that are being examined have typically been produced for a different reason, which is a plus content analysis clearly has a strength in being non-reactive and unobtrusive (though not for the research's purpose). The document may be structured in an inefficient manner, which leaves the researcher with the difficult task of organizing the data, which can also cause issues for the researcher. Ensuring the validity of the research is one of the main challenges, particularly when the analyst needs to discern between "witting evidence," or information that the document's author intended to convey, and "unwitting evidence," or any additional information that the analyst learns from reading the document. Finally, even though computers have made the process somewhat easier, content analysis is still known for being a very time-consuming and laborious process.

5.2. THE SCIENCE OF OBSERVATION? EPISTEMOLOGY AND RESEARCH DESIGN

Natural scientists who follow positivist principles acknowledge that repeated, methodical, and objective observations of naturally occurring phenomena are the best ways to learn about the natural world. Thus, for instance, by heating a piece of glass to various temperatures and noting any changes in color or texture, we may be able to learn more about the physical characteristics of glass. In this case, formal, structured, and objective observational methods would be used, and the experiment would be managed with the use of instruments like thermometers, stopwatches, and pre-made tables for recording data. Can these techniques be applied to the study of social phenomena, though? Social observation techniques were first created in the British Empire's colonial era. British anthropologists developed a research approach that included methods of observation, document collection, and interviewing because they were eager to learn about and comprehend the "exotic" cultures that existed in the recently established colonies. This method was later called ethnography. Even though the first anthropologists truly went on scientific expeditions into uncharted territory, the "armchair approach" became the norm and was more common. Instead of working in the field, they would use the notes that the teams of colonial administrators sent back to create a picture of life in the colonies while based in their libraries in London. The colonial administrators were guided in their actions by a manual that was first released in 1874 and gave the local district commissioners a list of inquiries to make of aboriginal informants.

Following the colonial era, American sociologists from the Chicago School of Sociology in the 1920s and 1930s revolutionized ethnographic methods. Notably, the researchers from the Chicago School added two essential components to the British anthropological approach. Initially, they added a pragmatist component to an otherwise highly positivistic approach. They embraced the idea that social life is dynamic and ever-changing rather than a static, unchangeable phenomenon (the kind of thing positivists like to study with their fixed measuring instruments). Formalism constituted element number two. This is the notion that social relationships represent underlying forms that can have similarities even though they will always differ in content. Therefore, rather than the individuals themselves, the interactions between people will be the main focus of any social setting. As a result, the Chicago School researchers' methodologies differed greatly from the anthropological one. They rejected positivism's rigid precepts and held the view that knowledge cannot come from a methodical process of hypothesis testing. Rather, they contended that one needs to make thorough and in-depth observations before drawing conclusions from the information. The researchers were then urged to map the layout of the city's streets using blank notebooks rather than clipboards and questionnaires, which asked fixed, static questions. Their goal was to make an effort to document and comprehend urban change.

Importantly, the Chicago researchers did not begin with a predetermined hypothesis that they intended to investigate. Instead, after gathering and analyzing the data, they came up with a theory. One of the main characteristics of ethnography is that the theory is developed from the data (instead of gathering data to support a theory). As the research develops, the researcher typically reformulates the research question. However, Hammersley & Atkinson (1983) point out that "substantive" or "topical" theory constantly interacts with one another theory created for particular empirical investigations) and "formal" or "generic" theory (i.e., more comprehensive conceptual theory). From the formal to the substantive, an ethnographic study can transition (see Hargreaves et al., study on classroom deviance). (1975), where label theory was used as a springboard and developed into a "shopping list" of topics specifically pertinent to educational institutions, or the other way around (Atkinson's study of industrial training units (1981) is a good illustration of this), wherein specific, topical research questions were connected to abstract ideas like stigma and labeling. Anyone thinking about using an ethnographic approach should understand that observation and ethnography are two different things; an observation study can be conducted without being an ethnography. Considering ethnography as a research strategy and observation as a research method may be the most beneficial approach.

Thus, an ethnographic study may use a variety of techniques, such as interviews, observation, and documentary research. Consider a study by Tomsen (1997), for instance, which examined the culture of drinking violence in Newcastle, Australia, by combining observations made in pubs and bars, interviews with bouncers, and the examination of police data. An ethnography's theoretical/epistemological foundation (the creation of theory from data) and the researcher's prolonged "immersion" in the social context are its distinguishing characteristics. Then, a "grounded theory" approach is used, in which the observer approaches the environment with an entirely open mind to whatever conclusions may be drawn. This method works especially well when the researcher wants to investigate and comprehend a situation or phenomenon that is unknown. An observer who takes an open observation approach assumes a neutral starting point and becomes more receptive to the relationships and surroundings that emerge in front of them. Making a list of concepts to observe or formulating theories in advance of the observation are not necessary. Rather, as the process progresses, the ideas, theories, and hypotheses become apparent. The observer has total control over what gets noticed and recorded right away and can let the process of observation take its natural course. Nonetheless, as we have previously highlighted, observation can be conducted independently as a research method and need not be a component of an ethnography. Research strategies of various kinds, including strongly positivistic ones, can incorporate an observation. In fact, there are study situations where a more structured and prescriptive approach to observation is more appropriate. For instance, if the objectives of the research project involved measuring pre-identified concepts and testing particular hypotheses, the observer would need to create a research tool or instrument to be used during the observation process as well as predetermine the concepts that are to be measured. In these kinds of studies, it is common for the observer to take on the role of a detached/non-participant observer and there are a number of good examples of this approach in criminology, including a street observation study by Shapland et al., (1994).

5.2.1. Role of the Observer

In an observation study, choosing the observer's role during the observation may be the most crucial choice you have to make. Two types of roles can be distinguished, broadly speaking: one in which the observer participates in the group and environment and another in which the observer is not involved in the group and is not attached to the environment. When it comes to the two roles, Robson points out that the main distinction is whether the participant observer acts as the instrument or the non-participant observer typically uses some sort of observation tool.

Numerous factors, such as the nature of the research question and the researcher's chosen epistemological stance, will influence the decision. The participant role is standard practice in ethnographic research. In other scenarios, a non-participant role is taken, particularly when preventing the "observer effect" is crucial. The decision to assume a covert or overt role will have been made by the observer. As we've already seen, there are obvious ethical concerns with taking on a covert role, so this is not a decision that should be made lightly. The benefit is that people are more likely to behave naturally because they are unaware that they are being watched. While it is typical to see the clear division between participant and non-participant observation, there is actually a range of observational roles that fall in between total detachment and full participation. The most helpful analysis of observational roles is frequently attributed to Gold's scheme of classification of participant observer roles (1958) in textbooks. Within it, he identifies four key roles:

1. **Complete Participant:** The full participant is an active participant in the situation and does not disclose to the other group members that they are an observer. Naturally, it is simpler in situations where the observer already plays a part in the group. Holdaway's work (Holdaway, 1983), which was mentioned earlier in the chapter, is a good example. Because Holdaway was a police officer at the time of his study, he was able to carry out his investigation discreetly from the other officers. The benefit in this case is that the observer can fully immerse themselves in the "real" social environment without worrying about how the research may affect group members' behavior. Even though it might seem like the "perfect" research environment, this requires a great deal of dishonesty, and it can be very taxing for the observer—both physically and psychologically. Additionally, there is a risk of "going native," a term used to characterize the circumstance in which a researcher loses their ability to remain objective because they become too emotionally invested in the setting, endangering the validity of their work. While it is difficult to find examples of this in the literature, there are instances where researchers have had difficulty remaining impartial.
2. **Participant-as-Observer:** In this capacity, the observer engages in full group participation, just like a full participant, but the other group members are aware that the observer is conducting research. It is not required—in fact, it is frequently preferable—that the group members be aware of the subject of the researcher's observation. Ditton's study of fiddling and pilfering in a bakery provides an illustration of this role. While his coworkers were aware that he was a research student, they were unaware that he was specifically observing their dishonest behavior (Ditton, 1977). If they had known, they might have acted differently.
3. **Observer-as-Participant:** The participant-observer does not genuinely take part in the group activities. Despite being able to be in the room, s/he does not contribute completely as a productive group member. In this capacity, the researcher is essentially conducting

interviews, as noted by Bryman (2004). He or she must question people as those acts or decisions happen to find out why they act in particular ways or make particular decisions because they have no say in the situation itself. Punch's study on police operations in Amsterdam serves as one example. He was unable to fully engage in police activities because he was not a trained police officer, but he was still allowed to go on patrol with officers and ask them questions (Punch, 1979). Robson (2002) raises concerns about whether individuals who engage in such interactions with group members can truly be classified as "not taking part" in the context. Consequently, caution must be exercised in evaluating the validity of the findings.

4. **Complete Observer:** The complete participant is at one end of the spectrum; at the other is the complete observer. He or she does not communicate in any way with the other members of the group and is totally cut off from them. Loftland's 1973 study, which examined street behavior through a window, is a classic example. Sampson & Raudenbush (1999) took an intriguing modern approach to this role, observing disorder on the streets of Chicago by driving slowly and methodically through the streets while covertly filming their surroundings with two cameras attached to each side of the car. Without trespassing into the areas they were observing, they were able to gather and examine their data.

Each of the four roles has distinct benefits and drawbacks, which the researcher must carefully weigh before selecting one to assume. Interestingly, despite being at opposite ends of the spectrum, Hammersley & Atkinson (1983) point out that there are certain benefits and drawbacks to both the complete participant and complete observer roles. Since the researcher does not engage with the subjects in the course of performing their research, both approaches minimize reactivity. However, it is unlikely that direct questioning will occur, so the researcher is forced to rely solely on his or her own interpretations of the observed interactions, exchanges, and events. They come to the conclusion that taking on a role at either extreme of the spectrum can make it challenging to develop and test theory in a rigorous manner. They do, however, raise a legitimate concern regarding whether there is a meaningful distinction between the observer and the participant.

5.2.2. Data Collection

The numerous methodological, ethical, and epistemological choices that must be made prior to starting an observation study underscored the significance of a carefully considered research plan. The observation can then start after these choices have been made. One last question remains to be answered, though, and that is how the data will be recorded and analyzed. The answer to this will vary depending on whether the observation is open-ended or structured, as well as whether the data is quantitative or qualitative. It is crucial for the observer to keep a record of their observations in all observational work because it can be very challenging to look back on an event days, weeks, or months later and remember every significant event. However, there are various approaches to data recording, which are discussed below.

5.2.2.1. Open/Unstructured Observation Studies

The notebook is the primary tool of the observer in unstructured, open observation studies. The ability to take notes is one that the observer must develop; there is a delicate balance between taking too many and too few notes. On the one hand, as Hammersley and Atkinson note:

> A research project can be as well organized and as theoretically well informed as you like, but with inadequate note taking, the experience will be like using an expensive camera with poor quality film. In both cases, the resolution will prove unsatisfactory and the results will be poor. Only foggy pictures result.

But you can't capture everything on camera. Despite the fact that it may seem apparent, this is a crucial point to remember. For 10 minutes, try to observe a television show (dramas or soap operas work best), noting everything you see, including the environment, people, and events. Try to note down your observations in a notebook and use a stopwatch to keep track of the time. You'll probably feel worn out at the end of the 10 minutes, and your notes will probably be long and disorganized. If you looked back on your notes six months later, would they still make sense to you? Even if something is not immediately understood, it is still important to document it. The majority of seasoned observers will concur that the best time to record events is as soon as possible after the action or event has occurred. If the observation is hidden, it will obviously be difficult to carry it out because the constant scribbler will undoubtedly raise suspicions (unless writing is part of the role being adopted, perhaps). While taking notes in an overt setting is easier when done in an open manner, it is still important to ensure that note-taking does not look strange or distracting in the context.

Though there are general guidelines to follow, the specific study will determine what should be recorded and what should be omitted from notes. In general, field notes ought to include specific accounts of social processes as well as contexts. According to Robson (2002), an observer can pose three different kinds of questions during an observation: what, how, and why. What are the simple facts and contexts that can be discovered through other means in addition to being observed and possibly recorded dobservation? records). Thus, for instance, if we were to observe a courtroom, we may ask about the cases scheduled for hearing that day, the number of witnesses called in a particular case, and a description of the court staff, including the names of the judges and barristers. The how questions address exchanges and occurrences that take place throughout the observation procedure. We may then inquire as to how the judge addresses the defendant (words used, tone adopted, facial expression) or how barristers present a legal argument (using statutes and cases to support their case), to return to the example of the courtroom. Investigating the causes of the behaviors being seen is frequently required to move things along a bit further. Perhaps the hardest questions to answer are the "why" ones since they call for the observer to make assumptions based on what is said or done. By genuinely questioning the participants about the circumstances, the observer who has taken on a participatory role will be able to expand on these deductions.

5.2.2.2. Structured Observation Studies

An observation schedule or coding scheme is typically used by the researcher to document his or her observations during a structured observation. All that is needed for a coding scheme is a list of pre-established elements that will be tallied or graded throughout the observation. Either a straightforward counting of items or events or a more intricate recording of behavioral sequences can be part of the coding scheme. It is true that careful planning and application of coding schemes are necessary to guarantee validity and reliability. Researchers frequently modify coding schemes that have already been employed in other studies. The categories that are employed ought to be precise, objective, comprehensive, non-exclusive, and simple to document. The purpose of this study was to investigate the patterns of crime in various parts of a city. They contend that it's critical to determine how people use various areas of a community and what opportunities there are for crime in order to investigate these patterns in the context of the physical environment in which they arise. Thus, an observation schedule was used for the street observations that were used in this study. To focus crime reduction efforts, the observation's findings were combined with information gathered from police data analysis and interviews.

Mapping an area gave the observers the ability to identify possible crime targets during the first observational phase. They paid special attention to mapping public spaces and properties, including those used for residential, commercial, and industrial purposes; routes for pedestrians and cars; parking; potential crime hotspots, such as car parks, pubs, and amusement arcades;

potential issues, such as litter, poorly maintained roads, abandoned buildings, and graffiti; and crime prevention measures, such as burglar alarms, secury lighting, CCTV, etc.). The observation proceeded to a series of 10-minute observations of street activity at various times of the day. Prior to commencing the observation, observers were mandated to record the overall environmental conditions, including the weather, lighting, overall atmosphere of the area, ongoing activities, etc. Every movement in the area, including traffic flow and social use, had to be recorded by observers during the ten-minute observation period (totals of each type of vehicle and pedestrian counted). The observation schedule was created in a way that allowed for the clear and individual logging of every item of interest, including pedestrians (women alone, families, or groups of children) and vehicles (cars, taxis, buses, or lorries).

Therefore, well thought-out observation schedules were employed in both phases of the study, which made it possible to gather valuable quantitative data. However, a coding scheme or schedule can be helpful in a variety of situations and is not always limited to gathering only quantitative data. It is especially helpful in situations where there are numerous distinct sample periods or when a team of observers is engaged to ensure consistency across observations.

5.2.2.3. Alternatives to Note-Taking

Using a tape recorder is the most efficient way to maintain an accurate record of circumstances in which a lot of speech is used. On the other hand, tape recording has a lot of drawbacks. People may become uncomfortable when they see a tape recorder; in fact, some may refuse to allow it to be there in the first place. Additionally, this method generates a lot of data that must be meticulously sorted through later. It might not be feasible to tape record and transcribe every observation study if it is going to take place over an extended period of time. Hammersley & Atkinson (1983) suggest that it could be more suitable to record only particular formal meetings or interviews using one method and use a different technique for other, less formal settings. An alternative method that has been effectively employed in certain research studies is video-taping (refer to Sampson & Raudenbush (1999), who drove through Chicago's streets and recorded people's behavior on camera to create social disorder scales, and Shrum & Kilburn (1996), who recorded the Mardi Gras festival in New Orleans on video to investigate instances of ritual exchange and nudity. Additionally, some researchers advise keeping a fieldwork journal to document the research process. It can be used in "de-briefing" sessions as a stress-reduction strategy and allows the observer to document methodological issues and developmental concepts (Johnson, 1975).

5.2.3. Data Analysis

After the data collection process has started, you need to give careful consideration to how to store and catalog the data. There are various methods to go about this. One option would be to organize the data in a chronological fashion. Nonetheless, it is frequently preferable to create a cataloging system based on theoretical ideas and themes that have been determined both before and during the study. Thus, for instance, you could arrange based on individuals, locations, or occasions. Making the choice to maintain computerized or manual records is another decision. Indexes, file annotations, and occasionally duplicate entries (when observations fall into more than one category) will be required. Some find it easier to operate a manual system, while others find it easier to use a computerized one. In contrast to other approaches, observation studies do not have a discrete phase for analysis. Rather, analysis happens all along the way in the research process. The precise methods of data analysis in an observation study will vary, depending upon the amounts of quantitative and qualitative data collected, but there are some basic principles which should be followed. All observation studies should start with the process of descriptive observation – a 'painting the picture' exercise (Robson, 2002). We saw an example of this in the street observation study where the observers 'mapped' what they could see before the 10-minute observation period began. The next stage is to go beyond the descriptive and identify concepts and develop theoretical frameworks. To give an example, in a study of the ways in which the police deal with disputes, Kemp et al. (1992) identified a series of different concepts which together form an 'incident': the arrival of the police at the scene, contact (when the police physically restrain someone), information-gathering, decision-taking and implementation, the conclusion and the aftermath.

You should be able to formulate some hypotheses by considering the relationships between various concepts and potential definitions for emergent "problems." The next step of the analysis is to test the initial hypotheses and determine the frequency and distribution of these observed concepts. The theories are revised and retested if they turn out to be false, which is often the case. The theories are reformulated until they are conclusively demonstrated. The more intricate modeling of relationships (and relationships between relationships) is required for the final analysis. This entails the development of "roles" and the relationships that link them so that they can eventually be expanded into comprehensive descriptions of social environments and lifestyles.

5.2.4. The Disadvantages of Observation

Despite some serious criticism over the years, observational methods are still widely used in criminological research. Thus, before starting any observational work, it's critical that you are aware of the possible objections. The process of observation requires a lot of time and resources, first and foremost. A participant observation study should last at least a year, according to Goffman (1961). Although we don't want to establish strict upper or lower bounds on this time frame, we must carefully weigh the demands of sufficient data collection against the constraints imposed by limited resources. Serious concerns have also been expressed by some observers regarding the moral dilemmas presented by both overt and covert observation (Bulmer, 1982; Norris, 1993). An additional prevalent critique is that observation is inherently subjective, thereby posing a substantial risk of the researcher's personal opinions influencing the study's conclusion. This occurs in the context of structured observations when the group or environment you are observing is given a conceptual framework that is wholly inappropriate. This is especially troublesome in cases where the goal of the study is to be exploratory and find new information. According to Bryman (2004), one way to approach this issue might be to begin with some unstructured observations and use the information gathered to create an observation schedule. This is not to argue that unstructured observations are less subject to subjectivity, though. Analytical induction may be argued to be a helpful tool in theoretical development, particularly in the context of grounded theory studies. However, we would join critics in challenging the notion that a researcher can approach a research study without contributing any theoretical ideas at all. Therefore, we believe it's critical to stress how important it is that the researcher incorporates validity checks into the research methodology whenever feasible.

Understanding the boundaries of what can be learned from observation is also crucial. The fact that you can only record what is "directly observable" is one of the main limitations of structured observation. This implies that you might not be able to gather much information about people's intentions or motivations and that you might miss the context in which an event or interaction takes place. Particularly participant observation has come under fire since it is primarily limited to working-class environments as a result of serious access problems, making it incapable of producing any meaningful analysis of power dynamics. This is especially frustrating for criminological researchers because it closes off intriguing research directions (such as examining the work habits of top criminal justice system officials or the ways in which executives in large corporations commit crimes and corruption).

5.3. RESEARCHING BY ASKING AND LISTENING

The approach of listening to what people have to say has arguably produced the most criminological research of any other method. Because we include questionnaires, which occasionally but not always result in non-verbal responses, we use the term "listening" in a colloquial sense here. However, we believe that answering questionnaires in writing is a means of listening to what is being said. This article covers three primary methods of listening: semi-structured interviews, questionnaires, and focus groups, which are a type of group interview. The fact that there is interaction of some kind between the researcher and participants unites them all. This is significant because it involves a reciprocal relationship. It is simple for a researcher to view the people they are interacting with as passive partners who are only there to provide them with the information they need in order to continue their studies. There are various reasons why this would be a grave error. One is that it involves objectifying participants, which makes it easier for unethical research practices to occur afterward. The second rationale is more practical in nature: you are more likely to obtain trustworthy and significant insights if you are cognizant of how others react. It's also critical to consider the potential uses of researchers by participants. This can occur in a number of ways. One is that the researcher might end up acting as an entirely unqualified, on-demand counselor.

People who participate in research have the chance to be heard, which they might not otherwise have, to express their opinions and feelings as well as perhaps to discuss some very private topics. A competent and skilled researcher will develop the ability to elicit information from subjects—victims, offenders, members of the public, or members of the legal system, depending on the situation. It's possible that a victim is confiding in someone about their experiences for the first time. It's possible that an offender is disclosing actions they regret taking. In this way, the researcher is being employed almost exactly as a listening post. This makes perfect sense, but in order to avoid unreal expectations, it's crucial to keep in mind and remind respondents of your true role as well as its limitations. Speaking with representatives of different branches of the criminal justice system may be part of the researcher's strategy to get their opinions heard by research consumers, such as the Home Office, which is funding the project, or by a larger audience that will read the research output. When interviewing court officials, for instance, about the impact of recent legislation or changes to criminal justice procedures, you should be mindful that the information you receive may represent the agency's "party line" on the matter. It could be that you are accepting of the agency's "party line" after learning what it is, or it could be that this is hiding what is actually going on. A competent researcher must make numerous decisions regarding the type of data they obtain and how to interpret it in the context of their own intervention.

Listening can take place in various methodological settings. A survey is typically far more structured than ethnography or participant observation, which are likely to involve the least structured types of research encounters.

Multiple listening techniques may be used in a research project, such as semi-structured interviews and structured questionnaires. This could be the result of various techniques complementing one another or because various techniques are appropriate in various contexts. For instance, relatively unstructured conversations with important figures and representatives of different groups of people could be the first step in a study of crime and law enforcement patterns in a given area. The findings from these could be added to a more formal questionnaire that is distributed to a greater number of individuals in order to determine whether the conclusions drawn from the small-scale investigations are applicable to a wider audience.

5.3.1. Interviewing

A questionnaire can be used to conduct a much more highly structured interview than one with very little structure. Three types of interview:

- the schedule standardized interview;
- the non-schedule standardized interview;
- the non-standardized interview.

The schedule standardized interview is extremely structured, with the same questions asked in the same order to each respondent. Nonetheless, thorough initial research, development, and pre-testing are necessary; the latter may initially require less structured interviewing techniques. A list of details that each respondent must provide is part of the non-schedule standardized interview, also known as the focused interview. The questions may be asked in any order or with different wording. It necessitates competent interviewing and acknowledges the unique nature of each interviewee's contribution. There are no predetermined questions in a non-standardized interview. As the interview goes on, the interviewer can delve into different topics and explore a variety of theories. It also implies that the interviewee is free to explore areas during the interview that the researcher had not previously thought of. The goal of unstructured, non-standardized interviews is typically to extract information from respondents with as little researcher intervention as possible. However, the researcher is probably going to follow an agenda even in this situation. Usually, the researcher enters a situation with some expectations and emergent theories.

Each of the three interview formats has a distinct purpose. For instance, the standardized interview allows for more generalizable hypothesis testing, while the non-standardized interview is better for exploratory work that aims to determine the meanings and definitions used by respondents. It's critical to understand which function is being used when throughout the investigation.

Every interview format has drawbacks, and how best to use them depends on the goal you want to achieve, the interviewers' experience, and the time and resources you have available.

5.3.1.1. Semi-Structured Interviews

In socio-legal research, this approach is widely used, particularly by individuals without prior training in social research. It is attractive because it seems less complicated than creating a questionnaire, but it should only be utilized when necessary because it is appropriate and not just handy. Instead of just "fishing" for information, the theoretical requirements of a study should be the primary factor in deciding whether to use such a data collection technique. To make the most of an interview without coming across as naïve, you must have done enough preliminary research and informal inquiries to gain sufficient knowledge about the subject. Semi-structured interviews are not a reliable way to learn about a problem. Semi-structured interviews can be utilized when comprehensive research is the primary goal, particularly when understanding the significance of particular items to individuals or when examining a procedure or series of events is desired. Semi-structured interviews are probably going to be especially beneficial when examining complicated phenomena that might have evolved over time. For instance, asking people about their activities during specific times after they left school or some other period of time could be helpful if you were trying to figure out the connection between employment and criminality. Likewise, a study examining the relationship between fine default and other debt issues may require that participants recall their debt status through a meticulous reconstruction of their circumstances (Crow et al., 1993). Examining the experiences that members of ethnic minorities have had with the criminal justice system could be another application for semi-structured interviews. In this case, walking people through the process step-by-step could be beneficial.

When conducting what are known as "elite" studies, semi-structured interviews are also appropriate in certain situations (Moyzer & Wagstaffe, 1987). A large portion of social science research targets "ordinary" people, or the weakest and least powerful members of society. Elite studies focus on the more powerful members of society, including senior police officers, judges, magistrates, and organization executives. If you are able to reach someone like that, they probably won't think filling out a questionnaire is for them. Making the most of the chance to interact with influential people is important, as is their desire to have some standing during the research process. These are probably circumstances that the researcher will need to handle carefully.

Semi-structured interviews can also be used when researching sensitive topics, which is a frequent occurrence in the field of criminology. These could include histories of abuse, mental illness, and both victimization and offense. Though not all situations can benefit from semi-structured interviewing, these examples should help illustrate some of the situations in which it may be suitable.

5.3.1.2. The Interview Schedule

The important aspect of the semi-structured interview is that the questions and their sequence are not entirely preset; we will address question construction in the context of questionnaire design in a moment. As a result, pre-planned "prompts" may come after the main questions, or the interviewer may use general prompts like "Could you tell me more about that?" or "Can you tell me what you mean by that?" to encourage the respondent to elaborate on a topic. This does not imply that questions in semi-structured interviews can be answered freely. The research process has produced hypotheses, which will influence the interview; however, the development of hypotheses is more likely to be aided by the interview than by testing them. The generalizability of the interviews determines how much of this occurs. Interviews can provide insight into a broader group of people, such as a bench of magistrates, when the interviewees are part of that group. However, the interviewees won't help you assess whether the information you learn from them is accurate in general unless they make up a trustworthy sample. For this to occur, a more methodical approach to data collection—such as distributing a questionnaire to every magistrate—might be required. What they say may be more conclusive, though, if you were interviewing people who are crucial to the topic of the study, like a chief constable, a judge at the Crown Court, or a senior civil servant in charge of a particular area of criminal justice policy.

5.3.1.2.1. Conducting the Interview

Depending on the situation, the interview will be conducted in a different manner. The interview will probably take place in the respondent's office if they work for a criminal justice system or another organization. It could be in their house, your office, or a mutually agreed-upon public place if they are a victim, an offender, or a member of the public. In any case, it's critical to make arrangements for both privacy and an uninterrupted interview (e.g., through phone calls). Cafés and bars are bad ideas. It is necessary to inform the interviewee ahead of time of things like the expected duration of the interview. The duration of the interview will depend on the specifics, and in some cases, it may be desirable and feasible to conduct multiple interviews with the same subject (for example, when attempting to piece together the subject's life history). If you are conducting an interview with a busy criminal justice practitioner, allow 45 to 60 minutes. One may be fortunate to receive 20 to 30 minutes if the respondent is an adolescent who has appeared in court. Even though most people dislike the idea of an interview going longer than planned, it is common for the interviewee to get carried away and talk for longer than planned. As such, you should be patient and ready to hear some things that will later turn out to be irrelevant.

The interview's recording method is a crucial factor to take into account. Ideally, a recorder will be used; however, this will rely heavily on the interviewee's consent. If at all possible, seek permission ahead of time rather than putting them on the spot during the interview. In the event that a recorder is being used, make sure the recording is clear and noise-free. Verify that the batteries are fully charged (or that there is a mains supply) and that there is adequate tape, disc, or memory on the recording medium being used for each interview. All of these might seem apparent, but tapes or batteries dying have ruined many a good interview. Taking notes is the best course of action if the interview is not being electronically recorded, but managing the rapport required to conduct an interview, pay close attention to the answers, and take notes at the same time is challenging. It might be better to have some very brief aide-memories because respondents won't open up if they have to wait for you to write things down. If you don't know shorthand, try creating your own shorthand codes. It is occasionally feasible to conduct an interview with a fellow researcher present, which facilitates the sharing of the interviewing and note-taking tasks as well as the subsequent note-comparing. Even taking notes may not be feasible in some circumstances; in these cases, your best option is to jot down as much information as you can as soon as the interview is over. One of us experienced this while researching drug users and dealers. It is a good idea to write it up as soon as possible, if not the same day, even after taking notes and recording the interview. After an interview, words and concepts stick in your head until the next night when you sleep. Writing a summary of the findings from a group of interviews at regular intervals is beneficial when conducting a series of interviews. It's also critical to consider the insights you are gaining and how they relate to the theories you are researching.

It might be necessary for your design that the interview's agenda or timetable be the same each time. This allows you to draw general conclusions about all respondents, but it can also be annoying because, once you've spoken with a few people, you might come up with additional questions. However, if you keep changing the interview, you won't be able to find out how previous interviewees might have responded.

5.3.1.2.2. Analytic Induction

The method referred to as analytical induction represents an alternative. By employing this method, the objective is to gradually advance your understanding and concepts from one respondent to the next rather than asking the same or comparable questions of every respondent. In order to accomplish this, you formulate a preliminary hypothesis before conducting an interview with the first respondent based on it. After that, you take into account what you've discovered from this respondent and adjust your hypothesis as necessary. Based on this revised hypothesis, the next respondent is interviewed, and the information gleaned from the second interview is utilized to further refine the hypothesis so that it is applicable to both respondents. Until diminishing returns are attained, this process is repeated. Denzin proposes that participant observation can be used to demonstrate causality through analytical induction. The participant observer looks to refute a hypothesis until every case in the study can be explained, whereas quantitative analysis using survey techniques can manipulate variables statistically to control factors that might affect the relationship between the dependent variable and independent variables.

Lindesmith employed this method to explain how opiate addiction started in 1947. As an illustration, one of us employed this method several years ago while conducting exploratory research to determine why some users of illegal substances, like cannabis and LSD, were reporting negative side effects. One first theory could be that there was some sort of contamination with the medication. While the respondent had a negative experience, friends who had taken the same drug had not, according to the first interview. The first theory was disproved, which gave rise to the theory that some of his friends were to blame for the unpleasant experience. Additional interviews uncovered a number of additional details, such as the environment in which the drug was used and any personal issues that were going on at the time. After conducting several dozen interviews, it became clear that negative drug experiences could be the product of a specific set of circumstances that differ from person to person. This allows for the provision of guidance to users regarding ways to lower their chance of experiencing negative effects.

Although analytical induction is a valuable technique, it is crucial to consider its limitations. The first relates to case selection, and the question of how far one can extrapolate from the cases interviewed remains relevant to social science research to this day. Denzin proposes that the maximization of the likelihood of finding a conclusive negative case should be the guiding principle when choosing cases to test a theory. A single instance is adequate to disprove or alter a hypothesis. That being said, a lot relies on the specific context of the research being conducted. Developing and improving hypotheses through analytical induction can be highly beneficial, as they can subsequently be verified on a larger and more representative sample. In a manner that is not possible with purely correlational analysis, it also offers the benefit of helping the researcher comprehend the mechanisms that influence the relationships between variables.

5.3.2. Group Interviews and Focus Groups

The second way to gather information through listening and asking is with groups of people. These come in two primary forms. It is helpful to start by defining the differences between the two methods—one uses focus groups, and the other employs group interviews. In its most basic form, group interviewing is simply conducting interviews with multiple subjects at once. You can record responses based on what each person says, you can use a schedule similar to one for a semi-structured interview, and you can analyze the data both quantitatively and qualitatively. It is more complex than doing interviews one by one, but the key features are:

- Group interviews are a way of saving time and resources;
- Several topics are usually discussed;
- The researcher is interested in the responses of the individuals involved.

Conversely, focus groups are typically employed to delve deeper into a particular subject, with the primary focus being on group dynamics. While there are some similarities between the two approaches, we will primarily focus on focus groups, with references to group interviews made when necessary.

5.3.2.1. When Are Focus Groups Appropriate?

sociologist Robert Merton created focus groups in the 1940s to assess the impact of propaganda during World War II (Merton et al., 1956). In the 1990s, they gained popularity once more as a research methodology and as a social and political policy instrument (Morgan, 1992; Morgan & Krueger, 1993). In semi-structured or unstructured interviews as well as questionnaires, people are questioned and listened to. However, opinions and perceptions, as well as actions within organizations, are socially constructed and don't happen in a vacuum. People frequently interpret their experiences, even the most intimate ones, in relation to other people. People's interactions with their neighbors, coworkers, family, and friends shape their ideas and the way they express them. Thus, gathering a group of them together is one way to find out how they feel about things like safety and crime in their neighborhood, for example. This allows you to become more familiar with the back-and-forth social interactions that occur in daily life. Also, the image is more lively. Individual interviews yield unchanging outcomes, suggesting that the subject has always thought or done this; however, communication alters people's understanding, perceptions, and conclusions. People are constantly creating their own theories and testing them in light of their surroundings in a (non-scientific) manner. Though limited in scope, focus groups offer some insight into this process. For this reason, focus groups are helpful when we want to learn how people solve problems or come to decisions. They enable us to learn how different groups of people interpret and give meaning to a phenomenon, and they aid in our understanding of why people feel the way they do.

5.3.2.2. Limitations of Focus Groups

However, opinions that one person may voice alone are likely to face opposition when discussed in a group setting, and people may become uncomfortable if the subject is very delicate. One disadvantage of gathering material from groups of people is that they might be reluctant to discuss personal experiences, like being victimized, in front of others and might not say what's really going on. For instance, it is less likely that someone in a mixed-race group will be truthful if we are investigating people's opinions and experiences regarding how the criminal justice system handles individuals from various ethnic backgrounds. In a mixed-sex group, there are topics that both men and women might find less interesting to discuss. Moreover, a group's dynamics and interactions can influence the direction of a discussion. We might see a very different picture than we would if the first, third, fifth, seventh, and ninth people were in one group and the second, fourth, sixth, eighth, and tenth people were in another group if 10 people are divided into two groups based on the first 10 in one group and the second 10 in another.

Group interviewing, including focus groups and group interviews, is a much more involved process than collecting data one-on-one. The researcher must be well-versed in interpersonal skills and has less control than in a single interview. A careful balance must be struck between enforcing just enough control to prevent the group from taking over and deviating from the subject and overly controlling the other. Should the latter occur, the researcher's influence might have an excessive amount of control over the group's responses. When multiple people are involved, the material is also more challenging to record and analyze.

5.3.2.3. Forming the Groups

It is usually necessary to conduct multiple focus groups in order to ensure that the discussions that emerge are not specific to that group. The number of groups you hold will rely on the resources at your disposal, but as a general rule, you should hold groups until you believe you can predict the topics the group will discuss (a process known as "category saturation"). A group will usually have six or eight people in it. Predicting how many people will actually show up on the day is a common challenge. The topic will determine how candidates are chosen. The idea behind focus groups is that, like any other type of social research, they should be as representative as possible of the subject matter being studied. This is where the sampling principles come in. Nonetheless, a fantastic advantage of focus groups is that they encourage conversation about shared interests (e.g., Judges discussing sentences or prostitutes discussing topics they'd prefer not to bring up in public. Asking a group of young offenders about their experiences with the criminal justice system is one example of the very purposeful sampling that is occasionally required. Morgan (2006) makes the case that homogeneous groups are better suited for discussing subjects that would be taboo in other settings.

5.3.2.4. Running the Groups

One way to encourage people to listen to what they have to say is to use a structured set of questions or to start with a few general questions that can be followed up with more specific inquiries and prompts (e.g., "What do you mean when you say that?" and "Can you give me any examples?"). Likewise, with regard to focus groups. An agenda is essential, even if the questions are not structured, to make sure that everyone stays on topic and that, in the event that multiple groups are being used, everyone is covering the same ground. The moderator's role is very important. He or she might be a researcher, but if funds allow, it might also be beneficial to have someone whose only responsibility is to facilitate. This frees up the researcher or researchers to focus on the action, both visually and verbally. The drawback of this is that a facilitator who isn't a researcher might not be as familiar with the demands of the study and less likely to lead participants in the right path. Two researchers should be present if there isn't an independent facilitator; one should moderate and the other should record, though this isn't as important if the session is being filmed.

The moderator should strike a balance between encouraging conversation and maintaining attention on the topics that will allow the study hypotheses to be investigated without being overly controlling. In addition to introducing themselves and outlining the goal of the study, he or she should also go over the session structure, recording methods, confidentiality policies, and what to do in the event that any participants have questions. In closing, the moderator will express gratitude to everyone present and explain what will happen to the data. Making sure there is a sufficient balance of participation in focus groups—both inviting more reserved participants and preventing more assertive individuals from becoming overly dominant—is one of the main concerns. However, there may be situations when sensitive topics are being discussed (e.g., family violence) when it is appropriate to offer participants the choice to stay silent. It is also important to note that focus groups may, whether on purpose or not, have an impact on participants. This is particularly important because criminological research frequently addresses difficult topics like victimization and crime. Sessions have the power to arouse memories or bring about shifts in attitude and perception.

It is a matter of good ethical practice to provide for handling this by carrying out any repercussions and, if necessary, directing participants to get assistance. Ideally, focus groups should be videotaped and/or audio recorded with a voice recorder. It's crucial to keep in mind that visual responses and reactions can teach us a lot in addition to what people say. In addition to eye contact and body language, people's expressions of anger, concern, and disgust can also be telling. This is especially crucial in situations where specific types of groups are being utilized. If, for instance, you were to gather a group of criminal justice professionals—judges, police, and probation officers—to discuss how local crime problems are being addressed, which members of the group seem more self-assured than others? Similarly, if the focus group consisted of young people, it would be intriguing to observe which members are more outspoken than others. This could reveal a lot about the influences of peer groups.

5.3.3. Questionnaires

A systematic approach to creating questions intended to elicit particular information, attitudes, behaviors, or opinions is required when creating questionnaires, which are crucial tools for effectively collecting data from large groups. To help with the development of pertinent and targeted questions, the process starts with precisely defining the study objectives. These questions can be left open-ended, allowing for more individualized responses and qualitative insights, or closed-ended, offering predetermined response options for quantitative analysis. To ensure clarity and prevent bias, questions should be formulated effectively and logically arranged to maintain a natural flow. Before a large-scale rollout, pretesting the questionnaire on a small sample size aids in identifying possible problems. The distribution strategy—online, offline, over the phone, or in person—should be determined by the study's objectives and target audience. It is crucial to take ethical issues—like getting informed consent and maintaining confidentiality—into account. After the data is gathered, it is cleaned to remove any inconsistencies before being analyzed to look at both the qualitative and quantitative responses thematically and statistically. The last stage entails presenting the results in their entirety, interpreting the data and coming to relevant conclusions through the use of narrative and suitable visual aids. All things considered, well-crafted questionnaires are effective tools for gathering thorough and trustworthy data in a variety of study domains.

5.3.3.1. Strengths and Weaknesses of Questionnaires

Firstly, they facilitate the relatively easy and quick collection of data about a large number of people, or whatever it is you are studying. Asking people to complete questionnaires at conferences, meetings, schools, colleges, or any other place where people are gathered can result in the collection of hundreds of completed forms in a comparatively short amount of time. You can achieve the same thing in a few days by sending people questionnaires. As a result, you can quickly obtain a vast quantity of information at your disposal. This seeming simplicity, though, could be misleading because there is no assurance that the method of administration you have chosen will yield consistent outcomes or a high response rate.

Second, it can be quite simple and quick to produce at least some of the results after you have your completed questionnaires. A software package can be used to carry out numerical analysis. Currently, it is relatively simple to enter data directly into a computer or set up a pre-coded questionnaire so that the responses can be scanned in to the computer. Entering data by hand can take some time. Once more, a word of caution: data errors can cause issues, and advanced statistical knowledge and data manipulation are frequently needed to produce more complex and valuable results.

Third, generalizations to a larger population are possible as long as the sample is a well-founded probability sample with a reasonable response rate. This is one of the survey's main advantages over alternative research methods. These factors have led to the widespread use of questionnaires as a method of inquiry. However, they also have disadvantages. One is that because they are now so popular, people may get "questionnaire fatigue" and find it difficult to fill them out.

They are also a very stilted way to do research. They tend to simplify things because of the same characteristics that make them relatively simple to finish. A questionnaire can be a handy tool for gathering factual data, classifying information, and creating rankings and scales, but it is less helpful for examining intricate processes and shades of meaning. Another issue is validity: it's hard to guarantee that every respondent understands a question in the same way. Therefore, it is probably best to use questionnaires when you know exactly what you want to know—possibly from prior fieldwork—and you want to be able to extrapolate the findings to a much larger population. Due to their limitations, questionnaires should only be created after a fair amount of planning and preliminary work has been done. It is also best to avoid attempting to use them in an attempt to accomplish an impossible task. Examples of when a questionnaire might be appropriate in criminology are:

- Crime surveys, where a study is being undertaken of people's experiences of, or views about, crime-related matters;
- Questionnaires for criminal justice personnel about some aspect of their work.

5.3.3.2. Collecting the Data

Actually, the word "questionnaire" refers to a wide range of data gathering methods. These differ based on the information's source and the manner of collection (Table 5.1). The most common image that people have when they think of a questionnaire survey is that of a researcher interviewing a respondent in-person from a sample using a clipboard. It's not the only way of administration, even though it's fairly popular. It is among the best because it allows for both visual and verbal interaction, allowing the participants to express themselves most effectively. A popular substitute is the quick and reasonably priced phone interview. The fact that not everyone had access to a phone in the past made telephone interviews problematic and resulted in a skewed sample. Landlines helped to lessen this issue, but the proliferation of cell phones in recent years has made things more difficult because people are more likely to rely on their phones, which make it more difficult for researchers to get in touch with them. Given that telephone surveys frequently rely on landlines, they may leave out specific populations that don't have access to personal landlines, such as those who are homeless, live in hostels, or don't have a place of their own. In addition, conducting interviews over the phone lacks the personal touch of in-person interviews and has lost value due to its increased use in marketing campaigns. However, it might still be helpful when interviewing individuals who are speaking on behalf of companies or organizations.

The internet has also been utilized to collect online questionnaire responses, which has the benefit of anonymity. When an organization wants information from its employees, students, clients, and so on, it is probably especially helpful; that is, if the person making the inquiry has access to a database or sample frame. Nonetheless, its applicability to general population surveys is restricted due to the greater challenge of obtaining a feasible sample frame. Moreover, a 2003 study discovered that even "even after very considerable weighting of the results has been undertaken or care exercised to ensure that those who are asked to complete an internet poll are demographically and politically representative of the whole population," results from online surveys are not always representative of the population as a whole. A convenient and reasonably priced method of surveying a large number of individuals or organizations is through postal questionnaires. However, response rates may be low, particularly if the questionnaire is received "out of the blue" by the recipient. Additionally, the researcher has very little control over how the questionnaire is completed, and there is no chance to clarify any questions that the respondent might interpret in an unclear way.

Table 5.1. *Data Collection*

Methods of collection	*Who produces the infromation*
Face-to-face	Researcher
Telephone	Researcher's assistants
Internet	Agency staff
Postal	Respondent

Source: http://ndl.ethernet.edu.et/bitstream/123456789/23015/1/228.pdf.

5.3.3.3. Who Produces the Information?

Who participates in the collection process is an additional crucial factor to take into account. When respondents choose self-completion, you have less control over how the questions are interpreted and must take care to ensure they understand what is expected of them. Self-completion involves respondents providing the data directly. If interviews are being used for collection, who is conducting the interviews? If assistants are being used, they must receive training to guarantee consistency in the process. Workers in an organization that assists the individuals under investigation may occasionally be able to gather or supply information. For instance, the mediators will probably be interviewing referrals anyhow if you are studying a victim-offender mediation program, and they can explain that they wish to ask questions that will also be used for research. Similarly, a large portion of the data for a study on offenders participating in employment and training programs may come from forms filled out by project staff members when participants join and discontinue the program. People may be reluctant to tell project workers certain things in such circumstances, so it's important to keep in mind that the relationship between the worker and client differs from that between the researcher and respondent. It is important to remember that although these employees might be skilled in their field, they may not have received training as researchers or be aware of the demands of the field.

Information extracted from agency records is one type of data collection that follows a similar principle. Data gathered for court or medical records is gathered to satisfy the needs of the relevant agency, not research needs.

There might be a lot of material to sort through, and some important pieces of information might not be available or might not be in the best format for researchers. For instance, the prior convictions of offenders may be a crucial piece of information in a study on sentencing in magistrate's courts. It is possible, though, that this information was kept by the Crown Prosecution Service or the police after the case was resolved, and is not currently in the court files. It may therefore be necessary to contact these agencies as well.

Apart from the aforementioned, it is imperative to take into account the conditions under which data is gathered. Which people will be interviewed, if a family, agency, or business is involved, for example? The mode of collection has an impact on the validity and reliability of the data as well as the expected response rate. Will it be in the street, on the doorstep, in offices? If respondents are not guaranteed privacy and confidentiality, it is unlikely that the information gathered is reliable. The information is unlikely to be trustworthy if different people ask the same questions in different ways. Response rates are significant because they can skew the results because individuals who choose not to answer a questionnaire might differ from those who do in some way. You will be less able to extrapolate from your chosen sample to the entire population if the response rate is low. Responses to surveys about one's intention to vote are one instance of this. Any extrapolation from the survey to likely election results may be incorrect if those who are likely to vote for a specific party also dislike being asked how they will vote. This is what happened during the General Election of 1991. It is inevitable that those who have broken the law will be reluctant to tell a stranger about it, which makes it challenging, but not impossible, to conduct reliable surveys of the offending rates based on self-report. If respondents are unprepared for postal questionnaires, they are especially likely to receive low response rates. Offering to pay respondents or rewarding participants with coupons or prizes has been one strategy used to address the response rate issue. This gives rise to accusations that people who accept these offers will respond in an untrustworthy manner because they are acting for the "wrong" reason or may provide information in an attempt to appease the person who is calling the shots.

The question that inevitably arises is, "What constitutes an acceptable response rate?" To which the inevitable response is, "There is no definitive answer." It is customary in social science research that, for a general population survey employing in-person interactions based on a reliable sampling frame, a minimum of 60% of respondents would be considered acceptable. However, this implies that four out of 10 sample participants are disregarded, which introduces a significant degree of uncertainty. Because you might be working with populations that are difficult to establish contact with, the circumstances for getting a good response in criminology aren't always ideal. Instead of accepting a low response rate, though, the solution to this is to minimize the possibility of non-response when designing the study. This can entail reaching out to individuals via a middleman, like an organization they are already in contact with. For instance, you could get in touch with known offenders by using the probation or jail services. An alternative route to access could be through organizations that assist victims or offenders.

5.3.3.4. Drafting the Questionnaire

1. **Content:** The theoretical underpinnings of the investigation and the hypotheses being investigated or tested dictate what goes into a questionnaire in any empirical study. Thus, you begin by enquiring as to what data is required in order to test or formulate hypotheses. Every question should ideally be considered a variable, with some variables serving as independent, some as dependent, and some as intervening factors. A few of the variables will be classificatory or demographic information, like marital status, age, sex, and ethnicity. These are probably going to be the independent factors that the dependent variables are measured against. The topics you are most interested in learning more about will be covered by additional questions, and these will probably make up the dependent variables. Thus, for instance, a very basic survey might be interested in learning what people think about different facets of crime and associated issues. This might lead to hypotheses such as:
   - whether younger people are more in favor of legalizing cannabis than older people;
   - whether people from higher income groups are more liberal towards convicted offenders than those from lower income groups;
   - whether men have more confidence in the police than women.

   The respondent's attributes (gender, income, and age) serve as independent variables in each of these cases, while their opinions on various subjects serve as dependent variables. Additionally, there might be some intervening factors that are considered. For instance, when comparing people's opinions on whether cannabis should be legalized, it may be crucial to take into account respondents' personal cannabis use histories and examine the impact of these factors in addition to age differences – a three-way analysis. It is also important to keep in mind that an item may be a dependent or intervening variable in relation to one hypothesis while acting as an independent variable in the context of another. For instance, income is the independent variable in the second hypothesis mentioned above regarding income and perceptions of offenders. However, gender would be the independent variable and income would be the dependent variable if our hypothesis were true—that is, that men generally make more money than women. When creating a questionnaire, take into account the purpose of each question. Regardless of the topic, it is generally a good idea to go over the final draft and consider the purpose of each and every question, how you plan to use it in the analysis, and what you want to do with the findings. This involves several considerations: theoretical (every question should have a theoretical justification somewhere along the line), pragmatic (having an excessively lengthy questionnaire that wastes a lot of material is pointless), and ethical (why are you asking someone something if it's not really necessary?).

2. **Sequence:** When drafting a questionnaire, it is quite important to think about the order in which questions will be asked. There are a variety of reasons for this:
   - One of them is to just consider what order will make the most sense and be most cozy for the responders. One of the issues with this is that you shouldn't start off by asking a lot of personal questions to people you don't know well. Conversely, it might be crucial to find out people's age and background to determine if they fit into any specific categories that are relevant to the discussion that follows. In addition, it's a good idea to record some important information in case the questionnaire isn't completed for any reason.
   - Another reason for giving careful thought to the sequence of questions is what is referred to as routing. Some questions may be not applicable to all respondents and they need to be directed to the next question that is appropriate for them, for example:
     - o Have you been burgled within the last six months?
     - o If yes, go to Question X; If no, go to Question Y.

     These are loop-related filter questions. To ensure that respondents will be guided through the questionnaire in the correct order and won't be left stuck, it could be helpful to create a flow chart.
   - The timing of events. If, as an example, you are interviewing

someone about their history of employment and offending, it may be necessary to have a question sequence that takes them through a sequence of time, such as since they left school, or over the past three years. This could be done diagrammatically by showing them a dated timeline. Remember that you also need to think about how it is going to be analyzed subsequently.

- Multiple events. It's possible that some people have had multiple experiences. Some people may have experienced multiple instances of victimization or a string of fines that preceded them becoming defaulters, for instance, if you are asking about their experiences. It might be necessary to ask someone the same set of questions multiple times, once for each experience that is to be recorded. It might be worthwhile to think about whether information is required regarding all of the incidents, those that occurred within a specific time frame (like the last year), the last three incidents, or just the most recent one. Even though you might overlook significant experiences for specific people, a well-sized probability sample will ensure that the overall picture is representative of the sample. Once more, careful consideration should be given to the analysis of a sequence of incidents.
- Lastly, the sequence in which questions are posed may have an impact on the responses that are received. If you were to ask people, for instance, what sentences they believe burglars should receive after asking them about the effects burglaries have on their victims, you might get different answers than if you asked people first what sentences they believe burglars should receive before asking them about the effects burglaries have on victims.

3. **Question Construction:** There are a number of important rules about question composition:
   - **Avoid Leading or Biased Questions:** A research inquiry is rarely, if ever, truly "objective," as asking certain questions instead of others implies that you are approaching the subject from a specific angle. But every effort should be made to ensure that the questions are as impartial as possible. Therefore, it is better to ask, "Are you for or against hanging?" as opposed to, "Are you in favor of hanging?"
   - **One Idea Per Question:** Attempting to squeeze too much

information out of each question is a common mistake made when attempting to keep questionnaires as short as possible. This may lead to an excessively complicated query. Asking someone how they typically get to and from work, for instance, is inappropriate because different people may have different commutes. Here, two questions are required as opposed to one.

– **Use Simple Sentence Construction:** Clearly defined terms, and avoid jargon. The more complex a question is, the more chance of a misunderstanding occurring.
– **Beware of 'Social Desirability' Effects:** For instance, asking someone, "Are you in favor of recycling?" is unlikely to cause them to disagree, but it might not accurately represent their actual opinions or actions. According to one study, kids learn how to control their reactions so they don't openly display their ethnic prejudices. In a similar vein, steer clear of questions that have "obvious" answers, like "Are you against cruelty to children?" or "Are you afraid of crime?" Instead, ask hypothetical questions, be more specific, or list potential concerns and ask respondents to rank the top two.

It is a good idea to put yourself in the position of the respondent and think about how you might answer a question.

5.4. SOURCES OF STATUTES

Statutes come from a variety of sources and are essential to a jurisdiction's legal system and legislative process. Gaining an understanding of these sources is crucial to understanding the creation, interpretation, and application of laws. The primary sources of statutes include:

- **Legislatures:** The legislature—whether federal, state, or local—is the main source of statutes. State legislatures pass state laws in the US, whereas Congress enacts federal statutes. Ordinances are imposed by local governments, such as county boards and city councils. These legislative bodies draft, discuss, and decide on bills that, once signed into law by the executive branch (e.g., either the mayor, governor, or president).
- **Executive Orders:** Executive orders signed by the president or state governors may have legal authority even though they are not statutes in the conventional sense. These directives are frequently used to carry out policies that fall under the purview of the executive branch

and to guide the activities of government agencies. Executive orders may occasionally have an impact on how current laws are interpreted and applied.

- **Administrative Agencies:** Statutory-created administrative agencies are empowered to promulgate regulations with legal force behind them. These rules interpret and carry out legislative directives. In addition, agencies possess quasi-legislative authority, which enables them to address matters not specifically mentioned in the statute. Particularly in intricate and specialized fields like labor laws, securities regulation, and environmental regulation, the ensuing rules and regulations are crucial sources of law.
- **Constitutions:** Both the U.S. Constitution and state constitutions are fundamental sources of statutory law. They establish the framework for government authority and set forth the basic rights and principles that statutes must adhere to. Constitutional provisions often require legislative action to be fully implemented and can also limit the scope of statutory law.
- **International Treaties and Agreements:** After they are ratified, international treaties and agreements are included in the statutes. Legislative action may be necessary to fully implement the provisions of these agreements, which have the potential to impact domestic statutes. Trade, human rights, and environmental protection are just a few of the many topics that treaties may address.
- **Judicial Decisions:** Statutory law is derived from judicial interpretations of statutes, not the statutes themselves. Court decisions have the power to effectively establish new legal principles or clarify those that already exist. Courts are crucial in interpreting the meaning and application of statutes. The interpretation and application of future statutes are guided by this corpus of case law.

Each of these sources contributes to the dynamic and evolving nature of statutory law, shaping the legal landscape and ensuring that laws remain relevant and effective in addressing societal needs and challenges.

5.4.1. Case Laws and Its Sources

Judicial precedent, or case law, is a corpus of law that is created by judges making decisions in court rather than by legislative acts or executive branch directives. It is an essential source of law, especially in common law jurisdictions where the interpretation and application of the law are determined by earlier court rulings. The opinions and decisions rendered by trial, appellate, and supreme courts constitute the main source of case law. These rulings interpret laws, rules, and constitutional clauses; they frequently close legislative gaps and shed light on murky legal matters. Furthermore, case law can originate from several judicial levels, with rulings from higher courts usually carrying greater weight and serving as legally binding precedent for lesser courts operating under the same jurisdiction. Legal principles established by common law, which is derived from enduring customs and judicial practices, are another source of case law. Judicial rulings continuously mold this corpus of unwritten laws, mirroring the changing social mores and customs. Additionally, case law is influenced by international judicial bodies like the European Court of Human Rights and the International Court of Justice, especially when it comes to issues pertaining to human rights and international law. All things considered, case law acts as a dynamic and interpretive source of law, making sure that legal systems continue to be adaptable to changing social norms and new situations.

5.4.2. Foreign Cases and Statutes

Statutes and court rulings from foreign jurisdictions are referred to as "foreign cases" and "enactments." These legal resources are essential for international legal practice and comparative law studies because they show how various legal systems handle related problems. International treaties, customary international law, and domestic laws as interpreted by foreign courts are all included in the category of foreign cases. When examining the ways in which various legal traditions—such as common law, civil law, or mixed legal systems—resolve legal disputes, these cases are especially helpful. International collaboration and harmonization are crucial in fields like commercial law, environmental law, and human rights, where foreign court rulings can have a significant impact on domestic case law. Legislative enactments from other countries are known as foreign statutes. Local governments, regional legislatures, and national parliaments have all passed laws that fall under this category. Legal academics and practitioners can compare legislative strategies, comprehend various regulatory frameworks, and find best practices that could be modified for their own legal systems by studying foreign statutes. Examining foreign labor laws, health laws, or environmental policies, for example, can provide fresh insights and creative solutions to typical legal problems. Foreign statutes are important for guaranteeing adherence to international obligations because international treaties and agreements frequently demand the implementation of particular statutes in participating countries. Furthermore, international business operations, immigration, and cross-border transactions may be impacted by foreign statutes, so a comprehensive understanding is necessary for efficient legal practice in a globalized society. All things considered, international cases and statutes contribute to the advancement of cross-jurisdictional understanding, legal innovation, and the creation of coherent international legal norms.

5.4.3. Analysis of Cases and Statutes

Investigation of cases in a designated problem area constitutes the majority of legal research. Setting legal trends is a difficult undertaking. Helping with the precise fact and its nature are very difficult issues. The proceedings in Coasts typically center on factual issues related to specific criminal trials. Court battles are won and lost according to which party can provide more evidence to support its claims. As stated by William J. Grode and Paul K. Hatt" an observation is considered an empirically verifiable fact. The fact could be a law, a behavior, or an attitude. What is the rationale behind accepting or rejecting something as fact? This aspect is criminal to the electric is a criminal case is the central question of doctrinal research on criminal justice. How are facts established? There are three common bases for establishing facts:

- Authority;
- Infusion; and
- Logic but these methods may lead us to false conclusion.

Therefore a scientific method has developed for establishing facts. Systematically collects data, undertake tests for their internal consistency and subjects them to empirical examination. Thus scientific information is based on reliable and valid observation.

The researcher must undertake case interpretation following the verification of facts. However, prior to that, the data must be broken down into its component parts in order to answer the research question or hypothesis. Using the legal system as an example, let's say a researcher believes there is a link between poverty and criminality. He gathers sociological information about the individuals found guilty in court cases over time from court records, and he then has to arrange, panic, and manipulate the information in order to find the answer to the research question or conjecture. He gathers sociological data from court records and case files about individuals found guilty of theft over time. He then has to arrange, deconstruct, and manipulate the information to find the answer to the research question. A study may also examine the judges' attitudes. While rendering a decision in a given case, a judge attempts to make generalizations (ratios) by connecting the case to more general social and historical concerns concerning that specific society in addition to discussing the land and circumstances (facts) of that particular case. He might make obiter dicta that have an impact on how people behave in social situations and how big-picture issues are handled.

REFERENCES

1. Arber, S. (2001). Secondary analysis of survey data. In N. Gilbert (Ed.), *Researching Social Life* (pp. 263–279). Sage Publications.
2. Atkinson, P. (1981). Transition from school to working life. Sociological Research Unit, Cardiff. (Unpublished memorandum).
3. Atkinson, R., & Flint, J. (2001). Accessing hidden and hard-to-reach populations: Snowball research strategies. *Social Research Update, 33*. University of Surrey.
4. Crow, I., Howells, G., & Moroney, M. (1993). Credit and debt: Choices for poorer consumers. In G. Howells, I. Crow, & M. Moroney (Eds.), *Aspects of Credit and Debt* (pp. 47–65). Sweet and Maxwell.
5. Denzin, N. K. (1988). *The Research Act: A Theoretical Introduction to Sociological Methods*. Prentice Hall.
6. Goode, W. J., & Hatt, P. K. (1952). *Methods of Social Research*. McGraw-Hill.
7. Kershaw, C. (1998). Interpreting reconviction rates. In *The Use and Impact of Community Supervision* (Research Bulletin No. 39, Special Edition, pp. 9–16). Home Office Research and Statistics Directorate.
8. Lewins, A. (2001). Computer-assisted qualitative data analysis. In N. Gilbert (Ed.), *Researching Social Life* (pp. 266–282). Sage Publications.
9. Maguire, M. (2002). Crime statistics: The 'data explosion' and its implications. In M. Maguire, R. Morgan, & R. Reiner (Eds.), *The Oxford Handbook of Criminology* (3rd ed., pp. 236–268). Oxford University Press.
10. Morgan, D. L. (1992). Designing focus group research. In M. Stewart (Ed.), *Tools for Primary Care Research* (pp. 203–220). Sage.
11. Morgan, D. L. (2006). Focus groups. In V. Jupp (Ed.), *The Sage Dictionary of Social Research Methods* (pp. 114–115). Sage.
12. Morgan, D. L., & Krueger, R. A. (1993). When to use focus groups and why. In D. L. Morgan (Ed.), *Successful Focus Groups: Advancing the State of the Art* (pp. 3–19). Sage.
13. Moyser, G., & Wagstaffe, M. (1987). *Research Methods for Elite Studies*. Allen and Unwin.
14. O'Leary, Z. (2004). *The Essential Guide to Doing Research*. Sage Publications.
15. Oppenheim, A. N. (2000). *Questionnaire Design, Interviewing and Attitude Measurement*. Continuum.

16. Rutland, A., Cameron, L., Milne, A., & McGeorge, P. (2005). Social norms and self-presentation: Children's implicit and explicit intergroup attitudes. *Child Development, 76*(2), 451–466.
17. Sampson, R. J., & Raudenbush, S. W. (1999). Systematic social observation of public spaces: A new look at disorder in urban neighborhoods. *American Journal of Sociology, 105*(3), 603–651.
18. Schuman, H., & Presser, S. (1996). *Questions and Answers in Attitude Surveys: Experiments on Question Form, Wording, and Context*. Sage.
19. Selltiz, C., Wrightsman, L. S., & Cook, S. W. (1964). *Research Methods in Social Relations*. New York: Holt, Rinehart & Winston.
20. Sherman, L. W., Gottfredson, D. C., MacKenzie, D. L., Eck, J., Reuter, P., & Bushway, S. D. (1998). *Preventing Crime: What Works, What Doesn't, and What's Promising*. U.S. Department of Justice, National Institute of Justice.
21. Smith, J. K. (1983). Quantitative versus qualitative research: An attempt to clarify the issue. *Educational Researcher, 12*(3), 6–13.
22. Spalek, B. (1995). Trust as an ideology: Exploring fear of white-collar crime. Paper presented at the British Criminology Conference, Loughborough University, July 18–21.

Chapter **6**

Crime Prevention and Control

Contents

INTRODUCTION

The topic of crime prevention is broad and includes a wide range of initiatives and programs. Crime prevention efforts can target a wide range of crimes, and their various approaches focus on different factors that contribute to crime. As a result, attempts to prevent crime will usually involve a variety of actors. Crime prevention has a lot of advantages. The human costs associated with crime victims are decreased when a criminal incident is prevented or does not occur in the future. It is possible to prevent bodily harm, save lives, and reduce financial loss. This is the reason why many governments and other organizations find crime prevention to be very appealing, and the reason crime prevention has grown in importance as a field of study and application. Nonetheless, there are issues with crime prevention. In the name of preventing crime, governments and private organizations may try to monitor and control the populace; crime prevention may turn into a commodity that is sold to the wealthy, making the poor even more vulnerable; the pursuit of crime prevention may stigmatize individuals and groups; and victims may be held accountable for causing their own suffering. As a result, it's critical to always take into account the unfavorable side effects of crime prevention initiatives. Recognizing that regional and local contexts differ significantly in terms of law, culture, and politics is crucial because it affects the way that crime prevention is thought of and implemented. Around the world, even the term "crime prevention" will be used differently, if at all. It is extremely problematic that the majority of the knowledge on crime prevention originates from a limited number of nations and areas. Certain methods may be beneficial in one situation but detrimental in another. Techniques used to lower crime in a community are referred to as crime control. Police work is standardized by crime control. In certain nations, crime prevention is also extensively enforced by government law enforcement as well as, frequently, private policing techniques like home defense and private security. Nevertheless, deploying the police or security forces might not always be the best course of action to stop a crime from happening.

6.1. CONCEPT OF CRIME PREVENTION

In today's common parlance, the word "prevention" has two meanings: "warn awareness" and "prevent, overtake and prevent something." Preventive criminology uses the word "prevention" in its original sense, meaning that the goal of employing various methods to stop delinquency is to stop the crime of falling into and emerging from delinquency. By addressing their various causes, crime prevention strategies and tactics aim to lessen the likelihood of crimes happening as well as their possible negative impacts on people and society, such as fear of crime. To effectively prevent conflict, violence, and violations of human rights, actors in the justice system must work in tandem with those in other sectors to address the underlying causes of disputes. This means that in terms of crime and violence, evidence-based prevention that lowers levels of violence—especially against women, children, and vulnerable groups—must replace punitive measures. In order to ensure effective communication and seamless referrals of specific cases to the right service providers that serve the interests of the parties involved, it also means that sectors that deal with offenders and victims, such as social workers, prosecution authorities, and defense attorneys, should be included in the implementation of prevention programs. The prevention of juvenile criminality and public delinquency is the most traditional form of prevention. This distinction states that adult offenders should be used as frightening and threatening punishment because their personalities have already been shaped, whereas children and adolescent juvenile offenders whose personalities are still forming should be used.

6.1.1. Types of Prevention

1. **Primary Prevention:** The main goal of prevention is to shield people from engaging in any criminal activity that is related to social development. People are making an effort to avoid crime at this point in the prevention process. The purpose of prevention at this level is to create values that strengthen healthy relationships and to make living conditions better so as not to offend anyone. Primary prevention focuses more on the crime event than the offender who initiated it. The lifestyle theory of Hendel Lang has also been connected to this method.
2. **Secondary Prevention:** Using strategies to safeguard vulnerable populations is secondary prevention such as addicts, homeless people, and street kids. By using appropriate and early measures, the goal of this type of prevention is to stop people who are in critical condition and likely to become victims from committing crimes. When it comes to preventing addiction, for instance, the emphasis is on people who amuse themselves recreationally and have not yet developed an addiction. Additionally, there is a higher likelihood of criminal activity among young people who have experienced domestic violence or who come from low-income families and poorly maintained neighborhoods.
3. **Tertiary Prevention:** Programs like family and child counselling, criminal interventions, and different groups are included in this type of prevention. In order for criminals to adapt to their social

surroundings and refrain from committing crimes again, prevention efforts at this point aim to stop criminal behavior. When operations are detected in order to apprehend the offender, house a convicted individual in jail, or sentence and rehabilitate a prisoner, the third prevention is used.

4. **Short-Term Prevention:** A collection of temporary fixes is known as short-term prevention. In addressing social and cultural issues, one cannot ignore short- and long-term preventive measures due to systematic and long-term planning. Examples of such measures include: increasing street and alley lighting, creating more deterrent criminal laws, establishing work institutions, offering decent recreational facilities, safeguarding children who are harassed and abused by their families, closing neighborhoods and crime scenes, prohibiting the broadcast of violent television shows, and arming law enforcement and police personnel.

5. **Social Prevention:** Through interfering with an individual's growth, enhancing their living circumstances, and normalizing social and natural norms, this type of prevention aims to eradicate or lessen the causes of crime and, consequently, prevent delinquency. This type of prevention is referred to as social prevention because it focuses on the shortcomings of juvenile offenders and their environment of growth while avoiding meddling in police and justice discussions. This is the result of social worker prevention experiences.

   This kind of prevention basically aims to help alter the state of delinquency in local and residential communities, with one of its objectives being to lessen or eradicate the social environment's role as a source of crime. Examples of this kind of prevention include the creation of parks and recreational areas, the establishment of educational, cultural, and recreational centers, the creation of jobs and income in neighborhoods, the reinforcement of religious beliefs through the appropriate and effective activation of local religious centers, the formation of local law enforcement, and the development of tools and programs like youth sports clubs and activity-based projects to deter current and potential offenders from making the same mistakes again. Coordinating community members with respect to social norms is another objective of social prevention, which has an "individual" focus. Put another way, social prevention is the same as criminal prevention, offender and individual, and it aims to instill in the individual the ability to recognize good and bad deeds and the power to evaluate their performance by means of education, persuasion, education, and punishment. The fundamental idea behind this prevention model is the specialization, thought, and duplication of effort. Due to the size and complexity of the issue, despite enormous and massive investments, the desired result in the reduction of crime is not achieved.

Advocates of this preventive approach contend that by identifying the social and personal factors that contribute to criminal behavior and addressing them through individual and societal reforms—such as treating illnesses and mental health issues, strengthening social institutions, and providing excellent access to housing, recreational, educational, and other opportunities—criminal tendencies can be avoided in people. As social environment has an impact on an individual's personality and motivations, social prevention is actually a set of controls over factors that influence the formation of crime. This is why some refer to it as Individual-Based Prevention. By influencing at-risk groups, social prevention also aims to reinforce the pillars that support socialization. Stated differently, social prevention aims to educate people so that they are in harmony with social norms. The goal of this kind of prevention should be to remove as many individuals from the criminal justice system as feasible. Social prevention, as a general term, refers to actions that modify the social, economic, and cultural context of crime in an effort to address the underlying causes of criminal behavior problems. Because of this, the best way to characterize primary prevention is through social prevention.

6. **Developmental Prevention:** Through early intervention in the child and his surroundings, this type of prevention aims to stop a child from committing crimes in the future if the child ever shows signs of criminal activity. Early psychosocial intervention and prevention during a child's developmental stage can reduce risk factors that could lead to an admission of guilt or a pattern of persistent criminal behavior in the future. A variety of personal and societal factors, including appearance, persistence, and sustainability of future criminal behavior in children and adolescents, are risk factors in this prevention. This type of prevention is characterized by its behavioral, personal, and general aspects. Its founders believe that early intervention can prevent delinquency and the persistence of criminal offenses against individuals exposed to particular circumstances because of specific situations. They also believe that early psycho-social interventions at the school, family, and social

environment can help identify individual and social risk factors and subsequently utilize supportive factors.

7. **Long Term Prevention:** The term "long-term prevention" describes procedures that are implemented over an extended period of time in order to lower the likelihood of future crimes. For example: Creating and executing general policies for community members' engagement; Developing family education programs to improve life skills; Strengthening the preventive role of schools through content promotion; Providing suitable platforms for individuals to access appropriate education opportunities. Police stations and police stations are required to use these types of planning to prevent various crimes such as theft, street harassment, evasion, and harassment. Other factors that affect social justice include the quality of education and training programs, efforts to close the economic gap among different classes of society, and quality of education. Policies that are structured, process-driven, and focused on specific and general crime factors in a broad and inclusive manner—including social, economic, cultural, political, and legal factors—are taken into consideration in this prevention strategy to eradicate or suppress offenders.
8. **Shame Prevention:** Certain standard preventive measures, like police warnings, are not precautionary or deterrent in nature; rather, they merely exert a passive influence on these behaviors. This is known as passive prevention. Social factors (social prevention) have no effect and don't play the slightest part in this type of prevention. Institutions that play a preventive role, like the police and the courts, also have very little influence.
9. **Active Prevention:** The primary goal of this type of prevention, which is implemented to deter crime and is also active at the social level, is the police force. In other words, when it comes to organizing and supervising a group of youth who are exposed to crime or deviance at a particular time and location, the police handle it. In the meantime, it is clear that deterrents of crime play a role in preventing crime or deviation at a given time and location. Active prevention involves long-term planning aimed at preventing and reducing delinquency. Government representatives act independently and play a significant role in society.
10. **Non-Penal Prevention:** Preventing the outcome of criminal intent and thought by altering the conditions under which a number of related crimes have occurred or might be committed is known as

non-penal prevention. Put differently, non-criminal prevention seeks to eradicate the underlying factors that contribute to crime and delinquency by tackling the problem of social control and its influence on criminal cognition, with the ultimate goal of raising people to abstain from crime. In this type of prevention, it's critical to consider the social, cultural, economic, and environmental elements that influence an individual's propensity for crime. In actuality, noncustodial prevention—for which the legal system's remedies are inappropriate—is the primary cause of crime prior to crime. Another name for this kind of prevention that opposes criminal prevention is "new prevention." Non-penal prevention, as it is actually called, is a non-criminal act that aims to prevent crime and crime by minimizing or doing away with criminal and improper ways of showcasing crime situations.

Therefore, preventive action features include:

- Effects on the factors or processes that play a decisive role in delinquency;
- Collective; in the sense that it targets the whole population or a certain group;
- Lack of coherence and action.

Thus, delinquents' elimination and neutralization as well as victim position changes or elimination constitute non-criminal prevention. Non-penal prevention essentially obstructs the process by which an idea turns into a criminal act from the outset.

11. **Penal Prevention:** Essentially, Penal Prevention is the subsequent phase that is implemented within the framework of Criminal Justice. Depending on the impact on society or the offender, this prevention is separated into two categories: "general reaction prevention" and "specific reaction prevention." General reaction prevention is a type of reactive prevention that works with groups or collectives to address citizens through horrifying and group-based learning in order to stop criminal delinquency. A specific reaction prevention is a reactive prevention of a criminal offender that aims to deter delinquent individuals by punishing the criminal and providing them with dreadful, individualized training. Reactive or criminal prevention, in general, refers to the use of the criminal justice system's mechanisms to reduce crime rates through criminal proceedings both before and after the crime.

A terrifying, individual, group, and educational tool to stop early delinquency and redress among people is the reactive prevention approach. By combining noncriminal preventive areas of crime and the use of both elements, this type of prevention can play a significant role in reducing crime in the community, even though it is not a sole response to the social and security needs of the community. The last line of defense against crime should be criminal prevention due to its numerous drawbacks and the impact it has on convicted felons' future lives in society. Criminal reform, community protection, intimidation, and general prevention through intimidating others are the general goals of criminal prevention.

12. **Judicial Prevention:** A sort of crime prevention known as "judicial prevention" is predicated on the endeavors of the government and the relevant institutions to lessen crime and eradicate its causes. This policy is analyzed within the framework of judicial prevention, wherein the state or the ruling apparatus takes the lead in combating crime and delinquent behavior by enacting laws and legislation that target the offenders. One method of preventing crime in policy-making is through crime prevention. "A process in which actions that are in conflict with their interests are prohibited and penalized" is how this approach is described. However, this restriction on people's lives shouldn't go beyond the parameters and intent of societal goals. One of the key components of the criminal justice system is the use of judicial prevention to reduce crime. In the executive and legal branches of government, judicial and legal prevention contributes to the criminalization and intimidation of criminals, particularly potential criminals, and until it does so, it essentially keeps criminals from committing crimes and from committing them again. The judiciary's efforts to prevent crime can include the drafting of suitable legislation for changing criminal policy and reforming the law from the perspectives of religious education and wisdom, including victimization, decriminalization, punishment, and the drawbacks of legalizing penalties.

13. **Disciplinary Prevention:** People's sense of security is based on the fact that every society has weaknesses. Because of their thoughts and intentions, a group of unhealthy people in the community cause conditions of weakness and instability in certain parts of society by acting in an unconventional way and against social norms. Governments and authorities have tried to control and reduce crimes through the implementation of crime prevention programs in order to prevent insecurity and increase social security. One of

the public security guards' primary responsibilities is to thwart law enforcement, which includes police and law enforcement. In order to deter criminal activity and lessen its recurrence within the confines of the law, police prevention measures include: "Inhibition and control of crime through police actions, such as: increasing police patrols and the concrete and effective presence of police at the city level." In order to take action against the offender, act quickly to combat delinquency and crimes, and collaborate with the relevant authorities to lower crime, it is also important to look into the causes of delinquency and its process. Because it protects social security and order, regulatory prevention is crucial. The government and other relevant institutions are crucial in creating and preserving security in the prevention of law enforcement, and they operate within the bounds of the law.

14. **Common Prevention:** In general, delinquent behavior can be prevented by taking steps to stop crimes from being committed. This definition will thus include any legal action, whether criminal or not, under the purview of delinquency prevention. General prevention is a type of crime-based prevention that concentrates on intimidating the public, deterring crime, and providing criminal education. This kind of prevention involves setting laws, deciding on penalties, and enforcing them against offenders in an effort to stop people from committing crimes. In public prevention, instilling in anyone who might be inclined to commit crimes feelings of fear, intimidation, threats, punishments, and fear of losing credibility. By putting the general public at the center of the group of people who might be inclined to commit a crime, this level of prevention aims to deter public crime by raising public awareness.

15. **Special Prevention:** It refers to how a punishment works to keep an offender from committing the same crime. By punishing the offender and making him suffer from punishment, this kind of prevention aims to stop retaliation for the same crime or other crimes. Therefore, the main goal of the specific prevention, which takes the form of steps for the training, rehabilitation, and rehabilitation of criminals, is to prevent crime from recurring and to instill fear in those who have already committed a crime. Short-term benefits of this type of prevention include reducing addiction and removing unaccompanied minors from the streets. "A set of measures and actions aimed at combating delinquency by reducing or eliminating criminal causes and influencing prospective opportunities, so that

it can be exploited by means of action mechanisms Personality of individuals and positions before crime was committed" is what special prevention entails, according to this definition.

16. **Situational Prevention:** A combination of non-criminal and criminal measures known as "situational prevention" work to deter crime by removing or minimizing favorable conditions for crime and erroneous prosecution. This method's tactics, which center on altering the surroundings, aim to protect the victims as much as control the offenders. In the 1980s, Clark, Cornish, and Heeur proposed Situational Prevention as a scientific theory to lower delinquency. In order to lessen the circumstances and opportunities that encourage criminal behavior, as well as to alter the dynamic between the offender and the victim, they must always take the right actions in their line of work. This preventive technique aims to stop someone from committing a crime by committing a crime themselves. It achieves this by altering the victimization and criminal circumstances of the individual or by altering the location and timing of the crime. By supporting someone who is at risk of crime, one can shield them from becoming a victim and keep them from realizing they have committed a crime. In certain instances, shifting environmental factors—like time and place—make it more challenging to identify the crime of deprivation or occurrence. Situational prevention entails removing some risks and hazards, minimizing risks by minimizing the extent of damage, and minimizing risks by implementing security measures like installing CCTV cameras or augmenting the police force to deter crime. Crime, the transmission of some of the hazards by means of facilitating insurance and the like, and accepting some of the risks that are inevitable or removing them from imposition of unwarranted costs. This kind of prevention will take action to eliminate or lessen the conditions and opportunities for committing the crime, depending on the facts of the crime, its type, its goals and issues, and the victim's characteristics.

    Physical security measures or the layout of communities and buildings are implemented in tandem with the reduction of opportunities and crime scenes, which eventually results in risky and expensive criminal activities. This preventive approach, known as crime prevention management, aims to neutralize criminal operations—which are actually such complementary measures of police work—by changing people's lifestyles and environments. Consequently, conditional prevention—also known as "crime risk management"—

is the process of anticipating, identifying, and evaluating the crime risk and then taking appropriate action to either eliminate or reduce it. Because it is easier to increase the safety factor of the victim in a sexual crime than it is to dissuade the offender from committing a crime motivated by uncontrollable natural instincts and intrusions, sexual crime appears to be more effective in preventing crime overall. Sexual assault; secondly, it can be used more actively as a potential victim for prevention due to the extremely detrimental effects of this crime on morale, psychological tragedy, and the concern of potential victims, especially women.

6.1.2. Applying SCP to Information Systems (IS)

Generally speaking, situational crime prevention (SCP) aims to disassociate itself from dispositional theories of crime commission the impact of psychological elements or the criminal's genetic composition, and to concentrate on contextual and environmental elements that may have an impact on criminal behavior. Therefore, SCP focuses on the conditions that encourage the commission of crime rather than the criminal. When these conditions are recognized, policies that change the surrounding conditions are introduced in an effort to lessen the likelihood of criminal activity. Other aspects of SCP include:

- Targeting specific forms of crime, e.g., cybercrime;
- Aiming to increase the effort and decrease potential risks of crime;
- Reducing provocative phenomena.

6.1.2.1. Safeguarding

The safeguarding principle is another facet of SCP that is more relevant to the cyber environment. The purpose of implementing these protections is to sway the prospective offender's perception of the advantages and disadvantages of committing the crime. If the perpetrator determines that there is little to no risk involved, they typically carry out a criminal act. Putting safeguards in place to the extent that a potential offender perceives the act negatively is one of SCP's objectives. For example, if there is almost a 100% chance of being caught trying to run a red light, drivers approaching a traffic intersection with speed cameras slow down. It has been suggested that using crime scripts is one way to implement safety measures. Originally created in the field of cognitive science, scripts center on the behavioral mechanisms underlying goal-oriented rational behavior. Consequently, scripts have been suggested as a tool for investigating criminal activity. Specifically, the application of a so-called universal script has been proposed to accurately identify each step in the criminal commission process.

6.1.2.2. Application to Cybercrimes

Assessing cybercriminals according to their criminal attributes—skills, knowledge, resources, access, and motives—has been proposed (SKRAM). Since cybercriminals typically possess a high degree of these characteristics, SCP may be more beneficial to combating crime than more conventional methods. Clarke proposed a table of 25 techniques of situational crime prevention, but the five general headings are:

- Increasing the effort to commit the crime;
- Increasing the risks of committing the crime;
- Reducing the rewards of committing the crime;
- Reducing any provocation for committing the crime;
- Removing any excuses for committing the crime.

These techniques can be specifically adapted to cybercrime as follows:

1. **Increasing the Effort:** Target reinforcement and access control measures include the use of firewalls, encryption, card-and-password access to ID databases, and the prohibition of hacker magazines and websites.
2. **Reducing the Rewards:** Target removal and cyberspace disruption: keeping an eye on websites and incoming spam, enforcing strict penalties for hacking, promptly reporting lost or stolen credit bankcards, and avoiding using ID numbers on any official paperwork.
3. **Reducing Provocation and Excuses:** Preventing conflicts and temptations; upholding good management-employee relations; and raising awareness of the policy on responsible use. Many of these methods don't call for a significant investment in cutting-edge IT expertise. Rather, what matters is how well current staff members are used and trained. It has been proposed that by lowering the rewards that criminals might anticipate from committing a crime, the theory underlying situational crime prevention may also be helpful in enhancing the security of information systems (IS). SCP theory aims to affect the motivation of criminals by means of environmental and situational changes and is based on three elements:
   - Increasing the perceived difficulty of crime;
   - Increasing the risks; and
   - Reducing the rewards.

   The frequency of computer crime that targets the information assets of businesses and organizations could be decreased by using the same tactics by IS professionals and other interested parties. A key component of SCP is designing out crime from the environment. Predicting criminal behavior and making it more difficult for the criminal to commit the crime is the most effective way to use computers to combat crime. SCP is superior to other IS strategies in that it does not consider crime from the perspective of the criminal. Information and communications technology (ICT) is a vital component of many businesses and organizations, and because information is so readily available, it is a highly valuable asset. For this reason, IS has grown in significance. Although users can easily access and share information stored on computers, computer crime poses a serious threat to this data, whether it comes from external hackers or "insiders," or dependable employees of a company or organization. Information theft, unauthorized access, and viruses rank second and third in terms of the total financial losses brought on by computer crime and security incidents. Businesses must safeguard themselves from these illicit or immoral activities, which can be carried out electronically or through other means. Information security technologies are essential to preventing tampering, unauthorized disclosure, and/or misuse of data. Since hackers can read, write, and modify files in addition to reading emails, computer intrusion fraud is a big business. However, if hackers could be stopped from accessing a system or detected in time, this kind of crime could be virtually eradicated.

There are regular reports of computer intrusions and data thefts at some of the most well-protected computer systems in the world, despite years of computer security research, enormous sums of money being spent on secure operations, and an increase in training requirements. Due to computers being used for a variety of illicit purposes, such as credit card fraud, software piracy, and email surveillance, there is a rise in criminal activity in cyberspace. An increasing number of web applications and services are being established as a result of the Internet's growing popularity and use in business transactions. Because they are using ineffective controls, even cautious companies or businesses that strive to create comprehensive and effective security measures may unintentionally create an environment that helps provide opportunities in the case of computer crime. Consequently, the IS will be vulnerable if the safety measures do not offer a sufficient degree of protection.

4. **Situational Crime Prevention and Fraud:** Risk assessment,

which involves monitoring clientele, business transactions, and circumstances for any signs of criminal activity, is one of the strategies employed in computer systems designed to design out crime from the environment. Credit card fraud is one of the most complicated crimes that has occurred in the world recently, and even with a lot of preventative measures in place, more work clearly needs to be done to find a solution. A wide range of tasks fall under the umbrella of fraud management, such as early warning systems, patterns and indicators of various fraud types, user profiles and behavior, computer security, and preventing customer dissatisfaction. The enormous volume of data involved, the need for quick and accurate fraud detection without interfering with business operations, the constant development of new fraud to circumvent existing techniques, and the possibility of false alarms are just a few of the problems that make developing fraud management systems an incredibly tough and challenging task. Generally speaking, there are two types of fraud detection techniques: statistical techniques and artificial intelligence techniques.

Important statistical data analysis techniques to detect fraud include:

- Grouping and classification to determine patterns and associations among sets of data.
- Matching algorithms to identify irregularities in the transactions of users compared to previous proof.
- Data pre-processing techniques for validation, correction of errors and estimating incorrect or missing data.

Important AI techniques for fraud management are:

- Data mining – to categorize and group data and automatically identify associations and rules that may be indicative of remarkable patterns, including those connected to fraud.
- Specialist systems to program expertise for fraud detection in the shape of rules.
- Pattern recognition to identify groups or patterns of behavior either automatically or to match certain inputs.
- Machine learning techniques to automatically detect the characteristics of fraud.
- Neural networks that can learn suspicious patterns and later identify them.

6.1.3. Crime Prevention Through Environmental Design

Creating a "Total Environment" is how this strategy prevents crime. It is closely tied to rational choice theory and the antithesis of the police's reactive tactics. Policies that persuade potential offenders to abstain from criminal activity, postpone their actions, or avoid a specific target can help reduce crime. Thus crime prevention can be achieved through one of three ways.

- Potential targets are carefully guarded;
- Means to commit crime are controlled; and
- Potential offenders are carefully monitored.

Because people are so mobile, efforts to prevent crime that target them directly, like general and targeted deterrence, are less likely to be successful. People move around a lot during the day; they are not permanent fixtures of an environment for very long. Buildings and other physical elements of the surroundings, however, are more or less permanent. Therefore, CPTED may have an impact on perceptions of personal crime risk as well as crime.

1. **Control Natural Access:** Encouraging people to go where they will do no harm or receive no harm, e.g., using hedges, shrubs, gates and fences to direct people to the entrance and exits of buildings.
2. **Provide Natural Surveillance:** Placing potential crime targets in places where they can be watched easily, e.g., making front windows on houses face those across the street.
3. **Foster Territorial Behavior:** Marking territorial areas so that they are easily observed and noted, e.g., do landscaping so that it is readily apparent where one apartment ends and another begins.

The three primary design philosophies are applicable to the natural, organized, and mechanical strategies. In natural strategies, space arrangement and design determine security. There are minimal capital and human costs. Security guards and police officers are used to implement organized tactics. It is costly and labor-intensive. Mechanical strategies are costly and use hardware and surveillance equipment to manage access and provide surveillance. By keeping crime from occurring in the first place, natural strategies are more advantageous economically and minimize conflict (Jeffery, 1977).

Research has shown that:

1. Much of the practical applications of CPTED have been in target hardening which have been largely successful
2. Increasing street lighting in crime prone areas reduced crime.
3. Creating cul-de-sacs in very dangerous areas of a city reduced the occurrence of drive-by shootings.

4. Making entrances and exits into public housing area one way reduced crime overall in those areas.
5. Placing strategic barricades of streets leading into a major drug neighborhood in order to limit access reduced drug related offenses.

6.1.4. Crime Prevention Through Defensible Spaces

According to the Defensible Space theory, this tactic suggests creating a residential setting that encourages and permits neighbors to watch over and take responsibility for their communities. The defensible space theory has practical applications such as enhancing resident visibility between homes and apartment buildings and establishing gathering areas for residents, which raises the possibility of resident surveillance. Reducing isolation and anonymity among individuals and locations within a community is the main objective. A key part of improving Defensible space is to improve the control of local Space. Newman divides local space into four different categories:

- **Public:** Places like streets where no one has control or dominion.
- **Semi-Public:** Places like sidewalks in from of home that people treat as having some responsibility over, despite their public ownership.
- **Semi-Private:** Areas like the backyard of a house that are controlled by a person(s) but are within view of the public.
- **Private:** Places like homes in which people have complete ownership and are able to watch completely and deny access to others.

This theory holds that the secret to preventing crime is private supervision. Items left in public or semi-public areas are more likely to be stolen. The Defensible Space concepts were used in housing and school projects across the United States as a result of this theory's practical application (Newman, 1996).

Studies on Defensible Space revealed that overall crime was lower in government housing areas with low-rise buildings than high-rise ones. Low fence use promoted territoriality and reduced theft and burglary rates in residential areas. In residential areas, narrow streets improved neighborhood watch and reduced criminal activity. By reducing large public areas where surveillance is inadequate, the number of small parks rather than the number of large parks reduced crime incidents. However, there was very little effect of design modifications on overall crime in neighborhoods other than public housing complexes.

6.1.5. Situational Crime Prevention Strategies

There are several strategies under Situational Crime Prevention:

1. **Increase Effort Needed to Commit Crime:** This is proposed by:
   - **Hardening Targets:** Making the potential target of criminal victimization more difficult to victimize, e.g., unbreakable glass on store fronts, locking gates, fenced yards
   - **Controlling Access to the Targets:** Limiting access to an area in order to reduce criminals chance of offending, e.g., parking lot barriers, secure doors to stores
   - **Deflecting Offenders from Targets:** Locating business and services so as to divert criminal opportunity, e.g., residential behind retail in mixed use.
2. **Increase Risks of Committing Crime:** This is done by screening entrances and exits, using formal surveillance by employees and natural surveillance.
3. Reduce Rewards of Committing Crime:
   - Remove targets;
   - Identify property;
   - Reduce temptation;
   - Deny benefits.
4. Induce Guilt or Shame for Committing Crime:
   - Set rules;
   - Alert consciences;
   - Control dis-inhibitors;
   - Assist compliances.

Although studies show that situational crime prevention strategies have been very effective, the findings should be interpreted cautiously because many of the studies focus on relatively minor crimes. Rather than being street crimes against individuals, many of the crimes where strategies have proven effective have been crimes against private organizations. There have been very few follow-ups and no control groups in the less than scientific methods used to assess the tactics' efficacy.

6.1.6. Community Policing

The goal of community-oriented policing, also known as community policing (COP), is to build relationships with the people that make up the community. It's a very personal full-service policing philosophy in which an officer spends a lot of time patrolling the same area and builds relationships with the public to jointly identify and resolve issues. The intention is for police to lessen low-level crime and antisocial behavior by fostering relationships with the community, sometimes through channels like local agencies. According to certain academic research, community policing can also lower serious crimes (broken windows theory, for example). In contrast to the reactive policing tactics that dominated the late 20th century, community policing is associated with intelligence-led and problem-oriented policing. There are teams within many police departments dedicated to community policing.

6.1.6.1. Method

A common feature of community-focused police systems is the assignment of officers to beats, or discrete geographic areas; beat profiling allows officers to get to know their beats. After that, the officers receive training on how to create customized patrol plans to address the various crimes that occur on that beat. These concepts are put into practice in a multifaceted manner by utilizing a range of techniques, including expanding the role of the police officer and customizing procedures to the community they are policing; redirecting police efforts to in-person interactions in smaller patrol areas with the primary objective of preventing criminal activity rather than responding to it; resolving issues with the community's input; and, lastly, attempting to increase service-oriented positive interactions with police.

Common methods of community-policing include:

- Encouraging the community to help prevent crime by providing advice, talking to students, and encouraging neighborhood watch groups.
- Increased use of foot or bicycle patrols.
- Increased officer accountability to the communities they serve.
- Creating teams of officers to carry out community policing in designated neighborhoods.
- Clear communication between the police and the communities about their objectives and strategies.
- Partnerships with other organizations such as government agencies, community members, nonprofit service providers, private businesses, and the media.
- Moving toward some decentralizing of the police authority, allowing more discretion among lower-ranking officers, and more initiative expected from them.
- Collaborating with social services to connect individuals to social workers, mental health resources, youth programs, and other supports

to address underlying issues like poverty, inadequate housing, and lack of youth opportunities

6.1.6.2. Community Alienation

Police officers' feelings of alienation from the community are strongly related to their experiences of mastery, which is a mental state in which they feel independent and confident in their capacity to control or affect outside events. In order to implement community policing, departments must flatten their organizational pyramid and give line officers even more authority and discretion. According to Taylor and Fritsch, there will be a commensurate decline in officers' sense of mastery in performing their expanded discretionary role as the degree of community alienation or isolation they encounter rises. Second, they assert that the fundamental goal of proactive law enforcement, which is community policing, appears to depend on police officers having a strong sense of community integration. The tendency of police officers to actively engage in crime prevention, community problem-solving, and a more transparent, dynamic, and quality-focused law enforcement-community partnership is known as proactive enforcement. Police officers felt increasingly alienated and apathetic as a result of the lack of community support. Police officers' feelings of alienation and level of inactivity were linked to both this lack of community support and their employment in a more populous area. Police officers became more jaded and lethargic as a result of alienation. According to research, police officers are more likely to retreat and develop bad feelings toward the people they serve when they experience social isolation from the community.

6.1.7. Crime Prevention Under the Routine Activities Theory

Routine Activity theory research has provided the following strategies that help prevent crime:

- Those areas where a higher percentage of residents are home during the day have lower property crime rates.
- Corner homes, usually near traffic lights or stop signs, are the ones most likely to be burglarized.
- Secluded homes, such as those at the end of a cul-de-sac or surrounded by wooded areas make more suitable targets.
- Criminals are more likely to drift towards a city center than move outwards to commit a crime.
- Communities that organize themselves restrict traffic, change street patterns and limit neighborhood entrances and exits will reduce property crime levels.

6.1.8. Combining Crime Prevention Approaches

There is no intrinsic superiority of one prevention strategy or underlying theory over another. There are benefits and drawbacks to each of them. Certain strategies for social development may need sustained dedication and financial support over an extended period of time. When it comes to keeping projects moving forward and involving citizens in constructive ways, community- or locally-based approaches may call for a great deal of patience. Because of their greater evaluability, it may be challenging to pinpoint precise and timely outcomes from interventions. Critics of situational prevention have frequently pointed out that it ignores the social and economic roots of crime issues and concentrates too much on opportunistic crime, target-hardening strategies, and surveillance. It has also been criticized for encouraging unequal access to security. Recent advances in situational prevention have centered on enforcing municipal and local by-laws and other regulations more effectively. This is seen to be a useful tool that motivates local businesses and residents to modify and control their own behavior. It is inappropriate to regard any one method of crime prevention as being better than any other. The advantages and disadvantages of each approach in a given context should be taken into account, and any approach chosen should be a part of a strategic and well-rounded plan. Therefore, a neighborhood project in a city, for instance, might incorporate a number of initiatives, like improving traffic patterns, lighting, hiring and educating young people to serve as guardians and community mediators, helping low-income families, and improving recreational opportunities and facilities in underprivileged residential apartments.

6.1.9. Collective Approaches and the Role of Governments

According to the UN guidelines for crime prevention, it is the duty of all governmental levels to establish, uphold, and encourage an environment that enables pertinent governmental institutions and all facets of civil society, including business, to more effectively contribute to the prevention of crime. The conventional belief that crime prevention is the police's job has significantly changed over the last few decades to one in which crime prevention is seen as a shared responsibility. There has been a growing body of evidence since the 1980s suggesting that proactive, community-based approaches to crime prevention are more advantageous, cost-effective, and effective. Both the Guidelines for the Prevention of Crime and the Guidelines for Cooperation and Technical Assistance in the Field of Urban Crime Prevention acknowledge the value of group effort. There are several strong arguments. First, governments at all levels cannot rely solely on the criminal law and justice system to ensure safety, as there are many social, economic, and environmental factors that influence the rise or fall in crime and violence. By establishing proactive rather than reactive strategies to prevent crime and victimization, multisectoral partnerships between ministries, including those in charge of housing, health, education and employment, recreation, social services, and the environment, as well as the police and justice sector, can all significantly impact crime levels. Second, evaluations of crime prevention programs, particularly in high-income countries, have demonstrated the limitations of the police role, underscoring the importance of collaborative approaches.

For instance, the vast majority of crimes go unreported to the police in practically every nation. Additionally, it has been shown that prevention lowers the expense of criminal justice interventions. The criminal justice system mostly takes action after crimes have been committed, or reactively. Proactive measures are necessary for crime prevention. Prompt prevention initiatives can also have other advantages, like enhancing community reconstruction and social functioning as well as job opportunities, all of which lower social and economic expenses in a city or nation.

6.1.10. Cost and Benefits of Crime Prevention

Any decreases in crime rates and the number of individuals going through the legal system are likely to result in savings on policing, prosecution, defense and court costs, as well as the significant costs associated with operating the prison and parole systems. This is because the criminal justice system is extremely expensive to maintain in all nations. In addition to the costs to the criminal justice system, crime has numerous long-term social and economic repercussions due to lost productivity and the social and welfare services that offenders and their families must pay for things like the placement of children in foster care or the imprisonment of breadwinners. In terms of their health, their capacity to work, attend school, or take care of their own families, victims of crime also bear a financial burden. The costs of crime to victims and society in terms of lost productivity, health, and income are estimated to be even greater than the costs associated with the criminal justice system.

Lastly, the costs of crime must account for all spending on preventive security measures like technological systems, private policing, fencing, and barriers. Numerous studies examining the advantages and disadvantages of crime prevention initiatives have been carried out during the last 10 years. For instance, research has demonstrated that early intervention programs, which offer assistance to children and families facing challenges, as well as work with youth to motivate them to finish their education, result in significant long-term reductions in criminal, social, and economic costs that outweigh the program's initial investments. As a return on investment, prevention initiatives cut costs for social service interventions as well as the criminal justice system. Other social and financial advantages they provide include higher earned incomes and cheaper medical expenses. These elements all serve to highlight the advantages of collaborative government work for governments. Therefore, national governments can assist in facilitating and supporting the development of strategic and planned responses at the subregional level, as well as with local governments and civil society, by developing a national strategy on crime prevention through a multisectoral partnership across ministries.

Local governments are in the best position to comprehend the needs and assets of their own community as well as the worries of the general public. It can be challenging to collaborate with local service providers, residents, and stakeholders, but doing so is probably going to be more successful than putting a plan into place. The significance of a localized approach to crime is emphasized in particular in the Guidelines for Cooperation and Technical Assistance in the Field of Urban Crime Prevention. However, the role of local communities is vital in preventing crime; it is not limited to national or local authorities and service sectors. Local civil society's participation and collaboration shows that government action is insufficient to establish safe and healthy communities. Governments must collaborate with civil society organizations and local communities. Therefore, a strategic approach and methodology for addressing safety and crime concerns is modern crime prevention. It acknowledges that crime has a significant impact on people's quality of life and has an impact on them on a daily basis at the local level.

6.2. CRIMINAL REHABILITATION

Rehabilitating criminals and getting them ready to reintegrate into society is known as rehabilitation. Reducing the rate of recidivism after prisoners are released from prison is the aim of addressing all of the underlying root causes of crime. It typically entails psychological techniques that focus on the cognitive distortions connected to particular types of crimes committed by individual offenders, but it may also involve more general education such as job training and reading comprehension. Reintegrating offenders into society is the aim.

6.2.1. Methods

A successful rehabilitation of a prisoner is also helped if convicted persons:

- are not placed in health-threateningly bad conditions, enjoy access to medical care and are protected from other forms of serious ill-treatment,
- are able to maintain ties to the outside world,

- learn new skills to assist them with working life on the outside,
- enjoy clear and detailed statutory regulations clarifying the safeguards applicable and governing the use and disposal of any record of data relating to criminal matters.

6.2.2. Psychopathy and Recidivism

Psychopathy and criminal recidivism have a strong correlation. An unrestrained gratification of criminal, sexual, or aggressive impulses as well as an incapacity to learn from mistakes made in the past are characteristics of the psychopath. People who suffer from this disorder don't feel guilty about their antisocial behavior because it gives them satisfaction. Research indicates that despite their higher likelihood of recidivism, psychopathic inmates have a 2.5 times greater chance of being released from jail than those without a diagnosis. Research indicates that employing punishment and behavior modification strategies is ineffective in modifying the actions of a psychopath. It has been frequently noted that psychopathic people grow more crafty and adept at disguising their actions. It's been proposed that conventional therapy methods actually make psychopaths worse, or at least much more skilled at controlling people and hiding their actions. They are typically regarded as being both incurable and untreatable [by whom?]. Psychopaths also exhibit a notably warped understanding of the possible repercussions of their actions on both themselves and other people. For instance, they are not fully aware of the possibility that their actions may be discovered, disregarded, or cause harm to themselves.

6.2.3. Criticism

Rehabilitative systems have been criticized for their ability to permit protracted detentions (to give medical professionals time to diagnose and treat patients) and for their broad presumptions about the authority of the state over the mental health of offenders. Furthermore, the absence of customary protections for defendants' procedural rights in rehabilitative processes may give rise to due process concerns. Certain restorative initiatives, like drug courts, have also come under fire for allegedly expanding the reach of the criminal justice system by sending more defendants to jail for breaking treatment plans than would have happened in the absence of the initiatives.

6.2.4. Presumption of Factual Guilt

Whether or not criminal rehabilitation is necessary is a further critique leveled at the practice. The resolution of this issue depends on the veracity of the crime. For example, the fundamental elements (e.g., the philosophical framework supporting the existence of a factually criminal behavior) for which an individual is charged with a crime might not exist. It may be debatable whether a crime actually happened or not, and the answer to that question will not always establish the existence of the crime. Legal systems necessitate that a burden of proof be met in order for someone to be found guilty, as evidenced by the fact that a conviction does not always follow from an actual crime. Rather, an allegation that a burden of proof was met does not guarantee that a crime was committed. Therefore, a defendant's factual guilt and legal guilt are not the same thing. An accused criminal offender will not be eligible for rehabilitation if there is no evidence of a crime.

6.3. DETERRENT THEORY OF PUNISHMENT

The word "deterrent" in the deterrent theory of punishment refers to refraining from any wrongdoing (Figure 6.1). This theory's primary objective is to discourage criminals from trying to commit the same crime or from attempting it again in the future. The main objective is to instill fear in order to deter crime. To put it plainly, the theory holds that anyone who commits a crime will face a harsh sentence; people will be aware of this and will refrain from committing any crimes or wrongdoings as a result of this fear in their minds. Every crime has an associated punishment. Punishment is primarily used to transform criminals into kindhearted, law-abiding citizens through reform. The utilitarian philosophy underlies the deterrent theory of punishment. For better understanding, consider the following example: "This person is punished not only to ensure that no crime will be committed again, but also because he has committed an illegal act." The deterrent theory seeks to lower the crime rate in society by educating potential offenders about the lack of value of crime.

"Deterrent" is a word with numerous meanings. Discouragement, which aims to divert evil minds from choosing immoral and unlawful paths, is a form of deterrent. Among the five theories of criminal jurisprudence—deterrent, retaliation, prevention, reformation, and expiatory—this theory identifies the grave repercussions, i.e., punitive measures against the offender in order to stop the threat. These measures also discourage criminals from committing the same offense in the future. It is evident that throughout the years, the death penalty has not been a very effective deterrent to society's most heinous crimes. It is quite upsetting that crime has not entirely stopped given the rise in rape cases over the previous few decades. It is possible, according to some socially rational thinkers, that crime has decreased somewhat. But will there be a place for a crime where the better half of society is denied the most basic human rights in a civilized society like ours, where we talk about internationalism, social networks at our fingertips, advances in modern high-tech science, and all that? The constant concern about the rising crime rate prevents the weaker (but stronger) sex of the society from living fearlessly.

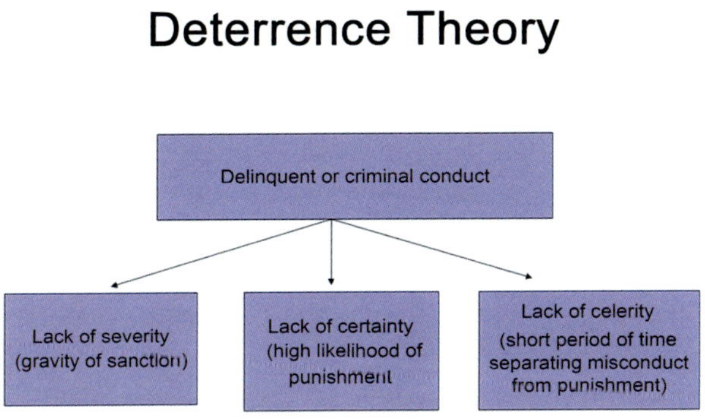

Figure 6.1. *The deterrence theory.*

Source: *https://www.researchgate.net/figure/The-Deterrence-Theory-Scott-nd_fig1_346831492.*

To reduce crime and elevate our society, the legal system is constantly refining its laws, policies, practices, and interpretations. This process will never stop. After all, human laws will only take effect when society has reached a civilized state.

6.3.1. Types of Deterrence

There are two types of deterrence:

1. **Specific Deterrence:** This kind of deterrence targets a particular person. The concept of specific deterrence posits that inflicting severe punishment on an offender for their misconduct will discourage them from committing similar crimes in the future. When an armed robber is sentenced to eight years in prison, for instance, the specific deterrence lessens the likelihood that he will carry out another armed robbery after his release. Research indicates that the efficacy of particular deterrents varies depending on the circumstances.
2. **General Deterrence:** The goal of general deterrence is to prevent people from committing the same crimes as those who have already been found guilty of them. The goal of general deterrence is to teach the public as a whole, not just those who are being accused of crimes. The theory behind harsh punishment is that when someone gets punished severely, the public will see it and be discouraged from partaking in the same or similar activities. The death penalty is

one such instance. The public is deterred from committing the same or similar crimes when a criminal receives a death sentence.

6.3.2. Components of the Deterrent Theory

6.3.2.1. Severity

The level of punishment is indicated by the severity. Criminal law must prioritize punishment in order to deter crime and motivate people to follow the law. Criminal behavior has long been thought to be largely deterred by the severity of punishments. Consequently, the legislature depends on applying severe penalties to discourage criminal activity. But until the 1960s, not many research looked at the deterrent power of severe punishments. The idea that severe penalties can discourage crime is supported by preliminary research. The harshness of the punishments for homicide serves as a deterrent, according to numerous studies looking at homicide rates. When the investigation was extended beyond murder, the situation changed completely. The severity of the sentence reduced the number of crimes including theft, robbery, burglary, battery, and rape. That is, crime was not deterred by the harshness of the punishment. It would, in fact, have the opposite impact. Strict penalties can be applied to criminal justice policy for other beneficial reasons. They have the power to publicly denounce certain acts, render someone incapable of committing crimes for a predetermined amount of time, or present a case for rehabilitative treatment. On the other hand, some research has shown that severe punishments hardly ever, if at all, have a deterrent effect. Severance basically means imposing a punishment that is so terrible that the audience will be afraid to receive it. If the penalty is too harsh, the public might protest and cry foul; if it is too light, test cheaters and pirates might still commit their crimes.

6.3.2.2. Certainty

A punishment's certainty is frequently deemed more significant than its severity. Studies reveal that assurance works as a much stronger deterrent than harshness. Subjective certainty carries greater weight than objective certainty when it comes to certainty. Put differently, one's perception of the likelihood of punishment trumps the actual likelihood of punishment. This subjective opinion may originate with the general public, but it is more likely to originate from firsthand knowledge or anecdotal evidence from members of the community.

The understanding of risk can be shaped by drug use, the presence of companions, and various factors that affect an individual's emotional responses. Correspondingly, as Becker illustrates, there's a delicate balance in relation to certainty. Enhancing the likelihood of apprehensions and convictions to an absolute 100% would entail substantial societal repercussions, including the necessity of maintaining a massive law enforcement force and relinquishing personal freedom and privacy.

6.3.2.3. Celerity

Any crime must have a prompt punishment in order to discourage future crimes. The literature has paid the least attention to celerity, or the speed at which someone is punished for breaking the law. According to research, punishment speed might not have a deterrent effect. According to at least one study, people would rather finish their punishment quickly. If this is true, then delaying punishment could be viewed as having worse effects than administering it right away. In conclusion, economic models of deterrents imply that most criminal activity is carried out by logical individuals who weigh the possibility of punishment against the crime itself. According to the theory, more people will commit crimes if they don't fear punishment. Academics contend that toughening up on criminal offenses will not effectively reduce crime. Thus, proponents of the deterrent theory contend that if punishment is swift, certain, and harsh, a reasonable person would consider the advantages and disadvantages before committing a crime. As a result, the individual will be discouraged from breaking the law and committing a crime.

6.3.3. Drawbacks of Deterrent Theory

The deterrent theory didn't work because the people who are killed, raped, etc., were powerless, and no one reported the accused. Deterrent theory is only effective against people who lack the will to follow through on their convictions. Even with a variety of deterrents, criminal minds occasionally act impulsively. Sanctions and penalties are now just barriers that criminals must get past. It is obvious that the Indian criminal justice system does not require this. Even with the severe fines and penalties, there are more criminal cases than ever before.

Some major drawbacks are:

- Punishment does not create fear in the criminal's mind once the punishment is over.
- This type of punishment does not create fear in the hardened offenders' minds.
- Arouse sympathy in the minds of the public for criminals.

According to the deterrent theory, the main goal is 'to deter crime by inciting fear or setting an example for society. Now, the death penalty is a severe punishment.

6.3.4. Relation Between Preventive and Deterrent Theory of Punishment

Justice Holmes claims that the goal of the preventive theory of punishment, which is also evident in the theory of deterrent, is to disabling the offender in order to deter crime. The preventive theory is favored by many utilitarians, including Bentham, Austin, and Mill, due to its ability to humanize. Because deterrence works to stop future crimes and ensure that those who have committed crimes do not repeat their bad behavior, the two theories are closely related. The idea of prevention, which seeks to stop criminals from committing the same or different crimes, gave rise to the development of penal systems. While it emphasizes more humane methods of punishment, it contradicts the deterrence theory by stating that no one has the right to take another person's life and that the death penalty is an extremely severe form of punishment. The best way to prevent crime, according to prevention theory, is to imprison offenders; this will likely prevent them from committing the same offense. It is reasonable to argue that the death penalty is an additional component of deterrence because it is a component of preventive theory. One seeks to dissuade society at large, while the other stops criminals from committing crimes. Punishing one individual won't stop others from committing the same offense. According to the deterrence theory, an offender may occasionally realize that his actions are not serving the interests of others as a result of punishment. It operates under the premise that people are only punished when their actions benefit society as a whole. Stated differently, it will be deemed successful if it shields society from potential future criminal activity.

The preventive theory clarifies that its objective is to deter crime rather than merely exact revenge. Its primary objective is to keep criminals behind bars, thereby removing any threat that their presence may pose to society. The goal of the deterrent theory is to create criminal discipline that keeps people from committing crimes in the future.

6.4. RESTORATIVE JUSTICE

The goal of restorative justice is to make amends for the harm that has been done to victims. By doing this, professionals seek to make sure that offenders accept accountability for their deeds, recognize the harm they have caused, offer them a chance to turn around, and deter them from doing more harm. The intention is to lessen the victims' sense of helplessness and anxiety while also allowing them to participate actively in the process. Unlike traditional methods of justice, which frequently center on retribution, restorative justice is based on an alternative theory. Programs for restorative justice can also be used in conjunction with more conventional approaches. However, some perspectives on punishment suggest that certain instances of restorative justice amount to punishment. Even though restorative justice has received positive academic evaluations, more recent research has revealed that academic performance suffers in school districts that use restorative justice. Advocates contend that the majority of research indicates it reduces the likelihood of reoffending by offenders. A 2007 study also discovered that compared to conventional methods of delivering justice, it had a higher rate of victim satisfaction and offender accountability. Practitioners have noted that there are now more opportunities for re-victimization in this field. Globally, its usage has increased during the 1990s. The study of restorative practices is influenced by and includes restorative justice.

Setting up a meeting between the victim and the perpetrator is one way to address a crime in a restorative justice program. Sometimes members of the larger community are involved in this. In order to reach a consensus on what the offender can do to make amends for the harm caused by the offense, they must first share their accounts of what transpired and talk about who was harmed by the crime and how. This could entail the offender giving the victim money, offering an apology or making other amends, or taking other steps to make amends for the harm done and to stop the offender from hurting people in the future. Restorative justice practices, on the other hand, are deeply based in the needs of the victim and may only advocate for sharing victim impact statements and holding offenders accountable without engaging in conversation.

6.4.1. Application

6.4.1.1. In Criminal Cases

In criminal proceedings, victims have the opportunity to provide testimony regarding the effects of the crime on their lives, get information about what happened, and take part in holding the perpetrator responsible. Offenders can share their story about why they committed the crime and how it has impacted their lives in the interim. They are offered the chance to directly make amends for the victim, to the extent that it is feasible. In criminal cases, these may take the form of cash, community service related to the offense or in general, education aimed at preventing recidivism, or the expression of regret. Pretrial diversion is a procedure used in court that dismisses charges following restitution. In severe situations, a sentence might come before further compensation. Concerned citizens gather with all involved parties in the community to evaluate the experience and consequences of the crime. Criminals pay attention to what victims have to say, ideally until they can relate to it. Next, they discuss their personal experiences and how they came to commit the crime. A strategy is developed to stop similar incidents in the future and to deal with the harm done to the victims. The offender(s) are held responsible by the community for following the plan. While an interaction between the offender and the victim is usually part of restorative justice, some organizations, like Mennonite Central Committee Canada, place more emphasis on the program's values than on its participants. Programs with a restorative framework that exclusively assist victims—or offenders, for that matter—may fall under this category. Indigenous groups are attempting to increase community support for victims and offenders, especially the youth, by utilizing the restorative justice process. For instance, various initiatives are carried out at the Pine Ridge Indian Reservation of the Oglala Lakota nation in the United States and at Kahnawake, a Mohawk reserve in Canada.

6.4.1.2. In Prisons

In addition to being a substitute for a civil or criminal trial, restorative justice is also believed to be relevant for criminal defendants who are presently serving prison sentences. Restorative justice is used in prisons to help inmates get better and eventually reintegrate back into society. Restorative justice aims to identify and address the circumstances that led to the crime in order to mend the damage that it caused to the relationships between offenders and victims as well as between offenders and the community.

This is believed to stop recidivism, which occurs when an offender returns to their previous bad behavior after being released from custody. After controlling for the self-selection bias, which is frequently challenging to overcome in research on restorative practices, recidivism was found to be lower in studies examining a restorative reentry planning circle process in Hawaii. It has also been demonstrated that the reentry planning circle process helps children whose parents were incarcerated deal with the trauma of losing a parent to prison. One of the best and most promising justifications for the application of restorative justice in prisons is its ability to lower recidivism.

However, restorative justice may not be feasible in a prison setting due to a number of theoretical and practical issues. These include the challenge of persuading victims and offenders to take part in mediation; the contentious impact of friends, family, and the community; and the high rate of mental illness among prisoners.

6.4.1.3. In Social Work

In social work cases, underprivileged victims, like foster children, are given the chance to discuss their aspirations for the future and create specific plans with their supporters to move out of state custody in a group setting. Restorative justice is used to solve issues in social justice cases.

6.4.1.4. In Schools

In certain schools, restorative justice has been introduced. It follows a model that is comparable to those employed by the criminal justice system. Preventive measures aimed at enhancing students' and adults' abilities and skills can also be included in restorative practices. Establishing community building in the classroom or working with teachers to jointly develop the expectations for the classroom are two examples of preventive measures in restorative practices. In addition, restorative justice emphasizes justice as needs and duties, broadens justice to include dialogues between the offender, victim, and school, and defines accountability as realizing the consequences of one's actions and making amends. With this strategy, agreements can be reached to satisfy the needs of all parties involved by educators, students, and the community. Since the group needs to come up with a plan of action to repair the damage and find a way to reintegrate the offender into society, collaboration is stressed.

The goal of restorative justice programs is to make the victim(s) whole, but they also have the added benefit of reducing the number of disciplinary actions, like suspensions and expulsions, which lowers the number of discipline cases reported to the state. Instead, more productive reformative and/or reconciliatory actions are imposed, like writing letters of apology, doing community service, or, in the case of bullying, writing a research paper on the harmful effects of bullying. Because the resolution of the conflict requires that all parties involved understand their needs, this approach helps to develop and foster empathy. With the help of the restorative justice partners, both the offending party and the wronged/victimized party can address and start to resolve their barriers to completing their education.

For instance, restorative justice programs may identify and acknowledge behavioral issues resulting from grief; in such a case, the party would be referred to a counselor for grief counselling. Theoretically, this will make it less likely that the offender will hurt people again. According to some studies, punishing a person who is grieving will make them feel worse, which will make them behave in more problematic ways. Through a restorative justice approach to student discipline, conflicts can be resolved to reduce student absenteeism, rehabilitate the offending party, and make amends for the wronged party while also meeting the district's funding needs. Encouraging students to take on roles as jurors or mediators in restorative justice circles fosters empathy and collective consciousness.

6.4.2. Method

In order to give victims a voice and hold offenders accountable, restorative justice advocates suggest methods such as arranging a voluntary meeting between the victim and the offender. The victim is encouraged to attend restorative justice conferences in person, but they are not required to, and in certain cases, the victim may be represented by a third party, according to a 2013 Cochrane review. There are, however, alternatives to the practice that lessen the possibility of additional harm or re-victimization, such as reading victim impact statements while holding the offender accountable. People from the larger community may also be present at the meeting.

Suggested reasons for why it can be effective include:

- The offender has to learn about the harm they have caused to their victim, making it hard for them to justify their behavior.
- It offers a chance to discuss moral development to offenders who may have had little of it in their life.
- Offenders are more likely to view their punishment as legitimate.
- The programs tend to avoid shaming and stigmatizing the offender.

Participants in many restorative justice programs, such as family group conferences and victim-offender mediation, are required to sign a confidentiality agreement. Typically, these agreements specify that information about conference discussions won't be shared with non-participants. Secrecy is justified on the grounds that it encourages direct and sincere communication.

6.4.2.1. Victim-Offender Dialogue (VOD)

Victim-offender dialogue (VOD)—also known as victim-offender mediation, victim-offender conferencing, victim-offender reconciliation, or restorative justice dialogue—usually consists of a meeting between the victim and the offender with one or two professionals acting as facilitators. For offenders who are incarcerated, this system frequently represents their only option and usually has few participants. In a case involving two accused vandals who met in person with their numerous victims in Kitchener, Ontario in 1974, the victim-offender dialogue was first implemented in Canada as an alternative court sanction. The South Yorkshire Probation Service operated one of the first victim-offender mediation programs in the United Kingdom from 1983 to 1986.

6.4.2.2. Family Group Conferencing

Compared to video over the internet (VOD), family group conferencing (FGC) includes additional participants who are not directly related to the main parties, such as friends, family, and professionals. Given the significance of the family in the life of a juvenile offender, FGC is most frequently employed in juvenile cases Examples are found in New Zealand under the 1989 Children, Young Persons, and their Families Act and in New South Wales, Australia, under the 1997 Young Offenders Act. The New South Wales Bureau of Crime Statistics and Research has given the New South Wales scheme a positive evaluation.

This type of mediation is used by Fiji in child sexual assault cases. Involving the victim's family in the process may seem advantageous, but there are a number of problems that result from it. For instance, in these cases, the victims know the great majority of the offenders. The concept of family is more expansive in Fiji than it is in the conventional Western understanding. As a result, involving the family in these situations may become difficult since they might not support the victim or because the procedure might stoke discord within the clan. Furthermore, rather than the offender making amends with the victim, the process as a whole emphasizes the victim's forgiveness of the offender. All in all, the existing procedure carries a high risk of greatly traumatizing the victim and re-victimizing them.

6.4.2.3. Restorative Conferences

Compared to VOD and FGC, restorative conferences (RC) involve a larger group of participants. These community-based meetings go by a variety of names and operating procedures. These can also be called Community Restorative Boards, Community Accountability Conferences, Restorative Justice Conferences, or Restorative Circles. The victim, the offender, and members of the community, who have usually undergone some training, will normally participate in a conference. Often invited are the victim's and offender's friends and family. RC expressly considers victims. Together with the offender, the community members talk about the nature and consequences of the offense. Until restitution is agreed upon, the conversation goes on; they might also witness the agreement being carried out. Between 100,000 and 500,000 people attended the largest-ever restorative justice conference during the 1990 reconciliation campaign that put an end to the blood feuds among ethnic Albanians in Kosovo. Under Anton Çetta's leadership, the reconciliation movement was able to bring an end to the blood feuds and record about one-third of Kosovo's population actively participating in restorative justice conferences over a three-year period.

6.4.2.4. Circles of Support and Accountability

A Mennonite church in Hamilton, Ontario called Welcome In was the original sponsor of Circles of Support and Accountability (CoSA). This method has proven to be effective in improving the safe reintegration of sex offenders into society who would otherwise be considered high-risk. In Canada, some sexual offenders are deemed too dangerous for any kind of conditional release, and they are kept in detention until they have completed their sentence. Being classified as a Dangerous Offender frequently follows a subsequent conviction. Many of these criminals were freed without any assistance or monitoring other than police supervision before 1994. CoSA helped well over 120 of these offenders integrate between 1994 and 2007. According to research, reducing recidivism by nearly 80% could be achieved by surrounding a "core member" with 5–7 trained volunteer circle members. Furthermore, compared to before the program, recidivist offenses were less harsh and intrusive. There are currently CoSA projects in every province in Canada as well as every significant city. CoSA projects are also operational in several U.S. states (Iowa, California, Minnesota, Oregon, Ohio, Colorado, Vermont) as well as in several United Kingdom regions (Cornwall, Devon, Hampshire, Thames Valley, Leicestershire, North Wales, North Yorkshire, and Manchester).

6.4.2.5. Sentencing Circles

Using the customary circle ritual and structure, sentencing circles—also known as peacemaking circles—involve all interested parties. Typically, the process goes like this: the offender applies for the intervention, the victim and the offender each have a healing circle, the offender receives a sentence, and then there are follow-up circles to track progress.

6.4.3. Social Movements

6.4.3.1. Positive Criminology and Positive Victimology

The Israeli criminologist Natti Ronel and his research team created the conceptual approaches of positive criminology and positive victimology, which have strong ties to the theories and practices of restorative justice. Both victimology and positive criminology emphasize social inclusion as well as the unifying and integrating forces at the individual, group, social, and spiritual levels that are linked to the reduction of crime and victimization recovery. The study of crime, violence, and related behaviors using traditional methods places a strong emphasis on the negative aspects of people's lives that are connected to victimization, deviance, and criminality. It is widely accepted that negative experiences have a greater impact on human relationships than positive or constructive ones. Three dimensions—social integration, emotional healing, and spirituality—that together make up positive direction indicators support the viability of a different strategy, according to positive criminology and victimology.

6.4.3.2. Prison Abolition

Aiming for the same goals as restorative justice, prison abolition demands not only the removal of cages but also new viewpoints and approaches to understanding crime. An impartial third party mediates the process, which involves all pertinent parties and is voluntary and unrestricted by professional or organizational requirements in an abolitionist style of restorative justice. The community's needs and strengthening are the main priorities.

REFERENCES

1. Agbiboa, D. E. (2015). Policing is not work: It is stealing by force: Corrupt policing and related abuses in everyday Nigeria. *Africa Today, 62*(1), 94–126.
2. Ajayi, O. J., & Longe, O. (2015). Public perception of the police and crime prevention in Nigeria. *British Journal of Education, Society & Behavioral Science, 6*(2), 145–153.
3. Akinlabi, O. M. (2017). Do the police really protect and serve the public? Police deviance and public cynicism towards the law in Nigeria. *Criminology & Criminal Justice, 17*(2), 158–174.
4. Alemika, E. E. O. (2012). Rethinking crime prevention and crime control approaches in Nigeria. *Journal of the Nigerian Sociological Society, 2*(1), 7–10.
5. Arvate, P., Falsete, F. O., Ribeiro, F. G., & Souza, A. P. (2018). Lighting and homicides: Evaluating the effect of an electrification policy in rural Brazil on violent crime reduction. *Journal of Quantitative Criminology, 34*(4), 1047–1078.
6. Baba, I. A., Babajo, H. H., & Namahe, U. Y. (2017). The role of local government towards crime prevention and control in Nigeria. *Saudi Journal of Humanities and Social Sciences, 2*(8), 696–700.
7. Bayat, B., et al. (2008). *Crime Prevention, Based on Social-Based Approach*. Tehran: Publication of Social Security Department of the Islamic Republic of Iran, Directorate General of Social Studies.
8. Brantingham, P. J., & Faust, F. L. (1976). A conceptual model of crime prevention. *Crime & Delinquency, 22*(4), 284–296.
9. Cane, P., & Conaghan, J. (2009). *The New Oxford Companion to Law*. Oxford University Press.
10. DeKeseredy, W. S., Donnermeyer, J. F., & Schwartz, M. D. (2009). Toward a gendered second generation CPTED for preventing woman abuse in rural communities. *Security Journal, 22*(3), 11–29.
11. Eberhart, A. O. (1913). Prevention of crime. *The ANNALS of the American Academy of Political and Social Science, 46*(1), 31–34.
12. Flew, A. (1954). The justification of punishment. *Philosophy, 29*(107), 291–305.
13. Hadadzadeh Nayeri, M. R. (2009). Situational prevention of the crime of sexual crimes. *Journal of Hearing, 13*(2), 45–58.

14. Harkness, A., & Larkins, J. (2020). Technological approaches to preventing property theft from farms. In A. Harkness (Ed.), *Rural Crime Prevention: Theory, Tactics and Techniques* (pp. 226–244). Routledge.
15. Hughes, G. (2001). Crime prevention. In E. McLaughlin & J. Munice (Eds.), *The Sage Dictionary of Criminology* (pp. 49–50). Sage Publications.
16. Jackson, J. (2009). A psychological perspective on vulnerability in the fear of crime. *Psychology, Crime & Law, 15*(4), 365–385.
17. Jeffery, R. C. (1977). *Crime Prevention Through Environmental Design*. Sage Publications.
18. Kaplan, H. M., Bickman, L., Pesce, E. J., & Szoc, R. (1978). *Crime Prevention Through Environmental Design: Final Report on Schools Demonstration, Broward County, Florida*. National Institute of Justice.
19. Mirkhalili, M. (2008). Urban development and the need for situational prevention. *Quarterly Journal of Private Law Studies*, University of Tehran.
20. Newman, O. (1996). *Creating Defensible Space*. U.S. Department of Housing and Urban Development.
21. Niazpur, A. H. (2004). Early prevention of sustainable criminal behavior. *Journal of Culture and Research, 161*(2), 103 118.
22. Packer, H. L. (1968). *The Limits of The Criminal Sanction*. Stanford University Press.
23. Petrovskiy, A. (2020). Safety, security, and crime prevention in rural areas of Krasnodarskyi Krai and the Republic of Adygea. *Journal of Criminal Justice and Security, 22*(3), 16–27.
24. Rajabipur, M. (2008) Student delinquency and the possibility of socially-inclusive growth. *Journal of Police Knowledge, 45*(3), 76–85.
25. Rayejian Asli, M. (2004). A new approach to the foundations of the prevention of crime. *Journal of Legal Justice, 12*(1), 34–50.
26. Rohami, M., & Heidari, A. (2005). The challenges of criminal policies for non-victims. *Journal of Faculty of Law and Political Science, University of Tehran*.
27. Sharma, R. K. (1998). *Criminology and Penology*. Atlantic Publishers.
28. United Nations Office on Drugs and Crime. (2010). *Handbook on the Crime Prevention Guidelines: Making Them Work*. United Nations Publications.

Chapter **7**

Juvenile Delinquency

Contents

INTRODUCTION

A young person who has committed a criminal offence is referred to as juvenile delinquent in academic literature, though the exact definition of this term varies depending on the local jurisdiction. Although the precise causes of these variations are unknown, it's possible that there isn't a recognized international standard. In this context, "juvenile" refers to a person who is under the legal age of majority, which is when a person is considered an adult, but who is over the minimum age of criminal responsibility and therefore legally able to commit a criminal offence. While the age of criminal majority is typically 18 years old, the minimum age of criminal responsibility varies between 6 and 18 years old internationally. Although the United Nations (UN) defines "youth" as those between the ages of 15 and 24, people over the age of 18 may still be considered juveniles in certain situations and be heard in juvenile courts. Although in other contexts "children" are frequently defined as those under the age of 18, the term "child delinquents" has been used to refer to children who have committed a delinquent act and are under the age of 13. The phrase "young offenders" has a broad definition; it can apply to offenders under the age of 18 or to young adults in their mid-20s. An individual who has engaged in criminal activity is referred to as a "delinquent." Therefore, delinquency covers a wide range of behaviors that are subject to laws that vary from jurisdiction to jurisdiction and that change over time. While serious interpersonal violence and theft are typically regarded as criminal offenses, there are very different levels of tolerance around the world for other behaviors, such as youth sexual behavior and alcohol consumption. These distinctions can occasionally be the result of historical or cultural causes, and in certain cases—like in some Middle Eastern nations—they may be supported by long-standing religious regulations. Certain crimes may be committed in different ways by different authorities in different jurisdictions. For example, in Singapore, the term "unlawful assembly," which is frequently used to quell riots, refers to when young people get together in public in groups of five or more as part of police efforts to combat youth gangs. Additionally, "status offences"—acts like drinking alcohol or skipping school that are acceptable for adults but illegal for children—not only differ amongst jurisdictions but also cause discontinuities when comparing juvenile delinquency with adult populations within the same jurisdiction. In jurisdictions where a young offender is handled through the welfare system as opposed to the youth justice process, ambiguity may also develop. Teenagers who engage in behavior that would typically be prosecuted and therefore classified as "delinquent" in other countries may not technically be considered criminals in those countries due to their high minimum age of criminal responsibility. Not every young person in prison is a "delinquent," as some may have been arrested before. All things considered, the term "juvenile delinquent" is widely used in academic literature, but it should be used with caution. It can be a potentially problematic term that, depending on the context, can convey a derogatory tone and falsely infer negative things. The term "children in conflict with the law" has been used by the UN for a number of years to characterize the diverse range of people under the age of 18 who have broken the law or are at risk of doing so.

7.1. OVERVIEW OF JUVENILE DELINQUENCY

Juvenile delinquency, commonly referred to as juvenile offending, is the act of engaging in illegal activity while a minor or someone under the legal majority age. If the people committing these acts were older, they would otherwise be seen as crimes. The word "delinquent" is often used to describe juvenile delinquency, but it can also be used more broadly to describe any young person exhibiting inappropriate behavior.

A person who commits a crime while under a certain age is considered a juvenile delinquent in the United States. The majority of states define a juvenile delinquent, or young offender, as someone under the age of 18, though some have slightly different upper age limits. In the late 18th and early 19th centuries, juvenile offenders were treated similarly to adult offenders, and the severity of the offense determined the severity of the punishment. This is when the term "juvenile delinquent" first appeared. Juveniles over the age of seven were tried in adult criminal courts prior to the 18th century, and they faced the death penalty if found guilty. Juvenile courts were first established in Illinois. This juvenile court established appropriate terminology for juvenile offenders, kept juvenile records private, and placed more emphasis on treatment goals than punishment. The maximum age was raised to under 19 in Michigan, New York, and Vermont in 2021. The Vermont law was then updated again in 2022 to include people under 20. There are still only three states that consider someone under the age of 17 to be a juvenile delinquent: Georgia, Texas, and Wisconsin. While the maximum age has gone up in some US states, it has gone down from under 20 to under 18 in Japan for juvenile delinquency. On April 1, 2022, a law lowering the nation's minor status age was put into effect by the Japanese Diet. States differ significantly in terms of the minimum age at which a child is deemed capable of delinquency or the age of criminal responsibility, in addition to the maximum age at which a juvenile delinquent may be found. While some states that have minimum wages have recently raised them, most states are still unclear about the minimum age at which a child can be classified as a juvenile delinquent. In 2021, the minimum age in North Carolina was raised from 6 to 10 years old, while in Connecticut the age was raised from 7 to 10 and in New York from 7 to 12. The minimum age varies by state depending on how serious the crime was. The crimes committed by juvenile delinquents, also known as juvenile offenders, range from status offenses like truancy, curfew violations, underage drinking and smoking, to more serious ones like property crimes, violent crimes, sexual offenses, and cybercrimes.

Several academics have observed a rise in juvenile arrests and have come to the conclusion that this may be due more to zero-tolerance policies and aggressive criminal justice practices than to behavioral shifts in young people. According to official US government statistics, youth violence rates in the country have decreased to about 12% of peak rates in 1993, indicating that the majority of juvenile offenses are non-violent. Environmental influences like peer pressure or family behavior can be held responsible for a large number of delinquent acts. The school-to-prison pipeline is one contributing factor that has drawn more attention recently. Approximately 75% of states have constructed more jails and prisons than colleges, according to Diverse Education. Additionally, CNN offers a diagram demonstrating how, in the majority of states, the cost per prisoner is much higher than the cost per student. This demonstrates that tax payer money is being used to support prisons rather than the educational system and the advancement of learning. The emphasis on punitive punishment has been found to be correlated with the rates of juvenile delinquency for each new school that is constructed. Some have proposed replacing zero tolerance regulations with restorative justice strategies.

The juvenile legal system often consists of juvenile courts, juvenile detention facilities, and electronic monitoring. Juvenile courts are designed to handle minor offenses as civil cases rather than criminal ones most of the time. States in the US have different procedures and formats for these courts. It is possible for someone under the age of 18 to be charged with and handled like an adult, depending on the nature and seriousness of the offense.

Juvenile delinquency, or offending, is often separated into three categories:

- Delinquency, crimes committed by minors, which are dealt with by the juvenile courts and justice system;
- Criminal behavior, crimes dealt with by the criminal justice system;
- Status offenses that are only classified as such because only a minor can commit them. One example of this is possession of alcohol by a minor. These offenses are also dealt with by the juvenile courts.

UNICEF estimates that over a million children are in some form of detention worldwide, but there isn't currently an organization whose responsibility it is to track juvenile delinquency worldwide. The United States has the highest number of juvenile delinquency cases among nations that maintain records on the number of delinquent or imprisoned minors. Many other countries do not maintain such records. Data on trends in juvenile delinquency is compiled by the Office of Juvenile Justice and Delinquency Prevention in the United States. In 2016, 7 out of 1,000 juvenile offenders in the US committed a serious crime, according to their most recent publication. The US Department of Justice classifies a serious crime as any one of the following eight offenses: robbery, aggravated assault, motor vehicle theft, larceny-theft, arson, rape (both legacy and revised), and murder and non-negligent homicide. Since its peak in 1994, the arrest rate for juveniles has been steadily declining, according to research compiled by James Howell in 2009. Probation is the most frequent outcome of juvenile delinquency cases that reach the court system, and men make up more than 70% of the caseload.

Moffitt's (2006) developmental research indicates that two distinct categories of offenders arise during adolescence. First, there is the age-limited offender, also known as the juvenile offender, whose juvenile delinquency starts and ends during their adolescent years. According to Moffitt, the majority of teenagers exhibit antisocial or delinquent behavior at some point during adolescence. For this reason, it's critical to take these behaviors into consideration during childhood in order to predict whether or not a child will engage in antisocial or delinquent behavior during adolescence or something more persistent. The second category of offenders is the repeat offender, also known as the life-course persistent offender, who starts committing crimes or acting in an aggressive or antisocial manner in adolescence or even early childhood and carries it through to adulthood.

7.1.1. Characteristics of Juvenile Delinquency

On the basis of these studies and on the basis of data compiled by National Crime Records Bureau, 1998, following characteristics of juvenile delinquency in India may be given:

1. Boys commit many times more delinquencies than girls do; in other words, girls commit fewer delinquencies than boys do. Up until 1987, the proportion of girls involved in juvenile delinquency was roughly 6–7%. Due to a change in the definition of juveniles, which limited the age range of 7 to 18 years for girls, this suddenly shot up to 13 points 4% in 1988. When we calculate the percentage of girls in the newly defined age range using the earlier years' data, we find that it is 13.1%, which is a good comparison to the 13.4% in 1988. Accordingly, the 1998 data points to an overall arrest ratio of 2.8 boys for every girl. In 1998, out of the 18,964 juveniles arrested for crimes under the IPC and SLL, 26.1% were female.
2. The delinquency rates tend to be highest during early adolescence

(12–16 years age group). After the new definition of the age of juvenile delinquency in 1988, if we calculate the average of 10 years from 1988 to 1998, about three-fifth delinquents (61.0%) fall in this age group of 12–16 years. Earlier (between 1978 and 1987), it was observed that a large number of delinquents (71%) belonged to 18–21 years (late adolescence) age group, 15% belonged to 16–18 years age group, 9% to 12–16 years age group, and 5% to 7–12 years age group. Now, the percentage share of two age groups has changed. About 17.5% belong to 7–12 years age group and 21.4% to 16–18 years age group (1998). The share of 12–16 years age group has increased from 10% in 1978–87 to 61% in 1998 because from 1988, 18–21 years age group has entirely gone out of the ambit of juvenile consideration.

3. Juvenile delinquency is more an urban than a rural phenomenon.
4. It has been observed that juvenile offenders are more likely to be living with parents or guardians. Three-fourths (73%) of the delinquents were found to be living with their parents at the time of arrest, followed by one-fourth (22%) living with guardians, and approximately one-twentieth (5%) living on the streets (1998). This demonstrates how the home environment affects juvenile delinquency.
5. A lack of education is the main factor contributing to delinquency. Of the juvenile population, about two-fifths (38.1%) are illiterate, two-fifths (39.3%) have completed primary school, one-fifth (18.5%) have completed middle and secondary school, and a very small percentage (4.1%) have completed high school or above (1998). That's why the majority of criminals come from lower-class, illiterate homes.
6. One more crucial aspect of juvenile delinquency in India is a poor economic background. Homes with an income below that of approximately half (52%) of the delinquents. Around 500 each month (i.e., impoverished and extremely low classes), with roughly one-fourth (27%) coming from households with mixed incomes 501 and 1,000 every month, that is, lower classes), roughly one-tenth (14%) of households with revenues in the middle 1,001 additionally 2,000 a month, (that is, lower-middle class) and a very tiny percentage (5%) from households earning in between (2,001 in addition to 3,000 every month, that is upper class) or those with a salary above it. Monthly income of $3,000 (2%) (i.e., middle-class] (1998). This indicates that young criminality is primarily a problem among the

lower classes. The lowest socioeconomic strata have been found to have the highest rates of juvenile delinquency, according to almost all of the research done in our nation on the topic.

7. Just 10% of juvenile offenders are recidivists or past offenders, while 90% of them are first-time offenders. Around 89% of the offenders in 1998 were first-time offenders. From 1988 to 1998, there were fewer and fewer juveniles arrested overall each year. The number decreased from approximately 38,000 (IPC + SLL) in 1988 to approximately 30,000 (29,591) in 1991 and approximately 19,000 (18,964) in 1998.
8. Not many delinquencies are committed in groups. In the United States, Shaw and McKay in their study found that 90% children had companions in their delinquencies. In India, it appears, a large number of delinquencies are committed all alone.
9. Though some delinquencies are committed in groups yet the number of juvenile gangs having support of organized adult criminals is not large in our country.

7.1.2. Types of Juvenile Delinquency

Delinquency manifests itself in a multitude of ways, including conduct patterns. Every pattern has a social context, associated causes, and recommended prevention or treatment methods that are most frequently mentioned as suitable for that particular pattern. There are four different kinds of delinquencies: situational delinquencies, organized delinquencies, group-supported delinquencies, and individual delinquencies.

7.1.2.1. Individual Delinquency

A child's conduct that involves them engaging in criminal activity on their own initiative without outside help is referred to as individual delinquency. Psychiatrists have significantly advanced the field of study on individual delinquency. Individual delinquency, in their opinion, results from psychological issues. Doctor Healy says that the delinquent's feeblemindedness is the main reason behind their behavior. A child's intellectual impurity prevents him from adhering to the moral standards that society sets, which forces him to engage in criminal activity. Children visualize the people and things around them when they adopt new behavioral patterns, so family dynamics play a big role in shaping a child's behavior. A child's mental and intellectual development is influenced by the family environment, way of life, and interpersonal dynamics. In the event that parents do not give their children the love, care, and support that is expected, the child may grow up to be antisocial. The primary causes of violent and antisocial behavior in children are poverty, illiteracy, drug abuse, and criminal history in the family. Another factor contributing to teenage delinquent behavior is heredity. Adopting bad behavioral traits from their ancestors is inherited by children. A change in the child's surroundings will, nevertheless, prevent the emergence of those criminal characteristics. With respect to Barun Chandra Thakur v. In the Master Bholu (2022) case, a 16-year-old slashed the throat of a 7-year-old boy in the Ryan International School restroom. Because of the accused's age, the case was moved from the Central Bureau of Investigation to the Juvenile Justice Board. The accused's social investigation report stated that he was frequently drunk, violent, irritable, and less stable. The accused has the mental capacity to commit an offense and can be tried as an adult, according to the board's assessment following the preliminary evaluation. Numerous appeals were made against the order, though, and the Supreme Court ruled that the Children's Court and Juvenile Justice Board have the authority to make an initial determination and that the Court is not permitted to investigate this issue.

7.1.2.2. Group-Supported Delinquency

The term "group-supported delinquency" describes a child's actions when they participate in antisocial behavior while they are with other people. Delinquents pick up this behavior as a result of social groups outside of their family and the culture that is prevalent in their immediate neighborhood. Teenagers who organize into gang-like groups are responsible for two thirds of all cases of juvenile delinquency, according to UN reports. Frederick Thrasher addresses group-supported delinquency in his book "Gang's Theory." Members of each group integrate their distinctive behavioral patterns—which set them apart from other groups—into their personalities. In order to protect and advance their interests, the groups incite hostility toward one another and spread illegal tactics during this process. People of similar ages form peer associations. Teens spend more time with their peers than with their families. Teenagers lack the mental and intellectual maturity of adults, which makes them more likely to have criminal tendencies. To fit in with the group, a person will participate in any immoral or unethical behavior that goes against social norms. When a child starts to value their peers' opinions over their parents,' parents lose control of the situation.

7.1.2.3. Organized Delinquency

Delinquency that is organized occurs when a group of adolescents joins together formally to commit crimes. These organizations are led by the group's established norms and values and feature a hierarchical structure. The first person to bring up organized delinquency was Albert Cohen. Albert Cohen developed the theory of subculture in his book "Delinquent Boys: Culture of the Gang." Cohen contends that juvenile involvement in crime is primarily caused by the delinquent subculture.

The socioeconomic divides that already exist in society give rise to subcultures. When a working-class person aspires to succeed and follow their dreams, they are frequently met with expectations and demands from the middle class; they quickly come to understand that their low social status and inflexible social structure impede their progress. In order to attain his objectives, an individual is forced by social injustices to reject accepted norms and values and affiliate with a subgroup. In their book "Delinquency and Opportunity," Cloward and Ohlin noted that young people who don't know how to cope with their inability to succeed through legal means will often turn to illegal means. Adolescents attribute their failure to the social structure rather than personal shortcomings. A deviant subculture is made up of people who share similar experiences and harbor a generalized hatred for the current system. The 1950s saw the emergence of these delinquent subcultures in America. In India, one of the main manifestations of organized delinquency is child trafficking. These organized groups pay juveniles in drugs for hiring them to deliver drugs and other substances.

7.1.2.4. Situational Delinquency

The reasons why young people commit crimes are deeply ingrained in the delinquencies described above. They are motivated by cultural, social, or psychological elements. However, the causes and solutions to situational delinquency are rather straightforward; it is not a deeply ingrained problem. A person who engages in antisocial behavior duc to a lack of impulse control or pressure from family and society norms. Situational delinquency is far simpler to manage than other forms of delinquency. Situational Delinquency was mentioned by David Matza in his book "Delinquency and Drift." Everybody has criminal tendencies, but they are suppressed because of social norms, according to Matza. A young person is torn between the worlds of the delinquent and the conventional; although aware of social norms and values, the young person succumbs to permissive temptations that lead him towards deviant behavior. Matza gave this process the name "Drift." According to David Matza, neutralization techniques make drift possible. Youth use the process of neutralization to rationalize their delinquent behavior. Nevertheless, there is a lack of development and consideration for the concept of situational delinquency in relation to the issue of juvenile delinquency. This kind of delinquency is exclusive to writing; it has no place in the real world.

7.1.3. Assumptions of Delinquent Behavior

Without a knowledge of the causes of adolescent criminal activity, it is impossible to create prevention programs that work. In the scientific and practical literature on juvenile crime and violence, various approaches are employed to characterize and elucidate delinquent behavior in young individuals. Juvenile delinquency, according to criminologists, includes all public wrongs perpetrated by minors between the ages of 12 and 20. Sociologists take a broader view of the idea, arguing that it encompasses a wide range of juvenile offenses against the law and social norms, from infractions to major crimes. Status offenses fall under the category of juvenile delinquency because they are closely related to the age of the offender; an action or behavior is only deemed illegal if it is carried out by a juvenile (truancy and running away are two examples). Sociologists link the particulars of adolescent behavior to the home, family, neighborhood, peers, and a host of other factors that collectively or individually shape the social environment of young people in an effort to explain the theoretical foundations of delinquency.

Antisocial behavior could be the start of a long-term criminal pattern or just a typical aspect of growing up. The vast majority of young people commit minor crimes at some point during their adolescence without this eventually leading to a criminal career, according to the United Nations Guidelines for the Prevention of Juvenile Delinquency, also known as the Riyadh Guidelines. These guidelines state that "youthful behavior or conduct that does not conform to overall social norms and values is often part of the maturation and growth process and tends to disappear spontaneously in most individuals with the transition to adulthood." Although delinquency is frequently associated with the stage and process of transitioning into adulthood, it is crucial to remember that young people frequently establish stable criminal organizations with a corresponding subculture and begin participating in adult criminal groups' activities, thereby selecting careers that involve delinquency.

Numerous countries' statistical data indicates that delinquency is primarily a group phenomenon, with members of different groups being responsible for between two-thirds and three-quarters of all juvenile offenses. Even young people who commit crimes on their own are probably a part of groups. The rate of criminal activity among juvenile offenders in groups is approximately three to four times higher than that of adult offenders, according to data from the Russian Federation. The frequency of juvenile group crime is lowest among 17-year-olds and highest among 14-year-olds. Premeditated murder and grievous bodily harm have lower rates than theft, robbery, and rape. The fundamental traits of young people's group behavior are similar in practically every class and cultural setting. Juvenile peer groups are characterized by high degrees of social cohesiveness, hierarchical structure, and a particular set of rules derived from the rejection of adult experiences and values. Rarely does the subcultural component of youth group activities receive the consideration it merits. A heterogeneous mix, or synthesis, of intergenerational (group-based) values that are ingrained in the family or neighborhood and dominant (class-based) values propagated by the entertainment industry is adopted by various juvenile groups. Specific lifestyle systems that emerge in groups and occupy structurally inferior positions due to pressure from dominant systems are referred to as subcultures.

Subcultures are a reflection of both collective and individual efforts to resolve systemic contradictions. Subcultures play a crucial role in shaping patterns of behavior that hold significant symbolic meaning for the members of the group. There are many subcultures today where violence and abnormal behavior are prevalent. Violence is frequently used by some groups and subcultures to resolve interpersonal conflicts, and the environment this creates plays a significant mediating role in the delinquent or criminal behavior that results from it. This could even be called a subculture of violence, where using aggression to solve problems is seen as brave, acceptable, and even preferred. Those who belong to territorial gangs are the most likely to engage in criminal activity. Empirical data indicates that their crime rate is three times higher than that of non-gang juveniles and juveniles. Studies show that fighting, street extortion, and violence in schools are the crimes that gang members commit most frequently. It must be acknowledged that there are always young groups in the communities where they live. Similar social traits among its members, such as belonging to the same social class or ethnic group, define a community. At the local level, urban neighborhood communities offer their members a certain level of everyday social comfort. Similar to rural communities, these neighborhood units are able to balance the social interests of the groups they contain in the face of social diversity and urban growth.

Sometimes, being a part of a young group is crucial to socialization. Numerous studies have demonstrated the potential for connections to form between delinquent groups and other social institutions—a "symbiosis" in which gangs, for example, could function to meet any need within a community. As was previously mentioned, juvenile delinquent groups frequently serve as a gateway to adult organized crime. Information at hand indicates a strong correlation between crime and delinquency and gender. According to police data, male juvenile and young adult offenders have crime rates more than twice as high as young female offenders, and they also have conviction rates that are six or seven times higher. For every 100,000 individuals in the targeted age group, there are more than six times as many male juvenile suspects as female suspects. The ratio of male to female juvenile suspects is even higher for those in the youth category, at 12:5 to 1. Young men are more likely than young women to engage in violent or criminal behavior for a variety of reasons. Fear of sexual assault is one of many stimulative and restrictive factors that push women to follow social norms that do not apply to men. Girls are more likely than boys to be under strict family control. Due to cultural conceptions, young women's deviant behavior is viewed with less tolerance by society overall than that of young men. Furthermore, in patriarchal societies, aggression and violence are crucial in the construction of masculinity and sexuality, with the main goal being to uphold and perpetuate men's status and authority. Male perceptions of violence can be downplayed, overlooked, rejected, or given justification. Males frequently do not view acts like verbal or sexual insults as violent behavior.

There are societies where the dominant masculinity is more or less overtly oriented toward dominance, control, and violent confrontation. Other cultures do not attach the same standards of physical strength, diligence, and combat readiness to the socialization of young men toward hegemonic masculinity. The street gang is the perfect setting for boys and girls to "do gender"—that is, to establish gender differences. As a result, girls who are involved in gangs are active contributors to the establishment of gender relations rather than merely passive objects of "patriarchy." Peer groups have a significant influence on how gender roles and relationships—including delinquent behavior—are constructed. The gendered power dynamics in society, as well as the associated discourse and practices that perpetuate them, are reflected in youth gangs. Consequently, the social construction of gendered dominance and subordination in gang arrangements contributes to the differences in behavior between men and women in this setting.

7.1.4. Classification of Juvenile Delinquency

Without precise data, we are unable to assess the problem's magnitude nationwide, and the data that is available does not fully reflect the problem's scope because the majority of these delinquent acts are either overlooked or go unreported in our records. It has also been said that all developed nations have greater rates of delinquency.

Various classifications of the juvenile delinquency have been enumerated by various authors. The following important classifications are listed below:

Characterize the various kinds of juvenile crimes/offences:

- Out of the home in late nights, disrespect of parents, and so on.
- Absentee, either from home or school.
- Damage done to both public and private property.

- Violence created in the society by using any means such as knives and guns.
- Sex offenses and activity like criminal assault and rape.

Classify the delinquents by the various kinds of offences such as:

- Traffic violations which include driving without license, drunk driving and any other such offence.
- Automobile theft, uncontrollable behavior and some minor traffic violations.
- Human addiction such as alcohol and drug addiction
- Violations related to property which includes all property thefts.
- Bodily hurt which includes homicide offenses that involve sexual deviation; such as rape and all other acts of violence against a person.

Classify juvenile who become delinquent in relation to three major variables:

- The individual social class
- The degree of comprehensible emotional pathology.
- The extent to which the offenders engage themselves in delinquent behavior.

Classified the delinquent behavior into two classes on the basis of kinds of offence under the class one list they included:

- Damages to property;
- Theft of property; and
- Physical and bodily injuries.

Under the class second, they include:

- Coercion.
- Property loss and property damage threatened.
- Victimization committed against any person.
- Victimization committed against a commercial establishment.
- Victimization which involve two individuals such as rape.
- No victimization which includes truancy.

7.1.4.1. Two Categories of Juvenile Offenders

1. **Neurotic Offenders:** Delinquency in neurotic offenders is caused by powerful unconscious impulses that, in many cases, cause guilt and spur them to engage in criminal activity within their community. For instance, people occasionally steal to appease their partners rather

than for their own financial benefit. It is recommended that these delinquents externalize their internal problems to the environment in order to address them.

2. **Character Disorder Offenders:** When this group of criminals commits small-time crimes, they frequently experience intense guilt and regret. Positive identification models are scarce in their environment, which prevents them from strengthening their resolve and acting on their desires when they get the chance. They are unable to restrain their impulses in a way that is acceptable to society. These troublemakers come from chaotic households and were raised in an unwelcoming environment. These offenders are self-centered, feel distant from others, and struggle to build lasting relationships. Classified juvenile offenders in the following five categories:

i. **Gang Organized Delinquency:** This classification states that children form groups and engage in illegal activity within those groups. These young people, who are from underprivileged backgrounds and frequently feel frustrated by their inability to fulfill middle-class aspirations, frequently express themselves and attempt to accomplish their goals through joining gangs.

ii. **Un-socialized Delinquents:** Those delinquents would be considered convicted felons and typically come from homes where they were abandoned and mistreated. These children's families are prone to physical abuse. Having witnessed hatred and violence in homes and families, they frequently carried it on to their own children, who by then had developed severe aggressiveness. These offenders are not taught impulse control skills that are acceptable in society.

iii. **Accidental Delinquency:** Delinquents fall into this category if they are generally law-abiding but occasionally make poor decisions. They unintentionally get himself involved in a criminal activity. Anyone can be affected by these delinquents because they stop acting in a delinquent manner when they become aware of their actions or are caught engaging in them.

iv. **Occasional Offender:** Similar to an accidental delinquent, an occasional offender or delinquent engages in minor infractions occasionally but does not develop a habit of it.

v. **Professional Delinquency:** In this category delinquent usually steals things for getting some profits. They have done stealing for economic gain and to satisfy their desire.

7.1.5. Factors in Juvenile Delinquency

The term "juvenile delinquency" refers to criminal behavior committed by a minor. This phrase has a wide definition that can cover anything from infractions like skipping school to more serious offenses like burglaries and violent crimes. To stop minors from committing crimes in the future, it is crucial to understand why they do so.

It may be possible to influence the minor child's future behavior by addressing the problems that contributed to the decisions they made. Adults may be able to prevent juvenile delinquency by addressing many of these problems early on. If delinquency has already occurred, resolving these concerns and erecting safeguards may enable the child to grow up in a more secure setting and steer clear of trouble both now and as an adult.

1. **Poor School Attendance:** One of the main things that leads to delinquency is absenteeism. In addition to being a place for learning and development, school follows a set schedule that gives kids daily objectives to meet. The daily routine of rising early, getting ready, going to school, finishing homework, and going home creates a foundation for making wise decisions in the future. Youngsters miss out on developing positive habits if they are not encouraged to learn this kind of routine. Additionally, they have a lot of free time at their disposal, which they can use to "learn" about other topics that won't improve their lives or their prospects. Children who do not embrace the routine of going to school are actually taught that they are free to do as they please and are not bound by social norms.
2. **Poor Educational Standards:** A child's educational background may also have an impact on their delinquency. Schools that are overcrowded and underfunded frequently lack order and discipline. Children become more defensive as a result of the chaos that these schools frequently experience because they are afraid of their surroundings. It has been discovered that parental involvement in schoolwork and school-related activities significantly discourages delinquent behavior. A child who has an involved adult in their life is more likely to do well in school and in social situations because they are aware that the adult will be observing them.
3. **Violence in the Home:** Violence in the family is one of the main causes of delinquency. Every juvenile criminal defense lawyer will tell you that children who witness violence grow up to be violent adults. It's not uncommon for people to become enraged at others for the violence they witness at home. Adolescents who experience

violent acts or witness others engaging in such behavior are more prone to act out of their frustrations and fears. Their "don't care" attitude often makes it easier for them to get into trouble.

4. **Violence in Their Social Circles:** Children are more likely to become involved in criminal activity if they grow up in a violent neighborhood. This is sometimes referred to as "street survival methods" because the child gets into trouble in order to avoid confrontation with local gang members or other violent individuals. When a child is taken out of this kind of environment, their propensity for misbehavior is frequently eliminated.
5. **Peer Pressure:** Just like neighborhood pressures, direct acquaintance peer pressure can influence a young person's response to negative circumstances. If the child's friends are all engaging in criminal activity, they might feel under pressure to follow suit in order to fit in. Being regularly involved in your child's social circle is the best way to prevent situations like this one. Be familiar with their pals. Are aware of the parents of their friends. This gives your child the confidence to make the right decisions and can assist parents in shielding their kids from negative influences.
6. **Socioeconomic Factors:** Adolescent criminality is more prevalent in impoverished areas. Delinquent behavior is not uncommon in any neighborhood, but it is thought to be more common in communities where kids believe that committing crimes is necessary for them to succeed. It's possible that theft and related crimes are the result of necessity rather than being small-time offenses. Making sure the kids in these communities have access to what they need and realize they don't have to commit crimes to succeed in life is the only real way to help this situation.
7. **Substance Abuse:** Drug abuse by the child or in the home is a major contributor to delinquency. When children witness substance abuse, they frequently lack the basic needs for survival and are compelled to obtain them in other ways. Some people who develop drug dependence might also need to commit crimes in order to support their habit. The only effective way to assist these kids in situations like this is through counselling and treatment. Their sense of self-worth may decline in such circumstances, leading them to consider actions they otherwise would not have.
8. **Lack of Moral Guidance:** The greatest influence in preventing delinquency is that of parents or other adults. A child is more likely to behave in a way that is not delinquent when they are interacting

with a parent or other adult who models appropriate behavior for them. A child's relationship with a good adult is crucial because this person will guide their behavior and help them understand the difference between right and wrong. Your child's life does not end when they commit a delinquent act. As their caregiver, you have the opportunity to transform their lives and teach them new behaviors. To guarantee that they are given a fair trial, the first step is to hire a reputable juvenile criminal defense lawyer. After the child has completed this process, you as the caregiver can start to alter the influences in their life, giving them a fresh start and a clean slate as they enter adulthood.

7.2. CAUSES OF AND CONDITIONS FOR THE FORMATION OF DELINQUENT TRAJECTORIES

The social, economic, and cultural context of a nation typically dictates the scope and gravity of juvenile offenses. There is proof that juvenile crime is generally rising at the same time that the economy is declining, particularly in large cities' impoverished neighborhoods. Street children frequently grow up to be juvenile offenders because they have already experienced violence in their immediate social environment, either as witnesses to violent crimes or as victims of them.

This group's average educational attainment is relatively low, their socioeconomic environment is characterized by poverty and underemployment, and the basic social experience they acquire in the family is frequently insufficient. Every level of the social structure, including society as a whole, social institutions, social groups and organizations, and interpersonal relationships, has conditions that contribute to and cause juvenile crime. A multitude of factors contribute to juvenile delinquency and their decision to pursue delinquent careers; the most significant ones are outlined below.

7.2.1. Economic and Social Factors

The detrimental effects of social and economic development, particularly political unrest, economic crises, and the disintegration of important institutions, such as the family, the public education and assistance systems, and the state, are the main causes of juvenile delinquency.

Young people with low incomes and prolonged unemployment are frequently associated with socioeconomic instability, which may raise the risk of their engaging in criminal activity.

7.2.2. Cultural Factors

Delinquent behavior frequently happens in social contexts where expectations of appropriate behavior have collapsed. Many of the customary laws that prevent people from engaging in socially unacceptable behavior may become obsolete for certain members of society in such situations. They resort to rebellious, deviant, or even criminal behavior as a response to the upsetting and destructive changes in the social reality. The modernization of traditional societies and the ensuing changes brought about by the application of new technologies are examples of such a setting. Shifts of this magnitude affect social characteristics, authority structures, modes of political participation, and even the types and organization of labor activity, as well as lifestyles and living arrangements. These changes can even affect people's perceptions of reality. The media has raised consumer expectations in both developed and developing nations, and most families are unable to meet them. Nevertheless, for many young people, these ideals become a virtual reality, and some of them will do whatever it takes to maintain a lifestyle that they cannot afford. Some population groups are unable to accomplish their goals through legal means because they lack access to the resources they need, such as professional training, education, good jobs and income, health care, and suitable housing. Many young people feel frustrated by the conflict between their idealized, socially acceptable goals and the occasionally scarce real-life opportunities to pursue them lawfully. Choosing to become a criminal is one way to deal with this contradiction. Therefore, an excessive focus on stated goals (achieving success) combined with inadequate means to achieve them is one of the causes of delinquent behavior.

The possibility of deviant behavior in this situation is largely dependent on the degree of access to illegal opportunities as well as the absence of legal opportunities. Some young people fall victim to the influence of adult offenders even though they are aware of the restrictions placed by following the law. Many young people turn to drugs as a psychological or emotional escape, withdrawing within the boundaries of their own groups. Juveniles who use alcohol and illegal drugs are more likely to become delinquent because they must commit crimes (usually theft) in order to get the money they need to support their substance use.

7.2.3. Urbanization

According to geographic analysis, nations with higher rates of urbanization also tend to have higher registered crime rates than do those with more robust rural communities and lifestyles. The variations in social cohesiveness and control may be the cause of this. Rural communities have significantly lower crime rates and deal primarily with antisocial behavior through family and community control. Formal legal and judicial measures are frequently used in urban industrialized societies; this impersonal approach seems to be associated with higher rates of crime. The way that different countries respond to the same offense can differ greatly due to cultural and institutional differences. Juvenile involvement in criminal activity is a result of the ongoing urbanization process in developing nations. The fundamental characteristics of urban environments encourage the emergence of new social behaviors, which are primarily caused by the decline in formal social relationships and authority, the growing reliance on media at the expense of unofficial communication, and the propensity for anonymity. The greater population density, degree of heterogeneity, and overall number of people found in urban environments are what cause these patterns.

7.2.4. Family

According to studies, kids who have enough parental supervision are less likely to commit crimes. Juvenile delinquency is strongly correlated with dysfunctional family environments, which are marked by conflict, insufficient parental supervision, poor internal connections and integration, and early autonomy. Offenders are disproportionately overrepresented among children from low-income families who have limited options for gainful employment and are more likely to experience social exclusion. Particularly upsetting is the situation of migrant groups and ethnic minorities, which includes displaced people and refugees in some regions of the world. In this regard, the transitional countries face unique difficulties, as the ensuing unrest and insecurity lead to a rise in the number of children and adolescents who are abused and neglected at home by their parents.

The family as a social institution is undergoing significant transformation right now; the rise in single-parent households and non-marital unions, for instance, is diversifying the family's form. Boys may look for examples of masculinity among their peers who are involved in criminal activities because fatherlessness is common in low-income households. These groups define masculine roles, act as a stand-in for the family in many ways, and help people acquire traits like strength, cruelty, excitability, and anxiety. The value of a healthy family is getting more and more acknowledged. The ability of parents to provide their kids "starting" opportunities—that is, the funds to pay for their studies and purchase books and manuals—determines how well their kids do in school. Low-income adolescents frequently experience feelings of exclusion. They may decide to join a juvenile delinquent group in an effort to boost their status and boost their sense of self-worth. These organizations favorably set themselves apart from families and schools, where adults hold positions of authority, by giving everyone equal opportunities. Young people have the chance to study delinquent behavior when they are exposed to the influence of adult offenders, and the likelihood that they will commit adult crimes increases. The decision to follow a delinquent path is influenced by the "criminalization" of the family. According to a study done in US prisons, families engaged in criminal activity often encourage their younger members to break the law. Over two-thirds of the people surveyed had family members behind bars; for 25% of them, it was a father, and for another 25%, it was a brother or sister.

7.2.5. Migration

Immigrants frequently turn to their own surroundings and culture for solace because they are frequently marginalized by society and the economy and have little chance of success within the confines of the current legal system. Cultural conflicts, which are one of the main causes of criminal behavior, are brought about by differences in norms and values as well as the differing degrees of acceptability of certain acts in various ethnic subcultures. Urban natives typically view immigrants as blatant outcasts.

7.2.6. The Media

The "cult of heroes," which upholds justice by physically eliminating adversaries, has gained popularity thanks to television and motion pictures. Numerous studies have found that young people who witness violence typically act more violently or aggressively, especially when provoked. Boys between the ages of 8 and 12 exhibit this the most, as they are more susceptible to these kinds of influences.

Media exposes people to violence in three different ways. Movies that show violent acts first thrill viewers, and this aggressive energy can later be carried over into daily life and encourage people to exercise on the streets. This kind of impact is transient, with a duration ranging from a few hours to several days. Second, violence committed on a regular basis by peers or parents (the punishment for not attending class or breaking certain rules or standards of behavior) can be shown on television.

There are no television programs that do not feature these kinds of violent themes because the public's acceptance of such content has guaranteed its continuation. Children are consequently constantly exposed to the use of violence in a variety of contexts, and there seems to be an increase in the quantity of violent acts on television. Third, the media's portrayal of violence is unrealistic and surrealistic; actual suffering and suffering from violent acts are rarely shown, and wounds bleed less; as a result, the effects of violent behavior frequently appear insignificant. Television gradually modifies the human value system, persuading children to believe that using violence to restore justice is noble and even brave. After analyzing the data, the American Psychological Association came to the conclusion that 10% of children's aggressive behavior is caused by violence on television.

7.2.7. Exclusion

The rise of "unwanted others" is a result of the widening wealth disparity. The accumulation of barriers, broken social bonds, unemployment, and identity crises is leading to a progressive increase in the exclusion of certain individuals. A "new poor" class has emerged in many areas as a result of welfare programs that have alleviated but did not eradicate the low socioeconomic status of specific groups and the growing reliance of low-income families on social security benefits. Juveniles who have committed even small crimes are symbolically excluded from society, which has significant effects on the trajectory of delinquent careers. Research indicates that the act of labeling can cause a delinquent image to become self-adopted, which can then lead to delinquent behavior.

7.2.8. Peer Influence

Youth policies rarely take into account the importance of peer groups as socialization institutions. Like belonging to any other natural group, being a member of a delinquent gang can happen as a person develops into an adult. An individual gains a sense of security and safety, learns about social interaction, and can exhibit traits like loyalty or leadership through these fundamental associations. While race, ethnicity, and private welfare are highly valued in "adult" society, every member of an adolescent group is essentially in an equal position and has comparable opportunities for advancement within the hierarchical structure. Individual traits like strength, determination, and self-control are the only factors that determine a group's well-being. Delinquent groups frequently have the ability to make up for the shortcomings of both family and education. Numerous studies have demonstrated that young people involved in gangs view their group as a family. For young people who are surrounded by violence on a daily basis, being a member of a gang can offer safety in the community. People who do not belong to gangs may live in constant fear of being attacked, subjected to abuse, harassed, or subjected to extortion at school or on the streets.

7.2.8. Delinquent Identities

Determining the elements that lead to a delinquent identity and the reasons why some teenagers who take on a delinquent persona do not shed that persona as they mature are crucial steps in figuring out the root causes of criminal conduct. In actuality, delinquent identity is an overlay of multiple identities related to ethnicity, race, class, gender, and delinquency itself. It is a very complex construct. The identity of a delinquent is invariably formulated as a substitute for the prevailing identity within society. Group and delinquent identities are formed through the use of violence and conflict. Maintaining conflictual relationships with other youth groups and society at large lays the groundwork for the development and reinforcement of group identity and activity. Violent interactions help members of a group fit in more quickly by strengthening their sense of identity and integrating them into the community. The potential for social and financial advancement is another factor that could encourage someone to join a gang. The delinquent lifestyle has been somewhat romanticized in many sociocultural contexts, and for underprivileged youth, joining a gang is one of the few avenues for social mobility. One view holds that communities marked by a dearth of social and economic opportunities benefit from the stabilizing influence of urban youth gangs.

7.2.10. Offenders and Victims

A victim's behavior is closely linked to criminal activity. An offender may occasionally be provoked by a victim's response, but "appropriate" behavior can stop a crime from happening or at least lessen its effects. As per scientific literature, the probability of becoming a victim is associated with the traits or attributes of an individual, a social role, or a social situation that incites or facilitates criminal behavior. Personal traits like financial prosperity, safety, and individual or family status, as well as logistical traits like the location and timing of a confrontation, can also determine the degree of victimization. People can unintentionally become victims because arguments are frequently had before an attack. Three categories of adolescent victims of violence are recognized by the psychological types classification: those who are predisposed to become victims, those who are accidental victims, and "inborn" victims. Research indicates that most cases involving physical harm have a known relationship between the perpetrator and the victim, which can include spouses, relatives, or friends. This is the case for 80% of homicides and 70% of sexual offenses.

7.3. CUSTODY OF JUVENILE DELINQUENTS

The term "arrest" is not used in reference to juveniles. Law enforcement can take a youth into custody. Three types of custody are:

1. **Temporary Custody:** Without a judge's order, police can place a minor under temporary custody for 12 hours, unless it's a Saturday,

Sunday, or holiday. Then, without a judge's permission, a minor may be detained for a full day. Parents, guardians, or custodians have the right to visit their minor until the court order is in effect, and law enforcement is required to inform them of this when the minor is taken into custody.

2. **Non-Secure Custody***:* Whether to place a minor in secure or non-secure custody is up to the court. The court may release the minor to a parent, guardian, custodian, or other adult if non-secure custody is requested.
3. **Secure Custody***:* The court must believe the juvenile committed the offense in the petition and also one of the following conditions must be met:

- The juvenile is charged with a felony and is a danger to property or persons;
- The juvenile is charged with a misdemeanor that includes assault on a person and is a danger to persons;
- The juvenile failed to come to court on a pending delinquency charge;
- The court believes the juvenile will not come to court on a pending charge;
- The juvenile has run away from a training school or detention center;
- The court believes the juvenile has or will harm himself/herself;
- The juvenile is undisciplined by being a runaway and may need secure custody.

7.3.1. Juvenile Detention and Custody

Any law enforcement official with a court order or reasonable suspicion that a minor has committed a delinquent act is authorized to arrest or detain a juvenile. It is mandatory for the law enforcement official to promptly inform the child's guardians, parents, or custodians. If the child provides a written commitment to appear in juvenile court, the law enforcement officer may release the child to his or her parent, guardian, or custodian. But if the law enforcement official has good reason to believe that the child is not likely to return, or if detention is necessary to safeguard the child or the community, or if the child is accused of murder or another Class A or Class B felony, then the child may be placed in detention. In addition, if the child has a valid reason for seeking detention or if the parent, guardian, or custodian cannot be found or refuses to take custody, the child may be placed in detention. The juvenile detention center or any other shelter care facility that houses people accused or found guilty of crimes cannot accept the child in such circumstances.

After placing a child under arrest, the Clark Superior Court #1 Juvenile Probation Department's Intake Officer looks into the circumstances surrounding the placement and may choose to release the child to guardians, parents, or other custodians in exchange for a written commitment to appear in juvenile court again. A detention hearing in Juvenile Court must take place in the event that the child is being held in the Juvenile Detention Center no later than 48 hours after the child is taken into custody, excluding Saturdays, Sundays, and holidays.

The Juvenile Court may, at the detention hearing, order the child to surrender his or her driver's license; dismiss the charges and release the child if there is no reasonable suspicion that the child committed a delinquent act; release the child to parents, guardians, or custodians upon a written promise to appear in Juvenile Court; or order continued detention if there is a reasonable belief that the child is unlikely to reappear; or if detention is necessary to protect the child or the community; or if the child has a legitimate reason for requesting detention. The child might not be granted bail to be released from custody.

7.3.2. What Happens in a Juvenile Case?

The process that is followed in a typical criminal case for juvenile offenders differs greatly from that used for adult offenders when a juvenile is suspected of breaking a law. Every state has established a distinct juvenile court system for young people who run afoul of the law. Additionally, even though these juvenile courts eventually find certain minors to be delinquent, the various parties involved in a typical juvenile case—police, prosecutors, and judges—have a great deal of latitude to reach different conclusions. While state-by-state procedures differ in handling juvenile delinquency cases, the following outlines the general process for a typical juvenile case.

7.3.3. How Police Deal with Juveniles?

A minor may interact with law enforcement in a variety of ways regarding an alleged criminal statute violation. While some minors are taken into custody by law enforcement, others are reported to them by guardians or educators. A police officer may choose to handle a minor in a number of ways, regardless of how they learn about a possible juvenile case:

1. **Issue a Warning:** The police officer can detain the minor, issue a warning, and then let the minor go. This is often referred to as the "counseled and released" alternative.

2. **Hold the Minor Until a Parent Comes:** Sometimes the police officer will detain the minor, issue a warning, and then release the minor to the custody of a parent or guardian.
3. **Refer to Juvenile Court:** The police officer may also place the juvenile in custody and refer the case to juvenile court.

7.3.4. When Cases Go to Juvenile Court

A prosecutor or juvenile court intake officer—typically a probation officer—takes charge of a case after a police officer refers it to juvenile court. That person has three options: file formal charges (also known as petitioning the case), handle the case informally, or dismiss the case.

In deciding how to proceed, the prosecutor or intake officer will typically consider:

- the severity of the offense;
- the juvenile's age;
- the juvenile's past record;
- the strength of the evidence in the case;
- the juvenile's gender (boys are more likely to be charged than girls);
- the juvenile's social history; and
- the ability of the minor's parents to control his or her behavior.

In an average year, about 20% of the cases referred to a juvenile court intake officer are dismissed and another 25% or so are handled informally. The remaining cases go through formal proceedings.

7.3.4.1. Informal Proceedings

In the event that the juvenile's case is taken up informally by the prosecutor or probation officer, the minor is typically required to appear before a judge or probation officer. Although no formal charge is entered against the juvenile, he or she will usually be required to do one or more of the following:

- Listen to a stern lecture;
- Attend counselling;
- Attend after-school classes;
- Repay the victim for damages;
- Pay a fine;
- Perform community service work; or
- Enter probation.

If the juvenile's abuse or neglect is suspected as part of the case, the juvenile court judge may initiate proceedings to remove the minor from parental or guardian custody.

7.3.4.2. Formal Proceedings: Petitioning the Case

In the event that the prosecutor or probation officer chooses to take formal action, a petition will be filed in juvenile court. After that, the minor is formally charged (arraigned) in front of a judge or referee in juvenile court. The juvenile may occasionally be sent to adult criminal court by the court. The minor's release or custody during the period preceding the initial hearing will also be decided by the court. A minor is permitted to stay at home while awaiting a hearing in approximately 80% of cases that are formally processed in juvenile court by the judge.

If the minor's case remains in juvenile court, one of three things may happen:

- **The Minor Enters into a Plea Agreement**: A plea deal frequently depends on the minor fulfilling specific requirements. For instance, a juvenile entering into a plea agreement might be required to follow curfews, go to counselling, or pay back the victim's damages.
- **The Judge "Diverts" the Case:** When a judge diverts a case, the judge still has jurisdiction over the juvenile while they complete an act (like community service or payment of restitution) or participate in a recommended program (like counselling). If the minor fails to comply with these requirements, formal charges may be brought again by the court.
- **The Judge Holds an Adjudicatory Hearing***:* In the event that the matter proceeds to trial (referred to as an adjudicatory hearing in a juvenile case), the attorneys present their cases and both parties submit evidence, much like in a criminal trial. A judge, not a jury, preside over the hearing in the majority of states. The judge will decide whether or not the minor is delinquent after the hearing. Sustaining the petition is the name given to a delinquency decision. If a juvenile is found to be delinquent, a probation officer will assess the minor, obtain diagnostic testing or psychological evaluations as needed, and present recommendations at the disposition hearing (which functions similarly to a criminal court sentencing hearing). The judge then decides what is in the best interest of the juvenile, and may order any number of things as part of the disposition, including:
- Counselling;

- Confinement in a juvenile detention facility;
- Reimbursement of the victim; or
- Probation.

The judge may also order the juvenile to appear in court periodically (called post-disposition hearings) so that the judge can monitor the juvenile's behavior and progress.

7.4. JUVENILE COURT CASE PROCESS

The normal course of a juvenile court case is mapped out in published materials by the Office of Juvenile Justice and Delinquency Prevention (OJJDP). The model case flow is fairly general because court decisions are highly personalized and many cases are processed informally; nonetheless, the fundamental steps outlined are the same across the country.

7.4.1. Arrest, Referral, and Initial Detainment

A young person's arrest by a member of the law enforcement community typically represents their initial interaction with the juvenile justice system. Probation officers, parents, schools, and victims of delinquency are some of the other ways that young people get into the system. After an arrest, a decision is typically made regarding the youth's placement in another youth welfare program, release from custody, or detention and prosecution. The juvenile's parents, the victims of the crime he committed, the juvenile himself, and any prior records the youngster may have with the juvenile justice system are all considered by the officer managing the case when making this determination. Federal laws mandate that minors housed in adult prisons must be kept out of the sight and hearing of adult inmates and must leave the adult facility within six hours of the juvenile's arrival (while officials try to get in touch with the juvenile's parents or arrange for a transfer). An intake officer will determine whether to dismiss, handle informally, or hear a juvenile court case formally when it arrives at the juvenile probation department. The officer considers all available evidence in the case before determining whether to proceed with the youth's trial. Whether the juvenile case should be heard formally or informally will be decided if the court finds sufficient evidence to consider the case. The case will be dismissed if there is insufficient information available.

A young person may be kept in a safe detention center pending trial. In a detention hearing, which is typically held 24 hours after the arrest, the judge will decide whether the minor should be held in custody prior to and during the trial, as well as define the purpose of the detention. If a young person endangers himself or the public, they will usually be placed in detention.

7.4.2. Informal Hearing and Disposition

Most juvenile justice cases that are heard informally—roughly 50% of all cases—are dismissed. When a minor acknowledges guilt and consents to resolve the charges by following the court's requirements as outlined in a consent decree, the case is handled informally by the judge. These prerequisites might include:

- **Restitution:** Juvenile is required to reimburse the victim or pay a fine to the community for damages he has caused.
- **Mandatory Curfew:** Juvenile is subject to a strict curfew.
- **School Attendance:** Juvenile is required to attend school regularly.
- **Rehabilitation:** Juvenile is required to participate in drug or other rehabilitation programs.

The youth will be released on probation so long as he complies with his obligations after all parties have approved the consent decree. An informal probation officer will be keeping an eye on his progress during this period. The juvenile court case will be dropped once he has complied with the consent decree's requirements. The youth might have to appear in person for a formal hearing if he disobeys the court's directives.

7.4.3. Formal Hearing

A preliminary determination regarding the mode of hearing must be made if an official hearing is judged necessary after evaluating the juvenile's case. Certain cases can be heard in either juvenile or criminal court in many states. The prosecutor is typically allowed to choose the venue for the case trial in such circumstances. The juvenile court has jurisdiction over the majority of cases involving minors. Still, some states have passed legislation mandating that especially serious crimes be tried in criminal court.

7.4.4. Juvenile Court Hearings

Delinquency and waiver petitions are the two types of petitions that prosecutors submit to juvenile courts. Delinquency petitions ask the court to declare a minor delinquent, while waiver petitions ask the juvenile court to give up jurisdiction over a case that would otherwise come before it and send it to criminal court.

7.4.5. Delinquency Petition

A delinquency petition notifies the court of the accusations made against a minor and requests that the case be heard in a formal hearing. The case's facts and witness testimony are heard during an adjudicatory hearing. A disposition hearing is set if the judge (or jury in some states) finds the minor to be delinquent. The probation office is responsible for assessing the young person and recommending a plan of action to the court in the interim. Probation officials will consider the findings of any research done on the young person. These frequently consist of diagnostic exams and psychological evaluations. The court receives advice from the disposition plan regarding which available options would be best for the youth and the community.

Probation officer, prosecutor, and juvenile may all suggest disposition strategies during the disposition hearing. Restitution, limited (weekend) confinement, drug rehabilitation, and residential placement are frequently suggested courses of action. A young person may be placed in a residential facility or on probation for a predetermined amount of time, or until the conditions of the disposition are fulfilled. The court will evaluate his progress at regular review hearings. The juvenile court case will end once the disposition's orders have been fulfilled. Adolescent offenders designated as state wards are housed in residential facilities. Different facilities have varying degrees of security; some are more like prisons, while others are more like group homes. A young person who has completed their stay in a residential facility is frequently placed in aftercare. Like parole, aftercare involves the juvenile corrections department keeping an eye on the youth's behavior and progress for a predetermined amount of time.

7.4.6. Waiver Petition

A waiver petition will be filed by a prosecutor or intake officer in the event that they determine that a case that would typically fall under the exclusive jurisdiction of the juvenile court should instead be heard in criminal court. After examining the case's circumstances and determining whether the juvenile would be better off under the juvenile justice system's care, the court will determine the location of the case's hearing. The juvenile's age, length of time youth services would have to work with the offender, past rehabilitation success, and criminal history (if the youth is a repeat offender) all influence the court's decision. The juvenile court forfeits its jurisdiction and the case is sent to criminal court if a judge grants a petition waiver. An adjudicatory hearing is set and the case is transferred to the juvenile court if the judge rejects a petition waiver.

7.4.7. Status Offenses

Status offenses are a common factor in many juvenile court cases. The main distinction between delinquent acts and status offenses is that the latter are crimes solely based on the offender's status as a minor. Some examples of status offenses are:

- Underage alcohol consumption;
- Truancy from school;
- General "ungovernability;"
- Violation of curfew;
- Running away from home.

Delinquent acts (which, if committed by an adult, would be crimes) are handled by the court in a different way than status offenses. Typically, the court interprets behavior related to status offenses as an indicator that a young person needs help. Social service providers and child welfare agencies frequently handle these cases. Since the Juvenile Justice and Delinquency Prevention Act has called for the deinstitutionalization of status offenders, these individuals are typically not housed in secure residential facilities.

7.4.8. Counseling of Juvenile Delinquents

A child under the age of 18 who engages in dubious and problematic behavior at home, school, or in social situations and has broken the law is considered to be a juvenile delinquent. If your child is acting in this way, handling the situation can be extremely difficult, and finding a solution may seem unattainable. Thankfully, you can do your part as a parent to stop your child's delinquent behavior by taking certain actions and enrolling them in programs.

1. **Define the Problems:** Reprimanding your child without taking the time to identify the issue at hand or acting to find a solution isn't constructive and may even encourage more delinquent behavior. Consider your child's particular circumstances as well as the particular behaviors they are displaying. Get truthful responses to your questions from your child's instructors or coaches, as well as from them directly. Teens who use drugs or alcohol and experience depression are often the ones who end up in legal trouble. Counselling might not be enough to help your child if substance abuse is evident in their behavior. Rehabilitation has been shown to be an effective strategy, particularly when the issue is dealt with quickly.
2. **Set Boundaries:** Children and teenagers who start acting out need to be taught that their behavior is inappropriate through both words and deeds. There will be repercussions for this. Setting limits for your child, such as curfews, chores, and the amount of time they can spend outside the house, is essential. If and when your child pushes those boundaries, you have to take away their privileges and make sure the punishment is appropriate for the offense they committed; otherwise, they'll have gained access and control over the situation.

3. **Be Their Support System:** You can still be there for your child during this important time even if you are taking on the role of enforcer. Think about your relationship with your child at home, any arguments that might have contributed to their erratic behavior, and what you can do to help your child feel comfortable and safe there. Children usually view their relationship with their parents as their most significant bond, and harsh love can only go so far.
4. **Get Your Child Involved in Activities:** Juveniles frequently run afoul of the law because they are bored or hang out with the wrong crowd. Your child's behavior and perspective will probably change if they are surrounded by kind and encouraging individuals. Programs for troubled teenagers are offered by groups and associations such as The Salvation Army and The Boys and Girls Club of America. Engaging in extracurricular activities such as music and art classes, church groups, and sports can guarantee that your child spends less time engaging in deviant behavior.
5. **Be Involved After an Arrest:** You might need to retain the services of a respectable lawyer if your child is placed in custody. Teens are less likely than adults to follow up on their paperwork and complete any court-mandated requirements, so there will probably be penalties and consequences following an arrest. Keep in close contact with all public officials involved in the case, including probation officers, community corrections officers, and corrections officers.

7.5. PREVENTING JUVENILE DELINQUENCY

Children's fundamental human rights are endangered by violence against them. Therefore, persuading people and organizations to devote the time, funds, skills, and other resources required to address this global issue is essential. A number of UN instruments show that social rather than judicial methods are preferred for reducing juvenile delinquency. The United Nations Standard Minimum Rules for the Administration of Juvenile Justice (the Beijing Rules) recommend implementing positive measures to strengthen a juvenile's overall well-being and lessen the need for State intervention. The Riyadh Guidelines assert that preventing juvenile delinquency is an essential part of overall crime prevention in society. The general consensus is that the most effective strategy for preventing juvenile delinquency is early-phase intervention. In order to prevent teenagers from breaking the law, prevention efforts must be made on an individual, group, and organizational level. Different strategies are employed in different nations to deter criminal and delinquent behavior. Some concentrate on punitive prevention, which aims to scare potential offenders by ensuring they understand the possibility of harsh punishment. Other measures to prevent recurrent crime include educating delinquents about the consequences of their actions and making efforts to make amends between offenders and their victims.

Many areas are implementing early preventive measures. Here are some of the most promising strategies, plans, and projects. Professional development programs are being established in the economic sector to offer legitimate options for generating income. Youth involvement in delinquent activities can be avoided by providing adolescents and young people with greater economic opportunities, professional training and education, new employment opportunities, and support in starting businesses. Youth education initiatives are assisting in the development of positive self-perception, conflict resolution, and aggression management skills. The shows dispel the stereotype of gang glamour and assist youth in avoiding criminal activity. Some work with young people who are troubled to help them acquire the social and cognitive skills needed to control their aggression and prevent conflict. These are the kinds of skills that kids who grow up in stable families, excellent schools, and wholesome communities usually naturally acquire. Law enforcement agencies, schools, local communities, and parents of teenagers participate in these programs in the United States.

The Riyadh Guidelines, which state that "a wide range of recreational facilities and services of particular interest to young persons should be established and made easily accessible to them," explicitly encourage youth development and recreation. The implementation of adolescent basketball programs resulted in a 60% reduction in crime rates in several American towns. A Boys' or Girls' Club can lower crime rates in public housing projects by an average of 13%, according to research from Columbia University in New York City. In Stevenage, a United Kingdom town with multiple youth clubs established and a sizable youth center and playground constructed, youth involvement has mostly remained away from criminal activity.

Often it is possible to reduce the level of juvenile delinquency by changing an urban environment, altering the physical features through architectural and landscape planning and providing opportunities to engage young people's interest. A research study conducted in a town in the United States revealed that most of the activities of juvenile delinquent groups were concentrated around the town's only park. The layout of the park was redesigned to create many more leisure and recreational alternatives for juveniles and their parents. The number of positive afternoon activities held in schools and parks was also increased. All of these measures led to a considerable reduction in juvenile delinquency; in the United States juvenile crime, including violent offences, peaks at around 3 p.m., generally right after school lets out.

More focus has recently been placed on the function and obligation of local communities in addressing juvenile delinquency. Programs are available to teach organizations and individual members of the local communities where juvenile delinquency has surged how to manage youth informally and involve them in positive activities. Over the past 10 years, there has been a growing acceptance of the notion that youth can and should collaborate with adults to better the lives of those in their communities. Young people are being asked to participate in community initiatives through organized (and occasionally mandatory) volunteer work, sit on boards, and submit ideas. The engagement of NGOs and volunteers (students and pensioners, along with well-known and authority figures such as sportsmen, politicians, and public figures) in social work with adolescents is a promising development in efforts to prevent juvenile delinquency and crime. Programs designed to stop youth gang involvement should generally aim to include kids and young people in structured group activities. This can be accomplished through independent boys' and girls' clubs, community centers, and social service organizations like the YMCA, YWCA, Girl Guides, Boy Scouts, and independent clubs. Recreational programs run by the local government can also help achieve this.

Collaboration amongst different prevention agents is becoming more and more crucial. The most successful multisectoral prevention programs are those that are created and carried out by entire communities; these include those that highlight youth interests and strengths rather than just their flaws or problems. In order to reduce crime in 10 high-crime neighborhoods, law enforcement officers, human service agency representatives, and local residents collaborated in one US city. The program, which also included the creation of youth sports leagues and a youth forum where young people could voice their concerns about neighborhood issues, among other preventative measures, resulted in a 29% decrease in crime in the targeted neighborhoods and a citywide decrease in violent crime. Institutional programs such as camps, group homes, alternative schools, and shelters are designed to offer social and psychological support to both individuals and groups. Individualized educational planning, individual, group, and parent counselling, health care and assignment to medical facilities, educational, behavioral, and psychological evaluation and diagnostics, and leisure activity planning are all provided in this context.

It seems that the family, as the main socialization institution, has the greatest influence on preventing child and adolescent delinquency. The most effective preventive initiatives concentrate on the families of problematic adolescents, including those with severe behavioral issues. When parents of troublesome children between the ages of three and eight in the United States received parent management training, the children's outcomes were significantly better than those of a control group that was placed on a waiting list for the program. All told, roughly two thirds to three quarters of the kids in the program made a clinically meaningful improvement and went back to operating within a typical behavioral range.

In this regard, children and teenagers living on the streets as well as those who lost their families during armed conflicts and never had proper family surveillance need to receive extra attention. Since most street child programs are ad hoc and provide food, clothing, shelter, and health services on occasion, they are primarily remedial in nature. It is necessary to supplement these symptomatic treatment initiatives with programs that address the root causes of streetism.

Special programmes are needed to tackle the problem of unaccompanied and homeless children, including rehabilitation schemes that take children off the streets. The United Nations Convention on the Rights of the Child provides a framework for improving the living conditions of children, focusing on the following four broad areas:

- **Survival Rights:** The basic needs—medical care, nutrition, shelter, and clothes—that children must have in order to enjoy good health and proper growth are covered in Articles 6.1, 6.2, and 24.1. Most of these needs are not met for children living on the streets.
- **Development Rights:** Articles 6, 26 and 28 relate to the opportunities and means for providing children with access to education, skills, training, recreation and rest, information, parental care and social security.
- **Protective Rights:** Articles 2, 19.1, 19.2, 32.1, 33, 34, 36 and 37 focus n the legal and social provisions that must be made by each country to protect children from exploitation, drug abuse, sexual abuse, cruelty, separation from family, discrimination, and the effects of all types of man-made or natural disasters.
- **Participation Rights:** The focus of Articles 12, 13, 14, and 17 is on giving children the tools and opportunities to voice their opinions on issues that impact their lives, such as the freedom of worship, the right to know one's own background information, and the right to testify (if necessary). Youngsters can come up with creative solutions to problems if they are given the opportunity to express their knowledge about their circumstances. Particularly, street kids have already mastered the ability to make critical decisions about their daily lives without adult guidance.

In slum and squatter settlements, community-based interventions have the power to keep kids off the streets and facilitate their reintegration into their communities. Aiding street children in developing positive attitudes and an optimistic self-perception is another goal of preventive work. Punitive prevention programs, which use surveillance (ongoing police observation) and prosecution to try to stop juvenile and youth offenses, gang recruitment, growth, and criminal activity, are still in place in many countries. One type of active intervention that the State has fully legitimized is suppression. This approach doesn't need any extra justification or outcome assessment because it is thought to be correct from the start. This kind of approach usually ignores attempts to encourage appropriate behavior in favor of preventing undesirable behavior. Nonetheless, in many instances, the use of force by authorities can facilitate young people's continued assimilation into criminal organizations.

For young people who are already in trouble, purely preventive (or suppressive) measures are not very effective. A relatively small number of repeat offenders, who usually exhibit severe behavioral issues in their early childhood, commit the majority of crimes. More comprehensive, customized care is probably needed for them. Restorative justice, which is typically implemented by non-governmental remedial organizations and local communities, is the most effective way to prevent recurrent crime. One alternative approach to criminal justice is restorative justice. It entails a procedure whereby all parties involved in a particular offense convene and decide together on the best course of action to address the offense's consequences and long-term effects. Through communication with the victim, the offender must come to understand the gravity of the situation. Then, in collaboration with the victim and social workers, a plan for reconciliation must be developed, including arranging for damages to be paid and offering the victim any necessary remedial support. If a successful resolution is reached, the young person is spared the influence of a setting (jail) that might encourage delinquent behavior by not being placed in a correctional facility or labeled as a delinquent.

The reconciliation process must be carried out very carefully so that the offender does not consider it a "deal" with the victim—a risk emphasized by various researchers. According to different studies up to 95% of juveniles who have participated in such programmes and agreed to provide restitution have fulfilled their obligations, and recurrence levels have been reduced by 50% in general. Moreover, restitution is much more cost-effective than confinement; in the United States the cost of keeping each juvenile in a correctional facility can be as high as $30,000 per year.

Reconciliation between the offender and the victim is a crucial component of restorative justice. It is a process that is required for both the offender's correction and the victim's restoration of justice. It is acknowledged that a fundamental component of comprehensive crime prevention and crime control strategies is the protection and assistance of witnesses and victims. Support measures are crucial for maintaining and safeguarding the role of victims and witnesses in the criminal justice system, as well as for lessening the impact of crime on those who are most immediately impacted. By promoting cooperation between victims, witnesses, and law enforcement and prosecution agencies, it also helps with criminal investigations and prosecutions. Experts say that in order for victims of crime to feel like they have their dignity and honor back, they need rehabilitation to help them feel like they have some worth again and to acknowledge the trauma they have experienced. Following a crime, victims typically get in touch with the police, immigration officials, welfare volunteers, representatives of non-governmental organizations, or laypeople; however, very few of these individuals are qualified to assist traumatized victims. People who are usually the first to interact with victims must receive the proper training. In particular, policies for witness protection must be developed and put into place with regard to organized crime and specific offenses like human trafficking, where intimidation or retaliation may be used against those who assist the police in preventing, investigating, or prosecuting offenses. More victim support services and awareness campaigns emphasizing victims' rights are required.

The effectiveness of a crime prevention system is generally contingent upon three factors: (a) a clear definition of the framework and contents of prevention efforts; (b) the appropriate utilization of functional opportunities offered by all agencies included in the system; (c) the development of mechanisms for administration, control, and coordination; and (d) the coverage of all subjects and targets of prevention work, including adolescents and their relationships in various spheres of society, with special attention to each unique characteristics.

In practice, many prevention approaches have proved ineffective. Studies show that shock incarceration (boot camp) does not reduce criminality. Short term, "quick fix" job training has not lowered arrest rates. Neither traditional psychotherapy nor behavior modification has shown great promise as a vehicle for redirecting delinquent and criminal youth. A few methods—especially scare-oriented approaches or programmes that place groups of delinquent youth together for extended treatment—have actually worsened the behavior of participants.

Experience has shown that the most futile efforts are made to combat gang membership. Numerous strategies have been proposed to change the gang environment, but they usually focus only on the criminal side of the issue, ignoring the socioeconomic and other factors that force young people to join gangs. Traditional social institutions are also rarely involved in the process.

However, there are many programs put in place to address the issue of gang membership; some evaluators claim these programs are effective, while others find them to be wholly insufficient. Some researchers claim that politicians looking to show that they are combating juvenile delinquency may find it appealing when several initiatives are put into place and received well. Adequate evaluation of prevention work is often hampered by political considerations, which means that ineffective programs may continue to run while the issues surrounding juvenile delinquency remain unresolved.

To achieve prevention at every level, consistency is crucial. It is a common misconception that juvenile delinquency is an individual problem, and the community component is frequently minimized or overlooked. But in actuality, young people who commit delinquent acts typically do so as members of a group, or at the very least within the parameters set by that group. Work on prevention needs to consider group cultural dynamics in addition to individual motivation in order to be effective. On a larger scale, juvenile delinquent groups may have close links to adult organized crime and local community members in some countries (like the Russian Federation). This must be taken into account when developing prevention programs.

Transferring prevention strategies from one societal and cultural context to another isn't always straightforward. Successful programs in one nation might fail to yield similar results in another; for instance, a method for restorative justice that demonstrates success in one country could fall short when implemented in another with disappointing outcomes. It's crucial to consider the unique subcultural aspects of a specific group of juvenile offenders when designing programs, and to precisely identify the intended audience for preventive interventions

To address the gang issue, communities need to employ a mix of prevention, intervention, and suppression tactics. Policies and programs should be designed with youth and institutions in mind, considering their relationship at that specific moment and location. This could mean concentrating on a specific young person's entry into or exit from a gang, or addressing the stage at which gang issues are becoming more prevalent in a given institution or community.

The desire to live within boundaries that are accepted by society is not entirely absent from gang members. They look to the gang as their only source of safety and acceptance, though, as they are frequently wary of and terrified of society at large. It is necessary to make attempts to steer young gangs toward socially acceptable behavior. The majority of rehabilitation programs currently in place are ineffective in refocusing gang members' potential or energies toward activities that are valued by society. In order to improve victims' status, one promising area of prevention work is to support victims' associations and create programs and training that are relevant to their needs. There is still a certain theoretical gap surrounding the issue of youth victimization. According to recent research, the distinction between victims and offenders is not based on age or sex but rather on variations within each gender; in other words, victims and offenders belonging to the same gender represent distinct facets of masculinity and femininity. The development of prevention programs must take these and other gender-related factors into account. In particular, addressing the needs of street and orphaned children, as well as victims of armed conflict, sexual abuse, and trafficking, would benefit from an expansion of efforts in this direction. Special measures are required for children and adolescents who are facing the latter three categories of challenges: roundtable discussions should be held to develop strategies for counter-trafficking and for integrating victims of armed conflicts (including adolescent former soldiers) and victims of harassment and sexual abuse into society; and the media, as the primary source of public information, should play a key role in informing the public about the destructive results of armed conflicts.

The creation and execution of prevention and rehabilitation programs require a proactive but thoughtful approach, with care taken to apply the lessons discovered via firsthand experience. Large public spending is necessary to bolster and broaden the youth-focused prevention agenda as well as to step up efforts to enhance and perfect the promise of prevention. However, it must be acknowledged that haphazardly spending money, time, or effort on impromptu or badly thought out solutions will not significantly address the issue; as a result, research and evaluation must be incorporated into all preventative initiatives.

REFERENCES

1. American Psychological Association. (1993). *Violence and Youth: Psychology's Response*. Summary report of the APA Commission on Violence and Youth. Washington, D.C.
2. Bartol, C., & Bartol, A. (2009). *Juvenile Delinquency and Antisocial Behavior: A Developmental Perspective* (3rd ed.). Upper Saddle River, NJ: Pearson Prentice Hall.
3. Bartollas, C. (2003). *Juvenile Delinquency* (6th ed.). NY: Allyn & Bacon.
4. Child Act 2001. (2006). Malaysia: International Law Book Services.
5. Dzikus, A., & Ochola, L. (1996). Street children in sub-Saharan Africa: Kenya's experience. *Habitat Debate, 2*(2), 16–22.
6. Federal Ministry of the Interior & Federal Ministry of Justice. (2001). *First Periodical Report on Crime and Crime Control in Germany*. Berlin.
7. Gilmore, D. (1990). *Manhood in the Making: Cultural Concepts of Masculinity*. London: Yale University Press.
8. Hague Convention on Protection of Children and Co-operation in Respect of Intercountry Adoption. (1993). Retrieved from: http://www.hcch.net/e/conventions/text33e.html (accessed on 16 August 2024).
9. Johnson, U. (1995). *Gang Violence Prevention: A Curriculum and Discussion Guide*. Pleasantville, NY: Sunburst Communications.
10. Klein, M. (1995). *The American Street Gang: Its Nature, Prevalence, and Control*. New York: Oxford University Press.
11. Machel, G. (1996). *Impact Of Armed Conflict on Children: Report of The Expert of The Secretary-General, Ms. Graça Machel, Submitted Pursuant to United Nations General Assembly Resolution 48/157* (A/51/306).
12. Office of Juvenile Justice and Delinquency Prevention, US Department of Justice. (2018). Victimizations by juveniles per 1,000 youth ages 12–17, 1980–2016. Retrieved from: www.ojjdp.gov (accessed on 16 August 2024).
13. Office of Juvenile Justice and Delinquency Prevention. (2015). *Characteristics of Delinquency Cases Handled in Juvenile Court in 2015* [PDF]. Retrieved from: www.ojjdp.gov (accessed on 16 August 2024).
14. Organization of African Unity & UNICEF. (1992). Africa's children, Africa's future: A background sectoral paper prepared for the OAU International Conference on Assistance to African Children, Dakar, 25–27 November 1992.
15. Pfeiffer, C. (1998). Trends in juvenile violence in European countries. *National Institute of Justice Research Preview Series*.

16. Regoli, R. M., & Hewitt, J. D. (2006). *Delinquency in Society* (6th ed.). Boston: Nelson Education.
17. Siegel, L. J., & Welsh, B. C. (2011). *Juvenile Delinquency: The Core* (4th ed.). Belmont, CA: Wadsworth/Cengage Learning.
18. Tolman, J., Pittman, K., Cervone, B., et al. (2001). *Youth Acts, Community Impacts: Stories of Youth Engagement with Real Impacts* (Community and Youth Development Series, Vol. 7). Takoma Park, MD: Forum for Youth Investment.
19. UNICEF. (1997). *MONEE Project: Children at Risk in Central and Eastern Europe: Perils and Promises*. Regional Monitoring Report No. 4. Florence: UNICEF Innocenti Research Centre.
20. UNICEF. (2001). *MONEE Project: Ten Years of Transition*. Regional Monitoring Report No. 7. Florence: UNICEF Innocenti Research Centre.
21. United Nations. (1990). *Guidelines for the Prevention of Juvenile Delinquency (The Riyadh Guidelines)*. Adopted and proclaimed by General Assembly resolution 45/112 of 14 December 1990.
22. United Nations. (2000). *Report of the Tenth United Nations Congress on the Prevention of Crime and the Treatment of Offenders, Vienna, 10–17 April 2000* (A/CONF.187/15).
23. United Nations. (2001). *Draft Plans of Action for The Implementation During the Period 2001–2005 Of the Vienna Declaration on Crime and Justice: Meeting the Challenges of The Twenty-First Century: Report of the Secretary-General* (E/CN.15/2001/5). Tenth session of the Commission on Crime Prevention and Criminal Justice, Vienna, 8–17 May 2001.
24. Venkatesh, S. (1997). The social organization of street gang activity in an urban ghetto. *American Journal of Sociology, 103*(1), 82–111.
25. Woolard, S. (2009). The legal regulation of adolescence. In R. Lerner & L. Steinberg (Eds.), *Handbook of Adolescent Psychology* (2nd ed., Vol. 2, pp. 345–371). New York: Wiley.

Chapter **8**

Causation of Crime Theories

Contents

INTRODUCTION

Theories of crime causation attempt to explain why people commit crimes and what circumstances lead to them being committed. These theories shed light on the intricate interactions between a range of environmental, social, psychological, and economic variables that affect criminal behavior. Over time, a number of well-known theories have surfaced, each providing a unique viewpoint on the reasons behind crime. The social learning theory is a prominent criminology theory that suggests people pick up criminal behavior from other people through their interactions with them, especially in their social surroundings. This theory states that the possibility of someone committing a crime can be increased by being around criminal family members, deviant peers, or media portrayals of criminal behavior. Social learning theorists emphasize how socialization processes shape criminal behavior by arguing that behavior is learned through observation, imitation, and reinforcement. The strain theory, which emphasizes how societal pressures and structural injustices affect crime, is another well-known theory. This theory holds that when people feel pressured or frustrated about not being able to accomplish culturally defined goals through legal means, they may turn to criminal behavior. A number of things, including discrimination, poverty, unemployment, and limited access to resources and education, can lead to stress. As a result, people may resort to criminal activity to succeed or get relief from their depressive symptoms. Psychological theories of crime causation look at personal traits and mental processes that could make someone more likely to commit crimes. For example, the psychodynamic approach contends that maladaptive personality traits or unresolved conflicts from early life can be factors in criminal behavior. Cognitive theories concentrate on the ways that criminal behavior can be influenced by cognitive distortions, flawed decision-making processes, or illogical beliefs. Furthermore, biological theories investigate how a person's genetic, neurological, and biochemical makeup may predispose them to engage in criminal behavior. Environmental theories also emphasize how social and physical environments affect crime rates. According to the routine activities theory, crime happens when competent guardians are absent, motivated offenders are present, and these factors come together in a specific location and time. Environmental criminologists examine how crime is distributed geographically and examine the effects of variables like neighborhood traits, urban planning, and law enforcement tactics on crime trends. Theories of crime causation provide useful frameworks for comprehending the complex nature of criminal behavior. These theories advance our knowledge of the motivations behind criminal behavior and information sharing by examining the interplay between personal traits, social dynamics, and environmental influences.

8.1. THEORIES OF CAUSATION OF CRIME

Theories of the causation of crime provide lenses through which we can see the causes and incentives of criminal behavior. They give us the ability to recognize and evaluate the elements that influence people to act in ways that are illegally deviant. The study of crime causation offers a great deal of depth and complexity, with many theories centered around various focal points, ranging from societal structures to biology and psychology. An illegal act that is subject to legal punishment is called a crime. An act that causes harm to both the victim and the state, society, or community is considered a crime. A person may be forced to commit a crime in order to satisfy their needs, for a variety of reasons that contribute to crime.

The entries that follow highlight this disciplinary among theories within five different kinds:

1. **Biological Theories:** Biological elements including physiology, neurology, and genetics are examined in biological theories of crime in an effort to explain criminal behavior. According to these theories, people may be more likely to commit crimes because of innate biological traits or anomalies. Biological theories highlight how biology shapes a person's predisposition for criminal behavior, without undermining the impact of social and environmental factors on crime. The genetic or hereditary perspective is a well-known biological theory of crime that posits a major role for genetic factors in predisposing individuals to criminal behavior. Research has indicated that specific genetic variations could heighten vulnerability to traits linked to criminal behavior, such as aggression and impulsivity. Genetic influences on criminal behavior have been demonstrated by twin and adoption studies, wherein identical twins have been shown to have higher concordance rates for criminal behavior when compared to non-biological siblings or fraternal twins. It's crucial to remember that environmental influences combine with genetic predispositions to influence criminal behavior rather than just genetics alone. The neurological perspective is another biological theory that examines the relationship between criminal behavior and the anatomy and physiology of the brain. Studies have revealed dissimilarities in brain architecture and activity patterns between those who commit crimes and those who don't. For instance, antisocial behavior and aggression have been linked to abnormalities in brain regions related to impulse control, decision-making, and empathy. Neurotransmitter imbalances, such as those caused by high dopamine or low serotonin, have also been linked to

sensation-seeking and risk-taking behaviors, which may be factors in criminal behavior. Hormonal influences have also been investigated as possible causes of criminal behavior. Specifically, testosterone has been connected to aggressive and domineering behaviors, which are frequently connected to criminal activity. Research has indicated a connection between high testosterone levels and a higher risk of acting violently or delinquently, especially in men. However, there is a complicated relationship between hormones and crime that is influenced by a number of variables, including social context, gender, and age. Furthermore, the development of criminal behavior has been linked to physiological factors like diet, substance abuse, and prenatal exposure to toxins or stressors. Inadequate nourishment, particularly in crucial stages of brain growth, can impact cognitive abilities and impulse regulation, elevating the likelihood of engaging in antisocial conduct. Abuse of substances, especially those with psychoactive effects, can change the chemistry of the brain, impair judgment, and cause impulsive or violent behavior exposure of an unborn child to drugs like alcohol or.

i. **Genetic Predispositions:** These are innate characteristics or susceptibilities that people inherit from their biological parents. These factors can affect an individual's tendency toward particular behaviors, traits, or health conditions. Genetic variations, such as differences in DNA sequences, patterns of gene expression, or mutations that can affect physiological functions and behavioral tendencies, are the source of these predispositions. Genetic predispositions can greatly influence a person's susceptibility to specific traits or conditions, such as behavioral tendencies linked to criminality, even though they do not deterministically dictate outcomes. Research in behavioral genetics and criminology has shown interest in the role that genetic predispositions play in criminal behavior. Research on genetic influences on criminal behavior has shown interesting results through twin and adoption studies. Identical twins tend to have higher concordance rates for criminal behavior compared to non-biological siblings or fraternal twins. These results imply that individual variations in susceptibility to criminal behavior are shaped by genetic factors. But it's important to understand that genetic predispositions interact in complex ways with other factors and the environment, which adds to the complexity of human behavior. It has been suggested that a number of genetic variations predispose people to characteristics linked to criminal behavior. For instance, impulsivity, aggression, and sensation-seeking tendencies are risk factors for criminality and have been related to genes involved in neurotransmitter regulation, such as those encoding serotonin transporters or dopamine receptors. Disturbances in the genes linked to monoamine oxidase (MAO), an enzyme implicated in neurotransmitter metabolism, have also been linked to conduct disorder and antisocial behavior. Moreover, genes that control stress response systems, like the hypothalamic-pituitary-adrenal (HPA) axis, may affect a person's susceptibility to environmental stressors and raise their chance of developing behavioral issues, such as violence and delinquency. Differences in stress reactivity and coping strategies have been related to variations in genes encoding receptors for stress hormones like cortisol. These variations can impact vulnerability to negative life experiences and encourage maladaptive behaviors. Nonetheless, it's critical to acknowledge the limitations of genetic determinism and approach genetic explanations of criminal behavior with caution. Genetic predispositions can raise the probability of particular traits or behaviors, but they do not guarantee results or relieve people of their personal accountability. Environmental influences that shape behavior include family dynamics, peer pressure, socioeconomic status, and resource availability. These factors can interact with genetic predispositions to affect results the genetic susceptibility.

b. **Biochemical Factors:** Emotions, cognition, and social interactions are just a few of the ways that human behavior is influenced by biochemical factors. These variables include the intricate relationships that exist between biochemical substances, including hormones, neurotransmitters, and other molecules, as well as the way in which the nervous system, endocrine system, and other physiological processes operate. Gaining an understanding of the biochemical foundations of behavior is crucial to understanding the biological basis of human behavior, including criminal behavior. Neurotransmitters, which are chemical messengers that carry messages between neurons in the brain and control a variety of physiological and psychological processes, are an important biochemical component of behavior. Neurotransmitters such as dopamine, serotonin, norepinephrine, and gamma-aminobutyric acid (GABA) are important for mood regulation, impulse control, reward processing, and making decisions. Psychiatric conditions like depression, anxiety, bipolar disorder, and attention-deficit hyperactivity disorder (ADHD), which are frequently linked to an increased risk of antisocial or criminal behavior, have been linked to imbalances or dysregulation of these neurotransmitter systems. For example, impulsivity, sensation-seeking behavior, and risk-taking tendencies—all of which are frequently connected to criminal activity—have been connected to abnormalities in the dopamine system. Aggression, animosity, and emotional dysregulation are linked to serotonin system dysfunction and can lead to violent or antisocial behavior. Furthermore, aggression and poor impulse control have been linked to changes in the GAB Aergic system, which controls inhibitory neurotransmission. Another class of biochemical factors that affect behavior is hormones, which do this by modifying the body's signaling and physiological systems. Hormones that affect mood, stress response, social bonding, and aggression include testosterone, estrogen, cortisol, and oxytocin. Particularly in males, testosterone has been connected to competitive aggression, territoriality, and dominance behaviors—all of which are characteristics linked to criminal activity. Higher testosterone levels have been linked to a higher likelihood of committing violent or criminal acts, especially in adolescence and the early stages of adulthood when hormone levels are highest. Moreover, the body's reaction to stress and misfortune is greatly influenced by cortisol, the main stress hormone. The hypothalamic-pituitary-adrenal (HPA) axis can become dysregulated after prolonged exposure to stressors or trauma. This can result in elevated cortisol levels and dysfunctions in the mechanisms involved in the stress response. The role of stress-related biochemical factors has been highlighted by the correlation between dysregulated cortisol levels and increased susceptibility to mood disorders, substance abuse, and antisocial behavior.

2. **Economic Theories:** There are many causes of crime, and an academic field like economics that is based on rational behavior finds it difficult to explain irrational events. The most challenging task is describing the global trend in crime rates in the majority of industrialized economies. Numerous social scientists have contended that there is a direct correlation between crime and poverty, unemployment among youth, and education. They have also suggested that these factors are consequences, if not the cause, of social exclusion. Most blue-collar criminals have little formal education and little experience in the workforce. These characteristics sum up most criminals' poor employment histories and low real incomes. Economists first examine the relationships between wages and the rate of unemployment and criminal activity. Economists have recently looked into the effectiveness

and rates of educational initiatives aimed at lowering crime. The rationale behind the economic model of crime serves as a model for making decisions in risky circumstances. Economists examine how the degree of illegal activity is influenced by people's attitudes toward risk. Convenience is a fundamental component; decisions are made regarding the appropriate benefit to be realized from a specific course of action. People are expected to be logical decision-makers who engage in either legal or illicit activity depending on the expected benefits of each activity. Therefore, the opportunity rate of illegal activity—a measure of the variables influencing the returns to unlawful activity—defines a person's involvement in illegal activities. The focus of economic models of criminal behavior has been on the relationship between employment and crime as well as the deterrent effects. One could argue that other factors influencing the crime rate are channeled through unemployment.

3. **Psychological Theories:** Distinctly psychological theories of crime are extremely difficult to define. Psychological theories place particular emphasis on the role that family and individual factors play in criminal behavior. Most psychological theories are based on longitudinal education, which tracks each individual over time, and attempt to explain how crime evolves from childhood to adulthood. These theories place more emphasis on continuity than discontinuity between childhood and adulthood. According to Lanier & Henry (1998), a fundamental premise is that people's positions on underlying concepts like illegal potential remain mostly stable over time.

   Psychologists examine offending as a type of behavior that shares many characteristics with hostile behavior. As a result, the theories, frameworks, and data regarding other forms of hostile behavior can be applied to the study of crime. The idea that offenses are among the many indicators of unfriendly behavior, such as drug use, excessive drinking, reckless driving, issues with institutions, problems at work, etc., was popularized by Lee Robins. Psychological theories typically cover decision-making, motivation, inhabiting, and learning processes. The most widely held belief that motivates people is that people, and children in particular, are inherently self-centered, self-indulgent, and pain-ignorant, which makes them naturally offensive. Another traditional theory holds that each person is driven to maintain an optional level of arousal; if it is above the optimal level, people will try to lower it, and if it is below the optimal level, they will try to raise it. Psychologists, in general, are dedicated to the scientific study of human behavior, with a focus on theories that can be verified or refuted through the use of empirical, quantitative data, gathered experiments, systematic observation, valid and trustworthy measures, etc. The following parts discuss the most important categories of risk factors that influence crime:

- Family impacts, like broken homes, poor child-rearing methods, and criminal parents.
- Individual impacts such as personality. The foremost important personality thinking about relevance crime is abandoned.

i. **The Psychological Perspective on Crime Causation:** The mental and emotional components that may influence criminal behavior are examined in psychological theories of crime causation. These theories, which have their roots in behavioral psychology, cognitive psychology, and psychodynamics, offer a multifaceted view of the causes of crime. For example, psychodynamic theories highlight how criminal behavior is influenced by unconscious forces, early experiences, and maladapted personality structures. They contend that unresolved internal conflicts and childhood traumas can lead to antisocial or deviant behavior. Subsequently, cognitive theories investigate how criminal behavior is affected by mental processes. They suggest that perception, comprehension, and interpretation of one's environment may influence one's propensity for criminal behavior. According to theories like moral reasoning, criminals frequently display a lower degree of moral development. Last but not least, behavioral theories propose that interactions with the environment teach criminal behavior. The importance of rewards and penalties, along with observational learning, in modifying behavior is highlighted by theories such as operant conditioning and social learning theory.

ii. **Psychodynamic Theory:** Sigmund Freud created psychodynamic theory, which provides a thorough framework for comprehending behavior, personality, and mental processes in people. The idea of the unconscious mind, which Freud proposed as a storehouse of suppressed memories, desires, and conflicts that influence conscious thoughts and actions, is fundamental to psychodynamic theory. Freud proposed that the human psyche is composed of three distinct parts, the id, ego, and superego, each of which has a unique role in controlling behavior and the formation of personality. The primal, instinctive aspect of the psyche known as the id seeks instant satisfaction for primal biological drives like hunger, thirst, and sexual cravings. It functions on the pleasure principle. It functions subconsciously and is propelled by the mind's basic processes, which include archaic mechanisms like fantasy and wish fulfillment. Irrational and impulsive, the id pursues its needs regardless of consequences or social norms. The id, on the other hand, gives rise to the ego during infancy. The ego is the conscious, logical aspect of the psyche that acts as a mediator between the id's demands, reality's limitations, and the superego's moral standards. The ego follows the reality principle, trying to satiate the id's cravings in ways that are both realistic and acceptable in society. It uses defense strategies like denial, repression, and rationalization to control internal conflicts and preserve psychological stability. The internalized moral principles and values that are ingrained by society and parental figures make up the final section of the psyche to develop. It serves as the conscience, using emotions of pride, guilt, and shame to enforce moral standards and social conventions. The impulses and desires of the id are frequently at odds with the superego's pursuit of perfection and adherence to moral principles. According to Freud, the id, ego, and superego interact to shape personality development, and early experiences are critical in the development of unconscious conflicts and psychological defenses. The idea of psychosexual stages of development was also introduced by Freud. These phases, which are oral, anal, phallic, latency, and genital, represent the development of libidinal energy. Specific developmental tasks and erogenous zones define each stage, and unresolved conflicts or fixations at any point can cause psychological disorders later in life. For instance, unresolved conflicts that arise during the oral stage, like difficulties with feeding or weaning, may later on in life present as oral fixation or dependency problems. In forming personality and behavior, psychodynamic theory places a strong emphasis on the role that unconscious processes, early experiences, and intrapsychic conflicts play. It holds that unconscious conflicts, motivations, and desires that can affect conscious feelings and thoughts are what drive human behavior.

iii. **Personality Theories:** Theories of personality offer frameworks for comprehending the composition, evolution, and dynamics of the human personality. Throughout psychology's history, a number of well-known theories have been put forth, each providing a distinctive viewpoint on the nature of personality and how it affects behavior. Some of the major personality theories include:

a. **Psychoanalytic Theory (Sigmund Freud):** The psychoanalytic theory of Freud places a strong emphasis on how early experiences, intrapsychic conflicts, and unconscious processes shape personality. According to Freud, the id, ego, and superego make up the structure of the personality, and psychosexual stages of development are involved in the development of the personality.

b. **Trait Theory:** It is concerned with figuring out and characterizing the essential qualities that comprise an individual's personality. According to trait theorists, individual variations in defining patterns of behavior, thoughts, and emotions can be used to analyze personality. Openness, conscientiousness, extraversion, agreeableness, and neuroticism (OCEAN) are the five broad dimensions that the Five-Factor Model, a well-known trait theory, suggests can be used to describe personality.

c. **Behavioral Theory:** This of personality emphasize the role of environmental influences and learning experiences in shaping behavior and personality. Behaviorists such as B.F. Skinner and Albert Bandura proposed that personality is largely determined by conditioning, reinforcement, and observational learning processes.

d. **Humanistic Theory:** These of personality emphasize people's innate goodness and capacity for self-actualization. Carl Rogers and Abraham Maslow's work serve as prime examples of these theories. Humanistic thinkers stress the significance of self-actualization, personal development, and realizing one's own potential in forming one's personality.

e. **Cognitive Theory:** The focus of cognitive theories of personality is on how cognitive functions—like memory, perception, and thought patterns—shape an individual's personality. According to cognitive theorists like George Kelly and Albert Ellis, individual variances in cognitive schemas, beliefs, and worldviews have an impact on personality.

f. **Biological Theory:** The influence of genetic, neurological, and physiological factors on personality is examined by biological theories of personality. According to these theories, hormonal regulation, brain anatomy and function, and genetic predispositions may all have an impact on an individual's variations in personality traits and behaviors.

g. **Social-Cultural Theory:** These of personality place a strong emphasis on how social and cultural elements shape personality. According to these theories, interpersonal relationships within a particular cultural context, society expectations, and cultural norms all have an impact on personality.

The intricacies of human behavior, personality, and development are all intricately explained by these personality theories. A more thorough understanding of personality and how it affects behavior can be obtained by taking an integrative approach that includes components from various theories, even though no single theory can adequately capture the richness and diversity of the human psyche.

4. **Political Theories:** Any approach to crime can be made to fit in with a certain political philosophy, which illustrates how any theory can be applied to further political goals. Therefore, any perspective on crime is a political theory in this broad sense. Furthermore, crimes of any kind could have political repercussions. It is true that some radical criminologists have contested the idea that all crimes are political at times. Furthermore, some theorists have provided justifications for crime that advance liberal or conservative political agendas and viewpoints. A different perspective on political theories of crime caution can be found in those that emphasize social conflict and government relations. Theories, as we've seen, can be used to form any kind of crime, but historically, they've focused more on explaining variations in crime rates and, in particular, on the various risks associated with being classified as a criminal than on solving specific criminal behavior. The politicization of all sins is deliberate inasmuch as the criminal law policy is perceived as an instrument of political power or repression. While it has occasionally been held that political sins are particularly agreeable to demonstrate through labeling and disputing theories, the counterargument is that political criminality is frequently explained by any theory that has an attachment to political philosophy Political beliefs and crime causation theories are in harmony, so it stands to reason that the more overtly political a philosophy is, the more probable it is that criminality will be given political significance. In order to explain crime and criminals in political terms, such as threats to political resistance to the political violation, theories sympathetic to radicalism and conservation seem more reasonable than theories sympathetic to liberalism. As a result, political offenders will be diagnosed by conservatives, liberals will conclude that they are often misguided individuals reacting to the stresses placed on them by weak social organizations, and extremists will conclude that political offenders are rational individuals who understand and uphold the oppressive and exploitative aspects of a plentiful democratic capitalist society.

5. **Sociological Theories:** Numerous sociological theories have been proposed regarding the causes of delinquency; these include theories based on differences in social class and/or family dynamics, theories addressing obstacles to educational and professional goals, theories addressing the influences of peers and the neighborhood, and theories addressing the consequences of official labeling. The majority of these theories agree that social interaction, not heredity or personality disorders, is what leads to delinquent behavior. Sociologists believe that a social context is necessary to understand delinquency. Thus, when researching delinquency, we need to take into account the time, place, audience, and type of behavior involved (Ardino & Vittoria, 2012).

There are three important sociological theories: strain, social learning, and control theories:

i. **Strain Theory:** This states that people who are under a lot of stress or strain, who become angry and perceive negativity around them, may become involved in or connect with criminal activity as a result. They might commit crimes in an effort to hide the stains they are dealing with. For example, in order to alleviate their financial difficulties, they might steal, stop being harassed by others, engage in violent acts, flee from their abusive parents, run away from home, or hurt themselves. In an effort to exact revenge on those who have wronged them, they might also be involved in criminal activity. In an attempt to feel better, they might begin abusing illegal drugs. Numerous sociological theories have been proposed regarding the causes of delinquency; these theories address a variety of issues, including social class and/or family dynamics, obstructed career and educational goals, peer pressure and the neighborhood, and the impact of official labeling. According to the majority of these theories, social interaction—rather than genetics or personality disorders—is what leads to delinquent behavior. Sociologists believe that a social context is necessary to understand delinquency. Therefore, when researching delinquency, we need to take into account the time, place, audience, and type of behavior in question.

   Cohen (1955) modified Merton's theory in an effort to provide an explanation for teenage gangs in the 1950s. He maintained that, particularly in the educational environment, adolescents from lower socioeconomic classes feel the pressure of failing in middle-class terms. Because it is difficult for many young people from lower socioeconomic classes to succeed in school, they reject middle-class ideals and engage in actions that are against middle-class norms in an attempt to rise in status. As a result, they create their own anti-middle-class moral code and organize into criminal gangs through mutual recruitment. In contrast, Miller (1958) emphasized the "focal concerns" (toughness, trouble, smartness, fate, autonomy, and excitement) of the lower social class as the sources of delinquent behavior. Miller disagreed with Cohen's theory that lower-class youth act in terms of inverted middle-class values.

Agnew revised strain theory once more in 1985. There are three strain types that could result in abnormal behavior. The first is the person's inability to meet objectives, and the second is the disappearance of a stable element (e.g., loss of a loved one), and the third happens when the person is exposed to unfavorable stimuli (e.g., inadequate academic performance). Furthermore, a lot of people just want to be treated fairly in accordance with their own abilities and resources, rather than working toward particular objectives. According to Agnew, people who feel they are not being treated fairly go through stress. Crime and delinquency may result from responses to this sense of unfair treatment. Victimization by the criminal justice system may rank among the most serious stresses that teenagers face and, as a result, may play a significant role in the development of delinquency. Predictions regarding the impact of victimization on subsequent delinquency arising from general strain theory. They came to the conclusion that, even after adjusting for an individual's prior involvement in delinquency, violent victimization significantly predicted later involvement in delinquency. Additionally, they found that the effects of victimization were significantly greater for juveniles with low self-control and slightly greater for juveniles with weak emotional attachment to their parents.

Baron (2004) investigated the relationship between crime and drug use and various forms of strain, such as emotional abuse, physical abuse, sexual abuse, homelessness, victimization from robbery, violence, or theft, relative deprivation, financial dissatisfaction, and unemployment, using a sample of homeless street youth. He also looked at the ways in which external attributions, deviant peers, deviant attitudes, self-efficacy, and self-esteem all influence strain. He came to the conclusion that any of the 10 strain types that were looked at could cause criminal behavior on its own or in combination with conditioning factors. The detrimental impact of experiencing violent victimization on subsequent delinquency. According to the strain theory, the authors discovered that a young person's subsequent delinquency was heightened when they experienced violence, and that the impact of this victimization on delinquency was partially mediated by the young person's anger. Delinquency involvement increased with feelings of anger. The direct effects of victimization on delinquency were lessened when anger was managed, and young people's ability to cope with victimization was correlated with their level of self-control; those who lacked self-control and were impulsive found it more difficult to cope.

Maltreatment and delinquency were found to be significantly correlated when parent-child issues were examined as a source of stress that contributed to delinquency. They discovered that negative emotions were significant intervening mechanisms in this relationship, which validated the strain theory. They observed, however, that the direct consequences of negative emotions were just as significant—if not more so—for involvement in delinquency than the direct consequences of maltreatment, defying the assumptions of the strain theory. Finally, there is some evidence to support the general strain theory, which found that Asian youth were more likely to engage in delinquent behavior in the future if they reacted angrily and frustratedly to stress related to school. However, the study did not find a meaningful connection between Asian youth gang involvement, negative affect, or strain. There was no evidence to support the theory that generational conflict-induced stress would lead to an increase in gang membership and delinquency. Rather, the findings indicated that young people involved in this kind of conflict had a lower likelihood of committing delinquent acts in the future. According to the researchers' hypothesis, Asian Americans' family relationships may be the reason for this. The strain/anomie theory has many detractors. It usually concentrates almost entirely on delinquency among the lower classes. It also downplays the impact of labeling and doesn't address the question of why so many young people, who surely feel pressure, don't resort to delinquency to achieve their objectives.

ii. **Social Learning Theory:** As per the social learning theory, individuals get involved in criminal activities because they pick up the skill from their friends and other people. They become aware of their propensity for crime and are exposed to criminal role models. This theory holds that young people learn about crime in the same way that they learn about sociability. Their learning is greatly influenced by primary groups, such as their peers, family, and friends. But, learning from others does not require a direct relationship with them.

Most social learning theory involves the three mechanisms by which every individual learns to involve in crime: differential reinforcement, modeling, and beliefs.

- **Differential Pillars of Crime:** People may guide others to get involved in crime through the support and punishments they provide for behavior. More probably, crime occurs when there is:
  - Frequently reinforced and infrequently punished;
  - Reinforcement in large amount (for instance, a lot of money or social approval);
  - More likely to be reinforced as the alternative behavior.
- **Beliefs that Encourage Crime:** Other people not only support our criminal activity, but they also instill in us beliefs that encourage crime. The majority of people are taught that crime is evil or immoral. As they finally come to terms with this belief, there is a decreased likelihood that they will be apprehended for criminal activity.
- **The Imitating of Criminal Models:** An individual's behavior is influenced by others around them as well as by the rewards, penalties, and beliefs they are subjected to. In particular, everyone imitates the actions of others; this is especially true when people respect or like others and have good reason to think that imitating their actions will be rewarded.

iii. **Control Theory:** According to control theories, in order for any of us to avoid giving in to the urge to commit crimes or engage in delinquent behavior, we need to be "controlled" or kept in check. There are two categories of systems that are used to monitor or rein in delinquent behavior: social (external) and personal (internal). For example, Reckless' containment theory highlights the significance of both internal and external constraints on self-concept. A negative self-perception is believed to increase the likelihood that a young person will become delinquent, whereas a positive self-perception is thought to shield the young person from engaging in delinquent behavior. Low self-esteem and negative self-concepts have also been widely identified as traits of child abuse and neglect. Critics of control theory, social learning theory, and strain theory take crime for granted. They contended that, in contrast to legal channels, every individual has certain needs and desires that are easily satisfied by crime. For example, stealing money is far easier than working for it. Consequently, control theorists contend that crime does not require a unique explanation because it is frequently the most practical means of achieving one's goals. Control theory emphasizes social factors (attachments and bonds) over internal controls. For instance, the term "attachment" describes a person's feelings toward other people or groups. One is less likely to commit delinquency the more attached they are to others who are not delinquent. The same kind of reasoning is used in relation to commitment (benefits of conformity vs. losses resulting from nonconformity), participation (in conforming vs. nonconforming behaviors), as well as convictions (in the traditional value system vs. A less traditional set of values. Hirschi argued that although these four elements of control theory could differ on their own, they usually vary in tandem. Strong negative ties increase the likelihood of delinquency, while strong positive ties reduce the possibility of delinquency in each of these four areas. Although some empirical evidence supports some aspects of the control theory approach, Hirschi's formulation has sparked a great deal of research, leaving many crucial questions unanswered. Are there longitudinal data that support the approach? How do some young people who seem to be well insulated from negative attachments and bonds commit delinquent acts? Do these bonds and attachments actually inhibit delinquent behavior, or are the bonds and attachments that law enforcement and criminal justice personnel perceive as simply a means of deciding whether or not to take official action?

iv. **Social Disorganization Theory:** A sociological theory known as "social disorganization theory" focuses on the disintegration of social institutions and the deterioration of social ties within neighborhoods in an attempt to explain why crime and deviance occur in urban areas. Social disorganization theory was created in the early 20th century by sociologists like Clifford Shaw and Henry McKay in response to the finding that certain urban areas with high rates of poverty, ethnic diversity, residential mobility, and social disorganization also have higher crime rates. The fundamental tenet of social disorganization theory is that patterns of criminal behavior and delinquency are shaped by the structural features of neighborhoods rather than by personal traits. The theory holds that societies with high levels of social disorganization are devoid of the collective efficacy, informal social control, and social cohesiveness needed to control behavior and preserve order. Social networks are disrupted, community ties are weakened, and the efficacy of formal and informal social institutions is undermined by factors that lead to social disorganization, including poverty, unemployment, residential instability, family disruption, and ethnic heterogeneity. Collaborative efficacy, or the ability of community members to work together to solve problems, enforce social norms, and achieve common goals, is a key concept in the theory of social disorganization. High levels of collective efficacy enable communities to effectively control behavior, deter crime, and address social issues. In contrast, because there are no informal social control mechanisms and a lack of social cohesiveness, communities with low collective efficacy are more prone to crime, disorder, and deviance.

Numerous neighborhood-level factors have been linked to higher crime and delinquency rates in empirical research that was motivated by the social disorganization theory. Residential mobility, financial hardship, family discord, population density, ethnic diversity, and physical disorder are some of these variables. According to studies, neighborhoods with higher degrees of social disarray also typically have higher rates of drug trafficking, juvenile delinquency, violent crime, and other antisocial behavior. Social disorganization theory also emphasizes the function of unofficial social control systems in preserving social order and reducing crime, such as neighborhood cohesiveness, mutual trust, and collective supervision. Communities that are well-connected to one another, have vibrant community organizations, and have unofficial social networks are better able to control behavior, discourage crime, and uphold pro-social norms and values. On the other hand, areas with a lack of social cohesion, social alienation, and mistrust are more prone to crime and disorder. Research and policy initiatives to identify and address the underlying causes of crime and delinquency in urban communities have been influenced by the social disorganization theory. Social disorganization theory emphasizes social cohesion, community resilience, and addressing underlying socioeconomic inequalities as strategies for community development and crime prevention by focusing on the social and structural determinants of crime. In summary, the theory of social disorganization offers a useful framework for comprehending the intricate interactions between environmental, social, and economic factors that lead to deviance and crime in urban neighborhoods. This theory clarifies the underlying dynamics of neighborhood crime and provides guidance for initiatives aimed at enhancing community safety, resilience, and well-being by highlighting the importance of social disorganization, collective efficacy, and informal social control mechanisms.

8.1.1. Causes of Crime

8.1.1.1. Poverty

One of the primary causes of crime is poverty. Crime rates are typically higher in economically deprived nations than in other nations. People engage in criminal activity because it is not only a simple way for them to obtain what they want, but it also does not require any other prerequisite talents, and they do not have the means to secure a living in the proper ways. An increasing number of the impoverished are turning to crime as a means of subsistence, which contributes to the widening gap between the rich and the poor that we are seeing. People become so frustrated with their inability to make enough money to support themselves and their families that they turn to illegal means of subsistence. Theft is one of the most frequent crimes in India, according to data gathered by the National Crime Records Bureau. All things considered, the poverty in India is pushing the impoverished toward a life of crime due to wealth inequality and a lack of resources for earning a living honestly.

8.1.1.2. Peer Pressure

The impact of peer pressure on the lives of all teenagers and young adults is well-established. During that stage of life, people often look up to their friends and think that what they do is either morally right or, more accurately, "hip and happening." Peer pressure forces them to jump on the bandwagon, therefore. These people's inexperience and lack of wisdom have only fueled the flames. Because of this, many young people are inadvertently drawn to vices like drinking alcohol and smoking by the way their peers behave. Peer pressure goes too far when it spreads to illicit drug use and other activities that could lead to addiction and ultimately ruin people's lives, rather than just involving alcohol and cigarettes.

8.1.1.3. Drugs

Drug misuse and crime are closely associated. When under the influence, people frequently engage in illegal activity that they might not have otherwise. The primary issue emerges when they develop a drug addiction and think they need the drugs to survive. Drug addicts will stop at nothing to obtain these illicit substances under such circumstances. Over 70,000 Americans lost their lives to drug overdoses in 2019 alone, according to data gathered by the National Institute on Drug Abuse, a division of the National Institute of Health in the United States of America. These numbers are concerning. People who are high have an inclination to do things that are not only against the law but also have the potential to ruin and occasionally even end their lives.

8.1.1.4. Politics

It is frequently ignored how politics and crime are related. This is troubling because a lot of people have dealt with political issues while committing crimes. Numerous politicians have a criminal history. Furthermore, a large number of politicians in developing nations have also been connected to murders and other violent crimes. A great deal of young party members are frequently armed and told to use force when in conflict. Any political disagreement, no matter how small, typically sparks widespread mob violence. This endangers the lives of numerous citizens in addition to exposing young people to criminal activity. Consequently, a nation's crime rate rises exponentially when its political climate is unstable.

8.1.1.5. Religion

Regretfully, religion continues to be a contributing factor in a number of societal problems and divisions. Many people are denied the opportunity to practice their own religion, even though it is a fundamental human right. The result is that believers start to feel resentful. In addition, a great deal of cases involving crimes against various schools of thought have also been documented. This conflict over ideological ideas that have existed for all eternity has claimed innocent lives.

This is a very depressing state of affairs, especially since we are already in the 21st century and humankind has advanced greatly in other domains. Religious extremists commit an enormous amount of crimes in the name of advancing their cause through the spread of their religion or, occasionally, demonstrating their superiority over other faiths through acts of vandalism and destruction.

8.1.1.6. Background

A criminal's upbringing and familial circumstances are frequently the driving force behind their criminal behavior. Those who feel that they have a duty to support their family and are unable to do so because of limited opportunities, inadequate education, or other disabilities turn to crime. This is a sad state of affairs because, in such circumstances, it is very likely that the criminal would not have committed crimes if they had enough money to support themselves and their family.

In addition to encouraging people to commit heinous crimes that endanger their freedom and lives, this problem also leads to theft and other criminal activity. Bribes and ransoms are used to generate large sums of money that individuals can use to support their families.

8.1.1.7. Society

Money is one of the most significant aspects of everyone's life in the modern world. The definition of money is not limited to a person's bank account balance; rather, it also refers to their social standing, self-worth, and even their moral principles. People now place a higher value on money than on their happiness and relationships. For some people, the opinions of others hold greater significance than their own emotions. Even educational institutions teach students how to increase their income rather than how to live happy and fulfilled lives, which subtly equates wealth with value. People who are in awe of students who choose to major in science instead of art because they typically have higher earning potential are one example of this. Because of this, those with lower incomes feel undeserving and are driven to lead criminal lives in an effort to increase their income and sense of worth.

8.1.1.8. Unemployment

Both developed and developing nations struggle with a shortage of job opportunities. A significant percentage of today's youth are unemployed, and the Confederation of Indian Industry reports that the rate of youth employment is rising steadily. The Centre for Monitoring Indian Economy's data indicates that the unemployment rate in our nation is steadily rising. Naturally, this frustrates the young people, who still struggle to find decent employment even after devoting a significant amount of time and resources to their education. Many young people experience this as a source of resentment towards the system, which later causes them to rebel and turn to crime at a young age.

8.1.1.9. Unequal Rights

Another important factor contributing to the rising crime rates is deprivation. When people are denied their fundamental rights, they turn to infamous activities because it makes it difficult for them to make a living the traditional and moral way. They choose to earn money and support themselves by hook or crook because they have few options and are already marginalized in society. Usually, this entails them taking part in illegal activity.

8.1.1.10. Unfair Justice System

Crime is also largely caused by an ineffective justice system. People become resentful of the system and begin to rebel when they feel that they are not treated fairly and that the system itself is not doing enough for them. This entails them acting against expectations and participating in illegal activity. When people perceive that the state is not going to treat them fairly, they attempt to obtain justice for themselves and often resort to committing different crimes in an effort to exact revenge and obtain what they feel is rightfully theirs. Because they lose faith in the legal system, a large number of innocent people turn to crime when they are falsely found guilty by the courts.

8.1.2. Examples of Theories of Crime Causation in Practice

An insightful dimension to their research is the examination of cases in which theories of crime causation are applied in real-world settings.

Here are a few examples:

1. **Application of Biological Theories in Profiling:** Sometimes, biological theories—such as the study of physiological reactions to stress—are applied by law enforcement organizations to develop techniques like lie detection during interrogations or polygraph testing. These methods highlight the applicability of the biological perspective on crime causation, even though they are not perfect.
2. **The Influence of Social Learning Theory in Gang Behavior:** It is evident from gang behavior that criminal behavior can be learned from peers. Gang members frequently imitate the illegal actions committed by their peers, illustrating how social learning can act as a trigger for criminal activity. Understanding how these theories relate to one another and overlap is essential to understanding these theories completely. For instance, a person's propensity for criminal behavior is frequently greatly influenced by the combination of biological predispositions, psychological factors, and social circumstances.

8.1.2.1. Diving Deeper into Variants of Theories of Crime

There are many different theories of crime, each with its own implications and based on a different premise. Understanding and dissecting these diverse viewpoints is essential to gaining a complete understanding of the phenomenon of criminal behavior. They cut across many academic fields, with sociology, psychology, biology, and economics making significant contributions. Comprehending these disparate theories facilitates the diagnosis of the complex issue of criminal behavior and the development of novel approaches for crime prevention and deterrence.

8.1.2.2. Evolution of Theories of Crime: A Historical Journey

- **Classical Theories of Crime (18th Century):** Jeremy Bentham and Cesare Beccaria, who are regarded as pioneers, proposed that people are rational beings who consider the advantages and disadvantages of their decisions. Therefore, the certainty, promptness, and severity of punishment serve as deterrents for criminal activity. The criminal justice system's foundation was made possible by this philosophy.

- **Positivist Theories of Crime (19th Century):** This school of thought, which was led by individuals like Cesare Lombroso and Enrico Ferri, maintained that psychological or biological factors that predispose people to crime cause criminal behavior. Unlike the classical school, Lombroso's theory of "born criminals" proposed physical characteristics as markers of criminal propensity.
- **Sociological Theories of Crime (20th Century):** These theories developed in opposition to positivist and classical schools' individualistic emphasis. Robert Merton's strain theory and Emile Durkheim's research on anomie highlighted the role that societal structures and inequality play in the causation of crime.
- **Contemporary Theories of Crime (21st Century):** The understanding of the causes of crime is still developing, incorporating ideas from many academic fields. Integrated theories, which combine sociological, psychological, and biological viewpoints, provide a more comprehensive understanding of criminal behavior nowadays. Every stage of evolution reflects an effort to improve our knowledge of the causes of crime, which affects criminal justice procedures and regulations.

8.1.2.3. Comparative Analysis: Traditional versus Modern Theories of Crime

A juxtaposition of traditional and modern crime theories highlights pivotal developments in understanding criminal behavior:

Traditional Theories of Crime	Modern Theories of Crime
Predominantly single-disciplinary, focusing either on individual or societal factors separately.	Are generally multidisciplinary, combining insights from psychology, sociology, biology, and more.
Less emphasis on empirical testing and more on anecdotal evidence.	Strong emphasis on empirical testing and statistical validation.
Societal solutions were often about retribution and deterrence.	Mitigating crime focuses on rehabilitation, prevention strategies, and addressing root causes.

Suggested static factors (e.g., biological traits) as primary causes of crime.	Recognize the dynamics of crime causation, considering changing factors like social environment or mental health status.

Although traditional theories have played a significant role in establishing the foundation for criminal theories, contemporary theories offer a more thorough understanding by incorporating insights from various disciplines and emphasizing the prevention and rehabilitation of criminal behavior.

8.2. CLASSICAL THEORIES OF CRIME

The classical school of criminology (also known as the free-will approach, or classical theory) first appeared in the writings of Jeremy Bentham and Cesare Beccaria in England and Italy in the latter half of the 1700s. This method of understanding and policing crime was predicated on the idea that people have free will and that their actions are the outcome of rationally weighing the benefits and costs in terms of pleasure and suffering. Put another way, a person considers whether a particular act will have pleasant or unpleasant results before committing it. It stands to reason that actions with unpleasant outcomes will be avoided. Therefore, society only needed to make the costs of punishment for violators' illegal acts greater than the benefits in order to control crime. Penalties therefore increased in severity in proportion to the seriousness of the offenses. The threat of punishment is thought to serve as a deterrent to criminals who logically consider the repercussions of their unlawful behavior, according to conventional theory. Beccaria's method was altered in the early 1800s after it was realized that not everyone could calculate benefits and costs in a logical manner. The modified strategy, also known as the neoclassical approach, advocated for lessening punishment for young people and the insane. Juveniles were considered less responsible than adults, at least until a certain age, and the insane were by definition incapable of making logical calculations. The classical approach holds that punishment should be appropriate for the crime, that juveniles and the insane should be treated differently from adults, and that punishment deters crime. These are fundamental tenets of our current criminal and juvenile justice system, so it is important to comprehend it.

8.2.1. Rational-Choice Theory

The rational-choice theory, also known as the postclassical theory of the 20th century, also holds that individuals weigh the benefits and risks in their minds before committing crimes. After observing an expensive mansion for several nights without any lights on and no police presence, a burglar may decide to break in because they rationally believe the risk is low and the potential rewards are worthwhile. The rational-choice model suggests that the state could create policies that better control crime and deviance and enhance quality of life by emphasizing the growth of rational thought, applying scientific laws, and utilizing empirical research. The idea that criminals have free will and consider the consequences of their actions logically aligns with conservative ideology and the "get tough" approach to dealing with delinquency. The threat of punishment, as opposed to the promise of treatment, may be the most effective deterrent for offenders if their actions are the result of free will and are not dictated by societal norms. Rational-choice theory may be used to characterize gang members who enter the drug trade with the obvious goal of profiting by outsmarting rivals and law enforcement.

8.2.2. Deterrence Theory

Another development of the classical method is deterrence theory. It focuses on the connection between misbehavior and punishment on both an individual and a group level. Specific deterrence pertains to stopping a specific person from committing crimes in the future, while general deterrence describes the impact of punishing one wrongdoer on stopping others from committing crimes. When we try to gauge the level of deterrence, what we're really doing is measuring perceived deterrence, or what people think will happen to them if they break the law (i.e., will they be caught? will they be punished harshly?). According to the majority of authorities, punishments that are swift and certain have a greater deterrent effect. Celerity (quickness) and certainty seem to mitigate the deterrent effect of harsh punishment. Regarding offenders, we might inquire as to whether the progressively harsher penalties proposed by "get tough" policies are likely to have a major effect on young people who do not think they will be caught for their delinquent acts or who do not think they will face consequences if they are caught. Regarding the deterrent effects of arrest, the data from longitudinal studies are solid and reliable. People who have been arrested before are at least as likely as those who have not to be arrested again, according to more than a dozen studies. Arrest therefore had the opposite effect of deterrence—it increased or maintained the rates of subsequent offenses. Another issue with the deterrence theory is that, in certain cases, people who are about to commit crimes do not think about the possibility of being caught or punished (e.g., those who act in a passionate or furious manner, those under the influence of alcohol).

8.2.3. Routine-Activities Theory

The idea that punishments and reasonable thought play a major role in shaping criminal behavior is furthered by the routine-activities theory. This method holds that criminal activity is merely a result of people's regular actions. When someone is in certain kinds of places that motivated criminals frequent, they become a prime target and, in the absence of strong parental figures, are more likely to commit crimes. The impact of hazardous activity participation on the violent victimization that juvenile offenders and non-offenders endure. Their findings indicated that there are some slight variations in the relationship between the chance of violent victimization and the consequences of regularly partaking in risky behaviors. Additionally, there is evidence to support the concept of "hot spots," or locations where crimes are persistently committed over time. In some instances, though, the victims' absence might be essential to the specific crime (e.g., break-ins are simpler when no one is home. The routine-activities perspective contends that risk is increased by being around criminal peers. Their research showed that variables related to family and peer context, net controls for unstructured and unsupervised activities, and demographic traits are correlated with an increased risk of violent victimization among teenagers. To ascertain the theory's validity, however, conceptualizing and measuring the variables related to routine-activities theory is essential.

The traditional method of reducing crime has never worked well for a number of reasons. The theory that the threat of punishment deters crime, at least as it is currently applied, is false, despite the approach appearing to make some sense. This premise has multiple potential sources of error. First, it's possible that people don't always weigh benefits and expenses sensibly. When someone commits what is known as a "crime of passion," such as killing their spouse after discovering they are having an extramarital affair or severely beating a child out of rage, they may not pause to consider the repercussions. The threat of punishment, no matter how severe, won't change this person's behavior if they don't stop to make these kinds of calculations. Second, a person may weigh benefits and costs in a way that makes sense to them—but maybe not to society—and determine that engaging in certain illegal activities is worthwhile despite the consequences of being caught (as in the case of a starving person stealing food, for example). Lastly, the person may weigh benefits and costs sensibly but not fear punishment because they think there is little chance of being caught (as is the case for many young people involved in alcohol and minor vandalism). The threat of punishment is meaningless if the offender thinks they will get away with their illegal activities. Furthermore, the person might think that, even if they are discovered, they won't receive any punishment (as is the case with minors who know that the majority of juvenile cases end in court and with parents who mistreat their kids under the pretext of discipline). The traditional theory of crime explanation and control has not proven to be effective, for whatever reason. Whatever chance of success this strategy may have seems to depend on punishing the offender fairly quickly and with a high degree of certainty. It is not surprising that our attempts to control crime and delinquency are unsuccessful because our society still primarily uses the classical approach and because there is no guarantee of apprehension or immediate punishment. Severe punishment does not seem to result in desirable behavior, but clearly, many child abusers think that their children will behave better as a result of such punishment. Therefore, emotional and/or physical abuse occurs when a child does not live up to the expectations of abusive parents, whether they are related to eating habits, toilet training, schoolwork, or demonstrating appropriate deference to the parents. This frequently results in the child having a lower sense of self, which further impairs their performance and prompts the parents to punish them more severely, and so on. Once started, this "cycle of violence" is hard to stop, and there's a chance the abused child will continue to abuse their own children in the same ways.

8.2.4. The Positivist School

In criminology, the positivist school first appeared in the latter part of the 1800s. As the "father" of modern criminology and the founder of the positivist school, Cesare Lombroso is widely acknowledged. Along with other positivists, Lombroso felt that criminals should be the subject of scientific investigation and that the foundation of criminal behavior is determinism rather than free will, as taught in traditional schools. While some positivists thought that genetics played a major role in determining criminal behavior, others thought that an individual's environment played a major role in determining whether or not they ended up as a criminal. In addition to highlighting the necessity of empirical research in criminology, positivists also emphasized the significance of the environment as a causative factor in crime. Even though their methodology was simple by today's standards, they made an indisputable contribution to the growth of contemporary criminology. Lombroso is also regarded as one of the pioneers of the biological school of criminology, at least in the early years of his career.

8.3. THE CONTROL THEORY OF CRIME: AN INSIGHTFUL EXAMINATION

When it comes to criminal theories, control theory provides an intriguing angle. It is based on the idea that people are inherently driven toward self-interest, which can show up as abnormal behavior, including criminal activity. It has strong roots in the sociology field. The social controls in place, such as the norms, regulations, and connections that bind people to society, prevent them from giving in to these tendencies.

8.3.1. Principles of the Control Theory of Crime

Travis Hirschi presented the Control Theory of Crime in 1969. Four fundamental components that influence a person's propensity to commit crimes are examined by this theory. These components are shown as social ties, which are frequently seen as the cornerstones of constructive behavioral guidance. These are described as follows:

- **Attachment:** This stands for the emotional connection a person has with other people, including friends, family, and teachers. Strong attachments frequently act as a deterrent to crime because people wouldn't want to disappoint or upset their loved ones by acting in an abnormal way.
- **Commitment:** A person's investment in their education, career, and other conventional endeavors that demand time and effort is a measure of their commitment to conforming to social norms. Serious repercussions, like losing one's job or being expelled, discourage criminal activity.
- **Involvement:** This is a reference to how involved a person is in traditional activities, like work or school. There is little time for criminal mischief when one is busy.
- **Belief:** This has to do with a person's belief in the standards and ideals of society. One is less likely to transgress these social norms the more strongly they believe they are morally right.

8.3.2. Critical Evaluation of the Control Theory in a Crime Setting

The Control Theory of Crime has faced various challenges from critics despite its resilience. Some claim that this theory ignores the impact of other domains like cultural practices, neighborhood characteristics, or economic conditions in favor of placing an excessive amount of emphasis on social bonds as control mechanisms. Moreover, some contest the idea that social ties are generally advantageous and deterrent to crime. Strong ties and commitments, for instance, can, in some circumstances, actually encourage criminal activity. This is demonstrated by gang memberships and corrupt organizational cultures. Furthermore, the Control Theory of Crime is less relevant to more serious and organized forms of crime because it primarily concentrates on explaining common juvenile delinquency and mild forms of deviance. The Control Theory is still a crucial foundation for comprehending why most people choose not to commit crimes in spite of the opportunities, even in light of these criticisms.

8.3.3. Real-World Application of Control Theory in Law Enforcement

Applications of control theory are evident in the tactics used by criminal justice and law enforcement organizations. Control theory serves as the foundation for many crime prevention and intervention initiatives, which work to fortify social ties and commitments as a means of discouraging potential or current offenders. The principle of attachment finds application in community policing tactics that strive to establish more robust relationships between law enforcement and community members. Strong ties to the local police can serve as a deterrent for criminal activity in this situation. Similarly, the promotion of school commitment and involvement in traditional activities is a common focus of intervention programs aimed at at-risk youth—two crucial components of the Control Theory of Crime. These initiatives seek to 'bind' these people to society more firmly by encouraging constructive interactions and involvement. The Control Theory of Crime offers a distinctive perspective that helps us comprehend criminal behavior. To get a more complete picture of crime and deviance, it is necessary to apply this theory in conjunction with other theories and understand it within its particular social and cultural context, as is the case with all theories.

8.3.4. Measures That Can Be Taken to Curb Criminal Activities

Since crime is something that people from all walks of life do in today's world and is not just a problem for the poor, it is critical to develop strategies and completely eradicate crime before it gets out of control. Here, the government is very important. In their role as representatives of the people, they should implement practical and effective measures to prevent crime in order to maintain social harmony. According to data gathered by the National Crime Records Bureau, the number of crimes reported in India is rising annually, even in spite of strict laws like the Indian Penal Code (1860) and other measures designed to reduce crime. Even though it appears to be working, these numbers show that harsh penalties by themselves are insufficient to make criminals fearful and discourage them from committing crimes. Therefore, it is imperative that the government reevaluate its efforts to reduce crime. The following list includes some actions that can be taken to stop criminal activity.

8.3.4.1. Speedy Justice System

Justice denied when it is postponed. Although not mentioned expressly in the Indian Constitution, Article 21, which guarantees the protection of Indian citizens' lives and personal liberties, implicitly guarantees the right to prompt justice. An assessment of the Indian legal system is long overdue. People's faith in the system has been eroded by the overwhelming backlog of cases and the inevitable delay in providing the victims with justice. Even a horrifying case like the Nirbhaya case (2017), which was expedited, took roughly 8 years to convict the offenders and provide the victim with justice. The fundamental tenet of the legal system—"innocent until proven guilty"—is one of the main causes of this delay. This allows offenders the chance to escape punishment for their crimes and, in the event that they are found guilty, to further drag out the legal system by appealing for a review. This regrettable circumstance not only incites criminal activity but also makes the situation worse for those who are the victims of crime.

Appointing a sufficient number of judges should be the first action taken to expedite the legal system. The primary cause of the backlog of cases in Indian courts is the insufficiency of judges in the country. The judges' bench in the 2002 case of Ramachandra Rao vs. State of Karnataka also made a note of this. Furthermore, Fast Track Courts must be established as soon as possible. This was one of the suggestions made in the 11th Finance Commission Report, which was published in 1998. In addition to filling judge vacancies, all courts must review their judges' working hours and yearly leave policies.

8.3.4.2. Creation of Job Opportunities

As was previously mentioned, there is a connection between criminal tendencies and unemployment. Criminals frequently commit crimes because they lack the financial resources to live otherwise. Research evaluating the relationship between unemployment and crime has shown that, rather than violent crimes, unemployment causes an increase in property crimes. This indicates that the criminals here engage in criminal activity to make ends meet. Therefore, in such cases, creating jobs would be an effective deterrent to crime.

8.3.4.3. Overcoming Economical Inequalities

The growing gap between the rich and the poor is a well-established fact. The wealthy appear to be living extravagant lifestyles that are never ending, while the impoverished continue to struggle to obtain the basic supplies and facilities they need to survive, such as food, clean water, shelter, and the like. Studies have shown that the impoverished then turn to small-time crimes in order to survive, so the government should intervene and take steps to lessen these economic disparities. In addition to lessening the negative effects of classism, closing the wealth gap would guarantee that all citizens have access to a means of subsistence and won't be forced to engage in illegal activity in order to do so.

8.3.4.4. Formulating Provisions for Cybercrimes

Everything has moved online since the invention of the internet. While this has many benefits, it also means that cyberspace is now a new, convenient, and accessible area for illegal activity. The rise in virtual violence is evident. It's time for the government to create sensible regulations to safeguard citizens online as well. For this, ineffective cyber security units are insufficient, and appropriate legislative measures must be developed.

8.3.4.5. Raising Awareness Among the People

It is important to inform the public of their rights and options. In addition, all young people should receive education on how to avoid becoming victims of crimes and how to be good citizens in addition to avoiding online transgressions. In addition, the public's trust in the legal system should be reestablished through systemic improvements as well as education about the proper course of action to take in case of a crime, in order to ensure that the victim receives justice. If the individuals who are the target of a criminal act are capable of handling the situation, criminals will also be discouraged from committing crimes.

8.3.4.6. Promoting Harmony Among Religions

India is a secular nation where religious beliefs are respected equally. Even so, are still a lot of cases of discrimination against specific ethnic and religious groups. The government has not addressed this issue or taken the required steps to resolve it. This might cause a number of issues in the years to come. In order to eliminate that, the government should protect the rights of all citizens without regard to their race or religion when passing legislation. There will undoubtedly be less crime in a community where everyone gets along.

8.3.4.7. Penalizing White-Collar Criminals

White-collar crimes are non-violent crimes with a financial motivation that are committed by people, companies, or even the government. A related type of white-collar crime is corruption. Despite the Prevention of Corruption Act (1988), which was later amended to become the Prevention of Corruption Act (2018), it is still pervasive in India. To put it simply, corruption is the abuse of authority by public servants for their own illicit personal benefit. It affects the entire nation negatively in a number of ways. First of all, it impedes economic expansion by discouraging investment and changing the structure of government spending to the detriment of the general populace. Regrettably, the government places less emphasis on corruption and other white-collar crimes than on other crimes. This is problematic because it creates a risky precedent that could result in an increase in bank thefts, money laundering cases, and other similar crimes. Even after the Fugitive Economic Offenders Act (2018) was passed, not much has been done to prosecute criminals such as Nirav Modi and Vijay Mallya. In this case, the government should be more proactive and take the lead by prosecuting all white-collar criminals as soon as possible.

REFERENCES

1. Ardino, V. (2012). Offending behavior: The role of trauma and PTSD. *European Journal of Psychotraumatology, 3*, 10.3402/ejpt. v3i0.18968.
2. Bernburg, J. G., Krohn, M. D., & Rivera, C. J. (2006). Official labeling, criminal embeddedness, and subsequent delinquency: A longitudinal test of labeling theory. *Journal of Research in Crime and Delinquency, 43*(1), 67–88.
3. Bouffard, J. A. (2007). Predicting differences in the perceived relevance of crime's costs and benefits in a test of rational choice theory. *International Journal of Offender Therapy and Comparative Criminology, 51*(4), 461–485.
4. Church, W. T., II, Wharton, T., & Taylor, J. K. (2009). Examination of differential association and social control theory: Family systems and delinquency. *Youth Violence and Juvenile Justice, 7*(1), 3–15.
5. Clark, P. (2010). Preventing future crime with cognitive behavioral therapy. *NIJ Journal, 265*. Retrieved from: http://www.ojp.usdoj.gov/nij/journals/265/welcome.htm (accessed on 16 August 2024).
6. Groff, E. R. (2008). Adding the temporal and spatial aspects of routine activities: A further test of routine activity theory. *Security Journal, 21*(1–2), 95–116.
7. Guo, G., Roettger, M. E., & Cai, T. C. (2008). The integration of genetic propensities into social-control models of delinquency and violence among male youths. *American Sociological Review, 73*, 543–568.
8. Hagan, J., & Parker, P. (1999). Rebellion beyond the classroom: A life-course capitalization theory of the intergenerational causes of delinquency. *Theoretical Criminology, 3*(3), 259–285.
9. Hollist, D. R., Hughes, L. A., & Schaible, L. M. (2009). Adolescent maltreatment, negative emotion, and delinquency: An assessment of general strain theory and family-based strain. *Journal of Criminal Justice, 37*(4), 379–387.
10. Kaufman, P. (2010). The long view of crime. *NIJ Journal, 265*, 26–28.
11. Moffitt, T. (1993). Adolescence-limited and life-course persistent antisocial behavior: A developmental taxonomy. *Psychological Review, 100*, 674–701.
12. Moffitt, T. (2003). Life-course-persistent and adolescence-limited antisocial behavior: A ten-year research review and a research agenda. In B. B. Lahey, T. E. Moffitt, & A. Caspi (Eds.), *Causes of Conduct Disorder and Juvenile Delinquency* (pp. 49–75). New York: Guilford Press.

13. Spano, R., & Freilich, J. (2009). An assessment of the empirical validity and conceptualization of individual level multivariate studies of lifestyle/routine activities theory published from 1995 to 2005. *Journal of Criminal Justice, 37*(3), 305–313.
14. Spano, R., Freilich, J., & Bolland, J. (2008). Gang membership, gun carrying, and employment: Applying routine activities theory to explain violent victimization among inner-city, minority youth living in extreme poverty. *Justice Quarterly, 25*(2), 381–408.

Chapter 9

Social Context of Crime and Punishment

Contents

INTRODUCTION

Crime is antisocial behavior that is frowned upon by society and is punished accordingly. Thus, all actions for which the government establishes penalties qualify as crimes. The sociocultural factors that mold people's experiences and have an impact on their behavior and health are referred to as the social context of crime. Sociological perspectives hold thassst external variables like a person's family, peer group, and neighborhood experiences have a significant influence on their criminal behavior. The social distribution of crime within a community is influenced by various factors, such as age, gender, race or ethnicity, family background, education level, and socioeconomic status. Poverty and unemployment rates are two local neighborhood characteristics that can have an impact on the frequency and kind of crime. Crime and Punishment by Fyodor Dostoevsky, which takes place in 19th-century St. Petersburg examines the moral conundrums and socioeconomic hardships of the era. The book explores the harsh realities that the lower classes must endure, especially as told by the protagonist Raskolnikov, a destitute former student. The atmosphere of the city is one of decay and desperation, mirroring the larger problems of injustice and inequality in society. Radical ideologies and utilitarianism are criticized through Raskolnikov's psychological anguish as he tests his theory of extraordinary individuals by killing someone. The novel's social context emphasizes the psychological effects of intellectualism, poverty, and isolation while highlighting the importance of moral integrity and compassion in the face of suffering and existential despair. By means of its striking depiction of St. Crime and Punishment provides a deep commentary on the philosophical and social currents of Dostoevsky's time, as well as on Petersburg and its people.

9.1. CRIMINOLOGY AS SOCIAL SCIENCE

As suggested by the etymologies criminal (accusation or guilt) and -ology (study of), criminology is the study of crime. A variety of academic fields have contributed to criminology as an intellectual field, including psychology, biology, anthropology, law, and, most importantly, sociology. Even though criminology's founding principles are derived from these many disciplines, modern criminology is increasingly entwined with other scientific disciplines and professions like public health, social work, and geography. The many causal hypotheses that make up theoretical criminology have been created and put to the test; in a similar vein, different quantitative and qualitative research techniques are frequently used to analyze crime phenomena. Thus, criminology both defines and provides theory–methods symmetry to the field of social inquiry. It is possible to refute inferential statements about relationships (the observed correlations) when a theory is considered scientific. To ensure that the theory is framed for methodical cause-and-effect observation, research involves data collection in accordance with the operationalization process. Next, a comparison is made between the conceptual logic of the theory and the analysis and conclusions regarding the existence, nature, and implications of relationships. A theory is proven false when the observations contradict its fundamental assumptions. Although it is customary to give more credence to observations that corroborate a theory's claims regarding the relationship between cause-and-effect statements, this does not imply that the theory is true because the same relationships could be explained by other theories.

The desire to identify causal relationships that may have an impact on criminal justice practice is reflected in the wide range of research questions that criminologists, in particular, are particularly interested in finding the answers to. Examples of these questions include: Will harsher punishments reduce the amount of crime in society? Do fines imposed on parents of truant children increase parental responsibility and ultimately lead to less truancy? Does a substance abuse treatment program in a correctional setting affect prisoners' rate of recidivism and drug relapse? In scientific theorizing, four main components must be demonstrated in order for there to be a causal relationship: (1) logical basis; (2) temporal order; (3) correlation; and (4) lack of spuriousness. Each of these is covered in turn in the paragraphs that follow. Like any other accurate explanation, scientific theory necessitates reasoned analysis. Believing that there is a causal relationship between observable phenomena requires a sound rationale. For example, when trying to explain an offender's behavior, criminologists are not concerned with the color of their eyes or hair because there is no logical correlation between these physical characteristics and criminal behavior. Temporal order, or the order in which cause-and-effect components occur, is a second component that is required for the construction of scientific theories. To put it briefly, as in the case of the correlation between morality crimes and religious participation, causal factors must come before outcomes. Initiatives rooted in faith are motivated by the conviction that religiously inspired policies will improve society overall and lower crime rates in particular. A decrease in the commission of these vice crimes (the dependent variable) would seem to indicate a causal relationship if offenders engage in religious programs (the independent variable) and adhere to religious doctrine condemning behavior like commercial sex, gambling, and recreational drug use and abuse. This is because the religious programming both preceded and logically prompted the decreased involvement in the specified behaviors.

The third necessary component of a scientific theory is correlation. Once more, correlation shows that there is a relationship between observable phenomena and that relationship's strength and direction. The requirement of spuriousness is the final crucial component for the development of scientific theories. For instance, the majority of subcultures are typically characterized by poverty, which obscures the causal relationship between subculture and crime because subcultures may actually originate within impoverished groups and crime is a result of poverty. Alternatively, it's possible that cultural norms promote actions that lead to both poverty and criminality. Thus, it is impossible to establish a cause and effect relationship between subculture, poverty, and crime. Therefore, theorists need to formulate relationship statements that show a lack of spuriousness. Criminologists raise the possibility or probability that relationship statements are true by upholding these four axioms.

9.2. SOCIAL INEQUALITY AND CRIME

Crime and social inequality have long been thought to be related. Edwin Sutherland (1947) made the claim that crime rates are higher in unequal societies with conflicting beliefs and lower in egalitarian, consensual societies more than 50 years ago. Inequitable societies probably have high crime rates because members of disadvantaged classes or groups commit crimes at disproportionately high rates. In contrast to wealthy urban neighborhoods and rural areas, extremely disadvantaged inner-city urban areas in the United States are strongly linked to high rates of crime and violence.

9.2.1. Inequality in the United States

The level of economic inequality in the US is very high and has skyrocketed in the last 25 years. Of the 30 developed countries that make up the Organization for Economic Cooperation and Development (OECD), only two—Mexico and Russia, which are regarded as developing nations—show more disparity in income. The US is one of the 28 OECD member nations that remain has the greatest disparity in income by far. In the United States salaries diverged in the latter part of the 1980s before stabilizing in the 1990s and 2000s. The rise in wage inequality over the last 20 years and the deteriorating status of the urban underclass in many American cities over the last 40 years are the two trends responsible for the unprecedented level of inequality. Four factors contributed to the rise in wage inequality in the 1980s: (1) Rising returns on higher education combined with skill-biased technological advancements to drive a need for highly educated managers and white-collar workers. (2) As a result of union declines, employees' bargaining power decreased, which, when taking into account the effects of union decline on both union and non-union pay, accounts for as much as 30% of the growth in wage inequality. (3) The

"Washington consensus" (1970–today) replaced the "treaty of Detroit" (1950–1970), which weakened labor unions, undermined the tripartite institutional framework, deregulated the financial industry, lowered taxes on non-labor and the highest income tax bracket, and stimulated unprecedented growth in the financial sector. The treaty of Detroit legitimized collective bargaining, created a tripartite institutional framework between labor, industry, and government, and as a result stabilized wage inequality. (4) The "Detroit treaty's" institutional framework and norms, as well as skill-biased technical changes, caused top executives' skills to shift from firm-specific to generalized, allowing them to accept offers from rival companies. This led to sharp rises in executive compensation.

At the same time, within the inner-cities of major metropolitan areas in the US.—particularly in rustbelt cities—problems such as concentrated poverty, joblessness, out-of-wedlock births, crack-cocaine use, and violent crime—worsened. Between 1970 and 1990, the urban underclass experienced a concentration of problems. However, the issue of the underclass became less severe during the 1990s due to the economic boom and modifications to public policy, including the expansion of the earned income credit and adjustments to housing assistance. This pattern has more recently been reversed by the Great Recession of the 2000s, which resulted in a 25% increase in the number of impoverished areas and the population residing in them. Furthermore, the welfare reforms of the 1990s made matters worse for the impoverished, though at first the economic boom obscured these effects until the recession years later. Furthermore, poor minorities were concentrated in inner cities and rural areas due to racial and class segregation. Extreme inequality has emerged in modern America as a result of these trends as well as trends in wage inequality.

9.2.2. Inequality of Crime

In contemporary industrial societies, the political system that gives the powerful the most influence determines the criminal justice system's content as well as how punishment is meted out. Therefore, political and economic inequality play a fundamental role in the definition of crime, as crime itself is ultimately shaped by these factors. This is not to argue against the widespread agreement regarding serious crimes. Legal scholars distinguish usefully between mala prohibita crimes—those that are strictly criminalized by statute law—and mala in se crimes, or those that are deemed wrong in and of themselves. Mala in se crimes, which are widely accepted, comprise most serious felonies, including rape, murder, arson, theft, and burglary, as well as violations of person or property. Mala en se laws originated in the oral common law tradition of medieval Europe and were later incorporated into U.S. criminal codes. Mala prohibita crimes, on the other hand, like tax laws or traffic infractions, are justified not because they are immoral but rather because they are required for a well-ordered society. These laws are usually passed by a legislature through a political process wherein a politically influential group manages to gather support in order to achieve their goals in the law—sometimes even in the face of popular opposition. Public policy and criminal law designed to deal with social control issues are rooted in a convergence of political-economic concerns, representations in the media, and political framing. These kinds of processes are usually driven by class interests. According to Garland, one must "appreciate the ways in which particular interests are interwoven with general ones" in order to comprehend how class is reflected in criminal law, since the defense of class interests is often concealed as the defense of universal interests.

When considering corporate crimes, the connection between class interests, social inequality, and the formulation and application of law is brought into stark relief. The term "white collar crime," which refers to crimes "performed by persons of respectability and high status in the course of their occupation," was first used by Edwin Sutherland in 1949 to call attention to a class of mala prohibita offenses that are generally disregarded by both criminologists and the general public. Sutherland demonstrated that the only distinction between these crimes—committed by upper-class individuals—and those committed by lower-class individuals is in the administrative processes that were employed to deal with the perpetrators. Even in cases involving relatively small amounts of money—such as burglary—street crimes are subject to relatively harsh and stigmatizing punishments when they are handled in criminal court. Contrarily, white collar crimes are typically handled in administrative or civil courts and, even in cases involving large sums of money, like antitrust cases, are typically punished with light penalties. Sutherland contended that there were two causes for this disparity. First off, corporate crimes frequently lack a definite victim like street crimes, which frequently have an enraged victim who is aware of the pain, suffering, and loss caused by the crime. For instance, victims of consumer goods misbranding, Ponzi schemes, and trade restrictions frequently aren't aware of their victimization or the consequences. Second, corporate actors give up a great deal of money and political clout in a free-market economy, which they can use to overturn laws and fight stigma.

There is evidence that big businesses will continue to get preferential treatment from the government and courts, even if the public can be inspired to take up the issue of corporate crime and demand stricter regulation and enforcement. A growing number of judicial decision-makers have established legal precedents for lax enforcement of actual compliance in the future by ruling that symbolic, as opposed to actual, adherence to the law by large corporations is sufficient. The financial reliance of public servants on big businesses and affluent contributors could potentially make it challenging to further regulate white collar crime. For instance, Congress's sluggish response to regulating the companies implicated in the savings and loan crisis of the 1980s was partly due to the close ties between lawmakers and the savings and loan industry, which included significant campaign contributions. With a few noteworthy exceptions, criminologists have tended to focus on street crime rather than crime in suites despite Sutherland's writings. According to definitions, criminal violence is a public health issue that is covered by National Institutes of Health research funding. Research funding on corporate and white collar crime has been relatively low. As a result, a vast body of writing has been produced to explain common crimes.

9.2.3. Inequality and Crime: An Integrated Social-Psychological Theory of Causal Mechanisms

Given the current definitions of crime, we try to explain the distinctions between criminal and deviant behavior in this section. In order to achieve this, we create a comprehensive social-psychological theory of the causal pathways through which structural factors—like income disparity—give rise to criminal activity and deviance.

9.2.3.1. The Influence of the Chicago School on Contemporary Criminological Theory

A large portion of Chicago school sociology is grounded in pragmatic concepts, which in turn serve as the foundation for a large portion of classical criminological theory and research. Examples of these theories include differential association, social control theory, social disorganization and cultural transmission, and labeling. However, there is no explicit social psychological theory of decision-making in situations in these classical theories. In this section, we briefly demonstrate how many well-known criminological theories, while devoid of a comprehensive theory of cognition and decision-making, have their roots in the pragmatist and Chicago school of thought.

1. **Social Disorganization Theories:** Shaw & McKay (1969) mapped the rates of juvenile delinquency by neighborhood and over time in the city of Chicago, building on the urbanization research of Park and Burgess. Based on these maps, they deduced that the city's center, where residential areas were being overtaken by industry, had the highest rates of delinquency; rates decreased monotonically as one moved from the center to the periphery; these patterns persisted

for decades despite the zone in transition experiencing a complete ethnic turnover. Shaw and McKay contended that social disarray in communities and the disintegration of social norms are caused by urban growth, particularly by businesses and industries encroaching on residential areas. In recent times, scholars have delineated the causal mechanisms, specifically informal social control, that lead to high crime rates when disorganization prevails. Shaw and McKay also discovered case study evidence that suggests juvenile offenders picked up delinquent customs from more experienced offending groups, as well as evidence of interlocking networks of delinquent groups over time. This intergenerational transfer of a criminal tradition—a process that was later refined by learning theories—was referred to as cultural transmission.

2. **Differential Association and Social Learning Theories:** According to Shaw & McKay's (1969) findings, delinquency is acquired through other delinquents, which is consistent with previous research on the spread of delinquency within gangs. Professional thieves can also teach others specialized skills and justifications for committing crimes. Sutherland (1947) formalized these concepts into his social psychology theory of differential association, which proposed that all crimes are acquired through associations with others in a process of communication in close groups. This process involves learning both definitions that are favorable or unfavorable to crime as well as techniques for committing it. The latter is a function of W. I. Thomas' idea of the situational definition: some people believe that crime is wrong in all circumstances, while others think it is right in some ones. In certain situations, these moral judgments justify crime. In order to explain overall crime rates, Sutherland also elaborated on his theory of differential social organization, which holds that a group's or society's crime rate is based on how much of it is structured in favor of crime (e.g., cultural transmission) as opposed to organized crime prevention (social organization, for example). Subsequently, criminologists tried to explain the differential association in terms of psychological learning theories. These theories included Skinner's operant conditioning principles and, more recently, Akers' (1985) social learning theory, which expands on Bandura's (1986) learning theory to specify that associational learning, vicarious reinforcement, and modeling are the ways in which crime is learned.

3. **Labeling Theories:** The origins of labeling theory can be found in the works of Tannenbaum (1938), who drew heavily from the

ethnographic research of Shaw, McKay, and Thrasher. Tannenbaum observed that a child's actions, which the child interprets as joy, excitement, and play, can occasionally be interpreted by the broader society as wicked, careless, and evil. As a result, the child is singled out for treatment or punishment by the adult community at large because they are perceived as troublemakers or bad kids. Recurrently bad interactions between the community and the youth can land the child in the juvenile justice system, isolate them from mainstream society, stigmatize them as deviants, and put them in the company of other similarly stigmatized youth who might encourage defiance and deviance. Therefore, the child would not have chosen a career in criminality if the early spontaneous acts had been accepted as a typical aspect of growing up. Put differently, the act of initially labeling resulted in a self-fulfilling prophecy, whereby the child ultimately confirmed the initial label of deviance. Lemert (1951); and Becker (1963) advanced labeling theory by formalizing the label as a definition of a situation and making a distinction between primary (initial acts of deviance) and secondary (deviance resulting from an initial label) deviance. Both authors drew on symbolic interactionism. In his theory of reintegrative shaming, Braithwaite (1989) has more recently integrated labeling theory. He contends that instead of punishing people severely—like locking them up—societies should choose public humiliation followed by forgiveness and reintegration into society at large.

4. **Social Control Theories:** The Chicago school is related to control theories as the individual level equivalent of the community level notion of social disorganization. The most well-known control theories are linked to Travis Hirschi's work from 1969. Hirschi separated control theories from other criminological theories by making two assumptions: first, that deviance motivation is constant across individuals and not a factor that can explain behavior; and second, that delinquent peers do not have a causal influence on delinquency. As a result, conformity is left up for explanation, while deviation is taken for granted—we would all, if we dared. According to Hirschi, people who have strong ties to traditional society—such as strong moral convictions, commitments and involvement in traditional activities, and strong attachments to others—are more likely to exhibit conformity. More recently, Gottfredson & Hirschi (1990) developed a theory of low self-control, according to which children acquire self-control by the age of culpability, which is typically 7 or 8. Self-control is a stable trait that guards against

crime. Children with strong self-control are raised by parents who actively supervise their behavior and voice their disapproval of it. In turn, having strong self-control makes people more likely to be in stable jobs, good marriages, pro-social peers, and educational settings throughout their lives. It also enables people to restrain their darker impulses. In contrast, people who lack self-control are often impetuous, focused on the here and now, and incompetent. They also find it difficult to restrain their abnormal tendencies and gravitate toward unfavorable situations, such as dropping out of school, hanging out with troubled people, having unstable jobs, having troubled marriages, and having high divorce rates. All these theories borrow from the philosophical tradition of pragmatism and the Chicago school of sociology, but they do not fully adopt pragmatist principles or provide a situational decision-making model of criminal behavior.

9.2.3.2. Differential Social Organization

In line with Sutherland (1947), we explain how macro-level structures and organization lead to crime by utilizing the theory of differential social organization. Social organization and crime are related, but different types of organization have different effects on crime: some suppress, regulate, and control crime, while others encourage it. Some organizations may even simultaneously promote and suppress some crimes. We employ the analytical categories organization against crime and organization in favor of crime to simplify the concept of organization. We then propose that the relative strength of each category determines the crime rate within a group or society. Matsueda has demonstrated how differential social organization, when viewed dynamically, transforms into a theory of collective action that uses structural ties, collective action frames, and resource access as explanatory concepts. According to this interpretation, cultural transmission represents strong organization in support of crime, while Shaw and McKay's concept of social disorganization represents weak organization against it. Rich communities that have a lot of resources, solid social networks, and group efficacy are well-organized to fight crime. In contrast, underprivileged inner-city neighborhoods with limited resources and a violent code of conduct dominate the streets are both strongly and weakly organized in support of violence and against crime.

9.2.3.3. A Pragmatist Theory of Situated Criminal Decisions

Mead (1934) emphasized the primacy of the group over the individual, stating that self-control and social control are identical processes merely viewed from different standpoints, the individual and the group, respectively. This focus on the problem of social control—how do organized and informal groups control the behavior of members—is one of the hallmarks of the Chicago School. We start with a situated interaction, where participants bring their biographical histories, including habits, attitudes, and preferences, and where crime is a possible outcome. A goal, which is continuously negotiated, tentative, and open to change, serves as the framework for the interaction. Pragmatist theories presuppose that ends can be changed through means negotiation and vice versa, in contrast to utilitarian theories which operate under the teleological assumption that ends are fixed and means are negotiated. Common institutionalized settings are characterized by shared goals, habitual behavior, and unproblematic situations. In the worst scenario, there is very little self-awareness, little introspection, and behavior is just a reenactment of previously acquired learned attitudes, scripts, and preferences. Professional pickpockets, for instance, coordinate their roles so that, in order to reduce the likelihood of being discovered, the "cleaner" removes the wallet from a pocket, the "stall" offers a distraction, and the "hook" takes it out. When such coordination is done repeatedly, unless something goes wrong, the behaviors become virtually automatic and habitual.

When an actor's routine behavior is disrupted—briefly stopped by a tangible or intangible object—the actor becomes uncomfortable and uses their cognitive faculties to work through their feelings. They may feel fear or disgust. In order to engage in cognition, an actor must engage in a creative rehearsal in which they assume the role of the other and brainstorm potential courses of action (such as attitudes, which are inclinations to act) from the perspective of the other. This is where the self as an object emerges: the self is pictured acting in the alternative way, which prompts a reaction from other people's perspectives. This reaction can be either positive, resulting in overt behavior, or negative, obstructing the alternative (attitude) and evoking another alternative (attitude) from other people's perspectives. Therefore, the process of reconciling opposing attitudes and the corresponding selves in the mind is known as cognition. This process is comparable to an exchange of gestures, which represent attitudes, between the self and the other, except it takes place internally rather than through overt communication. Until the problematic situation is resolved and habitual behavior is sufficient, or until the interaction simply fades, cognition persists. In the case of pickpocketing, occasionally an unforeseen circumstance thwarts the intended course of events. For example, the victim may become aware that their wallet is being taken, or a bystander may step in to protect them. Assuming the role of the group, the thieves find themselves in a difficult situation where they must decide between hiding the wallet, admitting to the theft, or threatening the victim and any onlookers. Giving back the wallet as a last resort would be a calculated move exhibiting street smarts or "larceny sense" to calm the mark down." After the difficult situation is resolved, the options, assessments of those options, and additional information utilized in cognitive processing are stored in memory and become part of a comparatively durable self that can be accessed later to resolve similar difficult situations. Similar situations become less problematic and behavior becomes more habitual as a person learns to adapt to their surroundings when they are encountered repeatedly and resolved in similar ways. At some point, initial attitudes become unblockable, cognition becomes redundant, and behavior becomes institutionalized, habitual, and predicated on initial attitudes. For instance, many urban street gangs turned to drug dealing during the 1980s crack epidemic in order to take advantage of lucrative opportunities. As they adjust to a new and unknown environment, gang members forge new relationships with local communities during the transition, including those with suppliers, customers, and other locals. This is a difficult process. These connections eventually institutionalize, become unproblematic, and the behavior becomes ingrained. According to this situational model, the result of an interaction is not just the sum of the biographical histories of the interactants; rather, it also includes an emergent process that arises from people reconstructing their current perceptual fields using their past experiences in order to prepare for their future. However, situated interactions are more often than not patterned rather than entirely original. The interaction becomes less unique and more patterned in an institutionalized setting. Most environments lie halfway between distinctiveness and predictability, having both a novel and an institutionalized element. The biographical histories of the participants, of which preferences, information, identities, and reference groups are important components, give rise to the patterned component of interaction.

9.2.3.4. Pragmatism and Rationality

Weak rationality is consistent with our model. This model of decision-making deviates from the rational choice utility-maximization model, which frequently takes preferences, beliefs, and tastes for granted, assumes actors have access to complete knowledge about the effects of their actions, and assumes individuals can maximize expected utility within certain bounds. Rather, we believe that preferences—which include attitudes, social identities, and habits—are significant and endogenous behavioral predictors. Furthermore, we make the assumption that people usually do not maximize utility or take into account the whole range of potential alternative choices due to information processing limitations. Pragmatists, on the other hand, believe that a model of bounded or limited rationality is more consistent with the criterion of choosing the first solution that occurs to mind that is not obstructed by the self as an object when solving a problematic situation. Actors usually satisfice based on sequential consideration of a few potential solutions, as opposed to undertaking an exhaustive search for complete information and then optimizing utility. Sometimes there are extremely difficult decisions to make, requiring lengthy discussions that ultimately approximate a utility maximization model in order to resolve the issue. In these cases, several opposing options may be called out.

The distribution of information is a crucial factor in bounded rationality. People's access to information about the effects of their actions is restricted due to cognitive limitations on information processing. Relying on the generalized other in cognition leads to a theory of learning, which is a natural consequence of a pragmatist theory of situated decision-making. After the problematic situation is resolved, the group's evaluations and the solution are kept as parts of the individual. In its most basic form, this kind of learning takes the form of updating: a person refreshes their understanding of the effects of decisions from the perspective of others. Such learning mostly takes place within social groups, which is consistent with the theory of social learning. Furthermore, habits are "standing decisions" for similar circumstances in the future, whether they are formed by conscious reflective decision-making or intuitive acts. Problematic situations are frequently resolved by applying basic shortcuts and rules of thumb, or social intuition, when long-standing decisions (habits) prove insufficient. Lastly, we postulate that social context influences the way habit, social intuition, and controlled reasoning interact. More complex choices that approximate utility maximization are a rare and exceptional situation where simpler answers are insufficient and a more involved and drawn-out solution search is required.

9.2.3.5. Reference Groups as the Source of Preferences, Information, and Identities

Therefore, the self is socially constituted (given meaning) as it emerges as an object in social interaction. According to Mead, the organized groups in which a person participates give the self a distinct social structure: "Inner consciousness is socially organized by the importation of the social organization of the outer world." The "generalized other," which includes the expectations, norms, and rules dictating the group's various roles and positions, makes up that structure. The best social control comes from adopting the role of the generalized other because it allows institutionalized norms and organized groups to permeate individual behavior. It also allows moral questions to be discussed by a wider range of people, moving toward a universal discourse. Mead (1934) believed that assuming the role of the generalized other is a necessary part of child development. The concept of the self is intricate and multifaceted. To make things simpler, we define information, preferences, and identities as the three overlapping concepts that make up the structure of the self. Knowledge pertinent to a problematic scenario, such as potential solutions and their associated costs and benefits, is referred to as information. Preferences are made up of routines, viewpoints, and assessments of available options. They are acquired through social interaction and observational learning in reference group interactions. Here, attitudes, or propensities to act, are important because they result in habitual behavior and constitute the building blocks of the sequential process of cognition. An attitude generates another evaluative attitude from the perspective of others, and so on. Organized groups are the source of attitudes, primarily through interactional learning.

This is where differential association and social learning theories come in: criminal behaviors, including attitudes or evaluations that are either in favor of or against crime, are learned through interaction in primary groups. We contend that assessments of crime are used to solve problems in both criminal and noncriminal ways, as the individual exercises agency by assuming the role of the other, taking into account alternatives from the standpoint of others, and coming up with a solution that will solve the problem. This contrasts with learning theories, which state that criminal behavior is strictly determined by such evaluations. Taking on a role implies that the self, viewed as an object from the perspective of others, is a central source of control over criminal behavior. Even though the self as an object emerges through interaction to resolve difficult situations, it has a multidimensional, enduring component that corresponds to the structure of organized groups in which the individual takes part. That structure encompasses the intricate relationships between the group's objectives and the roles themselves, as well as the standards, expectations, and penalties that govern each role.

Symbolic interactionists refer to the stable aspect of the self as "role-identities" to highlight how it relates to an individual's group roles and consists of how the individual perceives themselves from the perspective of others. Identity theories postulate that the ideas of role-commitments and role-identities connect individual behavior to structured groups. In an organized group, a strong commitment to particular roles increases the likelihood that the group will function as a generalized other and a source of social control in difficult circumstances. Through identities, commitment to roles is connected to the (stable) self. According to identity theorists, the self is made up of a hierarchy of role-identities. The corresponding role-identities are more salient and likely to influence habits, social intuition, and controlled cognitive processes in proportion to the degree of commitment to the role. Through repeated role-playing within structured groups, commitments to group roles are built up, corresponding identities are developed, and group-specific habits are formed.

These identities are constructed through social interaction. These role-identities gain prominence over time and increasingly direct both cognitive and habitual behavior. In the worst case scenario, there could be a "role person merger," wherein a person becomes so identified with a role that they attempt to act out the role even though it might not be appropriate.

Thus, identities connect criminal activity to organized groups. For example, in order to maintain his reputation as a tough guy not to be messed with, a debt collector employed by a loan shark will often threaten clients who have fallen behind on their payments. Since we belong to several groups that occasionally clash—either internally within groups or externally across groups—the self, which is composed of knowledge, identities, and attitudes, is generally multifaceted and occasionally at odds. This conflict arises in the serial resolution of conflicting identities, attitudes, and information that occurs in social cognition. For instance, Cressey (1953) discovered that embezzlers generally saw themselves as honorable businessmen and accepted positions of financial trust in good faith. But when faced with an unshareable financial issue—like an addiction to drugs or gambling, for example—and realized that the only way to address the issue was to betray the trust, they took off with the money. Their contrasting personas as a devout businessman and a financial embezzler were reconciled by means of motive vocabularies or evaluative definitions of embezzlement, like "I'm just borrowing the money." These embezzlers were deeply rooted in traditional society, but they faced a difficult circumstance and employed motivational language to subdue the authorities.

In order to explain crime, Cressey's (1953) study proposes two ideas that are not related to role-taking: the existence of a financial issue and the possibility of using crime to address the issue. These ideas can be applied more broadly by utilizing current criminological theory. First, an individual-level theory of strain or aversive stimuli and criminal behavior is provided by general strain theory, which is based on Merton's (1957) structural theory of anomie. Agnew argues that unless they have strong social support networks to help them deal with the strain, people who experience aversive stimuli—such as failing out of school, losing their job, or going through a divorce—are more likely to engage in deviant behavior. Pragmatically speaking, these strains prevent habitual behavior and create difficult circumstances that, depending on the individual and the knowledge, attitudes, and identities pertinent to criminal activity, may be resolved with criminal behavior. Second, routine activities and opportunity theories of crime specify that crime occurs at the intersection of a motivated offender, suitable target (e.g., a victim), and the lack of competent caretakers (e.g., police, or witnesses). As a result, the structure of objective opportunities limits crime. Of course, these opportunities are meaningless if one does not consider them to be such, and in the lack of capable guardians, motivated offenders frequently actively look for suitable targets. Motivation, perception, and search can all be explained from a pragmatic standpoint.

9.2.3.6. Causal Mechanisms of Classical Criminological Theories as Special Cases

The Chicago school of sociology is the source of many traditional criminological theories, which means that their causal mechanisms align with our pragmatist viewpoint. We contend that they frequently turn into particular instances of a broad pragmatist model of decision-making. Social control theories, for instance, stress that adherence to and attachments to traditional roles—such as new roles during the transition to adulthood—decrease the probability of criminal activity. However, criminogenic groups also exercise social control, and criminal behavior most likely results from the combined effects of these two types of group control on role-playing, thought processes, and habit formation. As a result, Heimer & Matsueda (1994) used the term "differential social control" to highlight how both conventional and delinquent groups influence behavior.

In order to solve difficult crime situations through role-playing, two special cases of learning information relevant to crime are differential association and social learning theories. This covers the necessary criminal abilities and methods in addition to assessments of crime and its likely effects. In addition, our model offers a situational decision-making mechanism that links conventional and criminal identities to the act of assuming the role of the other. A set of theories regarding the ways in which interactions with adult society and the legal system shape identities are offered by labeling theory. Based on our decision-making model that explains how this process leads to secondary deviance, the hypothesis of deviance amplification—which holds that negative labeling by adult society and the juvenile justice system may stigmatize youth, produce secondary deviance, and create a self-fulfilling prophesy—is therefore consistent with our perspective. As previously mentioned, our viewpoint is in line with a model of bounded rationality, in which choices are made pragmatically, frequently taking into account no more than two or three options rather than all available information, and frequently relying on standing judgments or shortcuts rather than utility maximization.

9.2.3.7. Inequality, Reference Groups, and Social Cognition

Individual behavior is controlled by formal or informal groups, according to our social psychological model. The crux of the matter within a group is whether certain roles—part of the role hierarchy—allow or even encourage criminal behavior. These roles will be structured to include identities, attitudes, and knowledge that encourage criminal activity. These roles' characteristics vary widely. Adolescent male peer groups, for instance, may play a largely conventional role in society, but they also play a minor role in the use of violence against outsiders—that is, until one of their members is in danger. On the other hand, violence is a key component of many inner-city turf gangs, as they have role-expectations of violence for anyone who even dared to enter their territory. Typically, embezzlement in financial organizations happens when a lone person uses justifications to solve a financial problem. Certain financial institutions, like Ponzi schemes, are specifically designed to deceive investors in order to generate profits. An individual's ability to participate in organized groups is limited by the larger social structure that surrounds them. Social inequality, which essentially influences the social distance between groups, is a crucial component of social structure. The divergence in communication networks, and consequently the divergence in information, attitudes, and identities, increases with social distance between groups. Divergent and sometimes conflicting identities, attitudes, and information are linked to such divergences, which in turn are linked to inconsistent and conflicting behaviors. Cultural differences intensify and subcultures emerge when divergences in communication networks become institutionalized, most likely as a result of persistent structural inequalities.

Rich and politically powerful groups have the most influence over the process through which laws are passed and upheld in the majority of democratic societies. Thus, a group's preferences, interests, and goals are more likely to coincide with the law the closer they are to the political-economic process that creates and upholds the law. Furthermore, if everything else is equal, those groups will have the lowest average crime rates, while the groups that are most removed from the process of creating and enforcing the law will, on average, have the highest crime rates. Crime rates will be high in societies where there is a relatively permanent class of people who are chronically poor, unemployed, and disenfranchised. This is especially true for the disadvantaged, but it also affects other classes because of spillover effects. Crime rates may depend on the overall degree of inequality in society, in addition to the absolute degree of disadvantage. High rates of between-group communication, generalized others' tendency to overlap, and homogeneous information, preferences, and identities all work against high crime rates in relatively egalitarian societies. High crime rates are strongly associated with societies that exhibit high levels of social inequality because intergroup communication is poor, generalized others are typically provincial, and group preferences tend to diverge.

9.3. GENDER AND CRIME

The nature and scope of male-perpetrated crime have been the focus of much research on crime's nature and extent. Programs, interventions, and sanctions that would be applied to all offenders have been developed using the findings of studies that were primarily conducted on males. Because of the presumption that a one-size-fits-all model of crime, punishment, theory, and intervention is effective for both genders, these male-based interventions have traditionally only been used to address the criminal activity of girls and women. The idea that female and male offenders are the same, that they commit crimes for the same reasons, and that the criminal justice system should handle them equally has, however, been contested by researchers in the 20th and 21st centuries. Gender and crime is a complicated, multidimensional topic that merits careful scholarly study. It describes the historical lack of particular focus on female criminality and the difficulties this lack of attention has consequently created for female offenders, specifically for the sake of coherence and general education. The field of gender and crime is informed by significant theoretical perspectives, female pathways to criminality, current trends in female criminality, and, lastly, women's experiences with the criminal justice system, including significant trends in the incarceration of girls and women.

9.3.1. Male-Based Criminology and Explanations of Female Criminality

We can state that a great deal is known about the type and scope of criminal offenses at the time this section is being written. Religious authorities and philosophers were the first to think critically about crime; their theories frequently touched on the causes, morality, and appropriate responses to crimes. Cesare Lombroso conducted the first real empirical studies of criminal offending because he thought there was a significant biological component to the causation of crime. Put differently, the belief was that certain individuals were destined to be criminals and could be recognized by physical characteristics like high cheekbones, baldness, or shifty eyes. Research on the causes and consequences of crime has advanced far beyond these biological variables based solely on appearance. Modern theories of crime causation are far more intricate and frequently combine psychological and/or sociological elements. Historically, male scholars have dominated the field of criminology, regardless of the extent of the theoretical perspective adopted or the variables included, with the goal of explaining the criminal behavior of other men. For far too long, women and girls who committed crimes were overlooked as guilty parties. In fact, feminist scholars frequently refer to the paucity of research and understanding regarding female offenders as the "invisible offender." Either women were removed from samples or their data was not included in analyzes aimed at explaining crime or determining how well the criminal justice system works. Theories of crime and justice were essentially theories of male crime and justice as a result of this androcentric focus. The work of feminist scholars played a major role in the 1970s in bringing attention to female offenders specifically. In fact, during this time, the number of academics classified as feminist criminologists has steadily increased, which has led to an expansion of the research agenda for those studying the relationship between gender and crime. Before this time, the majority of research on girls and crime was almost entirely focused on prostitution and was often plagued by stereotypes about "evil" and "bad" women. In contrast, feminist scholars focused on a broader range of offenses and started investigating whether girls and women committed crimes for different reasons than boys and men. Feminist research in this field thus included challenging male-based and male-informed criminological knowledge as well as creating a new criminology that places a focus on female offenders as the main subject of study. The experiences of girls and women in the criminal justice system, particularly those of women incarcerated, have also been studied by feminist scholars.

Feminist criminologists have long addressed the lack of theory and research on female offenders. They also brought attention to the fact that men have genders as well, which sparked the development of a new field of study known as masculinities research, which examines the part that expectations of masculinity play in some types of male criminality. Feminist criminology scholarship foregrounds gender, despite the term feminism's frequent negative connotations among the general public. Feminist criminologists do not necessarily assume that the same factors that are significant in explaining male criminal behavior will also predict female crime. Gender is constructed and shaped by history, culture, and the sociopolitical environment, according to feminist scholarship. Feminist criminologists place great importance on these systems of male privilege and how they interact with the policing of women, as gender frequently has a significant impact on opportunities and social participation.

The idea that girls and women in the criminal justice system are more likely than boys to have histories of sexual and physical victimization; the fact that women in the criminal justice system are frequently the only caregivers for dependent children; and, finally, the fact that the abuse that characterized their childhoods continues on into adulthood are some of the more salient aspects of gender in relation to crime and the criminal justice system that feminist research has highlighted. In addition to these distinctions, girls and women who have been criminalized have certain characteristics in common with their male counterparts: they are more likely to be from economically disadvantaged backgrounds, many have a very patchy work history, and a large proportion of the female inmate population belongs to a racial minority. Despite how significant these insights are, feminist criminology, as a subfield of feminist theory, has been influenced by a multitude of feminist viewpoints. Some academics have taken a liberal feminist stance when studying women, girls, and crime. According to this viewpoint, discrimination against women is the problem, and the solution is laws requiring equal treatment for men and women based only on their sex. The disadvantage that women face, along with other social issues, are the direct result of a society that sees women as inferior to men. Academics who follow this tradition frequently cite the numerous instances in which the criminal justice system treats men and women differently, such as the fact that women were not permitted to serve on juries until the middle of the 20th century and that women had a difficult time being admitted to law schools for the majority of the 20th century. Liberals combat gender inequality through integration, education, and legal action.

Radical feminists believe that understanding the current social structure is essential to comprehending women's status and crimes against women, particularly when that system is based in patriarchy, or institutional arrangements that uphold male privilege. As a result, radical feminists go beyond merely viewing the social structure as an explanatory framework and instead take aim at the current structure in an effort to improve the status of all women by equating the power and status of men and women in society. The nature and scope of female victimization—especially sexual assault and battery of the wife—at the hands of men, frequently in close and unequal relationships, has been shaped by academics who have adopted this viewpoint. Marxist academics believe that capitalism poses unique challenges to societies as a whole. The unequal class relations in which members of the upper classes can exert control over members of the lower classes (e.g., through pay and access to legislative processes and other power structures), present numerous challenges for those without authority. This viewpoint obviously concentrates on the crimes of the powerful, which are frequently not prosecuted, whereas the crimes of the weak are heavily publicized and subject to police enforcement. Marxist feminists hold that capitalism is the most significant social structure and that women are socially disadvantaged compared to men because they are even more economically marginalized than men. Socialist feminists draw attention to the fact that women are disadvantaged by two of the most significant social structural conditions: patriarchy and capitalism. As a result, these academics frequently adopt a more comprehensive perspective on the status and power dynamics of women in society. Socialist feminists believe that the disadvantages women experience are directly related to their overall placement of less power and status than men. According to this viewpoint, in order to address gender and class disparities, society would need to be totally reorganized away from both capitalism and patriarchy. Third-wave feminists concentrate on the ways that class, race, and gender interact to disadvantage some women more than others. Several feminist scholars considered this viewpoint to be a significant advancement over others since it implied that women were all situated equally in society. However, third-wave feminists have raised the crucial point that racial and class distinctions should be acknowledged. Put another way, while women are disadvantaged compared to men, not all women are treated fairly and valued in society. A person's position within the social, class, and power structures of a society is undoubtedly influenced by their gender, but so are their race, ethnicity, and class.

Remarkably, the study of masculinities also arose as feminists concentrated on the part gender plays in the causation of crime. Feminist scholars have refocused attention on male offenders and the role that male gender expectations play in crime through the study of gender, crime, and victimization. Once more, a lot of criminological theory has assumed that criminal behavior is exclusively associated with men. Few have ever asked how specific socialization—male or female—leads to involvement in violence and crime. Once more, it is crucial to remember that while there isn't a single feminist theory, gender—typically the female gender—is the primary focus of all of these feminist-based theories and the main focus of their scholarly investigation. These feminist theories specifically address the social disadvantages faced by girls and women and how these connect to victimization and criminal careers within the fields of criminology and criminal justice. Lastly, these theoretical stances frequently provide recommendations for enhancing the status of women and girls in society in order to lessen the need for them to commit crimes. Gender-specific explanations of female criminality, which incorporate ideas for change as well as theoretical frameworks for understanding offending behavior, draw from these and other significant feminist perspectives. The questions of whether male-based theories of crime actually explain female criminality, why gender matters so much in official measures of crime, why women victimize at significantly higher rates than men, whether or not women are treated differently within the criminal justice system, and why women appear over- and underrepresented in certain crimes have remained concerns for feminist criminologists. While by no means exhaustive, this list offers a condensed way to summarize the main issues raised by the majority of feminist criminological research to date.

Perhaps the feminist movement's initial emphasis on women was on how they were being victimized by a system that was primarily patriarchal. Unavoidably, the emphasis on female victimization resulted in the identification of a significant correlation between the victimization of girls and women and their subsequent criminal histories. This concentrated investigation on female offenders also brought to light the dearth of critical scholarly focus on women's criminality. Feminists have expressed particular concern about how a gender-based social structure (i.e., a patriarchal society) has negatively impacted women's participation in social interactions. Within this domain, gender is acknowledged as a social construct distinct from biological sex. There are ingrained societal expectations and meanings associated with gender, whether it be femininity or masculinity. It is noteworthy that feminist scholarship, in all its manifestations, has contributed to overcoming the binary opposition between crime as a male activity and victimization as a female one. Feminist studies have, in fact, brought men and crime—and what "doing gender" means for both—back into the spotlight. Regrettably, there have been negative effects from the lack of scholarly attention and research on women's crime. Firstly, academics have labeled women who commit crimes as "bad" instead of trying to understand why they do so. Undoubtedly, women have historically experienced excessively controlling treatment, particularly in patriarchal systems that place a high value on "good" women—that is, those who are primarily obedient to men and the institutions that men have established. Secondly, programs, policies, and practices intended for male offenders have been applied, mostly unrecognized, to female offenders. Even though their numbers have increased more quickly than those of men, little research or attention has been paid to the number of women who are arrested and incarcerated. However, research in the present era has progressed beyond the idea that female offenders are invisible. This section delves into the current understanding of women's criminal pathways, victimization patterns, the type and scope of female offending, and their involvement in the criminal justice system, including their incarceration and prison experiences.

9.3.2. Pathways and Women's Crime

The road to crime is a convoluted one for many people, and it's no different for women. Though there are many established gender-specific factors linked to women's involvement in crime and the criminal justice system, women do tend to share patterns with men. Once more, feminist scholarship has contributed to illuminating the ways in which women's roles in society have historically been disregarded by the criminal justice system and to explaining why women commit crimes. According to recent research, a woman's involvement in criminal activity and the criminal justice system is frequently a result of the complexity and context of her life. To put it briefly, compared to men, women have notably higher histories of trauma, addiction, abusive relationships, and economic marginalization. The pathways perspective, a subset of life course perspectives, currently provides the most insight into how women engage with the criminal justice system and commit crimes. Compared to their male counterparts, girls and women experience far higher rates of victimization and abuse (sexual, physical, and emotional). In contrast to less than one in five male prisoners, the majority of female jail inmates in the most recent national survey of correctional populations (including probationers and inmates) reported having experienced physical or sexual abuse at some point in their lives. In addition, abuse of females happens at disproportionate rates before and after they reach legal adulthood; put another way, women are more likely than men to experience severe abuse during their childhood and adolescence. Research already in existence indicates a connection between female criminality and victimization as children and adults, and women involved in the criminal justice system experience higher rates of abuse than women in general. According to trauma theorists, these violent past experiences compound one another and cause trauma that is rarely addressed by medical professionals. Women therefore respond to the trauma in ways that are considered illegal, particularly by abusing drugs and other substances and committing other crimes that fund their addictions.

Overall, women are incarcerated or otherwise placed under correctional supervision for drug and property offenses at a higher rate than men. According to a different nationwide survey of people behind bars, in 2006, women received sentences of 28.7% and 30.9%, respectively, for drug offenses and property offenses, while men received sentences of 18.1 and 20.1%, respectively. Drug-related property crimes are frequently connected to the multifaceted involvement of female offenders with drugs and other substances. Previous studies have indicated that a number of factors, including trauma, abuse, women's subservient roles in society, health issues, low self-efficacy and self-image, and relationship problems, are strongly associated with substance abuse and female offending. According to addiction theorists, if we addressed the gender-specific factors that contribute to drug-related crimes and addiction, we could actually lower the number of female offenders. Other academics have concentrated on the distinctions between relationships between women and how these relate to social and personal development. Girls mature into adulthood differently than boys do due to different socialization processes, and as a result, they end up in relatively vulnerable and disadvantageous positions. Girls who have experienced abuse often have lower levels of empowerment and self-worth, as well as a reduced capacity for meaningful relationships. It helps to understand the gender-specific strains that make girls and women more prone to crime and substance abuse to recognize the role that a patriarchal system plays in socializing female expectations and responsibilities. Moreover, women are more likely than men to be raising dependent children alone, and this, along with their own relationship issues, can frequently result in a dysfunctional cycle.

One especially good theoretical explanation for women's involvement in crime is the pathways perspective. This theoretical framework considers all of the gender-related risk factors that are believed to contribute to female criminality, taking a more comprehensive approach to the issue of women's involvement in crime. The transparency of women's problems in life and how they intersect with crime become evident when the context of female social participation is firmly placed within the framework of a patriarchal society, which restricts female participation in meaningful ways and labels females as "bad" when they do not follow gender-related rules. Girls and women in the criminal justice system experience higher rates of victimization than boys and men in their families of origin and in their intimate relationships, according to a pathways, or life trajectories, perspective.

Compared to men, they are more likely to self-medicate with both legal and illicit drugs, have fragmented family histories, experience physical and/or mental health issues, be single mothers of small children, have limited vocational skills, and have irregular employment histories. Individually or frequently all at once, these elements combine to have a beneficial impact on women's criminal behavior and interactions with the legal system.

These variables make it more likely for women to commit crimes and become involved in the criminal justice system overall, particularly for women of color and those from lower socioeconomic backgrounds. The opportunities that are perceived to be available to women who are marginalized in society are shaped by the socialization of girls and women. These restricted options frequently push women and girls into homelessness, substance abuse, prostitution or other sex-related crimes as a means of survival, abusive relationships, and more serious crimes. Gender has very strong but frequently unnoticed effects. Circumstances that devalue women and girls in comparison to their male counterparts limit and shape their lives.

Too long has passed without recognition regarding the process by which girls and women enter the criminal justice system, despite the fact that some of these consequences—like receiving less money for equivalent work—are now more widely known. Note that our point is that women who find themselves represented as offenders and other criminal justice participants are more likely than other members of the general population to exhibit the factors listed in this section. We do not, however, intend to imply that feminist scholars do not wish to suggest that women lack agency due to the pervasive histories of abuse and vulnerable positions within patriarchal societies.

9.3.3. Nature and Extent of Women's Crime

Gender is one of the best indicators of crime, particularly violent crime. A disproportionate number of reported crimes are committed by men. In 2006, for instance, men accounted for 68.8% of those arrested for property crimes (larceny theft, motor vehicle theft, and burglary) and 82.8% of those arrested for violent crimes (murder, aggravated rape, robbery, and aggravated assault). On the other hand, women accounted for 64.2% of arrests related to prostitution and commercialized vice, and girls accounted for more than half of all runaway arrests. Women make up about 25% of all official arrests, but their involvement in the criminal justice system has increased more quickly than that of men. There is no denying that women now account for a higher percentage of arrests overall. However, the true significance of these figures is more debatable. It's possible that the number of crimes committed by women has increased over the past 30 years. However, the body of recent research indicates that it is more likely that women's behavior has come under more scrutiny, especially in the area of assault, rather than that crime has increased dramatically. Historically and consistently, violent crime has been primarily the domain of men. This is true in spite of the attempts made by the media today to portray "bad" girls and rising rates of female aggression. Indeed, during the previous 40 years, there has been a notable decline in the proportion of females arrested for homicide. The number of women being arrested for drug offenses and property crimes—particularly fraud and larceny—has dramatically increased. Both of these shifts in female criminality are probably the result of increased attention to these behaviors by local and federal law enforcement, in addition to some degree of increased offending.

The majority of women who commit crimes and wind up in the criminal justice system are typically economically disadvantaged and lack access to opportunities for education and/or employment. It makes sense that the crimes that women tend to commit more frequently or in which they are otherwise overrepresented are those that could be classified as "survival crimes" given their economic standing and longer histories of abuse. For instance, property crimes like theft or larceny, fraud and forgery, and sex crimes like prostitution are feasible means of subsistence for women living on the margins of society. If a typical female offender exists, she is likely young, a woman of color, a single mother, undereducated, unskilled, and victimized in the past. In comparison to men, these factors influence the type and severity of crime experienced by women. Understanding women's involvement in drug use is essential to any discussion of women's criminality. Legal and illicit substances are more frequently used by women as a kind of self-medication for untreated emotional trauma, which is frequently linked to past abuse. Since the US has been enforcing harsher penalties for using illegal drugs, this has become even more problematic for women. The ensuing sections underscore that mandatory drug sentencing laws are primarily responsible for women's accelerated rate of incarceration growth. Girls and women have been more involved in the criminal justice system over the past few decades, making it harder and more unacceptable to ignore them. The way they should be handled by the criminal justice system and how they should be treated and supervised in the community is also affected by their increased presence in official arrest and conviction records.

9.3.4. Women and Equity in the System

Gender parity in the criminal justice system is a problem that hasn't gone away. The criminal justice system has only been applied to women and has been primarily defined and constructed around what is known about male offending. Many believe that this is fair treatment. Nonetheless, the "add gender and stir" approach to criminal justice policy is inequitable in light of what is known about female pathways to offending. Since laws, regulations, sanctions, and programs were primarily created with men in mind, it is assumed that they will also work for women.

Women are currently disadvantaged in comparison to men because of the way they enter and are handled by the system. For a female offender, equitable treatment would probably entail taking into account her needs unique to her gender and designing a system that would specifically address these areas. These gender-specific considerations are rarely brought up in conversations about criminal or penitentiary policy, so the potential harm to female offenders is not considered or examined in advance. Women are impacted by the system at numerous stages. For instance, women are generally less financially equipped than male offenders, so it is less likely that they will be able to post bail at the time of arrest. Due to their higher propensity for drug addiction and drug use as a form of self-medication, women are more likely to be subject to mandatory minimum prison sentences. When it comes to security risk classification schedules, female offenders are typically overclassified in comparison to their male counterparts. The 1997 Adoption and Safe Families Act, which permits the termination of parental rights if the parent has been consecutively without his or her child for 15 months, is more likely to affect women than men because they are more likely to have been the primary caregivers of their dependent children. Compared to men, who are much less likely to have continued to be the dependent child's caregiver, women are more likely to lose custody of their children permanently because the average sentence for women is currently longer than 15 months. Men have been the focus of prison supervision programs as well as probation and parole programs. In order to provide equitable treatment for women, supervision techniques tailored for female offenders would be implemented, taking into account the histories of abuse that the vast majority of women in the system exhibit. Furthermore, if the objective is to improve success while under community supervision, the competing demands of many female offenders in the community—child care, lower vocational skills and pay, familial responsibilities—often translate into a need for greater support.

Despite their outward appearance of gender neutrality, many academics contend that the current criminal justice laws—from which other criminal justice processes undoubtedly stem—involve gender discrimination. However, laws may not apply equally to men and women, or they may penalize men who victimize more severely than women (e.g., violent crimes as opposed to assaults associated with domestic abuse). Certain laws, like the one requiring an arrest in cases of domestic abuse, have inadvertently made things worse for women who are the victims of abuse. Certain academics have contended that women receive more severe punishment than men because they are perceived as "evil" or non-normative, while others claim that women are treated more chivalrously and receive lighter sentences than men. The evidence does not fully support either the evil-woman or the chivalrous theories. While there is evidence supporting each of these claims, the overwhelming body of research suggests that those making decisions about criminal justice, from law enforcement to corrections, typically take different factors into account when deciding how to treat men and women differently. In any case, the issue with differential treatment is one of translation—or the absence of it. Research on female offenders is becoming more and more prevalent, but it is rarely utilized in meaningful conversations about criminal justice treatment. The current body of research unequivocally shows significant qualitative variations in the type and severity of female criminality. In general, women commit crimes for different reasons than men and are overrepresented in certain offender groups (e.g., the viewpoint of the pathways). Therefore, the system's current challenge is to figure out how to use the information and research already in place to guide equitable treatment. The related difficulty is in making policymakers aware of the distinction between being exactly the same and being equitable—the two are not the same. Many people interpret "equal under the law" to mean "to be treated exactly the same," but treating women the same way as men does not amount to equitable treatment.

9.3.5. Female Inmates

Compared to men, women are incarcerated at a rate that is faster than that of other demographic groups. This requires particular attention because, despite a higher growth rate, female offenders may have remained the most invisible in this area. Even with the higher growth rate, there are still fewer women behind bars than men; additionally, they are frequently serving shorter sentences for less serious crimes, and they are seldom linked to rioting, violence in prison, or other aggressive behavior. Nonetheless, female offenders encounter significant issues unique to their gender during their incarceration. In the early jails and prisons, young offenders, male offenders, and female offenders were all housed in the same facilities without any consideration for issues of vulnerability or safety. The theory of penology evolved along with the ways that people were imprisoned. Males and females were typically kept apart in jails and prisons by the early 20th century, either in separate facilities or within the same facility. These previous distinct, and ostensibly equal, institutions were only equal on the surface. The original women's facilities were intended to rehabilitate criminals in a way that would make them comply with social norms related to gender. Stated differently, women were trained to perform tasks that are typically associated with women, such as cooking and cleaning, in order to become "better" wives or daughters. Their sentences were usually indeterminate, meaning they did not serve a set period of time (although there was usually a maximum sentence to be served), because the goal of their incarceration was rehabilitation. When it was determined that these female prisoners had recovered, they would be freed. However, during this same period of time, men were largely sentenced to prison for punishment and were released based on a set sentence. Women frequently served longer sentences than men for comparable offenses as a result of these disparate systems.

The main purpose of incarceration in the 21st century is still punishment, for both men and women. As a result, it would seem that both would experience the same kind of incarceration, but this is untrue. The fact that women have been incarcerated at a higher rate than men for the past 10 years may be the most concerning disparity. It is significant to note that female offenders appear to have been most affected by the "get tough" and severe crime control policies of the late 20th century. However, the policy pertaining to the war on drugs has been the most significant area that impacts female offenders.

The previous discourse on the pathways taken by female offenders brought to light the causes of the drug use and addiction issues that many women experience. For many women, untreated trauma, other mental health conditions, and underlying addictions are symptoms that lead to criminal behavior; consequently, comorbidity (i.e., having multiple issues) is a serious issue in prisons for women. The majority of "treatment" that many female offenders have received has been the war on drugs, which heavily relies on jail as a solution. Unfortunately, prison has not shown to be a successful setting for treating the extremely complex problem of drug addiction, particularly for the population of women who are likely to be uneducated, underemployed, economically marginalized, suffering from untreated physical or mental health issues, and caring for small children. Many academics—feminist or not—think that community-based social service-based treatment would be a better way to address the issues faced by addicts. It should be mentioned that, in contrast to less than half of men, over two thirds of women are in charge of raising their dependent children before being imprisoned. In addition, when a mother is imprisoned, her children are more likely to be looked after by a friend, relative, or other adult than their father; conversely, when a father is imprisoned, the mother is more likely to take care of the children. Therefore, it has long been believed that policies that disproportionately target female offenders in prison would have unintended consequences for the children who remain behind. There are fewer female facilities because there are fewer female prisoners overall than there are male prisoners. Facilities for both women and a large number of men are frequently too far away from families to permit visits. Since many of these women come from low-income homes and cannot afford to travel far from home for visits, many children will not have the opportunity to see their mother while she is behind bars. This is a sad state of affairs, as studies have shown that more family support and visits lower recidivism rates and promote general community success.

Compared to male incarceration, the nature of female incarceration has gotten substantially less attention. The literature currently suggests some significant differences in what it means to serve time in a female institution compared with a male facility. Often, the reason for the lack of research attention is the higher proportion of female inmates than male inmates. In male facilities, the prevalence of inmate-to-inmate sexual assault is significantly higher. However, the culture in a female-only facility is more likely to involve consensual sex and occasionally involve members of the pseudo families that are created there. If sexual abuse does happen in a prison, it usually happens with staff members. These mistreatments frequently go unreported or unchecked. These kinds of institutional-based abuse are not adequately addressed by the existing infrastructure. States that have recognized that women are inherently vulnerable to the authority and status of prison personnel and are never in a position to engage in consensual sexual relationships with staff have only recently started to criminalize the sexual abuse of female inmates by staff.

Like women in society at large, women in prison are excessively controlled. Inmates who are female typically receive more reprimands and misconduct violations than those who are male. But the purpose of write-ups and misconduct reports is to address minor infractions of the rules of the institution (e.g., disobedience to authority, and insubordination) as opposed to institutional violence. While women's prison environments are generally less violent than those of men, working with female inmates is still thought to be more challenging. Correctional staff frequently point to women's higher emotional needs and their unwillingness to follow orders blindly as the primary causes of this difficulty with female offenders. Compared to male offenders, women do in fact have higher unmet needs for both physical and mental health. This is frequently because women have experienced more emotional, physical, and sexual abuse in the past, as well as associated untreated trauma. Compared to male inmates, female inmates are much more likely to have experienced abuse as children and/or adults. Female inmates frequently receive inadequate care for their physical and mental health needs while incarcerated. The lower proportion of female prisoners has also resulted in less funding, research, and attention going toward women's prison programs. In addition to the previously discussed issues of mental and physical health in prison, women's vocational and educational opportunities have not kept up with those of their male counterparts. Programs that teach women vocational skills that will enable them to earn a livable wage after being released from prison are insufficient at the moment. Facilities that cater to men are far more likely to offer these kinds of programs. The fact that there are fewer female facilities is a significant effect of the decrease in female prisoners. Not only are these facilities far from the residences of the female offenders, but there are also infrequently facilities specifically designed for females according to risk level. The ability to classify female offenders by low, medium, and high risk is frequently lacking, despite the fact that the majority of them pose little threat to institutional security. Regardless of their classification, all female offenders are housed in the same facility during their sentence.

9.3.6. Women as Victims

It is complicated but crucial for researchers studying gender and crime to comprehend the relationship between a woman or girl's victimization and her criminal activity. Many women are frequently both offenders and victims, rather than just one or the other. As a matter of fact, a great deal of women were victims before they were ever offenders. Gender-focused research has brought attention to the victim roles played by female offenders. Women have frequently experienced physical, sexual, and/or emotional abuse at the hands of loved ones or family members. Girls who are abused at home frequently attempt to survive by committing "survival crimes," such as running away and having sex. These two actions provide practical ways for young people to leave abusive homes; the first is regarded as a status offense. Girls often don't think they have any other options. For young girls, life on the streets can be perilous and even lead to the pursuit of other means of survival, particularly those involving drugs and drug use.

Males are abused in similar ways to females, no doubt, but not to the same extent, and the abuse usually stops when the victim reaches adolescence (because they are stronger). Furthermore, male aggression is largely to blame for the victimization of women. When women reach adulthood, this victimization might also spread to the financial sphere, putting them in precarious relationships. Women who are parents face an even more difficult situation since they frequently cannot support their children financially on their own. Sadly, having less financial power as an individual or as a household means having less control and a decreased chance of feeling safe enough to leave an abusive relationship. Whatever the circumstances, women are frequently occupying roles that are seen as less powerful and subordinate to men. Girls and women are therefore more susceptible to different types of violence. Men abuse women in order to subjugate, control, and humiliate them as part of a patriarchal system that generally favors men over women. When women do inflict violence on men, it's usually in self-defense following an extended duration of being in a violent circumstance. It is no coincidence, according to feminist scholars, that men—often men the victim knows—have committed the majority of the violent crimes against women. This holds true for all kinds of abuse. Most female victims of sexual assault and rape are aware of their attackers. It is also more common for women who are already in physically abusive relationships to experience sexual assault. When we examine victims of physical abuse, similar trends are seen as well: the majority of women are aware of their attackers. In addition, the majority of serial killers are men, and the majority of their victims are women, making it statistically uncommon for mass murder victims to be men. The best explanation for why women are more likely than men to become victims of intimate violence seems to be that men who express violence against women do so as a means of subtly or overtly demonstrating their control and power over them. Rape laws used to be specific about who could be a victim—only women—and their existence stemmed primarily from the idea that women belonged to men. The purpose of punishment was to serve the interests of the person who "owned" the woman, not the woman herself. The messages from society have always been similar, if more subdued. More modern messages emphasize how women must be controlled by men and kept safe. This is just one example of how women are positioned in underprivileged positions that increase their susceptibility to abuse at the hands of men.

The fact that men they know frequently abuse women matters. First of all, it is more difficult for women who experience abuse at the hands of those who are meant to look out for them to establish healthy relationships. Secondly, the possibility of prosecution drops when the victim of sexual assault or physical abuse knows the attacker or is in close social circles with them. Stated differently, the likelihood of the attacker receiving punishment decreases with the strength of the social relationship. This reinforces social norms and gives men the impression that women are "safe" targets for abuse. Sexual and physical violence against women is a widespread issue that cannot be addressed on an individual basis. One of the most significant lessons from feminist scholarship is this. Both societal and personal issues are caused by the patriarchal system that permits so much victimization of women, frequently with no escape route available to them. Women will probably always be more likely to be victims than men, which raises the likelihood that they will abuse drugs, commit crimes, and interact with the criminal system until there is a major shift in how society views women.

9.4. AGE AND CRIME

One of the most consistent findings in criminology is the curvilinear relationship between age and crime; this relationship has been called a "resilient empirical regularity" and "one of the brute facts of criminology." The age-crime curve is the result of social statisticians' discovery of a significant correlation between age and crime as early as Quetelet in the 1800s. There is little disagreement over the general shape of the association between age and crime. According to aggregate studies, the official crime rate rises during adolescence, peaks in late adolescence, and then rapidly declines throughout adulthood. It is also evident that, in comparison to property crimes, the age-crime curve for violent crimes peaks somewhat later. Moffitt (1993) pointed out that while a lot of studies looking at the age-crime relationship have relied on official data and age-specific arrest rates, the general curvilinear pattern also applies more broadly to conduct disorder, antisocial behavior, and childhood aggression. Farrington (1986) and Hirschi & Gottfredson (1983) have observed that while academics concur on the age-crime curve's overall shape, they disagree on its interpretation and consequences.

9.4.1. Hirschi and Gottfredson's "Age and the Explanation of Crime"

Numerous academics have cited Hirschi and Gottfredson's groundbreaking work, "Age and the Explanation of Crime," published in 1983 as the starting point for a meaningful discussion on the connection between aging and criminal activity. Many theoretical and methodological issues are at the heart of this discussion. In particular, Hirschi and Gottfredson presented several fundamental viewpoints regarding the connection between criminality and age. The first and possibly most significant claim made by these authors is that the age-crime curve remains constant across a broad range of social and cultural variables, such as place, time, people, and types of crimes. While acknowledging that disparities in the severity of offenses between various groups (e.g., men and women), they disregarded this variance and came to the conclusion that the curve's overall shape is the same. This invariance argument has sparked a heated discussion among criminologists and has significant implications for methodological, theoretical, and practical issues in the field of criminology.

In response to criticism that theories should not be required to attempt to explain this relationship and should not be disregarded purely on the grounds that they are unable to do so, Hirschi & Gottfredson (1983) addressed theoretical attempts to contend with the age-crime curve. The authors further argued that there are no criminological theories out there that can account for the age-crime curve. Hirschi and Gottfredson proposed a direct relationship between age and crime, as well as other social factors put forth to explain crime, in the lack of compelling theoretical explanations. A supposed correlation exists only because people marry and start to age out of crime at the same time; in other words, the apparent relationship between reduced offending and marriage is spurious because age causes both. In conclusion, Hirschi and Gottfredson contended that understanding the correlation between age and crime in terms of a criminal career is superfluous and possibly deceptive, particularly considering that the reasons behind crime remain the same regardless of age. With significant implications for criminological research, theory, and policy, the arguments presented by Hirschi & Gottfredson (1983) in their article have generated a great deal of debate in the field. For example, Tittle & Grasmick (1998) contended that the perspective of Hirschi and Gottfredson poses a serious threat to many of the current directions in criminology, such as the perspective on criminal careers, longitudinal research, developmental theories, and social theories in general.

9.4.2. Methodological Implications of the Invariance Argument

Steffensmeier and associates observed disagreement regarding the degree and constancy of the age-crime relationship. Hirschi & Gottfredson's (1983) claim that the age-crime curve is constant across time, place, individual characteristics, offense type, and other factors is one of the primary methodological points of contention. In response to this argument, numerous criminologists argue that the assertion of invariance is exaggerated. In a summary of the discussion, Tittle & Grasmick (1998) discovered evidence of invariance only when examining the overall mathematical form of the curve; that is, the aggregate age-crime curve appears consistent across various locations, periods, person types, and offense categories. Every curve follows the same overall unimodal pattern, with rates increasing until they reach a peak in late adolescence and then decreasing until they reach adulthood. The assertions of parametric and individualistic invariance, according to Tittle & Grasmick (1998), have been categorically refuted.

Research investigating the particular characteristics of the age-crime curve (i.e., skewness, kurtosis, median, mean, and skewness) have revealed discrepancies. For instance, Steffensmeier and colleagues (1989) discovered that while the aggregate curves' overall shapes are similar, the curves' specific parameters do differ when using data from both the Uniform Crime Reports and self-report surveys. Specifically, they noticed that the age-crime curve's peak has moved to younger ages over time, and the curve has steepened. Farrington (1986), after examining the curve's individual components, also came to the conclusion that the age-crime curve is not constant. While some consider these variations to be unimportant, Gottfredson & Hirschi (1986) deemed them to be substantively interesting and worthy of consideration.

When the age-crime curve is examined at the individual level, the invariance claim has also been disproved. The modal age-crime curve has numerous individual deviations, as noted by Tittle & Grasmick (1998). According to Blumstein et al. (1988), the aggregate age–crime curve accurately depicts prevalence (e.g., the percentage of the population that commits crimes at a specific age), it only seems to be constant. At the individual level, however, there is a lot of variation in the relationship between age and crime. Farrington (1986) also mentioned individual differences in the trajectories of offenses, which have been confirmed in later studies.

The question of whether the correlation between age and crime results from prevalence (i.e., rates of participation) or incidence (i.e., specific trends in the frequency of offenses). Variations in the frequency or engagement rates of criminal activity suggest that the overall form of the age-crime curve arises from the fact that criminal activity differs among age groups. Put differently, the percentage of the population that commits crimes decreases for older age groups, but the percentage of adolescents involved in crimes rises. Conversely, an analysis of the incidence or frequency of offending indicates that the age-crime curve is a collective depiction of individual variations in the quantity of crimes committed at different ages. Put another way, people tend to commit fewer crimes as they get older and fewer crimes during their teenage years. It is now widely accepted that prevalence is the cause of the relationship seen in the aggregate age-crime curve. Research has shown that the frequency of offending can vary in its trajectory, as evidenced by the findings of Nagin & Land (1993) and subsequent studies. In agreement, Hirschi & Gottfredson (1983) contended that variations in prevalence (i.e., correctly differentiating between criminals and non-offenders) are the most crucial factors in criminology.

9.4.3. Age, Crime, and Criminal Careers

The question of the age–crime curve's invariance is at the center of additional methodological discussions about the correlation between age and criminality. The individualistic invariance claim has been refuted, and some researchers have taken into consideration offending within the context of a criminal career, acknowledging that there are individual variations in the age–crime relationship. Blumstein along with others. The term "longitudinal sequence of offenses committed by an offender who has a detectable rate of offending during some period" was used in 1988 to describe the criminal career. The criminal careers perspective addresses elements of a career like onset, persistence, and desistance and examines the relationship between age and crime at the individual level. The term "onset" describes the beginning of criminal behavior, and some scholars have highlighted the age of onset as a crucial component of a criminal career. Research has specifically looked at the likelihood that people who start offending at a young age will go on to commit crimes frequently or permanently. Desistance is the act of ending an offending career, whereas persistence is the continuation of that career for an extended period of time. Even so, Blumstein et al., claimed there is no reason to anticipate a specific pattern or tendency in criminal careers, and they recommended that the investigation into the existence of specific patterns (e.g., a rise in severity, expertise in specific criminal categories, etc., is amenable to empirical research.

The criminal careers perspective is a methodological and empirical approach that considers participation in offending separately from the frequency of offending among active offenders. It does not present any particular theoretical model, but rather allows for the possibility that different theoretical perspectives may be important in explaining different aspects of the criminal career. On the other hand, Gottfredson & Hirschi (1986) argued that the comparison between offenders and non-offenders (i.e., prevalence or participation) and that theories sufficient to differentiate between these two groups can do so without requiring the explanation of distinct aspects of a career. According to Gottfredson and Hirschi, the causes of crime are the same regardless of age or the presence of a criminal career, and questions about the incidence or frequency of offending have no bearing on our understanding of criminal behavior.

9.4.4. Longitudinal Research in Criminology

Long-term processes are implied by both the age-crime curve and the criminal career perspective. Cross-sectional studies have been replaced by longitudinal studies, which entail repeated measurement over time, for a number of reasons assessment at a specific moment in time) in the investigation of criminal professions. Blumstein et al. (1988) argued that longitudinal data is virtually necessary to understand dynamic patterns of offending, whether one is looking for variation or stability. They also pointed out that cross-sectional data is inadequate for studying criminal careers. Severinsmeier and associates (1989) contended that the age-crime curve's shape could be explained by a variety of social variables that vary with age. According to Greenberg (1985), depending on the stability or instability of the variable over time, the impact of dynamic factors will be understated in cross-sectional analyzes. When causal ordering is unclear, it may be most crucial to distinguish between longitudinal and cross-sectional data. Social control theories, for instance, contend that criminal behavior results from weaker social ties, but it is also conceivable that social ties could be weakened by offending. Longitudinal studies are more adept at ensuring the proper temporal ordering required to prove causation rather than merely correlation because they measure social factors and criminal behavior at different points in time.

Farrington (1986) brought up another crucial factor to take into account when deciding between cross-sectional and longitudinal research: cross-sectional research has a tendency to conflate period, cohort, and age effects. The term "period effects" describes the consequences of residing in a specific historical era. Regardless of age, people who experience specific eras (e.g., World War II) might encounter similar incidents or societal circumstances. Age effects and cohort effects can be confused more easily because people in the same cohort (e.g., born in the same year) might encounter comparable life circumstances (e.g., the generation of baby boomers). On the other hand, the phrase "aging effects" describes social circumstances that could change with age (e.g., alterations in social ties or peer networks, maturational reform, etc.) and would have an impact on people irrespective of cohort or time period. In order to accurately differentiate between these period, cohort, and age effects, Farrington argued that multi-cohort longitudinal studies are essential. Many of these arguments, however, have been contested by Gottfredson and Hirschi. Hirschi & Gottfredson (1983) contended that no particular methods are required to comprehend this relationship if the age-crime curve is the same for all individuals. Good cross-sectional studies, they contended, (e.g., true experiments) can address the same issues as longitudinal designs, particularly in light of the clear correlation between the dates of social events and crimes. This perspective rejects a key argument in favor of longitudinal designs, namely that temporal ordering should not be a major issue when studying criminal behavior. Since "crime cannot cause age, period, or cohort," they discounted the need to separate the effects of age, period, and cohort. Instead, they contended that criminology has been diverted from more important, policy-relevant issues by the focus placed on these problems. Additionally, Gottfredson & Hirschi (1987) argued that cross-sectional research findings and the correlates of crime found by longitudinal research are identical, meaning that cross-sectional study findings have only been validated by longitudinal research. They issued a warning, saying that longitudinal studies offer no additional value to the study of crime and are far more costly, ineffective, and time-consuming than cross-sectional studies. Additional challenges with longitudinal research have been highlighted by other researchers. These include the potential for testing and maturation or aging effects to be confused, as well as the high attrition (i.e., discontinuing their studies) of high-rate long-term offenders over an extended period of time.

This argument is far from over. According to Gottfredson & Hirschi (1987), it is more crucial to separate offenders from non-offenders, regardless of age, and that nothing useful has been learned from longitudinal studies because the age-crime curve is invariant. Conversely, researchers who are looking into the frequency of criminal activity (i.e., frequency) and criminal careers contend that in order to fully comprehend the patterns, longitudinal data is necessary as the curve varies significantly at the individual level. For example, Sampson & Laub (1995) proposed that while understanding differences between offenders is important, understanding differences within individuals over time is equally important. Individual-level, longitudinal designs are becoming more and more popular among scholars, particularly those in the criminal justice system or developmental/life course traditions. This study looks for more evidence of distinct criminal career patterns and investigates the possibility that these variations can be explained by various social factors.

9.4.5. Theoretical Implications of the Age–Crime Relationship

Criminological theory is significantly impacted by the age-crime curve debate. According to Hirschi & Gottfredson (1983), no social theory currently in use can account for the age-crime curve, which is invariant and the causes of crime are the same for all ages. The adolescent stage, which is when the age-crime curve peaks, has historically been the focus of traditional criminological theories like differential association and social control. Greenberg (1985) contended that crime does not simply level off after the transition to adulthood; rather, it consistently declines, which suggests the need for theoretical attention to the entire life span and to the decline and desistance from offending in addition to onset. This is understandable given that the majority of delinquent and criminal activity occurs during these ages. Traditional theories have frequently been evaluated based on their capacity to explain the trends visible in the age-crime curve, according to Hirschi & Gottfredson (1983). Some theories, for instance, are criticized for their inability to explain desistance, only the beginning and peak of criminal activity. The inability of theories to account for every facet of the age-crime curve is frequently interpreted as a fatal flaw. But Hirschi and Gottfredson contended that a theory that sufficiently separates criminals from non-criminals at a specific age (e.g., adolescence) might not explain the aging-out effect in all cases. Ageing out and refraining from crime are phenomena that all groups experience consistently, so a theory's inability to account for desistance shouldn't be disregarded, especially in light of the fact that no theory currently in existence, in their opinion, can adequately explain desistance.

Hirschi & Gottfredson (1983) further contended that, in the lack of a convincing theoretical justification, the only conclusion that can be drawn is that, independently of other social variables and devoid of an explanation from any social theory now in existence, age has a direct impact on crime. This would seem to imply a biological explanation of some kind, and they explained desistance in terms of a maturational reform process that is ubiquitous for all offenders. Farrington (1986) noted age-related differences in physical prowess and skills and further proposed that maturational reform reflects some biological forces. Once more, Gottfredson & Hirschi (1986) claim that attempts to explain these patterns with social forces—which are assumed to vary—are fruitless because the age-crime curve is invariant and aging out of crime occurs similarly for everyone. Ultimately, these authors questioned all criminological theories in existence, concluding that there is no real correlation between different social factors and crime.

9.4.6. The Age–Crime Relationship in Traditional Criminological Theory

Despite the critique leveled by Hirschi & Gottfredson (1983), the major theoretical traditions in criminology (i.e., stress, social control, and social learning theories) have all been applied to explain why criminal behavior varies throughout an individual's lifetime. Strain theory, for instance, contends that status frustration and strain are more common in adolescents and young adults and that these feelings lessen as they approach adulthood and gainful employment. When young people join the legal adult labor market, their relative deprivation decreases. In addition, strain theory has been partially adopted by theorists in their consideration of Easterlin's (1978) relative cohort size theory. Easterlin argued that larger cohorts (e.g., the Baby Boomers) have certain drawbacks, like competition for limited resources leading to increased rates of economic hardship for that generation. While pointing out the adverse economic circumstances that align with a strain perspective, Easterlin also made the argument that sizable cohorts might overburden social institutions, exposing cohort members to additional criminogenic social conditions like less supervision, less socialization, and lower levels of social control. These circumstances show to be particularly harmful for teenagers and young adults, and they could be the reason for rising crime rates when these sizable cohorts reach the most criminal years (i.e., late youth and the early years of adulthood).

According to Easterlin (1978); and Greenberg (1985), social control theory could also offer support for the idea that age-related variations in crime rates occur. Age differences exist in the effects of formal and informal social controls, as noted by Sampson & Laub (1995). According to this theory, social ties weaken during adolescence, giving people more freedom to defy social norms. Adolescence is therefore seen as a period of decreased attachment to conventional people and institutions, particularly parents. As people establish traditional ties through their employment and start creating their own families through marriage and parenthood, social ties may be reestablished as adults. Additionally, as people get older and have a stronger incentive to conform, the consequences of crime also get worse and exert a greater influence over their behavior. According to the theory of differential association, adolescent criminal activity may increase as a result of differing experiences with peers who have engaged in criminal activity. To bolster this viewpoint, Warr (1993) employed data from the National Youth Survey to show how exposure to delinquent peers varies with age. These changes include the proportion of friends who are delinquent, the amount of time spent with peers, and the self-reported significance of peers, and they correlate with the age-crime curve. According to the National Youth Survey, people reported having more delinquent friends later in adolescence, spending more time with them, and placing a higher value on peers. When peer variables were incorporated into multivariate models, the association between age and crime was lessened. According to Warr's research, alterations in peer associations may account for a portion of the age-crime relationship. More recently, Stolzenberg & D'Alessio (2008) looked at the implications of peer association from a different angle, asking whether age-related differences in criminal involvement are explained by changes in co-offending. Scholars have consistently observed that juvenile delinquency is predominantly a collective phenomenon. The aggregate age-crime curve's apparent rising prevalence rates during adolescence could be explained by this pattern of co-offending. According to Stolzenberg and D'Alessio, the reason why crime rates peak in adolescence and then start to decline in early adulthood after high school graduation is because juveniles are more likely to co-offend, which is partly due to the influence of peers who have criminal tendencies.

According to this viewpoint, the age-crime relationship should be most noticeable when examining crimes that involve co-offending; however, when co-offending is taken into account, the relationship should vanish. Put differently, an age-crime curve demonstrating a flat pattern for solo offenders should be seen, while a typical curvilinear pattern would be seen for co-offenders. However, Stolzenberg & D'Alessio (2008) discovered two intriguing findings using data from the National Incident Based Reporting System. First, solo offending is more common for all age groups, including juveniles, despite the majority of discussions about adolescent offending pointing to co-offenses as the most common pattern. Furthermore, a relationship between age and crime is evident for both solo and co-offending, indicating that taking co-offending into account does not lessen the general age-crime relationship. The age-crime curve does not seem to be explained by patterns of co-offending, according to Marvelll & Moody (1991), who concluded that while there is no shortage of conjecture regarding the reasons behind the age-crime curve, none of these explanations have much empirical backing. Despite looking at a number of age-varying criminogenic factors, Tittle & Grasmick (1998) concluded that the age-crime relationship could not be explained by including these factors. They concluded that it is difficult to explain away the age-crime curve after reporting their inability to reject the theoretical arguments put forth by Hirschi & Gottfredson (1983).

9.4.6.1. Propensity versus Developmental Theories

In addition to attempting to explain changes in crime levels over the course of the age-crime curve, more recent criminological theories have also attempted to explain the curve itself. Criminological theory appears to employ two strategies to account for variation throughout the life course: (a) propensity theories and (b) developmental or life course theories. According to propensity theories, crime occurs at all ages due to a single, enduring underlying characteristic. Gottfredson & Hirschi's (1990) general theory of crime, which contends that criminal activity and other risky behaviors at all ages are caused by a person's lack of self-control, is the most well-known and widely tested propensity theory in criminology. It may seem counterintuitive to use a theoretically stable trait to explain the clear age-related variation in patterns of criminal offending. Gottfredson and Hirschi argued that when criminogenic opportunities are present, criminal behavior results from a lack of self-control. Thus, even though levels of self-control are generally stable, opportunities for crime may change throughout the course of a person's life. Hirschi & Gottfredson (1995) proposed that a significant portion of the observed variation in actual criminal activity can be explained by differences in the opportunity for crime by age. Propensity theory contends that any association between age-varying social factors and offending is erroneous, supporting their previous claim that any relationship between social factors (e.g., aberrant peer relationships, and frail social ties), and misbehavior is unfounded due to self-control. Put another way, because self-control is the fundamental cause of all of them, offending is linked to deviant peer associations and weakened social bonds. People who lack self-control are also more likely to hang out with rebellious classmates and find it difficult to establish and maintain the kind of relationships that strengthen social bonds. Thus, they persist in their argument that criminological theories that link shifts in social factors to changes in offending over time are insufficient.

Developmental or life course theories of offending, in contrast to propensity theories, explicitly explain the age-crime relationship by pointing to age-related variations in criminogenic factors. Both life course theory and developmental theory consider the entire life course when explaining criminal behavior. For instance, the premise of Moffitt's (1993) developmental theory is based on empirical research and suggests that the age-crime curve indicates variations in prevalence by age, with a higher percentage of adolescents involved in criminal or delinquent behavior. Additionally, she contended that group differences in the association between age and crime are hidden by the aggregate age-crime curve. Put differently, she pointed out that the overall age-crime curve conceals individual differences in the frequency of offenses by age. According to Moffitt's (1993) typological perspective, there are two distinct categories of offenders, each with a unique age-crime curve. Therefore, the aggregate age-crime curve combines the characteristics of a larger group of people with a brief period of delinquent involvement during adolescence (referred to as adolescent-limited offenders), which shows the typical age-crime curve with a large peak during late adolescence, and a small group of long-term offenders (referred to as the life-course-persistent offenders), which has a relatively flat and stable age-crime curve. These two groups need different etiological explanations because they have different offending patterns. According to Moffitt, neuropsychological deficiencies, insufficient parenting, and the cumulative disadvantage linked to the unfavorable effects of early criminal involvement combine to cause life-course-persistent offenders to engage in criminal behavior early in life and continue to do so. On the other hand, juvenile offenders commit crimes for a comparatively short period of time. A maturity gap—a situation in which young people are biologically mature but still reliant on and controlled by their families—explains how people become involved in criminal activity. Imitating antisocial role models and striving for a degree of independence lead to minor offenses. In this group, persistence happens in the early stages of adulthood as social ties deepen and the penalties for criminal behavior get harsher.

Similar to this, life course theories of criminality emphasize societal forces and long-term offending patterns that persist throughout an individual's entire life. The age-graded theory of social control by Sampson & Laub (1993) examines how behavioral patterns both persist and alter over the course of a person's life, taking into account both inter- and intrapersonal variations. Many social factors, including poor social ties to family and school during childhood and adolescence, can explain the onset of delinquent behavior. The development of social ties, such as solid marriages, steady jobs, and other stabilizing influences, during the transition to adulthood, leads to a desire to abstain from delinquency. Staying Power (i.e., Conversely, continuity) arises from the compounding negative impact of early criminal activity. According to Sampson & Laub (1995), criminal activity weakens social ties even more by limiting opportunities within the normative society. Some academics contend that the emphasis on social bonding is overly limited and that a variety of life experiences may serve to modify peer association in a way that is more consistent with a learning than a social control perspective. According to Sampson & Laub (1995), this does not directly contradict their theory, and the most recent iteration of the theory has been expanded to take into account influences from routine activities, peers, and social bonding that change over the course of a person's life. For instance, marriage may increase social ties, lessen the influence of preexisting associations with deviant peers, and alter daily routines and criminal opportunities. Therefore, these life events explain why crime peaks in late adolescence and then sharply declines shortly after the transition to adulthood.

9.4.6.2. Variation in the Causes of Crime by Age

Whether the causes of crime are the same for all ages is one question that both traditional and life course/developmental theories fail to address. Hirschi and Gottfredson have contended, predictably, that the causes of crime are the same for all ages, i.e., age does not influence social factors that lead to criminal behavior. According to some theorists, there could be age-related differences in the causes of crime. Moffitt (1993) identified several theoretical factors, such as early neuropsychological deficits and parenting influences, negative peer associations in adolescence, and social control mechanisms in later adolescence and early adulthood, that may impact offending at different ages. The interaction thesis was investigated by Tittle & Grasmick (1998), who found no evidence that criminal behavior is produced by the interaction of age and criminogenic factors. They were unable to refute Hirschi & Gottfredson's (1983) claims, once more; nevertheless, there is still room for discussion and further research on this matter.

9.4.7. Practical and Policy Implications of the Age–Crime Relationship

Some useful and policy implications have also been brought to light by the discussion surrounding the association between age and criminality.

The consequences of the age-crime curve have frequently been taken into consideration when evaluating current criminal justice policies. Strategies like the three-strikes law, for instance, have drawn criticism because, by the time the penalty for a third strike is imposed, the offender is probably nearing the end of their criminal career and would have aged out of criminal activity regardless of the severity of the penalty. The law requires courts to impose a mandatory prison sentence on offenders who have been found guilty of felonies three or more times. Other concerns center on predicting future trends in crime rates and the proper crime reduction tactics suggested by the age-crime curve.

9.4.7.1. Targeting Participation versus Frequency

The distinction made in the criminal careers debate between frequency and participation turns out to be a crucial factor in crime policy. According to Hirschi & Gottfredson (1986), initiatives aimed at lowering participation rates (i.e., lowering the percentage of the populace involved in criminal activity) will have the biggest impact on crime rates. In particular, they promoted early intervention programs. Farrington (1986) also proposed that investing in early intervention programs is the best way to prevent crime from starting because the aggregate age-crime curve shows differences in participation. However, Blumstein and associates (1988) proposed that this is merely one strategy for reducing crime. Reducing the frequency of reoffending among currently active offenders would be a second strategy that would entail additional criminal justice tactics. These authors contended that the age-crime curve is comparatively flat and stable, and that there exists a small subset of offenders who commit crimes frequently. It may be advised to employ a tactic like selective incapacitation, which aims to lower the frequency of offenses committed by these chronic offenders. However, selective incapacitation is predicated on the difficult to achieve assumption that these chronic offenders can be accurately identified prior to their involvement in a large number of offenses. While Blumstein and associates acknowledged the challenges in identifying these career criminals, they maintained that criminological research on them should continue.

9.4.7.2. Forecasting Crime Rates

In order to predict future trends in crime and to explain changes in crime rates over time, age has also become a significant factor. For whatever theoretical reason, researchers have come to the conclusion that shifts in the frequency of criminal activity within specific age groups are reflected in the age-crime curve. Therefore, it makes sense that variations in the population's proportion of teenagers and young adults would result in variations in the crime rate. This offers the possibility of predicting shifts in crime patterns according to the population's age distribution. According to certain research, changes in the population's age distribution during the 1960s and 1970s may have contributed, at least in part, to the sharply rising crime rates during that time. Steffensmeier & Harer (1999) proposed that the decrease in adolescent population was a contributing factor to the reduction in crime that occurred in the first part of the 1980s. At this time, a significant portion of the Baby Boomer generation was emerging from the years with the highest rate of crime (i.e., aged out of criminality). Marvell & Moody (1991), however, pointed out that while projections indicated a significant decline as the Baby Boomers aged out during the 1980s, the decline actually only happened for the first half of the decade. Subsequently, even as the number of adolescents in the population decreased, crime rates rose once more, reaching all-time highs in the early 1990s. The 1990s saw a decline in crime rates, which were again largely attributed to the population decline of young adults, despite the apparent complexity and confusion surrounding the use of age as a predictor of crime rates.

Steffensmeier & Harer (1999) discovered that shifts in the population's age distribution did not seem to be responsible for variations in crime rates as determined by the National Crime Victimization Survey and the Uniform Crime Reports. Additionally, cross-national research by Phillips (2006) finds no meaningful correlation between crime rates and the size of the youth population. Most important, she found that the relationship between the percentage of young people in the population and homicide is attenuated when other criminogenic social conditions (e.g., little social supervision, and severe economic hardship) exist. She made the argument that there is a complex relationship between age and crime, and that the specifics of that relationship depend on other social and cultural factors. Levitt (1999) also came to the conclusion that, while it might make sense to predict crime rates based on the proportion of teenagers in the population, it is still unclear how much of an impact age structure has on crime. According to his research, variations in the population's age distribution only slightly affect annual variations in crime rates—no more than 1%. Marvell & Moody (1991) contended that demographic shifts shouldn't be utilized to predict crime trends because other criminogenic factors might be more significant and the age-crime relationship might not be strong enough to support predictions. Scholars and the mainstream media continue to predict trends in crime rates based on the age distribution of the population, despite the relationship's apparent complexity. For instance, Fox in 1996 warned of a "demographic time bomb" of crime and violence associated with the projected increase in the number of teenagers and young adults through 2010. This confirmed earlier theories that a large new generation of "super-predators" would be the driving force behind a new wave of crime. The number of teenagers was predicted to reach its peak in 30 years by 2005. Nonetheless, crime rates significantly decreased during the 1990s and continued to be low in the early 2000s. In their assessment of 90 studies, Marvell & Moody (1991) summed up this challenge by stating that "the age/crime relationship is far from established," limiting its usefulness in forecasting future crime trends based on the age distribution of the population.

9.5. THE PUNISHMENT RESPONSE

In all societies, punishment is the standard response to crime and deviance. It therefore takes on different forms. State authorities assign and impose criminal penalties, such as death sentences and incarceration. Additional legal sanctions include administrative decrees and civil lawsuits intended to make amends or mend fences between the parties, pay damages for injuries sustained, and/or stop future wrongdoing by limiting continuing practices. In order to further their own goals, extralegal groups like vigilante committees and paramilitary organizations, as well as friends and family, may also impose various forms of informal sanctions as a form of punishment. Punishments come in various forms and are applied for various reasons. Criminal penalties have several purposes, including upholding established norms and values, disabling and discouraging potential offenders, preserving power structures within a community, and neutralizing challenges to the established social order. Administrative and civil penalties also play a significant role in maintaining and regulating social order. Both official and informal sanctions can strengthen social cohesion against outside threats, highlight the negative effects of specific behaviors within a community, and fund social engineering initiatives aimed at raising standard of living. However, even a cursory examination of punishments shows that they differ greatly throughout space and time. In contrast to modern industrial societies, where social order is frequently only possible through a complex system of formal sanctions, earlier agrarian societies were largely devoid of formal sanctions from the state or other "official" bodies. Over time, there is also variation in the application of specific sanctions among nations. To gain a deeper understanding of this variation in punishment across time and space, a comparative historical approach is beneficial. A comparative historical analysis of punishments becomes even more crucial in light of the current state of world systems, global economies, and multinational penetration. A comparative historical approach challenges our ethnocentric views of "good" and "bad" practices based on our unique cultural and national experiences within this increasingly smaller and interconnected global system. Our knowledge of criminal sanctions and punishments in both Western and non-Western societies can be improved empirically by the possible discovery of punishment responses and principles that cut across time and space.

9.5.1. Punishment and Types of Sanctions

Every society and social group devises strategies to rein in norm-breaking behavior. A fundamental form of social control known as socialization involves learning processes and the internalization of group norms as one's own preferences in an effort to achieve conformity. Another direct method of achieving social control is through outside forces that threaten to have society react negatively if people don't conform. The use of threats and coercion ultimately leads to conformity, regardless of whether it is the result of external pressure or personal desires. Sanctions are a type of social control tool that come in different forms from different sources. Positive sanctions are incentives designed to promote norm compliance, while negative sanctions are penalties designed to deter norm breaking. Sanctions are regarded as "formal" depending on their origin; they can be imposed by the government or other entities that are legally able to do so (e.g., churches, educational establishments, and commercial associations).

Informal sanctions, on the other hand, are unofficial acts taken by organizations and people. These include penalties from friends, family, and quasi-legal organizations like neighborhood watch groups, paramilitary units, and local "regulators." Sanctions also differ in terms of their type and extent (*see* Table 9.1). Negative sanctions are meant to cause pain and can range in severity from small annoyances (e.g., tiny fines) to demise (i.e., the death penalty). These penalties can also take different forms, such as financial penalties, physical limitations, or even physical abuse. For instance, parents may decide to "ground" their children to their house (an incapacitative sanction), deny them their allowance (an economic sanction), or spank their children (a corporal punishment). Governments have the authority to impose death sentences, jail terms, and monetary fines in addition to other criminal penalties.

The severity of positive sanctions varies as well. Positive sanctions can vary from giving someone a pat on the back and some words of encouragement, to awarding multimillion-dollar mergers and acquisitions and giving significant pay raises and promotions for exceptional work performance. Unless one views criminal penalties like suspended jail sentences, the acquisition of "good time" credits while incarcerated, the pardoning of death sentences, and/or the reduction in the number of whipping lashes as a "reward," it is more difficult to see forms of incapacitation and corporal punishment as positive sanctions. "Even though both positive and negative sanctions are crucial for comprehending social control in societies, negative sanctions must receive more attention due to our focus on punishments. Furthermore, we mainly concentrate on state-sponsored sanctions (e.g., civil litigation verdicts, criminal penalties) as well as the deeds of different quasi-governmental organizations that apply extralegal sanctions.

Our goal is to gain insight into the similarities and differences between the ways that societies respond to deviation in diverse historical contexts by examining these punitive measures in distinct eras and locations.

Table 9.1. *Types of Sanctions (Examples)*

	Positive (rewards)	Negative (punishments)
Formal	Promotions Bonuses Awards/medals Honorary titles	Fines/forfeitures Probation/revocations Incarceration Torture/death penalty
Informal	Kiss/hugs Praise Respect Trust	Gossip Ridicule Ostracism "Street justice"

Source: https://catdir.loc.gov/catdir/samples/cam051/2004049271.pdf.

9.5.2. The Functions of Punishment

In any given society, the purposes of both criminal and civil penalties are primarily determined by the social, political, and economic circumstances that are present there. Sanctions are used to maintain social order in small, homogeneous societies that are defined by value consensus. They accomplish this by upholding the status quo and governing and controlling social relations. On the other hand, in more diverse societies, criminal and civil penalties are frequently seen as tools for protecting special interests as well as sources of maintaining order. Criminal penalties have been created for a variety of uses in various eras and locations. These goals include upholding societal norms, safeguarding the public by keeping convicted criminals physically incapacitated, rehabilitating the offender, discouraging reoffending behavior in the future (a tactic known as specific deterrence), and setting an example for others to follow in order to discourage them from committing crimes (a tactic known as general deterrence). Certain criminal and civil penalties (e.g., financial penalties, victim compensation) are intended to have a restorative effect. Furthermore, penalties imposed in public settings frequently serve significant symbolic purposes by emphasizing the wrongness of a certain behavior or demonstrating the impartiality of the judicial system. The conflict perspective on law and society holds that the main purpose of legal penalties is to uphold and defend the rights of the powerful. Through the creation and implementation of civil and criminal laws, this is accomplished in a number of ways. For instance, it has long been maintained that the purpose of the criminal code is to both criminalize and legitimize the avaricious acts of the weak and powerful. The same idea is expressed in Machiavelli's 17th-century remark, "Who steals a handkerchief goes to jail; who steals a country becomes a duke." More broadly, conflict theorists view social control as a primary goal of the law, serving as a tool for both restraining dissent and acquiring control over goods and services. Many civil, administrative, regulatory, and criminal laws reflect the use of legal sanctions to preserve one's cumulative advantage. In the US, for instance, the American Medical Association (AMA) has long opposed alternative medical providers (e.g., chiropractors, and herbalists) in order to protect their financial interests from the monopoly control over the provision of medical care. Groups like the tobacco and distillers industries, which aim to maintain their control over the legal drug market, are frequently the main opponents of marijuana legalization. For similar financial reasons, the main opponents of mass transit are typically the oil companies. While it is evident that the public is somewhat protected by the extensive use of licensing, external auditors and inspectors, building codes and ordinances, and other regulatory activities, these same measures are frequently suggested and created to maintain the combined advantage of a specific group. The use of criminal penalties, civil lawsuits, and different selection procedures are the main ways that legal sanctions are used to suppress dissent. In most nations, financial resources and social connections are the primary barriers to gaining political power. People or organizations that challenge the established order may be silenced or denied tangible advantages, among other tactics reducing student aid programs), civil commitments to mental health and rehabilitation facilities, and incarceration for criminal offenses are some ways to manage student dissension. A largely covert but equally effective means of suppressing dissent in the United States is offered by federal agencies such as the Internal Revenue Service (IRS), the Federal Bureau of Investigation (FBI), and the Central Intelligence Agency (CIA). Death squads and secret police groups are examples of coercive social control tactics used in response to dissident voices abroad. Social engineering, or "purposeful, planned, and directed social change initiated, guided, and supported by the law," is another tactic used by criminal and civil authorities. The ultimate objective of social engineering, however, differs depending on the theoretical viewpoint. Social engineering, from a functionalist perspective that emphasizes stability, collective solidarity, and interdependency among the units and institutions within social systems, aims to achieve maximum harmony for the greatest good and social integration. Conflict theories of social order only emphasize social integration when social engineering efforts help an individual hold onto their position. Conflict theorists believe that the social engineering function of both criminal and civil sanctions is responsible for controlling dissent and those who represent a serious threat to prevailing interest groups.

9.5.3. The Nature of Punishment and Societal Complexity

Sociolegal scholars generally agree that the social conditions that are prevalent in a society have an impact on the development and nature of criminal and civil penalties. Emile Durkheim's theories about punishment and social solidarity, Philippe Nonet and Philip Selnick's analyzes of transitional legal systems and the shift from repressive to responsive law, Donald Black's research on the behavior of law, Michel Foucault's theory on the evolution of the state's authority to control the body, mind, and "souls" of its subjects, and Norbert Elias's contention regarding the development of "civilized sensibilities" in contemporary society that influence the application of punishment are all examples of this relationship between punishment and social structure. There is general agreement that the nature of punishment changes throughout the historical transition from primitive or early tribal law to the development of modern legal systems, even though these authors differ in their focus on specific elements. The legal systems known as "primitive" or early tribal law are associated with small, uniform, and homogeneous societies. Informal sanctions rooted in common practices, conventions, and traditions uphold social order. These most cherished ideals and beliefs are reflected in and safeguarded by laws. While it's common to think of punishment as a straightforward, automatic reaction to deviation, Durkheim argues that, in some situations, punishments also function as social rituals that unite members of the community and offer a platform for reinforcing and strengthening their commitment to these shared values and a common identity. In these homogeneous societies marked by what Durkheim refers to as mechanical solidarity, repressive justice is frequently meted out in the form of diffuse ritual punishments meant to denounce "evil" and reinforce group values."

The social forces of urbanization, industrialization, modernization, and increased heterogeneity are frequently linked to the collapse of early tribal societies. New types of social organization emerge in the transitional stage of societal evolution in order to control and coordinate activities and preserve order. This period of transition is frequently linked to the emergence of the state as the main social institution, the application of laws based on jurisdiction or geography rather than kinship, and the definition of crime and deviance as harm to the public rather than private parties (e.g., in contemporary societies, the state is the "victim" of crime). This brief, transitional phase of societal development is characterized by the precariousness of both law and social order. It is frequently believed that the fundamental issue of integration in extremely diverse societies was the primary driving force behind the creation of a legally codified system. It is problematic to assume that informal sanctions (like interpersonal agreements, social customs, or moral precepts) alone are capable of regulating and maintaining social order because modern societies are typically so diverse and complex. Rather, in this particular context, societal integration calls for a legal framework that is all-encompassing, flexible enough to adapt to shifting political and economic circumstances, and widely acknowledged as the rightful authority. A significant portion of current theory and research in the sociological study of law centers on the central question of whether formalized codified legal systems are successful in fulfilling their various purposes.

It's generally accepted that shifts in the nature of social control and sanction types are reflected in the evolution of simple to complex legal systems. Since informal controls like customs, traditions, ridicule, gossip, praise, or verbal criticism are thought to be insufficient to maintain conformity in industrialized societies, a greater reliance on formal mechanisms of social control (like criminal sanctions, civil commitments, administrative and regulatory laws) is assumed to occur in modern societies. Sanctions changes are frequently linked to an increase in societal complexity. For example, the move away from repressive sanctions (e.g., penalties that aim to condemn, dehumanize, and discredit the offender) to restitutive penalties (e.g., penalties that don't stigmatize the offender in and of themselves, but instead work to mend or make up for the damaged relationship). An analysis of punishment from a comparative historical perspective offers the chance to directly assess the veracity of these theories about the social structure of societies and punishment. John Braithwaite characterizes these kinds of restitutive sanctions as attempts at "reintegrative shaming." Answers to these basic sociological questions about punishment and society require a comparative historical approach. For instance, have punishments become less punitive and more restitutive over time? Have formal sanctions replaced informal sanctions as the main force maintaining social order in modern societies? Do these patterns differ across specific countries in the modern world?

9.5.4. Effectiveness of Criminal and Civil Sanctions

Many scholarly works have addressed the efficacy of state-sponsored sanctions in promoting positive social change and preserving social integration. Over the past 20 years, civil litigation has increased dramatically in the US and most other Western democracies; some legal scholars have even dubbed this trend a "explosion." A growing number of people are using civil litigation to settle personal conflicts between people (e.g., disputes involving landlords and tenants, divorce, child custody, and forbidden employment practices). Employees who report fraud, waste, and abuse at work to external agencies are now entitled to civil remedies and other legal protections against retaliatory punishment from the majority of states and federal agencies in the country. Criminal penalties, including fines, imprisonment, probation, and suspended jail terms, are frequently applied to convicted offenders worldwide. When they achieve two objectives, civil and criminal penalties are generally regarded as useful tools for social integration and transformation. First and foremost, penalties ought to be derived from explicitly stated expectations of conduct, which should include rules and guidelines for the transgression. Second, citizens need to internalize these expected behavior patterns and adopt them as personal preferences (i.e., activities that people choose to perform) as opposed to merely following the letter of the law. Of course, sanctions can still be effective even in the absence of these prerequisites (e.g., by utilizing the state's coercive authority to manage criminal disobedience or control contractual agreements). However, it's generally believed that social control strategies that solely rely on coercion have a short lifespan. The quick ascent and fall of political regimes that primarily use force to enforce conformity serves as evidence of the long-term failure of this form of social control. It is common practice to evaluate the efficacy of criminal penalties in light of deterrence. Whether particular criminal penalties serve to discourage others from committing crimes or prevent convicted offenders from engaging in similar behavior has been the subject of numerous studies. While there is much disagreement regarding the precise and overall deterrent effectiveness of various penalties, criminal penalties are typically thought to be most successful for instrumental crimes (i.e., planned crimes carried out for future objectives) by individuals who are not very committed to crime as a way of life.

Examining the death penalty and other criminal penalties allows researchers to look at a number of factors related to how well laws work as social change agents. Let's start by discussing the historical applications of the death penalty to quell opposition and threats to established interests (e.g., China's increased application of the death penalty in the last 10 years in reaction to an increase in economic crimes). Second, the death penalty and extrajudicial executions, when carried out in specific nations and at specific times (e.g., lynchings in the South during the postbellum era; post-Mao China) ought to be particularly successful since the methods used to carry out death sentences in these situations (i.e., prompt, certain, harsh penalties in public) should optimize their deterrent effect. The current investigation will also demonstrate the efficacy of criminal sanctions in diverse historical and cultural contexts by means of a comparative and historical analysis of lethal and nonlethal punishments.

9.5.5. Disparities in Criminal and Civil Sanctions

The topic of discrepancies or unequal treatment in the application and accessibility of criminal and civil law has been extensively covered in the literature. Studies of disadvantaged groups' varying access to civil remedies (e.g., the impoverished, racial and ethnic minorities); the variations in the outcomes of individual litigants and corporations in civil cases; and the kind and extent of discrepancies in the application of criminal penalties based on gender, race, and class. The topic of differential treatment in the context of the criminal justice system pertains to whether decisions about charges and sentences differ based on group membership following modifications for a wide range of legal factors (e.g., factors (such as the gravity of the charge, the defendant's past behavior) that ought to affect these choices. Research on American court practices frequently reveals disparities in both gender and race, with African Americans and men being the most negatively impacted by unequal treatment. Both studies on the death penalty and studies on other forms of criminal sanctions highlight these social differences. The behavior of law theory developed by Donald Black provides an intriguing framework for analyzing disparities in the application of criminal penalties. Black claims that the amount of law (e.g., how frequently it is used) and its manner (e.g., retributive, compensatory, therapeutic, or conciliation) differ depending on specific facets of social life. When applied upward (e.g., when a higher ranking individual kills a person from a lower social position), the law, for example, takes the form of a compensatory system rather than a penal one. Law has a conciliatory style among individuals of equal status. A clear platform for assessing Black's theory of differential legal treatment across various social and political contexts is the comparative analysis of criminal sanctions.

9.5.6. The Value of a Comparative Historical Approach

While punishment and crime are commonplace in modern society, it would be a grave error to think of punishment as a predetermined or consistent response to specific kinds of misbehavior. In actuality, the definition of an act and the way it is treated by the law at any given time reflect the social, political, economic, and historical context of the society in question. Certain criminal acts (e.g., drug abuse, rape, adultery, and political corruption) may be viewed as normatively acceptable in some cultures while being heinous crimes deserving of the harshest penalties in others. Certain criminal offenses have different legal acceptance rates depending on the circumstances, even within the same nation over time. For instance, drug offenses were not always punishable by death in the United States, England, or China throughout history. A comparative historical analysis is strongest when it can find patterns that hold up over time and space, extending beyond the comparative and historical contexts. The identification of such patterns helps us to more precisely define the nature of the relationship between crime and punishment, which is important from a theoretical and practical standpoint. Even though they serve to limit our universalism claims and demand more research into the reasons behind them, exceptions to these patterns are nonetheless significant. The current context for a deeper understanding of crime and punishment from a comparative historical framework is provided by the dramatic globalization of the modern world and the emergence of a world system perspective in various spheres of social life. The choice of specific comparative cases and the sufficiency of the data that is currently available constitute the main limitations of a comparative historical perspective. As the number of comparable cases rises, issues with the lack of information on the prosecution of criminal or civil cases and the historical documentation of these procedures become more severe. The conclusions' generalizability is called into question by the choice of specific comparative cases. The current study aims to provide enough diversity in the selection of comparative cases to enable a thorough comparative analysis of crime and punishment by choosing nations with different legal and cultural traditions for in-depth examination.

REFERENCES

1. Alarid, L. F., & Cromwell, P. (2006). *In Her Own Words: Women Offenders' Views on Crime and Victimization*. Los Angeles: Roxbury.
2. American Bar Association & National Bar Association. (2001). *Justice by Gender: The Lack of Appropriate Prevention, Diversion and Treatment Alternatives for Girls in the Justice System*. Chicago and Washington, DC: Authors.
3. Belknap, J. (2001). *The Invisible Woman: Gender, Crime, and Justice*. Belmont, CA: Wadsworth.
4. Bloom, B., Owen, B., & Covington, S. (2003). *Gender-Responsive Strategies: Research, Practice, And Guiding Principles for Women Offenders*. Washington, DC: National Institute of Corrections, U.S. Department of Justice.
5. Braithwaite, J. (1989). *Crime, Shame, and Reintegration*. New York: Cambridge University Press.
6. Brame, R., & Piquero, A. R. (2003). Selective attrition and the age–Crime relationship. *Journal of Quantitative Criminology, 19*, 107–127.
7. Brown, L. M. (2003). *Girl Fighting*. New York: New York University Press.
8. Durkheim, E. (1933). *The Division of Labor in Society* (G. Simpson, Trans.). New York: Free Press. (Original work published 1893)
9. Durkheim, E. (1938). *The Rules of Sociological Method*. New York: Free Press.
10. Kruttschnitt, C., & Gartner, R. (2003). Women's imprisonment. In M. Tonry (Ed.), *Crime and Justice: A Review of Research* (Vol. 31, pp. 1–82). Chicago: University of Chicago Press.
11. Laub, J. H., & Sampson, R. J. (2003). *Shared Beginnings, Divergent Lives: Delinquent Boys to Age 70*. Cambridge, MA: Harvard University Press.
12. Mauer, M., & Chesney-Lind, M. (2003). *Invisible Punishment: The Collateral Consequences of Mass Imprisonment*. New York: New Press.
13. Miller, J. (2001). *One of the Guys: Girls, Gangs, and Gender*. New York: Oxford University Press.
14. Miller, J. M., Schreck, C. J., & Tewksbury, R. (2008). *Criminological Theory: A Brief Introduction*. Boston: Allyn & Bacon.
15. Phillips, J. A. (2006). The relationship between age structure and homicide rates in the United States, 1970 to 1999. *Journal of Research in Crime and Delinquency, 43*, 230–260.

16. Pollock-Byrne, J., & Merlo, A. (2006). *Women, Law, and Social Control.* Boston: Allyn & Bacon.
17. Renzetti, C. M., & Goodstein, L. (2000). *Women, Crime, and Criminal Justice: Original Feminist Readings*. New York: Oxford University Press.
18. Renzetti, C. M., Goodstein, L., & Miller, S. L. (2007). *Rethinking Gender, Crime, and Justice*. New York: Oxford University Press.
19. Sabol, W. J., Couture, H., & Harrison, P. M. (2007). *Prisoners in 2006* (Report No. NCJ 219426). Washington, DC: Bureau of Justice Statistics.
20. Sprague, J. (2005). *Feminist Methodologies for Critical Researchers: Bridging Differences*. Lanham, MD: Alta Mira Press.
21. Stolzenberg, L., & D'Alessio, S. H. (2008). Co-offending and the age–Crime curve. *Journal of Research in Crime and Delinquency, 45*, 65–86.
22. Vago, S. (1994). *Law and Society* (4th ed.). Upper Saddle River, NJ: Prentice-Hall.
23. Van Voorhis, P., & Presser, L. (2001). *Classification of Women Offenders: A National Assessment of Current Practices*. Washington, DC: National Institute of Corrections.
24. Vold, G. B., Bernard, T. J., & Snipes, J. B. (2002). *Theoretical Criminology* (5th ed.). Oxford, UK: Oxford University Press.

INDEX

D

N

O

P

FSC
www.fsc.org
MIX
Papier | Fördert
gute Waldnutzung
FSC® C083411

Kolibri 360 GmbH
Ferdinand-Jühlke-Straße 7
99095 Erfurt, Deutschland
produktsicherheit@kolibri360.de